The Semantics of Derivational Morphology

Linguistische Arbeiten

Edited by
Klaus von Heusinger, Agnes Jäger,
Gereon Müller, Ingo Plag,
Elisabeth Stark and Richard Wiese

Volume 586

The Semantics of Derivational Morphology

Theory, Methods, Evidence

Edited by
Sven Kotowski and Ingo Plag

DE GRUYTER

ISBN 978-3-11-162852-3
e-ISBN (PDF) 978-3-11-107491-7
e-ISBN (EPUB) 978-3-11-107643-0
ISSN 0344-6727
DOI https://doi.org/10.1515/9783111074917

This work is licensed under the Creative Commons Attribution-NoDerivatives 4.0 International License. For details go to https://creativecommons.org/licenses/by-nd/4.0/.

Creative Commons license terms for re-use do not apply to any content (such as graphs, figures, photos, excerpts, etc.) not original to the Open Access publication and further permission may be required from the rights holder. The obligation to research and clear permission lies solely with the party re-using the material.

Library of Congress Control Number: 2022950208

Bibliographic information published by the Deutsche Nationalbibliothek
The Deutsche Nationalbibliothek lists this publication in the Deutsche Nationalbibliografie; detailed bibliographic data are available on the Internet at http://dnb.dnb.de.

© 2024 the authors, editing © 2024 Sven Kotowski and Ingo Plag,
published by Walter de Gruyter GmbH, Berlin/Boston.
This volume is text- and page-identical with the hardback published in 20XX.
This book is published open access at www.degruyter.com.

www.degruyter.com

Contents

Sven Kotowski & Ingo Plag
The semantics of derivational morphology: Introduction —— 1

Rochelle Lieber
Ghost aspect and double plurality: On the aspectual semantics of eventive conversion and -*ing* nominalizations in English —— 15

Viktoria Schneider
Eventualities in the semantics of denominal nominalizations —— 37

Verginica Barbu Mititelu, Gianina Iordăchioaia, Svetlozara Leseva & Ivelina Stoyanova
The meaning of zero nouns and zero verbs —— 63

Ingo Plag, Lea Kawaletz, Sabine Arndt-Lappe, Rochelle Lieber
Analogical modeling of derivational semantics: Two case studies —— 103

Richard Huyghe, Alizée Lombard, Justine Salvadori, and Sandra Schwab
Semantic rivalry between French deverbal neologisms in -*age*, -*ion* and -*ment* —— 143

Sven Kotowski & Martin Schäfer
Quantifying semantic relatedness across base verbs and derivatives: English *out*-prefixation —— 177

Olivier Bonami & Matías Guzmán Naranjo
Distributional evidence for derivational paradigms —— 219

Martin Schäfer
Splitting -*ly*'s: Using word embeddings to distinguish derivation and inflection —— 259

Index —— 301

Sven Kotowski & Ingo Plag
The semantics of derivational morphology: Introduction

1 Setting the scene

In some way or other, most authors will agree that derivational morphology is characterized by processes that relate particular forms to particular meanings, and vice versa. More specifically, all morphology textbooks will tell their readers that a hallmark of derivation is its concept-creating nature, i.e. that derivation concerns operations on lexical semantics, which crucially sets derivation apart from inflection (see e.g. Haspelmath & Sims 2013: ch.5, Plag 2003: 14f.). Traditionally, however, research in the field has been biased in favor of formal aspects over semantic aspects. Although derivational semantics has gained some more attention recently (see e.g. the volumes Arndt-Lappe & Plag 2015; Bauer et al. 2015; Rainer et al. 2014), many of the fundamental questions remain under debate. In various ways, the articles compiled in this volume contribute to under-researched aspects of the semantics of complex words. All contributions have a sound empirical footing, and many of them present innovative methodological approaches that allow for formulating and testing new, and more adequate, models of how complex words mean.

In this introduction, we will first present some major questions of derivational semantics, and illustrate them with pertinent phenomena from English. Second, we will discuss how these problems have been addressed methodologically in the past and how more recent methodological developments offer possibilities for more adequate treatments, including novel types of semantic representations. Third, we will introduce the articles in this volume with a special eye on how their methodologies contribute to new insights in their different domains of inquiry, and how the empirical results speak to theory.

Sven Kotowski & Ingo Plag, Heinrich-Heine-University Düsseldorf, email of corresponding author: ingo.plag@uni-duesseldorf.de

2 Fundamental problems of derivational semantics

The first general issue can be captured under the label of form-meaning mappings and comprises three interrelated phenomena: polysemy, affix rivalry, and form-meaning mismatches. The majority of morphological processes are polysemous (see e.g. Lehrer 2003; Rainer 2014), i.e. one form maps onto more than one meaning or reading. A classic example of a polysemous derivational process is the English suffix -*er*, which gives rise to various semantic classes of nouns, including agents (*dancer*), locations (*diner*), instruments (*computer*), or person nouns indicating residence or origin (*Londoner*) (cf. e.g. Lieber 2004; Plag 2003). However, a fully satisfactory analysis of the polysemy of -*er* is still pending, and the suffix allows for the illustration of problems posed by derivational polysemy in general (see Olsen 2020; Rainer 2014). Most broadly, different categories of meaning raise the question of whether they are in fact based on the same underlying meaning, or whether they merely share a form by historic accident (see Olsen 2020 on the agent and instrument readings of -*er*), or have developed into distinct affixes. Moreover, related to the question of whether affixes are considered linguistics signs, it is unclear what is to be taken as polysemous: an affix as such or the derivatives it occurs in. In particular, attempts at assigning to an affix a core meaning representation that is applicable to all semantic patterns is notoriously difficult. As shown by Rainer (2014), assuming a highly underspecified meaning for an affix, such as 'person or thing having to do with X' for -*er* (see Plag 2003, 89), may cover all attested meaning categories, but oftentimes has to be so vague that it overgenerates massively and predicts categories of meaning not attested for the affix.

The second facet of form-meaning mapping concerns affix rivalry. This term has been applied to cases where different affixes can take the same kinds of item as base and overlap regarding the interpretations the resulting derivatives give rise to (see Rainer et al. 2019). Or, from another perspective, we find bases that can take different affixes to derive sometimes equivalent, sometimes different interpretations of the derived word. Hence, one is faced with a many-to-many mapping of form and meaning. Well-known examples concern competition between affixes such as -*ness* and -*ity* (e.g. *opaqueness/opacity*; see Arndt-Lappe 2014) or -*ing* and conversion nouns (as in $cutting_N/cut_N$; see e.g. Lieber & Plag 2022). Rivalry can be challenging to account for, as a multitude of factors may have a say in the distribution of the rivals (e.g. phonological, semantic, analogical, lexical strata). The frequent existence of doublets, sometimes with a meaning difference, sometimes without one, complicates matters further.

The third type of form-meaning mapping to be considered concerns mismatches. We will focus here on morphological processes that are marked by a change in meaning that does not go along with a change in form, i.e. conversion phenomena as in *saddle*$_N$/*to saddle*$_V$ (see e.g. McIntyre 2015; Valera 2015).[1] The classic problems posed by conversion include the issue of whether these processes should be analyzed as zero-marked cases of affixation (and an underlying form-meaning pairing), and which syntactic category should be analyzed as the respective base in the first place. Although several authors stress that assigning conversion a single semantic representation is misguided as, e.g., English verbs converted from nouns show far too much semantic diversity (see e.g. Lieber 2004, ch.3; Baeskow 2021), the identification of the factors that constrain possible interpretations remains a desideratum.

These different facets of the mapping from form to meaning are related to a set of arguably broader problems of derivational morphology. One concerns affix-base interaction and the degree to which the semantics of a derivative can be modeled compositionally via the semantics of the base and the semantics of the affix. For example, most -*able*-adjectives in English are semantically highly predictable regarding affix-base interaction: they denote the capacity of the base verb's PATIENT/THEME argument to undergo the process denoted by that verb (e.g. *imaginable*, *adjustable*) (see Bauer et al. 2013, 307f.). However, not all bases of -*able* formations are verbs, and the meaning of non-deverbal derivatives seems less well predictable (e.g. Plag 2004). In fact, many derivational processes are far less homogeneous than -*able*: they are either far more selective with respect to the bases they are attested with or far more polysemous. Arguably even more so than sentential semantics, word formation semantics appears to be characterized by a high degree of idiomaticity, lexicalization, underspecification, and lack of predictability.

A second general issue, directly related to the question of compositionality, concerns semantic coherence (see Aronoff 1976; Spencer 2013). Coherence itself can be understood as the degree of lexical relatedness between sets of derivatives as well as between sets of bases of a derivational process. The possible links to both polysemy and compositionality are directly evident. First, the more polysemous a morphological process is, the lower the degree of relatedness between its derivatives can be expected to be. Second, there is evidence that coherent subclasses of bases often go together with different senses among derivatives. For example, English nouns in -*ship* can denote several categories, such as relations

---

[1] We will leave aside the reverse case where a form does not seem to have a proper meaning correlate, as e.g. in the synonymous pair *cyclic*/*cyclical*.

and skills. As shown by Aronoff & Cho (2001), if the base is a relational noun, the derivative denotes the relation that underlies it (e.g. *friend–friendship*), while person nouns that semantically include skills as base give rise to derivatives that denote these skills (e.g. *airman–airmanship*). Such constellations, where morphological processes are characterized by a predictable semantics as well as a related predictable feature in their respective bases, show that coherence may also concern the relationship between bases and derivatives (see also the deverbal *-able-* adjectives that allow for fairly straightforward decomposition).

Two related perspectives on derivational semantics touch upon the fundamental question of how semantic knowledge is organized in the morphological system to begin with. First, the inflection–derivation divide is widely regarded as a basic opposition between morphological processes. Distinguishing factors that are typically assumed to be characteristic of derivation include changes in semantic structure, possible changes in part of speech, and semantic idiosyncrasies (see e.g. Spencer 2013; Stump 1998). At the same time, various morphological processes have been described as borderline cases between inflection and derivation. For example, *-ing* clearly forms part of English verb paradigms (as in the progressive, e.g. *Peter is filming$_V$*), but also derives nominalizations and participial adjectives (cf. *the filming$_N$* and *the filming$_A$ crew*, respectively).

Second, the dominant approach to inflectional morphology is onomasiological and understands the organization of inflected forms as paradigmatic in nature. On such an account, a predefined set of categories, such as different PERSON categories in verb conjugation, are related to particular realizations on the form side (e.g. Stump 1998). In contrast, derivational systems are often regarded as too irregular and unpredictable for a paradigmatic organization. Thus, derivation is typically approached in the form of word formation rules that are both semasiological and syntagmatic in nature: particular forms are related to the categories of meaning they encode, while complex meaning is understood as a composition of the semantics of different units which arises through the concatenation of bases and affixes. However, numerous studies (see e.g. Bauer 1997; Bonami & Strnadová 2019; Booij 2017; Hathout & Namer 2022; Spencer 2013) argue for morphological unity and that derivation, too, allows for a paradigmatic analyses. This view is supported by evidence for morphological families, such as morphologically related lexemes that do not share a base or root (e.g. English *aggressive–aggressor–aggression*, for which no base form is attested). So far, however, a paradigmatic analysis of derivational morphology has focused mostly on formal properties, neglecting semantic relationships.

Finally, no matter what kind of fundamental problem the analyst wants to solve, there is the crucial, and perhaps most fundamental, question of all: what *is* meaning and how can we represent it? Traditionally, there have been different approaches to meaning in morphology. Syntactically oriented approaches like Distributed Morphology have treated derivational formatives as rather clearly defined semantic entities that operate at the sentential level. This approach necessarily glosses over many of the questions touched upon in the previous paragraphs. These questions are questions of lexical semantics proper, only that the lexical items are either complex (under a word-based view), or concern sublexical meaningful units (in a morpheme-based view). The lexicalist position that the articles in this volume adopt holds that morphology resides in the relation between words in the lexicon, or in the processes that relate form and meaning in the lexicon.

Addressing the fundamental challenges of the semantics of derivation raises important concerns with regard to methodology. To these concerns we now turn.

3 Methodologies

Until fairly recently, the research focus in derivational morphology was largely on theory-building, and methodological considerations took a back seat. Most troublesome, many a theoretical analysis was (and still is) based on self-generated data with the occasional supplement of examples from the literature, dictionaries, or reference works (see Lieber 2014 for an overview on methodology). This kind of methodology is arguably particularly problematic with respect to derivational morphology, where processes are often sketchy, show diverging productivity, and do not allow for generalizations or theory-building based on insufficient sets of data. For example, Plag (1999) and Lieber (2004) show that verbalizing *-ize* is highly polysemous, and that causative interpretations (as in *standardize*) form the majority pattern among derivatives, but not the only one. Given the paucity of activity interpretations (as in *philosophize*) and inchoative interpretations (as in *oxidize*), Lieber (2014) argues that the extent of polysemy of *-ize* would necessarily remain obscure when relying on self-generated data.

The increasing availability of corpora, and thus very large amounts of naturally occurring data, is tantamount to a methodological turning point. With respect to semantics, larger corpora have the capacity to remedy the inadequacies of insufficient data bases in two ways, in particular when paired with appropriate coding of the generated data and statistical measures. First, they allow to lay bare the actual range of attested readings of a morphological process. Second, they allow for quantifying phenomena, such as the relative distribution of different senses of a particular affix, as well as comparing different phenomena, such as determining the actual overlap between competing processes. For example, as shown quantitatively by Lieber & and Plag (2022) and contrary to prevalent claims in the literature, the majority of English conversion nouns encode eventive readings (as in *during a drive*). At the same time, conversion nouns and *-ing*-nominalizations largely encode the same kinds of semantic categories, and it tends to be specific feature constellations of the bases' semantics that determine fine-grained preferences.

Unsurprisingly, the appropriateness of the empirical groundwork also sheds light on how well different modelings of derivational semantics fare. For example, categorical approaches that are committed to hard-and-fast rules oftentimes do not stand the test of broader empirical scrutiny. In particular, approaches that represent the meaning of complex words via syntactic projections (e.g. Distributed Morphology; see e.g. Harley 2012, or the Exoskeleton model; see Borer 2013) rely on unambiguous compositionality. Due to this commitment, they typically cannot adequately handle the range of readings and variability we find in larger data sets (see e.g. the critique in Lieber 2016). In contrast, the inheritance mechanisms of schema- and construction-based approaches more adequately capture the variability found in the lexicon (e.g. construction morphology; see Booij 2010, relational morphology; see Jackendoff & Audring 2020, or constraint-based models such as HPSG; see Bonami & Crysmann 2016). However, such approaches typically refrain from representing semantics in a structured way, and the semantic paraphrases they content themselves with fall short of the semantic categories needed for devising plausible models of the meaning of complex words. Yet other frameworks, such as Lieber's Lexical Semantic Framework (see Lieber 2004) or frame semantics (see Andreou 2017; Kawaletz 2021; Plag et al. 2018) are inherently decompositional and are explicit about semantic structure. However, they have two downsides. They are rather unconstrained, and thus potentially overgenerating, and they cannot predict probabilities or tendencies of derivational processes.

There are at least two methodological approaches involving computational modeling to the organization of meaning that promise to overcome some of these shortcomings. The first one, distributional semantics, is a decidedly semantic approach that is grounded in the hypothesis that the meaning of a word is reflected in its distribution (see Boleda 2020 for an overview). This meaning can be modeled as a numeric vector generated automatically from large enough corpora. While distributional semantics has no explicit formalism to represent semantic structure, it has been employed for several of the derivational phenomena discussed above, and excels at establishing patterns among non-categorical data. For example, Huyghe & Wauquier (2020) investigate the morphological and semantic coherence of French agent nouns by comparing the semantic vectors of derived nouns with the vectors of different classes of non-derived verbs and nouns. Bonami & Paperno (2018) use similarity measures to disentangle derivationally and inflectionally related word pairs. Other studies follow a compositional route and model affixes as matrices that are then multiplied with the semantic vector of a given base to create the vector of the derived word (e.g. Marelli & Baroni 2015).

The second approach, analogy, is part of the classic toolbox of morphology (see e.g. already Paul 1909). In its modern form, it is a concept that can be implemented using computational analogical algorithms such as TiMBL (see Daelemans et al. 2007) or AML (see Skousen & Stanford 2007). Such analogical models perform classification tasks that decide between different possible outcomes of, for example, a complex word depending on its similarities with pertinent properties of other complex words in the lexicon. While a number of studies employ analogical models using the formal properties of complex words (see e.g. Eddington 2000; Arndt-Lappe 2014), they have not yet been used for semantic classification tasks, and the obvious challenge of such an endeavor lies in the appropriate coding of the semantic properties that are used for establishing degrees of similarity.

Let us now have a closer look at what the articles compiled in this volume have to say about the semantic phenomena described above, and how they arrive at their insights. We will first discuss different articles along the lines of the methodologies they predominantly use and then focus on their theoretical contributions.

4 The articles in this volume: Theory, methods, evidence

4.1 Methods

Simplifying somewhat, we can divide the articles of this volume into corpus-based, distributional, and analogical contributions. Four articles included in this volume are what we may call corpus-based in their methodology. They all deal with nominalizations, but differ greatly with respect to how they make use of their respective corpus data.

Mitetelu, Iordăchioaia, Leseva & Stoyanova's contribution **The meaning of zero nouns and zero verbs** presents a detailed study on the semantics of English noun-to-verb and verb-to-noun conversion. The article makes use of WordNet and the OED as a combined data sources and provides descriptive statistics on the predictability of semantic categories based on the respective direction of conversion.

Based on attestations from the OED and various corpora, **Viktoria Schneider's** article **Eventualities in the semantics of denominal nominalizations** uses frame semantic formalizations for the decomposition of English -*ee*-derivatives. The author presents a reference shifting mechanism on the bases' semantic structures which is shown to account for the semantics of both common deverbal -*ee*-forms and of less frequent denominal -*ee*-forms. The denominal forms frequently present ontological clashes between base and derivative, and the article's deep decompositional approach facilitates the necessary retrieval of embedded eventive structure.

Rochelle Lieber's article **Ghost aspect and double plurality** investigates eventive count-quantified -*ing* and conversion nominalizations in English and their aspectual properties. Building on a carefully compiled data set of more than 800 forms, Lieber provides both quantitative and qualitative evidence for diverse patterns of affix-base interaction and underspecification.

Finally, based on a set of neologisms, **Huyghe, Lombard, Salvadori & Schwab's** article **Semantic rivalry between French deverbal neologisms in -*age*, -*ion* and -*ment*** employs a variety of statistical measures to shed light on the nature of affix competition. The study builds on a very careful coding procedure for semantic properties of more than 500 nominalizations and their respective base verbs. The authors statistically tease apart factors that influence the suffix distribution and the degrees to which different affixes compete with each other.

A second group of three articles makes use of distributional semantic measures. **Kotowski & Schäfer's** contribution **Quantifying semantic relatedness across base verbs and derivatives: English *out*-prefixation** investigates the semantics of English *out*-prefixed verbs along the lines of semantic coherence between bases, between bases and derivatives, and between derivatives. The authors present two classic corpus-based studies that show that underspecified meaning components of *out*-derivatives are largely predictable via classes of base verbs. In two further studies, distributional cosine similarities show that *out*-derivatives are even more similar to each other than bases are to their respective *out*-derivatives and that *out*-prefixation differs in this respect from a number of other English prefixes.

Bonami Guzmán Naranjo's article **Distributional evidence for derivational paradigms** explores the potential of distributional semantic evidence for a paradigmatic analysis of derived words in French. The authors make use of distributional models in which a lexeme's vector is used to predict a morphologically related lexeme's vector. Their investigations into the interpredictability of all words in triplets of the kind *racler–racleur–raclage* provide good semantic evidence for both syntagmatic and paradigmatic organization.

Finally, **Martin Schäfer's** contribution **Splitting -*lys*: Using word embeddings to distinguish derivation and inflection** investigates the question whether the semantics of the English adverb-forming suffix -*ly* can shed light on the debate on the status of this suffix as derivational or inflectional. By means of various distributional semantic measures, the author teases apart functional and semantic similarity, and demonstrates that *-ly* displays variable semantic behavior depending on the semantic class of bases.

Schäfer's article is also representative of an approach that applies classic analogical reasoning on the basis of distributional semantic models (see Mikolov et al. 2013; Pennington et al. 2014, but also Bonami and Guzmán's article in the present volume). Specifically, Schäfer establishes distributional similarities between morphologically related pairs of words, and asks which target word shows analogous similarity to a given base word.

A different approach is taken by **Plag, Kawaletz, Arndt-Lappe & Lieber's** article **Analogical modeling of derivational semantics: Two case studies**. These authors employ the analogical algorithm AML to two of the mapping phenomena described above, affix rivalry and affix polysemy. Using data sets taken from their own previous research, the authors first tackle affix rivalry and use the algorithm for predicting the choice between conversion and *-ing* nominalizations based on semantic features: the interpretation of the derived noun and the aspectual properties of the base. Second, AML is used to predict the different readings of English *-ment*-nominalizations depending on the verb class of the respective base. This contribution is pioneering, insofar as it is the first one to use analogical modeling in the realm of derivational semantics. Overall, the article shows that by finding analogical sets for appropriate semantic features, AML is very successful at predicting both the choice between competing forms and the possible readings of derivatives that contain a polysemyous suffix.

4.2 Theory

With regard to the theoretical problems posed by derivational semantics sketched in section 2, the articles in this volume provide interesting new perspectives on these problems. Let us start with problems of form-meaning mappings.

Rochelle Lieber's article on the aspectual properties of conversion and *-ing* in English adresses all three problems of form-meaning mapping: polysemy, affix rivalry, and mismatches. She demonstrates that nominal *-ing* both turns a verbal base into a noun and adds the feature [+durative], while conversion makes no aspectual contribution of its own. The analysis of conversion nominalizations demonstrates that even with processes that have no formal expression, there are intricate interactions of context and base properties with the process at hand that generate the reading of a particular token.

Mitetelu et al.'s contribution tackles the problem of mismatches by looking at zero-derived nouns vs. zero-derived verbs. Their analysis of a huge number of such verb–noun and noun–verb pairs shows that morphosemantic relations associate with one direction or the other, and that zero-derived verbs are semantically more heterogeneous. Overall, however, either direction is partly predictive of distinct patterns of polysemy.

Semantic rivalry is at the heart of Huyghe et al.'s study of French deverbal neologisms in *-age, -ion* and *-ment*. They demonstrate that lexical aspect, semantic role assignment properties, and nominal semantic type are all influential in predicting suffix selection. Rivalry turns out to be a gradient, probabilistic phenomenon, while each suffix comes with its own set of preferences. For example, *-age* typically refers to strictly dynamic eventualities, while *-ion*-nouns preferentially denote gradable changes of state.

Practically all articles deal with the semantic coherence of morphological categories. Their results boil down to the conclusion that coherence (or non-coherence) can only be understood by a detailed analysis of the interplay between the meaning of the base and the semantics of the morphological category. For instance, the reading of a nominalization is heavily dependent on the semantic properties of its base, as, for example, demonstrated by French nominalizations (Huyghe et al.), English zero-derived nouns (Mitetelu et al., Lieber), *-ing* nominalizations (Lieber, Plag et al.), or *-ment* nominalizations (Plag et al.). Similarly, the semantic properties of prefixed verbs (Kotowski & Schäfer) and *-ly* adverbs (Schäfer) can only be grasped by taking into account both the contribution of the morphological process and peculiar properties of different classes of base forms.

The organization of semantic knowledge is specifically addressed in the articles by Bonami & Guzmán, by Schäfer, and by Schneider. Building on her frame approach to affix-base interaction, Schneider extends her shifting mechanism and argues that the semantics of some *-ee*-forms are best understood as operations on the semantic structures of paradigmatically related nouns. For example, she shows that it is feasible to account for the meaning of *tutee* via a referential shift on the structure of nominal *tutor*. Thus, the article provides arguments in favor of assumptions of substantial amounts of shared semantic structure in morphological families. Bonami & Guzmán address the question of paradigmatic organization by putting paradigms to the test. The authors measure the semantic similarity between bases and affixes and between derived words and compare the similarities that can be found along each of the two axes. It turns out that both the syntagmatic and the paradigmatic axis are important dimensions of morphological organization. Thus, different morphological categories differ in the strength of the respective organizational axis, and some complex words show interpredictability that is larger than either forms' interpredictability with the respective base, while base-derivative interpredictability is larger in other triplets. While these results may have been expected by some readers, this study is unique in the kind of solid empirical evidence brought up by its authors.

Schäfer's study re-opens the debate on the distinction between inflection and derivation by investigating a well-known controversial case, English *-ly*, from a semantic perspective. His complex results seem to indicate that the alleged inflection–derivation divide may not be a useful way of understanding morphological organization.

Finally, let us turn to the largest question of all: what is meaning? The articles give or assume different answers to this question. With regard to the question where meaning resides, a number of papers consider meaning in derivation a property of words, others assume that meaning resides in affixes and bases. Some articles represent meaning as being compositional and built on the bases of discrete semantic units, other articles treat meaning as a dynamic, emergent property.

We still lack an answer to this largest question of all, but the articles in this volume show that each type of approach, when combined with rigorous empirical methods, may lead to very interesting new insights concerning the nature of meaning in derivational morphology.

5 Conclusion

To summarize, this volume brings together state-of-the-art research on the semantic properties of derived words and the processes by which these words are derived. As suggested by the subtitle of the volume, all contributions have a theoretical orientation in that they address important issues in morphological theory that relate to the interpretation of derived words.

Each article addresses an under-researched problem of the semantics of complex words, and all articles make use of empirically solid data bases. Several of the applied methodologies are innovative and several articles complement one another in making use of different methods in investigations of similar phenomena. For example, affix rivalry is tackled via analogical means (see Plag et al.) as well as by using classic statistical means on neologism data (see Huyghe et al.). Semantic coherence is investigated via distributional similarity measures (see Kotowski & Schäfer) as well as by statistical analyses of lexical data bases (see Mititelu et al.). Paradigmatic relationships between derived words are approached from the perspectives of both decompositional modeling (see Schneider) and distributional interpredictability (see Bonami & Guzmán).

The editors believe that the volume at hand will be a valuable contribution to the field of derivational semantics, presenting a broad range of theoretically and empirically well-motivated approaches to meaning, and, above all, highly interesting new insights into how complex words mean.

Acknowledgments

This volume grew out of a workshop of the same title at the *43. DGFS-Jahrestagung*, held at the University of Freiburg from February 23-26, 2021. We are very grateful to our contributors for the smooth collaboration over the past one and a half years. A special thanks goes to the reviewers and to series editor Klaus von Heusinger for their very helpful comments on earlier versions of the contributions in this volume. Finally, we thank the Deutsche Forschungsgemeinschaft for the partial funding of our research (Grants SFB 991/2-C08 and PL 151/11-1 'Semantics of derivational morphology' to the second editor). Finally, we thank the Open-Access-Fonds of Heinrich-Heine-Universität Düsseldorf for funding large parts of the costs for the Open Access publication of this volume.

Bibliography

Andreou, Marios. 2017. Stereotype negation in frame semantics. *Glossa: a journal of general linguistics* 2(1). 1–30. 10.5334/gjgl.293.

Arndt-Lappe, Sabine. 2014. Analogy in suffix rivalry. The case of English *-ity* and *-ness*. *English Language and Linguistics* 18(3). 497–548.

Arndt-Lappe, Sabine & Ingo Plag (eds.). 2015. *The semantics of derivational morphology* (=Special issue of Morphology 25.4).

Aronoff, Mark. 1976. *Word formation in generative grammar*. Cambridge, MA: MIT Press.

Aronoff, Mark & Sungeon Cho. 2001. The semantics of *-ship*. *Linguistic Inquiry* 32. 167–173.

Baeskow, Heike. 2021. Noun-verb conversion as a metonymic metamorphosis. *Skase Journal of Theoretical Linguistics* 18(1). 2–34.

Bauer, Laurie. 1997. Evaluative morphology: A search for universals. *Studies in Language* 21. 533–575.

Bauer, Laurie, Lívia Körtvélyessy & Pavol Štekauer (eds.). 2015. *Semantics of complex words*. Dordrecht: Springer.

Bauer, Laurie, Rochelle Lieber & Ingo Plag. 2013. *The Oxford reference guide to English morphology*. Oxford: Oxford University Press.

Boleda, Gemma. 2020. Distributional semantics and linguistic theory. *Annual Review of Linguistics* 6. 213–234.

Bonami, Olivier & Berthold Crysmann. 2016. Morphology in constraint-based lexicalist approaches to grammar. In Andrew Hippisley & Gregory T. Stump (eds.), *The Cambridge handbook of morphology*, 609–656. Cambridge: Cambridge University Press.
Bonami, Olivier & Denis Paperno. 2018. Inflection vs. derivation in a distributional vector space. *Lingue e linguaggio* (2). 173–196.
Bonami, Olivier & Jana Strnadová. 2019. Paradigm structure and predictability in derivational morphology. *Morphology* 29(2). 167–197.
Booij, Geert. 2017. Inheritance and motivation in construction morphology. In Nikolas Gisborne & Andrew Hippisley (eds.), *Defaults in morphological theory*, 18–39. Oxford: Oxford University Press.
Booij, Geert E. 2010. *Construction morphology*. Oxford: Oxford University Press.
Borer, Hagit. 2013. *Structuring sense. Vol. III: Taking form*. Oxford: Oxford University Press.
Daelemans, Walter, Jakub Zavrel, Ko van der Sloot & Antal van den Bosch. 2007. Timbl. Tilburg memory based learner, version 6.0, reference guide. ilk technical report 07-03.
Eddington, David. 2000. Spanish stress assignment within the analogical modeling of language. *Language* 76(1). 92–109.
Harley, Heidi. 2012. Semantics in distributed morphology. In Claudia Maienborn, Klaus von Heusinger & Paul Portner (eds.), *Interfaces*, 143–168. Berlin and Boston: De Gruyter.
Haspelmath, Martin & Andrea D. Sims. 2013. *Understanding morphology. 2nd ed.* London and New York, NY: Routledge Taylor & Francis Group.
Hathout, Nabil & Fiammetta Namer. 2022. ParaDis: a family and paradigm model. *Morphology* 32(2). 153–195.
Huyghe, Richard & Marine Wauquier. 2020. What's in an agent? *Morphology* 30(3). 185–218.
Jackendoff, Ray & Jenny Audring. 2020. *The texture of the lexicon: Relational morphology and the parallel architecture*. Oxford and New York: Oxford University Press.
Kawaletz, Lea. 2021. *The semantics of English -ment nominalizations*. Düsseldorf: Heinrich-Heine-University Dissertation.
Lehrer, Adrienne. 2003. Polysemy in derivational affixes. In Brigitte Nerlich, Zazie Todd, Vimala Herman & David D. Clarke (eds.), *Polysemy*, 217–232. Berlin and New York: De Gruyter.
Lieber, Rochelle. 2004. *Morphology and lexical semantics*. Cambridge: Cambridge University Press.
Lieber, Rochelle. 2014. Methodological issues in studying derivation. In Rochelle Lieber & Pavol Štekauer (eds.), *The Oxford handbook of derivational morphology*, 85–94. Oxford: Oxford University Press.
Lieber, Rochelle. 2016. *English nouns: The ecology of nominalization*. Cambridge: Cambridge University Press.
Lieber, Rochelle & Ingo Plag. 2022. The semantics of conversion nouns and -*ing* nominalizations: A quantitative and theoretical perspective. *Journal of Linguistics* 58(2). 307–343.
Marelli, Marco & Marco Baroni. 2015. Affixation in semantic space: Modeling morpheme meanings with compositional distributional semantics. *Psychological review* 122(3). 485–515.
McIntyre, Andrew. 2015. Denominal verbs. In Peter O. Müller, Ingeborg Ohnheiser, Susan Olsen & Franz Rainer (eds.), *Word-formation*, 434–450. Berlin and Boston: De Gruyter.
Mikolov, Tomas, Ilya Sutskever, Kai Chen, Greg S Corrado & Jeff Dean. 2013. Distributed representations of words and phrases and their compositionality. In Chris J. Burges, L. Bottou, Max Welling, Zoubin Ghahramani & Kilian Q. Weinberger (eds.), *Advances in neural information processing systems*, vol. 26, https://proceedings.neurips.cc/paper/2013/file/9aa42b31882ec039965f3c4923ce901b-Paper.pdf.

Olsen, Susan. 2020. The relatedness of meaning in derivational patterns. In Jenny Audring, Nikos Koutsoukos & Christina Manouilidou (eds.), *Rules, patterns, and schemas. MMM12 online proceedings*, 64–76. University of Patras.
Paul, Hermann. 1909. *Prinzipien der Sprachgeschichte. 4th edition*. Leipzig: Niemeyer.
Pennington, Jeffrey, Richard Socher & Christopher D Manning. 2014. Glove: Global vectors for word representation. In *Proceedings of the 2014 conference on empirical methods in natural language processing (EMNLP)*, 1532–1543.
Plag, Ingo. 1999. *Morphological productivity: Structural constraints in English derivation*. Berlin: De Gruyter.
Plag, Ingo. 2003. *Word-formation in English*. Cambridge: Cambridge University Press.
Plag, Ingo. 2004. Syntactic category information and the semantics of derivational morphological rules. *Folia Linguistica* 38(3-4). 193–225.
Plag, Ingo, Marios Andreou & Lea Kawaletz. 2018. A frame-semantic approach to polysemy in affixation. In Olivier Bonami, Gilles Boyé, Georgette Dal, Hélène Giraudo & Fiammetta Namer (eds.), *The lexeme in descriptive and theoretical morphology*, 546–568. Berlin: Language Science Press.
Rainer, Franz. 2014. Polysemy in derivation. In Rochelle Lieber & Pavol Štekauer (eds.), *The Oxford handbook of derivational morphology*, 338–353. Oxford: Oxford University Press.
Rainer, Franz, Francesco Gardani, Wolfgang U. Dressler & Hans Christian Luschützky (eds.). 2019. *Competition in inflection and word-formation*. Cham: Springer.
Rainer, Franz, Francesco Gardani, Hans Christian Luschützky & Wolfgang U. Dressler (eds.). 2014. *Morphology and meaning: Selected papers from the 15th International Morphology Meeting, Vienna, February 2012*. Amsterdam and Philadelphia: John Benjamins.
Skousen, Royal & Thereon Stanford. 2007. *Am:: Parallel*. Available from http://humanities.byu.edu/am/.
Spencer, Andrew. 2013. *Lexical relatedness*. Oxford: Oxford University Press.
Stump, Gregory T. 1998. Inflection. In Andrew Spencer & Arnold M. Zwicky (eds.), *The handbook of morphology*, Oxford, UK and Malden, MA: Blackwell.
Valera, Salvador. 2015. 17. Conversion. In Peter O. Müller, Ingeborg Ohnheiser, Susan Olsen, Franz Rainer, Gerold Ungeheuer & Herbert Ernst Wiegand (eds.), *Handbücher zur Sprach- und Kommunikationswissenschaft = Handbooks of linguistics and communication science*, vol. 40, 322–339. Berlin: De Gruyter.

Rochelle Lieber

Ghost aspect and double plurality: On the aspectual semantics of eventive conversion and -*ing* nominalizations in English

Abstract: This paper considers the aspectual semantics of -*ing* nominalization, comparing -*ing* to conversion nominalizations in both the singular and the plural. Based on a corpus of eventive count-quantified -*ing* and conversion nominalizations that are matched for verbal base, I argue that nominal -*ing* does have an aspectual component to its semantics, but that this semantic contribution is neither imperfective nor imperfective as has been claimed sporadically in previous literature. Rather, I argue that -*ing* is aspectually durative. Durativity is only one of several semantic components that can be attributed to progressivity in English (Huddleston & Pullum 2002), and it is distinct from imperfectivity (Comrie 1976). Claiming that -*ing* nominalizations bear a feature of durativity makes sense of some hitherto unnoticed semantic patterns displayed in these nominalizations, specifically that -*ing* has clearer and more visible aspectual effects on punctual bases (achievements and semelfactives) than on durative bases (states, activities, and accomplishments), and that plural -*ing* nominalizations on semelfactive bases can exhibit a reading that might be characterized as doubly plural, denoting multiple sets of multiple events.

Keywords: derivation, aspect, nominalization, conversion, plural

1 Introduction

In the last six decades there has been a great deal written about -*ing* nominalizations as in, for example, *Hillary's climbing of Everest*. Much of this literature concerns their syntactic structure, as compared either to sentences (Lees 1960), or to other sorts of nominalizations (Grimshaw 1990; Alexiadou 2001; Borer 2013; Lieber 2016, among many others). Much less has been said about the semantics of -*ing* nominalizations, and in particular about the aspectual semantics of nominal -*ing*, although there have been a few brief treatments of this topic in the literature (Asher 1993; Pustejovsky 1995; Brinton 1995, 1998; Alexiadou et al. 2010; Alexiadou 2013; Plag et al. 2023). Andreou & Lieber (2020) consider the aspectual semantics of -*ing* more systematically, looking at whether nominalizations with -*ing*

Rochelle Lieber, University of New Hampshire, email: rochelle.lieber@unh.edu

∂ Open Access. © 2023 the author(s), published by De Gruyter. [CC BY-ND] This work is licensed under the Creative Commons Attribution-NoDerivatives 4.0 International License.
https://doi.org/10.1515/9783111074917-002

differ from conversion nominalizations in terms of boundedness/completiveness. But there are other facets of aspectual semantics that have not been looked at systematically.

In this paper I look in more detail at the aspectual contribution of *-ing* nominalization, comparing it to conversion nominalizations in both the singular and the plural. In particular, I use corpus data to compare eventive *-ing* and conversion nominalizations that are count quantified. I argue on the basis of these data that nominal *-ing* does have an aspectual component to its semantics, but that this semantic contribution is neither imperfective nor imperfective as has been claimed sporadically in previous literature. Rather, I suggest that *-ing* is aspectually durative. Durativity is only one of several semantic components that can be attributed to progressivity in English (Huddleston & Pullum 2002), and it is distinct from imperfectivity (Comrie 1976).

Claiming that *-ing* nominalizations bear a feature of durativity will allow me to explain some hitherto unnoticed semantic patterns displayed in these nominalizations. One pattern that I document is that *-ing* has clearer and more visible aspectual effects on punctual bases (achievements and semelfactives) than on durative bases (states, activities, and accomplishments), and indeed that *-ing* sometimes seems to have no aspectual effect at all on durative bases — a phenomenon that I dub here *ghost aspect*. Further, I argue that plural *-ing* nominalizations on semelfactive bases can sometimes exhibit a reading that might be characterized as doubly plural, denoting multiple sets of multiple events. I try to show that both ghost aspect and double plurality make sense if we treat *-ing* as aspectually durative.

Section 2 reviews the claims that have been made in the literature and sets out the research questions to be explored in the paper. In section 3 I provide a brief introduction to the semantics of the imperfective in English, to the distinction between imperfectivity and durativity, and to the semantics of the plural. Section 4 explains the methodology used in the study, including the composition and coding of the database. Section 3.2 presents the patterns uncovered in the data, and section 5 develops the analysis.

Two points need to be clarified before I begin. First, I look here only at examples of *-ing* and conversion nominalizations that have eventive interpretations. It has been argued elsewhere (Lieber 2016; Lieber & Plag 2022), that *-ing* and conversion nominalizations can display either eventive or referential readings, but I exclude the referential cases here, as they would not be expected to show aspectual semantics; nominalizations with referential readings are frequently concrete, they sometimes refer to products or event participants, and are more prone to lexicalized meanings than eventives are. Second, although I look both at *-ing* and conversion nominalizations, my main focus is on the semantics of *-ing*; conversion serves here as a point of comparision. My strategy is to compare carefully matched *-ing* and conversion nominalizations, specifically ones that occur on the same verbal bases, and share eventivity and count quantification, so that the only difference is the presence or absence of the *-ing* suffix on the nominalization. This methodology will allow me to tease out differences between the types of nominalizations that might otherwise not be noticed.

2 Literature and research questions

Although there have been quite a few claims in the literature that touch on the aspectual contribution of nominal *-ing*, many of those claims are also tangled up with questions of quantification (count versus mass interpretation) and aspectual class of the verbal base (state, activity, accomplishment, achievement, semelfactive). Andreou & Lieber (2020) review these claims in some detail, so I will only highlight here the claims that bear on what is to follow.

First, it is well known, contrary to the claims in Grimshaw (1990) that conversion nouns do allow eventive interpretations and that eventive readings do occur in both *-ing* and conversion nominalizations in the plural (Alexiadou et al. 2010; Andreou & Lieber 2020). Andreou & Lieber (2020) and Lieber & Plag (2022) also show that eventive *-ing* nominalizations do not prefer bases that are activities as claimed by Brinton (1995), nor do they disprefer accomplishments and achievements, as Alexiadou (2001) suggests; indeed Andreou & Lieber show that *-ing* nominalizations occur on bases of all sorts.[1]

There has also been sporadic discussion in the literature about what, if anything, is the semantic contribution of nominalizing *-ing*. Asher (1993) claims that nominal *-ing* is similar to imperfective *-ing*, denoting on-going events. Pustejovsky (1995), however, argues contrary to Asher that *-ing* nominalizations can denote completed events. Siegel (1997) considers the aspectual contribution of *-ing* to be one of progressivity and durativity. Brinton (1995) and Alexiadou (2001) both suggest that nominal *-ing* is an imperfectivizer. But Alexiadou et al. (2010) argue that the *-ing* suffix itself has no aspectual effect, and rather that *-ing* nominalizations can be pluralized only on telic bases, preserving the telicity of the base. According to Borer (2013), *-ing* has the property of 'homogeneity,' her term for atelicity. Finally, Andreou & Lieber (2020) suggest that both *-ing* nominalizations and con-

---

1 *-ing* nominalizations on stative bases are quite rare, however.

version nominalizations may be aspectually either bounded (completive) or unbounded (incompletive), so that in that respect, they are aspectually identical.²

There is more to be said about the aspectual contribution of -*ing*, however. Only Andreou & Lieber (2020) have tried to tease apart the contributions of the aspectual class of the base verb, the kind of quantification, and possible aspectual readings in these nominalizations. But in terms of aspect, Andreou & Lieber considered only boundedness, and not other sorts of possible aspectual contributions. In this paper, I go beyond Andreou & Lieber in two respects. First, I set up a controlled comparison of -*ing* and conversion nominalizations, looking only at nominalizations that are count quantified and eventive in interpretation, and where the two types of nominalization occur on the same verbal base. In terms of aspectual contributions, I look beyond boundedness to other distinctions, teasing apart the semantics of imperfectives and imperfectives to see if any or all of the semantic facets of those types of aspect are relevant to the interpretation of -*ing* nominalizations.

In what follows I will try to answer the following questions. First, I ask whether nominalizing -*ing* has any distinctive aspectual contribution at all, and if so, whether this -*ing* bears any similarity to imperfective -*ing* in English. I also consider whether possible readings of eventive count conversion and -*ing* nominalizations differ systematically in any way, and if so, whether aspectual class of the verbal base has anything to do with these differences. Finally, I look at the semantic effects of pluralizing -*ing* and conversion nominalizations and consider the relationship between these effects and the aspectual class of the base verb.

3 A brief interlude on imperfectives and plurals and verb classes

Since some past claims about the aspectual contribution of -*ing* have attributed imperfective or imperfective semantics to the affix, I begin by looking at the semantics of the imperfective in English and at the relationship between progressivity and other distinctions such as imperfectivity and durativity.

---

2 One pervasive problem in the literature is that authors are not always explicit about what they mean by terms like imperfective, imperfective, completive, telic/atelic, etc. In what follows I will try to be precise about my own use of the terms, which largely follow those of Comrie (1976) and Huddleston & Pullum (2002). See also Andreou & Lieber (2020) for a discussion of the difficulty of defining what boundedness means when discussing nominalizations.

Huddleston & Pullum (2002, 163) tease apart several strands that pertain to the English imperfective:

> imperfective aspectuality involves the following features, two of which are strong implicatures rather than part of the meaning proper:

(1)   i. The situation is presented as in progress, ongoing, at or through T_r.
     ii. The situation is viewed imperfectively.
     iii. T_r is a mid-interval within T_{sit}. [implicature]
     iv. The situation is presented as durative.
     v. The situation is presented as dynamic.
     vi. The situation is presented as having limited duration. [implicature]

Leaving aside the implicatures, what is most important for our purposes is that the English imperfective presents a situation as non-stative, as ongoing with respect to the reference time of the event, and as both imperfective and durative.

Comrie (1976) offers useful clarification of the distinctions between progressivity, imperfectivity, and durativity. For Comrie (1976, 24), imperfectivity involves "explicit reference to the internal temporal structure of a situation, viewing a situation from within..." He notes as well (1976, 33) that imperfectives in languages other than English often allow for a purely habitual interpretation, which is not the case for the English imperfective. Comrie (1976, 41–42) also clarifies the distinction between imperfectivity and durativity: "We may therefore make a distinction between imperfectivity and durativity, where imperfectivity means viewing a situation with regard to its internal structure (duration, phasal sequences), and durativity simply refers to the fact that the given situation lasts for a certain period of time (or at least, is conceived of as lasting for a certain period of time);... ." What will be important for our purposes is this: although imperfectivity implies duration, duration does not necessarily imply imperfectivity. durative situations may be perfective, which is to say completive or bounded. Progressivity includes both imperfectivity and durativity, but also other nuances.

Since I will be looking at both singular and plural count nominalizations, it is also useful to look briefly at the semantics of the plural. Rothstein (2017), reviewing the vast model theoretic literature on the subject (Link 1983; Krifka 1989; Landman 1995; Chierchia 1998, among many others), says that plural count nouns denote sets of atoms. These 'atoms' can be naturally atomic, in the sense that the noun in question denotes something that is an individualizable entity (something that might have to do with its perceptual qualities or ontological status), or they can be semantically atomic, in that the context dictates that the noun consists of individual units (Rothstein 2017, chapter 4), such as when a typically mass noun is made count by using it with an indefinite article (for example, *a wine*). Eventive nominalizations are by definition not concrete nouns, and therefore do not necessarily have what Rothstein would consider natural atomicity. When they are construed as count nouns in context, their atomicity may be purely semantic, that is, dependent on or induced by context. Adding a plural marker to a nominalization can coerce that semantic atomicity, something which will prove important in the data we examine here.

Finally, since the analysis I present below pertains to the lexical aspect of the verbal bases on which the nominalizations are built, it is worth pausing to clarify our understanding of lexical aspect. Although it is well known that the overall aspectual interpretation of a verb depends not only on its lexical meaning but on the syntactic context in which it is deployed (see for example, Verkuyl 1993), it is nevertheless possible to focus on just those elements of meaning that are contributed by the verb. It is typical to distinguish five lexical aspects (Smith 1991; Brinton 1995, 1998; Filip 2012): states, activities, accomplishments, achievements, and semelfactives:[3]

(1) states: love, doubt
    Activities: embrace, sail
    accomplishments: wash, transfer
    achievements: kill, find
    semelfactives: knock, blink

states are distinguished from the other four lexical aspects in that they require no input of energy, whereas all other aspects (grouped together as 'events') do require an input of energy to be sustained (Comrie 1976). Activities and semelfactives do not involve transition or change of state, whereas accomplishments and achievements do involve transition. states, activities, and accomplishments imply temporal duration, whereas achievements and semelfactives are construed as momentaneous/punctual, that is, they do not imply any linguistically significant passage of time. accomplishments and achievements imply some endpoint, whether or not that endpoint is actually reached in a given context. states, activities, and semelfactives do not imply an eventual endpoint.

It is often useful to decompose the lexical aspect of verbs according to three binary features (Smith 1991; Brinton 1995; Lieber & Plag 2022, among others). Different names for these features appear in the literature, but the way in which the

---

[3] A reviewer asks why degree achievements are not included in this study. The original Andreou & Lieber (2020) dataset from which my data were extracted looked only at deverbal nominalizations. Degree achievements are typically deadjectival, and therefore did not form part of that dataset.

three features are used to distinguish the five main classes is always more or less the same, as given in Table 1.[4]

Tab. 1: Aspectual features

	[+/-dynamic]	[+/-durative]	[+/-implied endpoint]
state	-	+	-
activity	+	+	-
accomplishment	+	+	+
achievement	+	-	+
semelfactive	+	-	-

The feature [+/-dynamic] distinguishes states from events. The feature [+/-durative] encodes whether an event occurs over a linguistically significant stretch of time, with [+durative] denoting some appreciable amount of time and [-durative] denoting a stretch of time that is not linguistically significant. Finally, [+/-implied endpoint] encodes whether the event suggests a natural endpoint or not.

4 Methodology

For this study, I analyzed a subset of the data used in Lieber & Plag (2022), which is itself a subset of the dataset used in Andreou & Lieber (2020). All data were originally extracted from the Corpus of Contemporary American English (COCA, Davies 2008-) and the British National Corpus (BNC, Davies 2004). The Andreou & Lieber (2020) dataset contained over 57,000 tokens of *-ing* and conversion nominalizations derived from 106 base verbs. These verbs were chosen from all aspectual classes and also from a range of frequencies. The Lieber & Plag (2022) dataset contained over 7000 tokens taken from the larger set and coded for aspectual class, quantification, and eventivity. Since my aim was to compare the aspectual nuances of *-ing* nominalizations with conversion nominalizations derived on identical bases, I extracted tokens of nominalizations from the Lieber &

---

4 Smith (1991) uses the features [+/- static], [+/- durative], and [+/- telic]. Brinton (1998) distinguishes static/dynamic. durative/punctual, and telic/atelic.

Plag database that were coded as both eventive and count, and that were matched for the verb base of the nominalization in either the singular or the plural.[5] [6]

From the 106 verbal bases in the original dataset, there were 29 verbs that showed eventive count readings in the singular (258 tokens in total) for both types of nominalization and 38 verbs that showed eventive count readings in the plural (549 tokens in total) for both types of nominalizations. The verbal bases found in the singular and plural sets overlapped, but were not identical, as some bases were attested with both types of eventive nominalization only in the singular or only in the plural. In both the singular and plural datasets, all of the [+dynamic] verb classes were reasonably well represented; only one state verb was attested in the plural and none in the singular, so the analysis here looks only at the [+dynamic] classes. The verbal bases for the singular and plural datasets are shown in Tables 2 and 3 (verbs in italics occur in both the singular and plural datasets). Table 4 shows the numbers of tokens for singular conversion nouns, singular -*ing* nouns, plural conversion nouns, and plural -*ing* nouns. Table 5 breaks these down by aspectual class:

Tab. 2: Verbal bases of singular nominalizations.

Aspectual class	Verbal bases	N
state		0
activity	*embrace, gurgle*, hurt, rise, sail, *stir*	6
accomplishment	bend, burn, *change, fix*, rise, transfer	6
achievement	*break*, find, *kill*, slam, split	5
semelfactive	*blink*, drip, *kick, knock*, punch, *tap*	6
sem/act	beat, shake	2
acc/ach	cast, shift	2
act/ach	pass	1
sem/ach	strike	1

Several verbs in the dataset could belong to either of two lexical aspects, often depending on particular senses of verbs. For example, the verb *cast* is an achieve-

---

[5] Lieber & Plag (2022) analyzes only singulars in this dataset, but their dataset contained plurals as well.
[6] Lieber & Plag (2022) are concerned with semantic eventivity, rather than with what have been called in the literature Complex Event Nominals (Grimshaw 1990) or argument structure nominals (Borer 2013). In coding nominalizations as count and eventive, (Lieber & Plag, 2022, 8f) used a number of criteria, given in (2) and (3) below.

Tab. 3: Verbal bases of plural nominalizations.

Aspectual class	Verbal bases	N
state		0
activity	account, climb, *embrace*, *gurgle*, ride, run, spin, step, *stir*, stretch, stumble, swim	12
accomplishment	change, *fix*, report, spread, take, wash	6
achievement	*break*, burst, finish, fracture, *kill*, split	6
semelfactive	*blink*, flash, *kick*, knock, poke, *tap*	6
sem/act	beat, *shake*, shove	3
acc/ach	cast, *cut*, shift	3
act/ach		
sem/ach	pop	1

Tab. 4: Numbers of tokens.

	Singular	Plural	Total
conversion	176	309	485
-ing	82	240	322
Total	176	549	807

ment (punctual) when it refers to fishing, but an accomplishment (durative) when it refers to metallurgy. In comparing *-ing* and conversion nominalizations for such verbs, care was taken to make sure that the sense of the verb was the same in both nominalizations.

Each token in the dataset was coded for verb class, quantification, and eventivity, as in the dataset used in Lieber & Plag (2022). The criteria for count quantification are given in (2) and the criteria for eventivity are given in (3):[7]

(2)   Evidence for count qualification:
   a. A determiner *a/an* precedes the noun.
   b. There is an ordinal like *first, second*, etc. or the cardinal *one*.
   c. There is a modifier like *final, last,* or *single*.
   d. There is a quantifier like *many, each, every*.
   e. The noun is plural.

(3)   Evidence for eventivity:
   a. syntactic: kinds of PPs, possessives or other modifiers, synthetic compounds

---

[7] Coding for quantification and eventivity for the singulars in the Lieber & Plag (2022) database was done by both authors. Coding for eventivity for the plurals was done by Lieber, as was the coding for aspect discussed below.

Tab. 5: Breakdown of types and tokens by aspectual class of verbal base.

	Aspectual class	N types	N tokens	N tokens conv./-*ing*
Singular	activity	6	51	34/17
	accomplishment	6	35	26/9
	achievement	5	35	25/10
	semelfactive	6	75	57/18
	mixed	6	62	34/28
Total singular			258	
Plural	activity	12	178	98/80
	accomplishment	6	64	37/27
	achievement	6	119	71/48
	semelfactive	6	70	41/29
	mixed	7	118	53/65
Total plural			549	

   i. The context shows a tensed verb that suggests an eventive reading for the nominalization.
   ii. There is a temporal adjectival or adverbial modifier like *frequent, continuous, repeated* etc. that suggests an eventive reading.
   iii. There is a possessive subject or a *by* phrase with an agentive interpretation.
   iv. There are other PPs that indicate participants in an event (e.g., *of* PPs).
   v. There are manner modifiers like *intentional, personal,* or *nervous* that suggest eventivity.
   vi. There is a temporal preposition like *after* or *before* that suggests eventivity.
   vii. The nominalization occurs as the second element in a synthetic compound and the first element is construed as the internal argument of the base verb.
 b. semantic: paraphrases that suggest eventivity
   i. The feeling of
   ii. The state of
   iii. The activity of
   iv. An instance of

In addition to the coding for eventivity and quantification, the singular and plural datasets were coded for a number of possible aspectual readings. First, each token was coded for whether the event denoted was bounded (context implied that the event was finished or had reached an endpoint) or unbounded (context gave no indication that the event had come to an end). Factors involved in determining boundedness included the tense of surrounding verbs and modifiers that occurred in context.[8]

(4) a. Event is bounded
         BNC 1991: He's right, he has the body of a whippet topped by the face of a bulldog that's been given a severe KICKING.
         Mitigating Circumstances 1993: Feeling the eyes on her, Lily threw her arms around John's neck in an awkward EMBRACE, then stepped back.
     b. Event is unbounded
         Outdoor Life 1996: With the approach of spring, gobblers begin a round-robin KICKING that breaks up their large, fairly peaceful winter flock into smaller, more compatible groups.
         Nights in Black Satin 2007: Some guy she couldn't see clasped her around the waist from behind and enfolded her in a dance-club EMBRACE, moving his body sinuously with hers as they writhed with the music.

Each token was also coded both for the durativity of the base verb (where states, activities, and accomplishments were [+durative] and achievements and semelfactives were [-durative]) and for the durativity of the resulting nominalization, that is, whether the nominalization implied an event that occurred over a linguistically appreciable amount of time or not. Singular tokens were also coded for iterativity. Plural tokens were coded for whether they implied multiple sets of events. Examples illustrating these distinctions can be seen in (5):

(5) a. Nominalization interpreted as durative
         Hellboy 2004: After a moment, a weird GURGLE emanates from the creature's innards.
         Highlights for Children 2011: Suddenly, the rumbling stopped. A giant GURGLING came up from the bay.
     b. Nominalization interpreted as punctual
         New England Review 2007: The sound of the ball echoing with each solid KICK, and the George Harrison song, his guitar on "My Sweet Lord," how perfect it was, how fine!

---

8 See Andreou & Lieber (2020) for further discussion of issues involved in determining boundedness in deverbal nominalizations.

c. Nominalization interpreted as iterative
Esquire 1997: He would flicker into view and then, just as suddenly, disappear with a nervous TAPPING on the coffee cup.
d. Nominalization interpreted as implying multiple sets of events
A grown-up kind of pretty 2012: She responded by digging her toes into the sand, and I could read savage KICKINGS and the wailings of the damned in her face.

Finally, all tokens were coded for whether there was special focus on the kind of activity or the activity viewed as a type rather than a specific event. Factors involved in determining focus on the kind of activity included the presence of qualitative modifiers like *gentle* or *bearable*, the presentation of the event as generic, hypothetical, or typical, or the listing of the nominalization alongside other types of events, as the examples in (6) illustrate. This category is not meant to be an aspectual category, but rather implies that the event is viewed as not being anchored at a specific time.

(6) Emphasis on kind of activity:
   a. *US News and World Report 1996*: But in each case, says Nissenbaum, Christmas exchanges amounted to a PASSING of goods from master to servant, patron to apprentice and wealthy to poor.
   b. *Fantasy and Science Fiction 2004*: When the evening news came on with its roster of rapes and KILLINGS, he turned off the set, escorted his protesting daughter through her evening rituals, tucked her into bed, and then went to his room and lay sleepless.
   c. *Chicago Sun-Times 1995*: Knowing that a new crop of pears is right around the corner makes the fading of summer and its glorious bounty a bearable PASSING.

In example (6-a) the event is described as generic or hypothetical rather than as actual occurring events. In (6-b), *killings* is part of a list of event types, alongside *rapes*. And in (6-c), we have a qualitative modifier that focuses attention on the type of event.[9]

---

[9] The presence of a qualitative adjective modifying the nominalization often forces the focus on activity, but it is neither necessary nor sufficient to produce that reading. Instead, the activity reading seems to depend on a subtle combination of factors that requires further study.

5 Results

As has already been argued by Andreou & Lieber (2020), both conversion and -*ing* nominalizations can express either bounded or unbounded readings, and boundedness is independent of whether the verbal base is durative or punctual or the nominalization itself is construed as durative or punctual. (4) shows examples of the -*ing* nominalization *kicking* and conversion nominalization *embrace*, which can be bounded or unbounded depending on the context in which theyhttps://www.overleaf.com/project/63569319352b43463349e1a7 are deployed. Interested readers can find further discussion in Andreou & Lieber (2020) of the complex issue of boundedness in nominalization as well examples that show that both conversion and -*ing* nominalizations based on all of the lexical aspects can occur with either bounded or unbounded readings.

What has not been examined systematically in previous literature is the effect of durativity on the interpretation of these two types of nominalization. I begin by comparing singular conversion and -*ing* nominalizations on different types of bases, first on activities and accomplishments, then on achievements and semelfactives.

On durative bases (activity and accomplishment), we can observe two possible effects. One possibility is that the conversion and -*ing* nominalizations can turn out to be more or less semantically equivalent or interchangeable, as the examples in (7) suggest:

(7)   a.   *Fortune 2019*: Some of the leagues' positions are in line with casino industry groups like the AGA, including an EMBRACE of mobile betting and support for cooperation between the leagues and bookmakers on detecting irregular betting patterns that could signal "integrity issues" with certain games and contests.
       b.   *NPR_ATC 1994*: Tuesday in terms of those who cast their vote, but I think we as Republicans need to be somewhat careful that we don't read this as a total EMBRACING of a strict conservative ideological agenda, that more of the people want to see things in Washington get fixed.

In the examples in (7) the -*ing* and conversion nominalizations seem to be virtually the same in meaning, and for all intents and purposes interchangeable. This suggests that sometimes nominal -*ing* has no aspectual effect.

A second possibility that we see is that the -*ing* nominalization, while still durative, seems to be deployed in contexts that place a stronger focus on the type of activity denoted by the nominalization as compared to the conversion nominalization. In other words, the -*ing* nominalization seems to be preferred in generic contexts.[10]

(8) a. *Analog Science Fiction & Fact 2010*: I'll fire a quick BURN, push myself above and behind you.
 b. *Ugly Ways 1993*: On leaving this city the characters have a vision of its demolition by fire, or rather, as it burns we are given a series of famous fictional burnings of cities, libraries, and books. This constitutes a ritualistic BURNING of the books in which the characters were conceived; they are thus taken out of the 'old world' of their origins and made to embark on an adventure in the 'new world' of Brooke-Rose's novel.

(8-a) has a clear 'instance' reading of an actual event – the example describes the rapid firing of some sort of burner on a spaceship. In contrast, the -*ing* nominalization in (8-b) denotes a type of event, as suggested by the modifier *ritualistic*. This is not to say that genericity is actually contributed by the -*ing* suffix, but rather that the -*ing* form is preferred in these sorts of generic contexts. The conclusion to be drawn here is that -*ing* on durative bases sometimes has the effect of focusing on the nature of the activity, but in other cases seems to be aspectually invisible. The latter non-effect is what I have termed ghost aspect.

In contrast, -*ing* seems to show more robust aspectual effects on punctual bases (semelfactives and achievements). Here we find that conversion nominalizations typically have a punctual interpretation as their bases do, unless there is a modifier in context that suggests otherwise, as we see in (9):

(9) a. *Golf Magazine 2004*: "Cheater," he says without a BLINK. "You're a zero. You should wear a mask."
 b. *1634: The Galileo Affair 2005*: Richelieu clasped his hands behind his back and turned further. A long BLINK, then, both eyes closed for a whole breath before they opened, and he leaned forward a little.

In (9-a), the conversion nominalization on a semelfactive base is interpreted as punctual. In (9-b), the modifier *long* coerces a durative interpretation, which is not possible with the nominalization alone. The evidence that this durative reading is the result of coercion rather than something inherent in the verb base *blink* is that with semelfactives, the addition of durativity with -*ing* would naturally lead

---

10 Note that I do not mean to say here that for a given -*ing* type (say, *burning*) all tokens in the dataset will display the same reading. In other words, the example in (8-b) has a generic reading, while other tokens of *burning* in the dataset might simply be durative in interpretation.

to an iterative reading. In other words, *blinking* typically refers to a sequence of blinks, rather than a single on-going blink. which is what (9-b) implies.

On the other hand, *-ing* nominalization on a punctual base always has some semantic effect. Sometimes this effect is one of simply adding a durative interpretation, as we see in (10-a); here *splitting* in context suggests continuation over some time. Where the verbal base is semelfactive, however, the effect of *-ing* is to yield an iterative interpretation (10-b):

(10)   a.   *ABA Journal 1998*: Thus, joint custody can encompass anything from an equal SPLITTING of expenses and decision-making to arrangements that are in fact indistinguishable from sole custody with visitation.
        b.   *Leprechaun 1993*: There is a sudden loud KNOCKING on the door and Bill turns and goes to the door.

What we see then on the singulars is that the effects of *-ing* on punctual bases are always visible in some way, whereas on durative bases *-ing* sometimes merely nominalizes with no aspectual effect.

Let us turn now to the plural conversion and *-ing* nominalizations. Where we find plurals on the accomplishment and activity bases, we again find two possibilities. As was the case in the singulars, one possibility is that the conversion and *-ing* nominalizations can have identical readings, as illustrated in (11), where *washes* and *washings* are virtually interchangeable:

(11)   a.   *Good Housekeeping 2010*: Very absorbent but also quick-drying, these cotton towels looked and felt lovely even after multiple WASHES, though they did shrink some (three to four inches in length and about an inch in width).
        b.   *New England Review 1999*: He had on camouflage pants whose earth-tones had faded from countless WASHINGS and heavy-soled combat boots.

The second possibility, as we saw with the singulars, is that there is a slight difference of interpretation between the two types of nominalization, with the *-ing* nominalization suggesting a stronger focus on the type of activity, as compared to the conversion nominalization. This is illustrated in the examples in (12):

(12)   a.   *Climber and Hill Walker (BNC)*: Second ascensionist Steve Reid reports the crag to be of good, rough rock, although further cleaning would make the CLIMBS more enjoyable.

b. *Michigan Quarterly Review 2001*: All through one lunch she watched the workers bringing down the tiers of planks and ropes and metal tubing, their teamwork a delicate dance of CLIMBINGS and lowerings.

Where the conversion nominalization in (12-a) simply denotes multiple instances of a 'climb' event, (12-b) places more emphasis on the kind of activity: as an event it is *a delicate dance*.

On achievement or semelfactive bases, the plurals can exhibit several possible readings. Plural conversion nominalizations on semelfactive bases frequently receive iterative interpretations, as we see in (13):

(13) *American History 1991*: Weird light illuminated them in FLASHES, and it was almost too noisy to hold a conversation.

For *-ing* nominalizations, if a punctual base already has received a durative interpretation in the singular through the affixation of *-ing*, the plural might simply denote multiple durative events:

(14) *San Francisco Chronicle 2006*: Police said that tension over drug corners is still a factor in some KILLINGS, particularly in several neighborhoods just north of the West Oakland BART Station.

Or the *-ing* nominalization might put a special focus on the type of activity, as we see in (15):

(15) *Saturday Evening Post 1997*: However, many people know someone who is chronically suicidal and has had many treatments for suicidal threats or attempts, usually involving overdoses or wrist CUTTINGS.

Perhaps the most interesting reading we find occurs in plural *-ing* nominalizations on semelfactive bases. Recall that singular *-ing* nominalizations on semelfactives frequently have an iterative interpretation, which is to say that they denote multiple repeated punctual events. When such nominalizations are pluralized, what we find is an interpretation that we might describe as doubly plural; they denote not simply iterations of punctual events but multiple events of iterated punctual events.

(16) *A grown-up kind of pretty 2012*: She responded by digging her toes into the sand, and I could read savage KICKINGS and the wailings of the damned in her face.

A *kicking* typically involves more than one *kick*. But *kickings* here refers to multiple instances of multiple kicks.

To summarize, it appears that -*ing* sometimes has an aspectual contribution to make in nominalizations and sometimes does not. Specifically, when -*ing* nominalizes a verbal base that is an activity or an accomplishment, nominalizing with -*ing* can potentially have no aspectual effect at all. This is what I call ghost aspect: the nominalizing affix has an aspectual component to its meaning, but sometimes you don't see it. In contrast, when -*ing* nominalizes an achievement or semelfactive base, we find more robust aspectual effects. In the next section, I turn to what that specific aspectual component is and the question of why the ghost aspect option is available at all for -*ing* nominalizations.

6 Analysis

I propose that the observations I have made here can be explained on the basis of three assumptions. First, lexical aspect can be represented featurally, as we saw in Table 1, with activities and accomplishments bearing the feature [+durative] and achievements and semelfactives bearing the feature [-durative]. Second, along with changing the verbal base to a noun, -*ing* contributes the feature [+durative] to its verbal bases, whereas conversion adds no special aspectual feature.[11] Finally, pluralization has the semantic effect of imposing a part structure, that is, creating or imposing a structure of semantic atoms, using Rothstein's (2017) term. In eventive abstract nouns the imposition of a part structure can lead to an inference of multiple events, which in turn necessitates an assumption of temporal duration. In other words, plurals are not [+durative] per se but durativity can be inferred from the adding of a part structure to an event.[12]

This analysis predicts that -*ing* nominalization should have more consistent semantic effects on punctual bases than on durative bases. If a base is already lexically [+durative], adding [+durative] -*ing* would add nothing new to the aspectual semantics of the nominalization and the resulting -*ing* nominalization might potentially be construed as synonymous with a conversion nominalization on the same base. Alternatively, adding [+durative] -*ing* to an already [+durative] base might invite an inference to place further focus on the generic nature of the nom-

---

11 See Lieber (2016) for semantic representations of both -*ing* and conversion nominalization within the LSF framework.
12 This analysis could be formalized in a number of ways, for example, as is done in the Model Theoretic literature; see Rothstein (2017) for a thorough review of various approaches to this formalization. It can also be formalized in lexical semantic frameworks, such as in Jackendoff (1991) or Lieber (2004) by using an individuating feature ([+i] for Jackendoff, [+CI] for Lieber). Nothing here hinges on the precise means of formalization.

inalized event. Such an inference might follow from the tendency to avoid synonymy between the two kinds of nominalizations.[13]

Turning to nominalizations on achievements and semelfactives, that is, the [-durative] bases, we should expect -*ing* to have a more consistent and robust aspectual effect, as the value of the durative feature of the verbal base would necessarily undergo a change in the derived word. And indeed we do see consistent semantic effects of nominalizing with -*ing* on punctual bases, including both simple durativity and iterativity. In contrast, conversion nominalizations on punctual bases should never be interpreted as having temporal duration, but rather should have a simple 'instance' interpretation. Indeed, as we have seen, we only get a durative interpretation from a conversion on a punctual base when there is a modifier such as *long* (*a long blink*) that coerces a durative interpretation that is not available from the conversion form alone. In other words, durativity in this case is not an effect of conversion.

We turn now to plural nominalizations. Here we would expect that the part structure imposed on by the plural on the nominalization should lead to semantic effects under two circumstances. First, with conversion nominalizations on punctual bases, imposing a part structure through pluralization might lead to an inference of multiple events with temporal duration. On semelfactives, an interpretation of iterativity would then result, as we find with nominalizations like *flashes* in (17-a). The plural conversion noun should therefore come close to the singular -*ing* on a semelfactive base. That this is a plausible prediction is confirmed by the data in (17):

(17)   a.   *Esquire 2010*: ...she can still see and feel and hear the pop and whine of the cameras, the blinding fusillade of FLASHES, the bump and jostle, the chaotic din: Paris, over here!
          b.   *Persephone (BNC)*: As the light withdrew from the grass and the dips in the turf and those paths that were beneath overhanging branches, and collected higher in the sky, the FLASHING and the music of the fairground became more prominent.

The other place where we would expect to find a special effect of pluralization would be on nominalizations that already have an iterative interpretation, as we find with -*ing* nominalizations on semelfactive bases. Here, if the plural mor-

---

[13] At this point the appearance of the generic reading under these conditions is more on the level of of a descriptive observation; why just this reading follows from adding a [+durative] affix to a [+durative] base still awaits explanation. One possibility suggested by a reviewer is that the -*ing* serves to generalize over time indices giving rise to the generic reading.

pheme partitions an already iterative event, we interpret the result as multiple iterative events -- our double plural.

Interestingly, there are two situations where it is predicted that we should find doublets between conversion and *-ing* nominalizations on the same bases, specifically in either the singular or the plural where the two types of nominalizations are built on [+durative] bases, that is, on activities or accomplishments. Although it is probably more typical for the *-ing* nominalization to invite a further inference of focus on activity, thus distinguishing itself from the corresponding conversion nominalization, such doublets do occur, as I have shown by the examples in (7) and (11). Those are cases where *-ing* has become an aspectual ghost.

7 Conclusion

I began with several questions. My first goal was to determine whether nominalizing *-ing* makes any distinctive aspectual contribution to the nouns it derives. Here, we have seen that *-ing* does have distinctive effects as compared to conversion nominalizations on the same bases, contrary to the claims of Alexiadou et al. (2010), Alexiadou (2013), and Andreou & Lieber (2020). However, the aspectual effect of nominal *-ing* is neither imperfectivity (Brinton 1995; Alexiadou 2001) nor progressivity (Asher 1993). Neither does telicity enter into the semantics of conversion versus *-ing* nominalization (Borer 2013). Rather, the effects of *-ing* have to do solely with temporal duration. Nominal *-ing* both changes a verbal base to a noun and adds the feature [+durative]. Conversion changes category, but makes no aspectual contribution of its own.

My second goal was to determine whether the aspectual class of the base verb had any systematic effect on the aspectual interpretation of *-ing* and conversion nominalizations. I have shown here that *-ing* on [-durative] bases (achievements and semelfactives) shows subtle but systematic semantic effects, whereas on [+durative] bases (activities, accomplishments) *-ing* sometimes shows a semantic effect (a focusing on the kind of activity) but sometimes shows no effect at all. In effect, adding a [+durative] feature to an already [+durative] verbal base can simply be redundant. Those cases where the [+durative] *-ing* suffix adds nothing to the nominalization as a whole are cases of what I have dubbed ghost aspect -- it's there, but it doesn't seem to be there.

Finally, I looked at the effect of pluralization on both *-ing* and conversion nominalizations. One striking finding is that plural *-ing* nominalizations on semelfactive bases can have a sort of double plural reading. I also observed that we sometimes find a similarity between plural conversion nominalizations like *knocks* and singular *-ing* nominalizations like *knocking*. Both observations can be explained by the proposed analysis: nominalizing *-ing* adds the semantic feature of durativity to a punctual base and the plural imposes a part structure that allows for an inference of durativity. Thus, a plural conversion nominalization on a semelfactive base can receive an interpretation similar to a singular *-ing* nominalization, and a plural *-ing* nominalization can yield a doubly plural interpretation on a base that is already interpreted as iterative. What we see, then, is that there is a complex interplay here between the aspectual durativity of base verbs, the durativity of the nominalizations, and the implied durativity that sometimes results from pluralization.

Bibliography

Alexiadou, Artemis. 2001. *Functional structure in nominals: Nominalization and ergativity*, vol. 42 Linguistik Aktuell/Linguistics Today. Amsterdam and Philadelphia: John Benjamins.

Alexiadou, Artemis. 2013. Nominal vs. verbal *-ing* constructions and the development of the English progressive. *English Linguistics Research* 2(2). 126–140.

Alexiadou, Artemis, Gianina Iordachioaia & Elene Soare. 2010. Number/aspect interactions in the syntax of nominalizations: A distributed approach. *Journal of Linguistics* 46(3). 537–574.

Andreou, Marios & Rochelle Lieber. 2020. Aspectual and quantificational properties of deverbal conversion and *-ing* nominalizations: The power of context. *English Language and Linguistics* 24(2). 333–363.

Asher, Nicholas. 1993. *Reference to abstract objects in discourse*. Dordrecht: Kluwer.

Borer, Hagit. 2013. *Structuring sense. volume iii: Taking form*, vol. 3. Oxford University Press.

Brinton, Laurel. 1995. The aktionsart of deverbal nouns in English. In Pier Marco Bertinetto, Valentina Bianchi, James Higginbotham & Mario Squartini (eds.), *Temporal reference, aspect, and actionality, vol. i: Semantic and syntactic perspectives*, 27–42. Turin: Rosenberg and Sellier.

Brinton, Laurel. 1998. Aspectuality and countability: A cross-categorial analogy. *English Language and Linguistics* 2(1). 37–63.

Chierchia, Gennaro. 1998. Plurality of mass nouns and the notion of 'semantic parameter'. In Susan Rothstein (ed.), *Events and grammar*, 53–103. Berlin: Springer.

Comrie, Bernard. 1976. *Aspect*. Cambridge: Cambridge University Press.

Davies, Mark. 2004. British National Corpus (from Oxford University Press). https://www.english-corpora.org/bnc.

Davies, Mark. 2008-. The Corpus of Contemporary American English (COCA): 520 million words, 1990-present. http://www.americancorpus.org/.

Filip, Hana. 2012. Lexical aspect. In Robert I. Binnick (ed.), *The Oxford handbook of tense and aspect*, 721–751. New York: Oxford University Press.

Grimshaw, Jane. 1990. *Argument structure*. Cambridge, MA: MIT Press.

Huddleston, Rodney & Geoffrey K. Pullum. 2002. *The Cambridge grammar of the English language*. Cambridge: Cambridge University Press.
Jackendoff, Ray. 1991. Parts and boundaries. *Cognition* 41(1-3). 9–45.
Krifka, Manfred. 1989. Nominal reference, temporal constitution and quantification in event semantics. In Renate Bartsch, Johan van Benthem & Peter van Emde Boas (eds.), *Semantics and contextual expression*, 75–115. Dordrecht: Foris.
Landman, Fred. 1995. Plurality. In Shalom Lappin (ed.), *Handbook of contemporary semantics*, 425–457. London: Wiley-Blackwell.
Lees, Robert. 1960. *The grammar of English nominalizations*. Bloomington: Indiana University Press.
Lieber, Rochelle. 2004. *Morphology and lexical semantics*. Cambridge: Cambridge University Press.
Lieber, Rochelle. 2016. *English nouns: The ecology of nominalization*. Cambridge: Cambridge University Press.
Lieber, Rochelle & Ingo Plag. 2022. The semantics of conversion nouns and *-ing* nominalizations: a quantitative and theoretical perspective. *Journal of Linguistics* 58(2). 307–343.
Link, Godehard. 1983. The logical analysis of plurals and mass terms: A lattice-theoretical approach. In Rainer Baeuerle, Christoph Schwarze & Arnim von Stechow (eds.), *Meaning, use and the interpretation of language*, 302–323. Berlin: De Gruyter.
Plag, Ingo, Lea Kawaletz, Sabine Arndt-Lappe & Rochelle Lieber. 2023. Analogical modeling of derivational semantics: Two case studies. In Sven Kotowski & Ingo Plag (eds.), *The semantics of derivational morphology. Theory, methods, evidence*, 103–141. Berlin: De Gruyter.
Pustejovsky, James. 1995. *The generative lexicon*. Cambridge, MA: MITPress.
Rothstein, Susan. 2017. *Semantics for counting and measuring*. Cambridge: Cambridge University Press.
Siegel, Laura. 1997. Gerundive nominals and the role of aspect. In Jennifer Austin & Aaron Lawson (eds.), *Proceedings of the 14th eastern states conference on linguistics*, 170–179.
Smith, Carlota. 1991. *The parameter of aspect*. Dordrecht: Kluwer Academic Publishers.
Verkuyl, Henk. 1993. *A theory of aspectuality*. Cambridge: Cambridge University Press.

Viktoria Schneider
Eventualities in the semantics of denominal nominalizations

Abstract: This paper deals with eventuality-related, denominal nominalizations. The term 'eventuality-related nominalizations' refers to nominalizations in which an eventuality plays a central role for the interpretation of the derivative. This paper will argue that a nominalizing affix requires an eventuality or a participant of an eventuality from the semantic representation of the base word. For deverbal nominalizations, the required eventive elements are straightforwardly available as verbs are typically eventive in nature. However, concerning nominal bases, the semantic representation of the base word is in many cases not straightforwardly eventive. This study aims at finding the required eventive structures for the nominalizing suffix -*ee* in nominal base words. In order to do so, data for denominal derivatives with the suffix -*ee* from previous research on the suffix are used and analyzed using a frame semantic approach. It can be observed that it is indeed possible to reveal eventive structures in nominal bases which are accessible for the process of nominalization.

Keywords: nominalization, semantics, suffix -*ee*, semantic representation, frame semantics

1 Introduction

Many English nominalizing suffixes, such as -*ation*, -*ee* or -*ment*, give rise to derivatives that denote either eventualities[1] or participants of eventualities. In this paper, such derivatives are called EVENTUALITY-RELATED. The examples in (1) and (2) illustrate that the base words denote eventualities which are, in both examples, central for the meaning of the derivatives.

(1)   Salary and bonus information for every **employee**. (COCA; see Davies 2008; BLOG, 2012)

---

[1] The term 'eventuality' includes events, processes and states. For a fine-grained distinction of the different types of eventualities see, for example, Bach (1986); Van Valin & LaPolla (1997/2002).

Viktoria Schneider, Heinrich-Heine-Universität Düsseldorf, email: viktoria.schneider@uni-duesseldorf.de

∂ Open Access. © 2023 the author(s), published by De Gruyter. This work is licensed under the Creative Commons Attribution-NoDerivatives 4.0 International License.
https://doi.org/10.1515/9783111074917-003

In (1), the derivative *employee* denotes a participant of the *employing-eventuality* denoted by the base *employ* as an employee is a person who is employed by someone.

In (2), on the other hand, the derivative with the suffix *-ment* denotes the whole eventuality denoted by the base to form the meaning of *befoulment*.

(2) Markham sets down the rules about park **befoulment**. (Plag et al. 2018: 474)

In general, eventuality-related nominalizations, as the examples in (1) and (2), denote either a (sub-)eventuality or a participant of an eventuality. The category of eventuality-relatedness is a rather broad category as several more fine-grained classes, which are to be found in the literature, such as, for example, participant, result, or eventive readings, are merged together in this umbrella term (see Lieber 2017 for an overview of the several diverging classification systems for the semantic categorization of nominalizations).

Research on nominalizations observed that such eventuality-related readings arise systematically from eventualities denoted by the base (see, e.g., Bauer et al. 2013, 213, Plag et al. 2018; Kawaletz 2023). There is an implicit consensus that suffixes which lead to eventuality-related readings prefer verbal bases because of the strong association of verbs and eventuality semantics (see, e.g., Haspelmath 2001; Van Valin & LaPolla 1997/2002; Szabó 2015; Moltmann 2019 on the preferential concurrence of word classes and ontological categories). Due to this strong link between verbs and eventualities, studies on eventuality-related nominalizations tend to focus on verbal bases (see, e.g., Grimshaw 1990; Alexiadou 2001; Lieber 2016; Plag et al. 2018; for overview articles with the same bias, see Alexiadou 2010; Lieber 2017).

However, such a narrow focus on only one possible word class of the base for a word-formation process is problematic. First, in English, the word class of a base is oftentimes not unambiguously identifiable. Determining the directionality of conversion poses a notoriously difficult problem for the identification of the word class of a base (see, e.g., Balteiro 2007; Bram 2011, Plag 2018, 87, see also Barbu Mititelu et al. 2023). Second, less ambiguous cases indicate that the majority of English word-formation processes operate on more than one word class (see, e.g., Plag 1999, 2004, 2018, 87, Bauer et al. 2013, ch. 10). Several authors suggest that it is the semantics of a word-formation process that determines potential bases regarding semantic compatibility of word-formation process and base. Conversely, the word class of the typical base of a process should be understood as an epiphenomenon of this word class's typical semantics (in particular Plag 2004; see also Barker 1998; Bauer et al. 2013). This also holds for nominalizations that produce eventuality-related readings on bases other than verbs. Some clearly denominal examples are given in (3).

(3) a. ozonation, sedimentation
    b. biographee, debtee

The problem which arises for a semantic account of the word-formation process with eventuality-related nominalizations is that nouns usually do not denote eventualities, in contrast to verbs (Haspelmath 2001; Van Valin & LaPolla 1997/2002; Szabó 2015; Moltmann 2019). Nevertheless, nominalizations based on non-deverbal bases also produce eventuality-related readings. For example, the bases for the derivatives in (3), like *sediment*, do not denote an eventuality, but the derivatives, like *sedimentation*, do. To the author's knowledge, to date there is no systematic study on denominal nominalizations with eventuality-related readings available (cf. Plag 2004). Since nominal bases, such as the noun *biography*, are not eventive, it remains unclear where the origin of the eventuality-related nature of the derivative lies.

Different approaches to nominalization semantics might suggest different solutions to the problems posed by examples such as those in (3). In syntactic approaches, such as Alexiadou (2001) or Borer (2013), dedicated functional projections are responsible for (sub-)eventive or participant readings. In lexicalist morpheme-based approaches, such as the framework of Lieber (2004; 2016), affixes come with a semantic representation of their own, for example, with feature specifications such as +DYNAMIC to mark eventive semantics. In word-based approaches, in contrast, affixes are not linguistic signs on their own, and it is only (abstractions of) complex words that have meaning (as, e.g., in Booij 2010; Koenig 1999). In this paper, a form of word-based morphology that has recently been employed successfully in the analysis of the semantics of deverbal English *-ment*-nominalization is followed (see Plag et al. 2018; Kawaletz 2023). In this approach, the semantic contribution of the suffix is modeled as its potential to induce referential shifts on the semantics of its base.

In this paper, I will extend Plag et al.'s (2018) and Kawaletz's (2023) reference shifting approach and show that denominal nominalizations are also dependent on eventualities in their respective bases. The focus here lies on denominal nominalizations with the suffix *-ee*. The examples in (4) illustrate further denominal derivatives with the suffix *-ee* mentioned in the literature (Barker 1998, Plag 2004, Mühleisen 2010).

(4) biographee, covenantee, festschriftee, mentee, tutee

Previous research on eventuality-related nominalizations with the suffix -ee already illustrates that an eventuality in the base is essential to form the participant reading of the derivative (Barker 1998, Plag 2004). This assumption of the necessity of an eventuality in the base leads to the following question for the analysis of the word-formation process with nominal bases:

> How can the semantic representation of nominal bases be modeled to reveal the eventive structures needed to induce the referential shift to create the meaning of the derivative?

In order to reveal the eventive structures in the nominal base, the semantic representation of the base needs to be decomposed. frame semantics will be used to model the semantic structures of the derivatives and bases. In particular, the reference shifting approach suggested by Plag et al. (2018) and Kawaletz (2023) will be followed.

Some of the examples chosen in this paper might also have a verbal variant of the base. A frequency criterion was chosen to determine the word class of the base. The nominal base forms of the chosen examples for this study are by far more frequent than the verbal forms. This difference in frequency leads to the assumption that the nominal form is more likely chosen as the base for the nominalization than the verbal option (see, e.g., Plag 2018, ch. 3). Furthermore, new -ee formations are often based on -er formations (Bauer et al. 2013, ch. 23) which then may pose the same problem, e.g., *aggressor, mentor, executioner.*

The next section of this paper discusses the theoretical background. Section 3 gives exemplary frame semantic analyses of eventuality-related nominalizations with nominal bases and the suffix -ee for non-derived bases in 3.1 and paradigmatically related cases in 3.2. Section 5 evaluates the findings of these analyses and discusses implications for further work on eventuality-related, non-deverbal nominalizations.

2 Theoretical background

2.1 Eventuality-related nominalizations

Eventualities are complex semantic entities of which participants, like AGENTS and PATIENTS, are part of. Henceforth, the term 'eventive elements' will be used to refer to participants, eventualities, sub-eventualities and eventualities in the broader sense, including states. Theoretically, sub-eventualities, for example, RESULT-STATES, can also be contained in the eventive structure of one eventuality. For the creation of the meaning of an eventuality-related nominalization, either the eventuality or one of its participants from the semantic representation of the base word is required. Table 1 illustrates possible derivatives based on the verb *employ*.

Tab. 1: Derivatives based on the verb *employ*.

derivative	eventive element
employer	AGENT
employee	PATIENT
employment	EVENTUALITY

It can be observed that the nominalizations with the different nominalizing suffixes, *-er/-ee/-ment*, refer to different eventive elements from the eventuality denoted by the base. The eventive elements are inherited from the semantic representation of the base verb (Löbner 2013; Plag et al. 2018). The derivative with the suffix *-er* denotes the AGENT, and the derivative with the suffix *-ee* denotes the PATIENT of the *employing-action*.[2] The derivative with the suffix *-ment*, then, denotes the whole eventuality.

As illustrated, the derivational process of eventuality-related nominalizations is straightforward with verbs, as verbs are eventive in nature. Verbs denote eventualities which can be decomposed into several eventive elements that are relevant for the construal of the derivative's semantics: The semantic representation of the verb *employ* in Table 1 consists of an eventuality and its participants. The word-formation process can refer to one of these eventive elements to create the meaning of the derivative.

Turning to nominal bases, nouns are not always as straightforwardly eventive as verbs. Especially nouns which denote concrete objects or artifacts seem not to be eventive at all. Nonetheless, it is possible to take a noun like *biography* as the base word for a nominalization to form the derivative *biographee*. The derivative shifts the references from the book or its content to a person, the person whose life is described. In order to achieve this change in meaning, a participant of an eventuality which fulfills the requirements of the word-formation process with the suffix *-ee* is needed. This referential shift is similar to the verbal process in the example derivative *employee* which denotes the PATIENT of the *employing-action*.

---

[2] An alternative analysis would say that an *employee* is someone who is in a state of being employed. A detailed analysis of *employee* is beyond the scope of this paper. I use this derivative only for exemplification of my approach.

Nevertheless, although the referential shift from the object *biography* to a participant of an eventuality in the derivative *biographee* seems similar to the process with verbal bases, it is unclear where the eventuality with the required participant comes from. Thus, the process does not seem to be as straightforward with nominal bases compared to verbal bases. The problem has been mentioned rather vaguely in the literature:

> The verbal relation is implied by context or can be inferred from the nature of the non-verbal base. [...] Such interpretations follow from the sort of activities that the base nouns could conceivably be involved in. (Bauer et al. 2013: 233)

It remains unclear if and where an eventuality in a nominal base is inherent in the semantic representation of the nominal base.

One approach that does incorporate eventualities in lexical entries in nouns is Pustejovsky's Generative Lexicon (1996, ch. 6; for different approaches on eventualities in nouns see, e.g., Larson 1998; Winter & Zwarts 2012). For example, for the artifact noun *biography*, the approach by Pustejovsky would posit two eventualities in the lexical entry. In one eventuality, the artifact came into being as a result of the writing of the book (AGENTIVE-QUALE). The second eventuality is what Pustejovsky (1996, ch. 6) has labeled 'qualia' (more specific: TELIC-QUALE) and other people have called 'affordance' (see, e.g., Löbner 2013, 315). Affordances describe what artifacts are used for and they function as an integral part of the meaning of the noun. The second eventuality would thus describe the presumed usage of this book, that is, the reading of the book. Both eventualities relate to the idea by Bauer et al. (2013) that the base noun could be involved in an activity. The analysis by Pustejovsky does not go into detail about the eventive structures itself. For the purpose of this study, the eventualities in the nominal base need to be further decomposed as the word-formation with a nominalizing suffix can refer to a whole eventuality, an embedded sub-eventuality or a participant taking part in the eventuality. Hence, further decomposition of the eventuality is needed to identify the eventive element for the word-formation process. To achieve this necessary degree of decomposition of eventive structures, frame semantics is used to model the inherent structure of the nominal bases to clarify the referential shift from base to derivative. This will be explained in the following section.

2.2 Semantic frames

The semantic frames used in this study are based on Barsalou's (1992b, 1992a) theory of cognitive frames. The general idea behind semantic frames is that meanings are concepts, and that such concepts in human cognition are stored as 'frames'

(Petersen 2007, Löbner 2013, 2014, Gamerschlag et al. 2014). Research on deverbal nominalizations has shown that frame semantics is a useful tool to analyze the semantic representation of a base word and its derivative in a unified format (e.g., Kawaletz & Plag 2015, Plag et al. 2018, Kawaletz 2023).

The central building block of frames are attribute and value structures as known from other frameworks (e.g., HPSG, Pollard & Sag 1994). Attributes describe a concept and each attribute then takes a specific value (Löbner 2013, 303). For example, the sentence *John employed Paul* describes an employing-eventuality that is specified for the attributes AGENT with the value *John* and PATIENT with the value *Paul*. The semantic representation of the verb *employ* can be depicted in an attribute-value-matrix (AVM) as in Figure 1:

$$\boxed{0} \begin{bmatrix} employing\text{-}action \\ \text{AGENT } \boxed{1} \ John \\ \text{PATIENT } \boxed{2} \ Paul \end{bmatrix}$$
$$\text{REF} = \boxed{0}$$

Fig. 1: Exemplary AVM for the verb *employ*.

The AVM describes an *employing-action* as the semantic representation of the verb *employ*. The action is specified for two attributes, an AGENT and a PATIENT. These two attributes are further specified with the values *John* and *Paul*. The numbers in the AVM are indices which serve as labels for and reference to the elements in the frame. The index $\boxed{0}$ labels the *employing-action*, the index $\boxed{1}$ labels the AGENT, and the index $\boxed{2}$ labels the PATIENT. Reference of the lexeme is specified by the REFERENCE-attribute (REF). For the lexeme *employ*, reference is on the whole event, i.e., on node $\boxed{0}$. Frames are recursive, as a value can have further attributes which then have further values (Löbner 2013, 307).

Moving on to the description of participant-denoting derivatives in semantic frames, a shift of reference is necessary from the action itself to a specific participant in the eventuality denoted by the base. This referential shift of the base word to the derivative is indicated in the REFERENCE-attribute (REF) in the semantic frame (Plag et al. 2018, Kawaletz 2023). Figure 2 depicts an AVM for the derivative *employer*.

In order to form the derivative *employer* from the base verb *employ*, the reference shifts from the *employing-action* indexed with $\boxed{0}$ to the AGENT-attribute indexed with $\boxed{1}$. Hence, the meaning of the derivative describes the AGENT of the *employing-action*, *John*, and not the whole action of the verb *employ*. The deriva-

$$\boxed{0}\begin{bmatrix} employing\text{-}action \\ \text{AGENT } \boxed{1} \ John \\ \text{PATIENT } \boxed{2} \ Paul \end{bmatrix}$$
$\text{REF}=\boxed{1}$

Fig. 2: Exemplary AVM for the derivative *employer*.

tive *employee*, on the other hand, would shift the reference of the base to the PATIENT-attribute *Paul* indexed with $\boxed{2}$.

2.3 Restrictions on the suffix -ee

Before the formalization of the base and the derivative will be described in detail, an explanation on what is already known about the restrictions for the suffix *-ee* in general is needed. Phonetically, the suffix *-ee* is autostressed (e.g., Plag 2018, 89). Verbal bases are frequent and nominal bases are not uncommon for formations with the suffix *-ee*. Looking at the semantics, the meaning of a derivative with the suffix *-ee* is rather clearly discernable. The denoted participant follows three known restrictions. First, the derived noun denotes a sentient participant of an eventuality. For example, the PATIENT in the *employing-action* (see, e.g., Table 1) is necessarily a sentient being. The sentience constraint is an important semantic requirement for derivatives ending in the suffix *-ee*, but it can be violated in domain-specific terminology (Barker 1998, 710).

Second, another known restriction for the word-formation process with the suffix *-ee* is the necessity of an eventuality in the base. Barker (1998) calls this constraint "episodic linking":

> The intuition behind episodic linking is very simple: the referent of a noun phrase headed by an *-ee* noun must have participated in an event of the type corresponding to the stem verb. For example, in order to qualify as a *gazee* it is necessary to participate in a certain role in a gazing event. This requirement is a crucial part of explaining how the meaning of an *-ee* noun can depend on the meaning of its stem without depending on the syntactic argument structure associated with the stem. (Barker 1998, 711)

The necessity of episodic linking shows that eventualities and their participants are indispensable for the creation of the meaning of the derivative with the suffix *-ee*. More specifically, the derivative denotes a participant of the base's eventuality. Due to the other requirements of the word-formation process with *-ee*, not all participants involved in the eventuality in the base word are possible candidates for the word-formation process. The same restrictions hold for denominal -*ee* derivatives (Barker 1998, Plag 2004).

Third, the participant denoted by the suffix -*ee* is restricted by a lack of volitionality. Hence, the participant which is described by the derivative must be non-volitional. This lack of volitionality is usually defined as the lack of control the -*ee* participant has over an eventuality. The lack of volitional control is not an absolute property but rather up to a certain degree, in contrast to the sentience requirement or the episodic linking (Barker 1998, 719). More precisely, a participant does not have to be completely non-volitional but rather more non-volitional than other possible targets for the suffix -*ee*. For instance, a PATIENT is less volitional than an AGENT. As a consequence, exceptions to the volitionality constraint can be found. For example, *escapee* denotes the AGENT of the *escaping-action*. This violation is possible for -*ee* derivatives with bases that are either intransitive verbs or verbs that can be interpreted as having a non-volitional subject participant (Barker 1998, 719f.). For new formations with the suffix -*ee*, the volitionality constraint is expected to be satisfied.

As mentioned previously, nominalizations with the suffix -*ee* are attested for nominal bases. The list in (5) illustrates some -*ee* nominalizations with a nominal base. Note that this list is not exhaustive.

(5) *Non-deverbal* -ee *derivatives* (Barker 1998, Plag 2004, Mühleisen 2010)

aggressee	asylee	bargee	benefactee
biographee	blind datee	covenantee	custodee
debtee	executionee	festschriftee	inquisitee
laryngectomee	letteree	malefactee	
mentee	moneylendee	optionee	
patentee	philanthropee	politicee	
return adressee	tutee	wardee	

Summarizing, previous research has established three restrictions for nominalizations with the suffix -*ee*, which hold for all kinds of bases (Barker 1998, Plag 2004):
– the meaning of the derivative is a participant involved in an eventuality in the base word
– the participant must be sentient (sentience requirement)
– the participant lacks volitional control with some exceptions, for example, intransitive verbs (non-volitionality constraint)

This paper focuses on two types of denominal nominalizations. First, the denominal derivatives *debtee, biographee* and *covenantee* will be analyzed to illustrate the word-formation process with non-derived bases in section 3.1.

Second, section 3.2 illustrates the word-formation process with bases that appear to be derived, like *tutor* or *mentor*. These bases look as if they are already derived with the suffix *-or/-er*. However, they are loan words either from French or Latin. The suffix *-ee* replaces the suffix *-er/-or* to refer to a different participant from the eventuality given by the loan word.

3 Frame formalization

In Figure 3, a frame representation of the derivational process with the suffix *-ee* is shown. It includes the constraints given by Barker (1998)(see section 2.3). The frame illustrates which elements are needed in the semantic representation of the base to successfully form a nominalization with the suffix *-ee*. Part of this descriptive generalization is an eventuality in the base. This eventuality then includes a participant which, in turn, is referred to by the derivative.

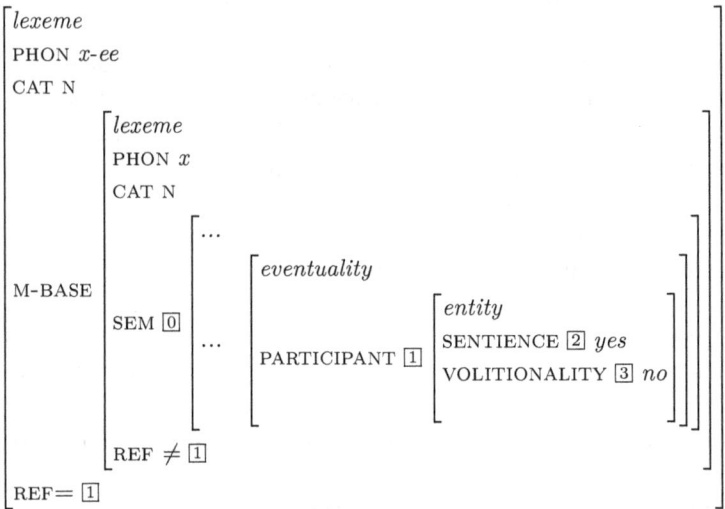

Fig. 3: Generalized derivational process for denominal *-ee* nominalizations.

The type *lexeme* at the top of the frame stands for the derivative and base under investigation. This derivative has the phonological form[3] (PHON) of the base *x* and the suffix *-ee*. The derivative has the syntactic category noun (CAT N). The attribute M-BASE describes the morphological base of the derivative. The base is also a *lexeme* which has a phonological representation (PHON) and is also a noun (CAT N) indicating that we are dealing with a denominal derivative.

Additionally, the base contains a semantic attribute (SEM) which illustrates the semantics of the base. In order to successfully derive an *-ee* nominalization, the semantic representation of the base needs to contain an *eventuality*. Importantly, the base word does not have to consist of this eventuality directly in the node indexed with ⓪, but the eventuality can be more deeply embedded in the semantic representation of the base word. This potential embedding is represented by the three dots (...) in SEM ⓪ which serve as placeholders for a potentially different semantic type of the base. Moreover, this eventuality in the base needs to have one PARTICIPANT such as the one indexed with ①. The PARTICIPANT is an *entity* which has to be sentient and non-volitional. The SENTIENCE-attribute indexed with ② has the value *yes* for indicating that the entity is sentient. The VOLITIONALITY-attribute indexed with ③ has the value *no*, thus indicating that the entity described is non-volitional. The PARTICIPANT indexed with ① meets the restrictions of the suffix *-ee* described in section 2.3 and is hence required for the referential shift to create the meaning of the *-ee* nominalization.

At the bottom of the representation of the base and the derivative, the potential referents of the lexemes are indicated by a REFERENCE-attribute (REF) for each lexeme. The reference of the base word is not fixed in the rule with the exception that it cannot refer to the PARTICIPANT indexed with ①. The reference of the derivative, however, is the node indexed with ①, as the reference shifts towards the PARTICIPANT.

The frame in Figure 3 is the template for the frame representations of the individual words in the remainder of this section. The analysis will show that the derivational process is not always as straightforward as assumed in the generalized frame.

For the semantic decomposition of the individual bases, the definitions of the base words in the *Oxford English Dictionary Online* (OED 2021) were used as a starting point. This source was chosen as it is based on solid empirical evidence (i.e., actual attestations). The entries are accessible for verification and provide

---

[3] The phonological form given in Figure 3 is only short-hand for a more complex representation that would have to include, for instance, the necessary adjustments in stress. As this paper focuses on semantics, the phonology of *-ee* derivatives is not described in detail (see, e.g., Bauer et al. 2013, 227).

paraphrases detailed enough to derive semantic descriptions from. The usage of derivatives is illustrated with attestations from the *Corpus of Contemporary American English* (COCA, Davies 2008) and the *British National Corpus* (BNC, Davies 2004).

3.1 *-ee* nominalizations with non-derived bases

3.1.1 *debtee*

The first derivative under investigation is *debtee*. Its base word is the noun *debt*. A *debtee* denotes a person as illustrated in (6):

(6) The "**debtee**" is an old word for the creditor or payee. (BNC; see Davies 2004; ACAD, 1992)

As indicated in the definition in (6), the *debtee* has an eventuality-related interpretation as it denotes an entity to whom the money is owed. This eventuality suggests a potential *paying-eventuality*. More precisely, the *debtee* can be construed as the recipient in a future money transfer eventuality. Since *debtee* denotes a participant in an eventuality, the assumption is that the eventuality to induce the referential shift of the derivative is in the semantic representation of the base word *debt*. This assumption leads to the question where the eventuality and the required participant for the word-formation process with *-ee* is to be found in the nominal base. The paraphrases in the OED (2021) already provide a clue for the eventuality in the semantic representation of the base word *debt*:

1. That which is owed or due: a sum of money or a material thing; a thing immaterial.
2. A liability or obligation to pay or render something; the condition of being under such obligation.

In the second definition, *debt* is defined as an obligation. Semantically, obligations can be analyzed as states, i.e., non-dynamic eventualities with at least one participant. I will refer to this eventuality as an obligation-state. This link leads to the representation of base and derivative in the frame in Figure 4. The derivative has a phonological representation (PHON) and the syntactic category noun (CAT N). The base (M-BASE) *debt* is also a noun.

The semantics of the base (SEM) is depicted as a so-called multi-AVM and consists of two frames with different source nodes, indexed with [1] and [2]. Both AVMs illustrate states, an *obligation-state* ([1]) and an *expectation-state* ([2]). First,

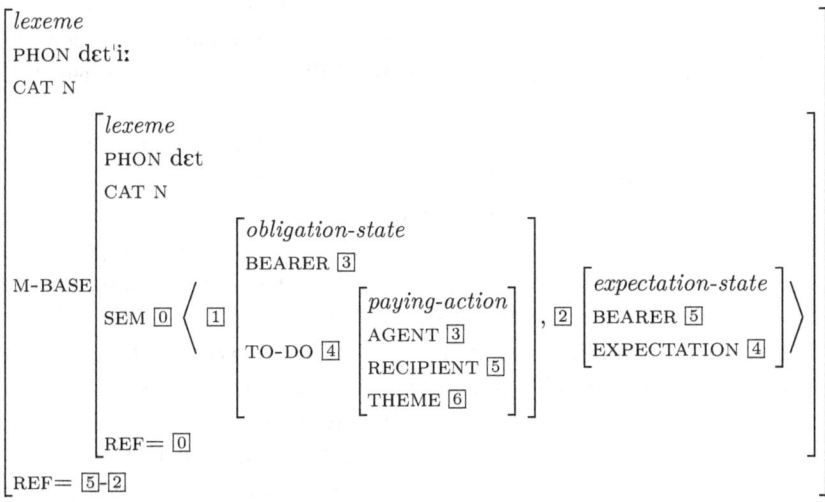

Fig. 4: Representation of the lexeme *debtee*.

the *obligation-state* has two attributes; a BEARER[4] of the state, indexed with ③, and an attribute TO-DO, indexed with ④. The attribute TO-DO specifies what the BEARER has to do in order to fulfill their obligation. The TO-DO attribute has the value *paying-action*, which is a sub-eventuality in the semantic representation of the base *debt*. This *paying-action* has at least three attributes; an AGENT indexed with ③, a RECIPIENT indexed with ⑤ and a THEME indexed with ⑥. The indices indicate that the BEARER of the *obligation-state* is the same person as the AGENT of the *paying-action* indicated by ③. The BEARER in the *obligation-state* is the one who has to pay.

The second state in the base is an *expectation-state* which describes the circumstance that the *paying-action* (④) has not been finished. The *debtee* expects to get their money back. The *expectation-state* has at least two attributes, a BEARER indexed with ⑤ and an EXPECTATION indexed with ④. Note that the BEARER of the *expectation-state* is co-indexed with the RECIPIENT of the *paying-action* (⑤) and the EXPECTATION is co-indexed with the whole *paying-action* (④).

Moving on to the process of derivation, the question of how the word-formation process with *-ee* knows which node to pick as the reference node (REF) arises. The

---

[4] The label BEARER is only one option to name the participant in a state. Different notations for the participant in a state are known (see, e.g., Van Valin & LaPolla 1997/2002). The label of the participant does not play a crucial role for the analysis provided in this paper, as long as this participant role fulfills the sentience and volitionality restrictions of *-ee* in pertinent cases.

restrictions for nominalizations with the suffix -ee state that the referent has to be sentient and non-volitional (see section 2.3). In the semantic representation of the base *debt*, two possible targets for the shift of reference are present, the BEARER of the *obligation-state* and the BEARER of the *expectation-state*, as BEARERS are sentient and non-volitional. The participant indexed with ③ is not only a BEARER of the *obligation-state* but also an AGENT in the embedded eventuality, the *paying-action*. Hence, the participant in ③ is not only a non-volitional participant as a BEARER in the *obligation-state* but also a volitional participant, an AGENT in the *paying-action*. The BEARER of the *expectation-sate*, on the other hand, is co-indexed with the RECIPIENT of the *paying-action*. As the BEARER of the *obligation-state* is co-indexed with the AGENT of the *paying-action*, it is more likely for the derivative to refer to the BEARER of the *expectation-sate*. The entity indexed with ⑤ is only represented as a non-volitional participant. According to the volitionality constraint, the more non-volitional participant is chosen as a referent for the word-formation process if two possible targets exist. Hence, ⑤ is the reference node for the interpretation of *debtee*. Note that the derivative does refer to the element indexed with ⑤ in the *expectation-state* ② as the payment of the *paying-action* has not been completed.

The frame for *debtee* illustrates that nominal bases can be eventive themselves. Accordingly, an eventuality can exist in the semantic representation of a nominal base. The eventuality and its participants provide possible targets for the word-formation process.

3.1.2 *biographee*

As shown in 3.1.1, the derivational process of -ee derivatives with nominal bases can be rather straightforward in the case of eventive bases. However, what happens if a base is not clearly eventive? This will be illustrated by the derivative *biographee*. The examples in (7) illustrate the use of this derivative:

(7) a. [...] version of the Petraeus biography, whose biographer is admitted to have lain with the **biographee** in the Biblical sense. (COCA, BLOG, 2012)
 b. [...] who noted that 'politicians are happiest when talking, at their most miserable when making up their minds.' His **biographee** would dissent (BNC, MAG, 1985-1994)

The base for the derivative is the noun *biography*. The base noun is not clearly eventive as it denotes, among other things, an object. As Pustejovsky (1996, ch. 8) already pointed out, artifacts, like *books*, also serve as objects which contain information. Such objects which can be of two different types are so called 'dot-objects'. *Books*, for example, can be described as physical objects and as containing information at the same time. This also applies to the specific type of book, *biography*, which is not only a concrete object but also a thing that contains information. This information concerns the life of a person and the derivative *biographee* denotes this person. The referential target of the suffix *-ee* is the person about whose life a book is written.

Moreover, a *biography* has to come into being and it is used for a specific purpose. These two processes are eventualities that are part of the semantic representation of the base word *biography*. These different aspects of the meaning of the base *biography* and the derivative *biographee* are represented in Figure 5.

The semantic representation of the base *biography* is more intricate than that of *debtee*. The base noun *biography* is labeled as a *text* in the semantic representation as the frame for the base illustrates *biography* as an information object. This *text* has the attributes PRODUCTION indexed with 1, AFFORDANCE indexed with 2, and TOPIC indexed with 4. The structure in the base is based on Pustejovsky (1996, ch. 6). This illustration of the base shows which elements can be assumed in a nominal base in general. A look at the properties of the participants in these eventualities will show which of them are compatible with the suffix *-ee*. The PRODUCTION-attribute is analogous to the AGENTIVE-QUALE in Pustejovsky, and the AFFORDANCE-attribute is analogous to the TELIC-QUALE in Pustejovsky. Hence, a biography is a *text* about something (TOPIC) which is produced by someone (PRODUCTION/AGENTIVE) for a special purpose (AFFORDANCE/TELIC).

The PRODUCTION-attribute and the AFFORDANCE-attribute have eventualities as their value. The PRODUCTION is a *writing-action* and the AFFORDANCE is a *reading-action*. Both eventualities contain an AGENT; in the *writing-action* the agent is the writer of the text and in the *reading-action* the agent is the reader of the text. The two AGENT-attributes refer to different persons and are therefore given different index-numbers (3, 5).[5] In contrast, the THEME-attributes (indexed with 0) represented in both eventualities refer to the same entity, namely the *text* itself, which is the referent of *biography*. This THEME contains the TOPIC-attribute indexed with 4.

---

[5] The frame-format does not prohibit co-indexation of these two elements. The writer can read their own work as well. The non-co-indexed version is probably the more natural one.

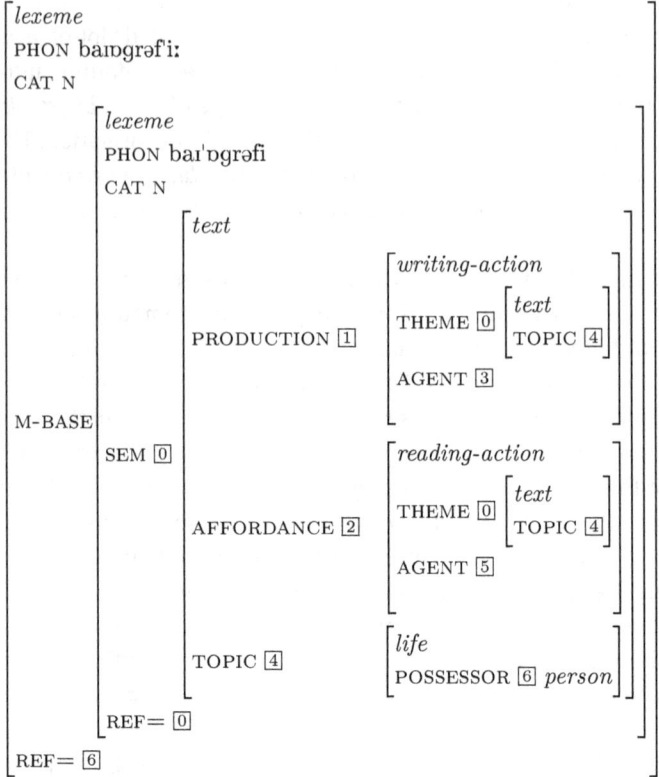

Fig. 5: Representation of the lexeme *biographee*.

Finally, in order to account for the specific genre of text instantiated by *biography*, the topic-attribute is typed *life*. In turn, the type *life* has a POSSESSOR,[6] indexed with 6, which is a person.

The REFERENCE-attribute is specified for an element with the required semantics to form the meaning of the derivative *biographee*. The reference is on the element indexed with 6, the POSSESSOR. Of the seven different nodes in this frame, only this one adheres to the restrictions posed by -*ee*. All other nodes are either volitional (AGENT: 3, 5) or non-sentient (THEME 0, PRODUCTION 1, AFFORDANCE 2, TOPIC 4). Thus, the aforementioned restrictions on derivatives with the suffix

---

6 The label POSSESOR is only one option to name the participant in 4. Other analyses for this participant might be available. The label of the participant does not play a crucial role for the analysis provided in this paper.

-ee successfully narrow down which part of the base's semantic structure can be used as reference for the derivative.

3.1.3 *covenantee*

The next derivative analyzed in this paper is *covenantee* as in example (8). The base is the noun *covenant*.

(8)   a.   It was argued on behalf of the respondents that the doctrine applied to a covenant which was imposed for the benefit of the trade of the **covenantee** and which either forbids the covenantor to carry on his trade or restricts the way in which he may carry it on. (BNC, ACAD, 1991)
       b.   However, even if the **covenantee** would not have entered the agreement without the covenant, the contract may not be invalidated as a whole [...]. (BNC, ACAD, 1991)

According to the definition from the OED, a covenant is "a mutual agreement between two or more persons to do or refrain from doing certain acts". The derivative *covenantee* denotes a person who is under an obligation to fulfill such an agreement, regardless of whether the agreement authorizes or prohibits something. Interestingly, *covenantee* can refer to two entities, namely to both parties that are involved in the covenant. This is opposed to *debtee* and *biographee*, for which only one possible referent can be identified. Figure 6 illustrates the frame for *covenantee*.

Focusing on the representation of the base, a *covenant* is a different type of obligation than the one in the base *debt* described above (see section 3.1.1). The obligations denoted by a *covenant* are *mutual-obligations* and *expectations*. These *mutual-obligations* and *expectations* are analyzed as a state in ④, which is a sub-eventuality that results from a *causation*-eventuality. The *causation*-eventuality consists of a CAUSE, which is an *agreeing-action* and a RESULT-STATE. The *agreeing-action* has at least two attributes, an AGENT indexed with ②, a CO-AGENT indexed with ③. Two agents are realized as the agreement on the *covenant* as the RESULT-STATE is made by two parties. These parties can be on equal level as assumed in the frame notation. The RESULT-STATE has at least two attributes, a BEARER indexed with ②, and a CO-BEARER indexed with ①. The two BEARERS are co-indexed with the two AGENTS in the *agreeing-action*.

In this representation, two possible targets for the suffix *-ee* are available as two non-volitional sentient beings are represented in the RESULT-STATE of

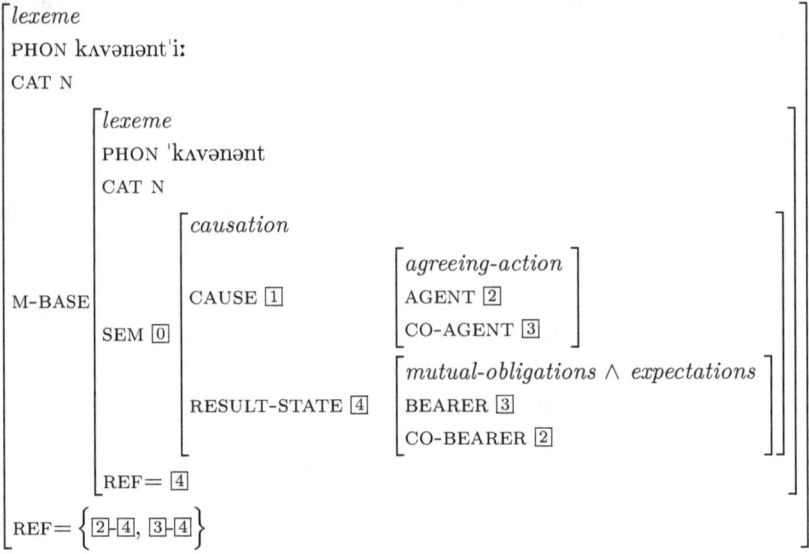

Fig. 6: Representation of the lexeme *covenantee*.

the base, the BEARER 3 and the CO-BEARER 2. The REFERENCE-attribute (REF) shows that the meaning of the derivative *covenantee* can either be on the element indexed with 2 or 3 in the RESULT-STATE 4 (2-4, 3-4). Interestingly, both participants are symmetric in the frame representation as both occur as AGENTS in the CAUSE and as BEARERS in the RESULT-STATE. It is not possible to tell apart which participant an *-ee* form refers to because they behave identically in all sub-eventualities. Thus, two possible referents in their non-volitional reading in the sub-eventuality 4 are the expected result.

3.2 *-ee* nominalizations with *-er/-or* bases

The data on denominal *-ee* derivatives show an interesting subset with *-er/-or* forms as their bases. For example, the derivative *tutee* is most likely constructed on the noun *tutor*. According to Bauer et al. (2013, 524) these nouns are paradigmatically related to each other. This relation arises when the new word has the same base but a different suffix. This is especially interesting as the data show that many *-ee* derivatives come into being not by suffixation to a base (i.e., a syntagmatic process), but by a paradigmatic process (see also Bonami & Guzmán Naranjo 2023). The analysis proposed here will show that the process operates on the same eventualities. Hence, the paradigmatic process is shown by the switch of the reference from one participant to another in the same eventuality. Some of the bases in this subset appear to be derived but are non-derived. For example, according to the OED, the word *tutor* was loaned from French or Spanish as a complex word and not derived within the morphological system of English. Nonetheless, it is possible to form *tutee* parallel to *tutor* by changing the apparent suffix although the *-or* form is non-derived. The semantic representation of the *-er/-or* bases and the reference shifts to a different participant are more straightforward due to the fact that the eventuality is already given by the respective *-er/-or* forms and is therefore more readily available.

The example illustrated in detail in this paper is the *-ee* derivative *tutee* as in (9):

(9) 'I used to have a **tutee** who lived there.' she told Guido. 'A tutee.' Guido laughed at that. 'Little miss schoolmistress.' (BNC, FIC, 1993)

The derivative is based on the noun *tutor*. The noun *tutor* is sufficiently more frequent than the verb to assume that the noun serves as the base. The word *tutor* occurs as a loan word around 1500[7] and *tutee* in the 1920's (OED). The verb *tutor* occurred in 1590. However, the meaning of the verb is definitely based on the eventuality given by *tutor*N. Due to the fact that the verb is built on the eventuality denoted by the loan word and the immensely higher frequency of the noun, the assumption of a paradigmatic relation between the two nouns, *tutor* and *tutee*, is straightforward. Additionally, this relation is visible due to the change of the alleged suffix. Figure 7 illustrates the frame for *tutee*.

The *teaching-action*[8] is directly accessible from *tutor*. The reference of *tutor* is on the element indexed with [1] as *tutor* denotes the AGENT of the *teaching-action*. The derivative *tutee*, on the other hand, has a different REFERENCE-attribute which points to a different entity, namely the PATIENT of the *teaching-action* indexed with [2]. The two lexemes refer to different participants in the same eventuality to create the meanings of *tutor* and *tutee*.

A second example of an *-ee* derivative with a pseudo-derived base is the derivative *mentee* in (10):

---

[7] It occurred even earlier in nowadays obsolete contexts.
[8] The special interaction of student and tutor is probably not entirely described with the label *teaching-action* as this relation may contain more than teaching. However, for the illustration of the derivational process, the label is sufficient.

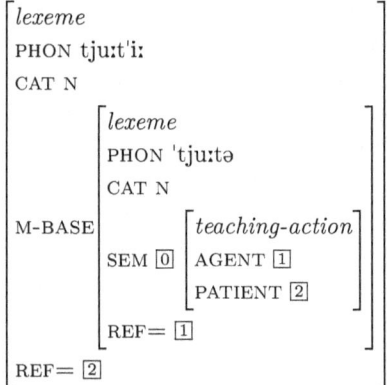

Fig. 7: Representation of the lexeme *tutee*.

(10)   One corporate lawyer scratched his tradition of grabbing Christmas drinks with a female **mentee**, and opted for the safer alternative of lunch. (COCA, NEWS, 2018)

The derivative *mentee* denotes the person who is supervised. The related word *mentor* is, as well as *tutor*, a loan word from French. The noun *mentor* is sufficiently more frequent than the verb which leads to the assumption that the noun serves as the base. The first attestation of *mentor*N in the OED is from 1750 and *mentee* occurs in 1965. The verb *mentor* occurred in 1918 and is based on the eventuality given by *mentor*N. The paradigmatic relation between the two nouns is straightforwardly visible due to the change of the alleged suffix and the operation on the same eventuality.

The semantic representation of *mentee*, then, looks similar to the one of *tutee*. The specification of the eventuality is changed into a *supervising-action*. Mentor denotes the AGENT and *mentee* the PATIENT. Both forms operate on the same eventuality but target a different participant of this eventuality (*supervising-action*). Thus, the word-formation process with the suffix *-ee* works similarly for the bases in section 3.1 and *-er/-or* bases as a non-volitional and sentient participant is referred to.

3.3 Formalization of the semantic restrictions on -*ee* formations

The restrictions for the suffix -*ee* described in section 2.3 are that the derivational process with the suffix -*ee* requires a participant which has to be sentient and non-volitional. These restrictions also underlie all of the examples formalized in sections 3.1 and 3.2 and can be regarded as the basis of the regular semantics of -*ee* nominalizations. However, exceptions to the non-volitionality constraint can be found in the literature on -*ee* for deverbal and denominal nominalizations. More precisely, Barker (1998) pointed out that some derivatives with -*ee* can also refer to volitional entities. One example is *escapee* which, just as the also existing derivative *escaper*, denotes the AGENT of the *escaping-action* from the verb *escape*. According to Barker (1998), this is possible for -*ee* derivatives with bases that are either intransitive verbs, or verbs that can be interpreted as having a non-volitional subject participant, like *stand*, for example. The data on denominal derivatives (Barker 1998, Plag 2004, Mühleisen 2010) also shows -*ee* derivatives which denote AGENTS, for example, *bargee* in example (11).

(11)   'I'm a **bargee**, owner-operator, that's my ship down there,' she said, pointing down the side of the quay. (BNC, FIC, 1985-1994)

Divergent semantic classes of a word-formation process can be captured in inheritance hierarchies (Riehemann 1998, Koenig 1999, Booij 2010, Bonami & Crysmann 2016, Plag et al. 2018). Figure 8 shows such an inheritance hierarchy for denominal nominalizations derived by the suffix -*ee*. The abbreviation *n-n-lfr* stands for noun-to-noun lexeme formation rule and indicates that the categories under this node describe denominal nominalizations. The hierarchy severs the phonological component (PHON) of the word-formation process from different semantic (SEM) categories.

On the left side of the inheritance hierarchy, the phonological realization (PHON) of the derivative is described. The phonology of the base is modified by adjusting the phonological form according to the information of the suffix, in this case the suffix -*ee*. On the right side, the semantic specification of a lexeme-formation rule is illustrated. The left node describes the *regular semantics* investigated in this paper. In order to derive the *regular semantics*, a *non-volitional-participant-noun*, the base (M-BASE) must provide but not necessarily denote an eventuality with a participant which is non-volitional and sentient (PARTICIPANT). This constraint is described by the reference (REF) which is on the element indexed with $\boxed{x}$. The individual derivatives discussed in this paper have their reference on a participant which meets the constraints given in the *regular semantics* node in

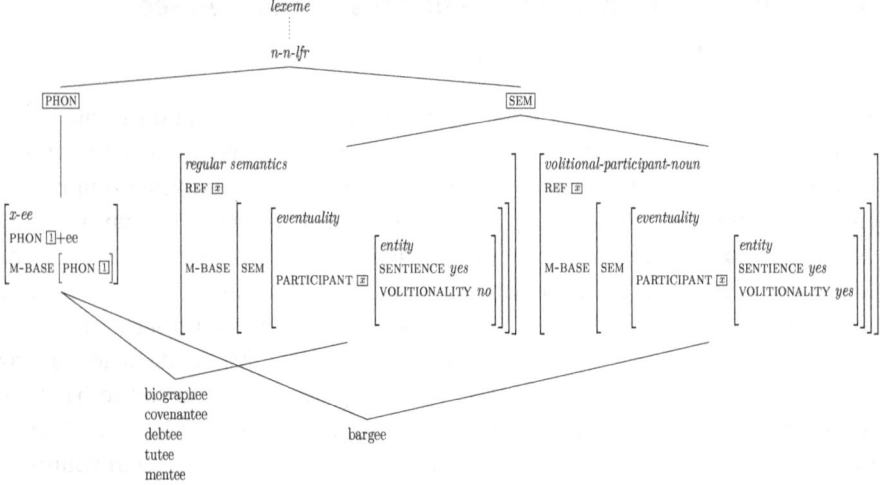

Fig. 8: Inheritance hierarchy of lexical rules for *-ee* including regular semantics and volitional exceptions.

the inheritance hierarchy. The derivatives discussed in sections 3.1 and 3.2, e.g., *biographee* and *tutee*, connect the phonological component of the word-formation process with its regular semantics. These forms are listed below each other.

The right semantic node illustrates the semantic make-up of the exceptions. The participant which is referred to by the *-ee* derivative is sentient and volitional which leads to a *volitional-participant-reading* as in *bargee*.

4 Discussion and outlook

The aim of this study was to investigate denominal nominalizations with the suffix *-ee*. The research questions asked whether it is possible to find an eventuality in the nominal base and how the assumed referential shift induced by the word-formation process can be explained and modeled. A word-formation process can attach to several different word classes (e.g., Plag 2004). However, eventuality-related word-formation processes clearly prefer verbal bases. In turn, this preference is grounded in the fact that verbs denote eventualities themselves. Nouns, on the other hand, usually denote things or participants in eventualities (see, e.g., Haspelmath 2001; Van Valin & LaPolla 1997/2002; Szabó 2015; Moltmann 2019). Moreover, conversion in English makes it in many cases impossible to decide unambiguously to which word class the base belongs. However, for the semantic approach in this paper, the word class of the base is not of paramount importance. The analysis of denominal derivatives with -*ee* demonstrates that nouns can, as well as verbs, provide the eventive elements that are required for the word-formation process. In contrast to verbs, deeper decomposition of the semantics of nouns might be necessary to reveal the required eventive elements. Consequently, the word class of a base does not have a central role for eventuality-related nominalizations. Rather, the semantics provided by the base word is crucial. Assuming that the semantics are central for word-formation processes in general, every word that has the eventive elements for the process in its semantic representation can serve as potential base, regardless of its word class. The word-formation process can then shift reference to an eventive element in the eventuality in the semantic representation of such a base.

The approach applied in this paper is one of semantic decomposition and reference shifting and thus similar to the approach by Plag et al. (2018) and Kawaletz (2023) for deverbal nominalizations with the suffix -*ment*. This approach allows us to decompose the base into its semantics which consists of eventive elements like (sub-)eventualities and participants. In some cases, the eventive elements that are used for the nominalization process are deeply embedded in the semantic structure. Applying the analysis to denominal derivatives and their base words in this paper demonstrates that seemingly non-eventive nouns like *biography* have eventualities embedded in their semantic representation. The REFERENCE attribute allows for the inclusion of the reference of base and derivative in one frame. The approach used in this paper is a non-coercive approach. Coercion of eventive elements is not needed, as such elements have been shown to already be provided by the respective bases. Thus, the analyses presented in this paper are in line with frameworks that assume embedded eventualities in the semantics of non-eventive nouns (see, e.g., Pustejovsky 1996, ch. 6).

As a consequence of the exceptions to the volitionality constraint for suffixation with -*ee*, the inheritance hierarchy in section 3.3 does not only depict the *regular semantics* for derivatives with the suffix -*ee* but also the possibility of such derivatives to refer to volitional participants. The restrictions that a volitional participant can only be the target for a nominalization with the suffix -*ee* if no non-volitional participant is present in the semantic representation of the base word needs systematic testing. For bases lacking a non-volitional participant in their semantic representation, affix competition between -*ee* and -*er* might be involved in the process of -*ee* referring to a volitional participant as well. Similar problems of mismatches between eventuality-denoting derivatives and their nominal bases arise with other suffixes like -*age, -ance, -ation, -er, -ment, -ure* (Plag 2004, 2018, ch. 4). The approach proposed in this paper can potentially be used for the analysis of other nominalizations as well.

Acknowledgments

This research was funded by the Deutsche Forschungsgemeinschaft (Grants SFB 991/2-C08 and PL 151/11-1 'Semantics of derivational morphology'). The author is grateful to the audience of two conferences (Event semantics 2020; 43. Jahrestagung der Deutschen Gesellschaft für Sprachwissenschaft 2021), the reviewers and the colleagues at the Department of English Language and Linguistics at Heinrich-Heine-Universität for valuable input.

Bibliography

Alexiadou, Artemis. 2001. *Functional structure in nominals: Nominalization and ergativity.* Philadelphia: John Benjamins.
Alexiadou, Artemis. 2010. Nominalizations: A probe into the architecture of grammar part I: The nominalization puzzle. *Language and Linguistics Compass* 4(7). 496–511.
Bach, Emmon. 1986. The algebra of events. *Linguistics and Philosophy* 9(1). 5–16.
Balteiro, Isabel. 2007. *The directionality of conversion in english: A dia-synchronic study.* Bern and New York: Lang.
Barbu Mititelu, Verginica, Gianina Iordăchioaia, Svetlozara Leseva & Ivelina Stoyanova. 2023. The meaning of zero nouns and zero verbs. In Sven Kotowski & Ingo Plag (eds.), *The semantics of derivational morphology. Theory, methods, evidence*, 63–102. Berlin and Boston: De Gruyter.
Barker, Chris. 1998. Episodic -ee in English: A thematic role constraint on new word formation. *Language* 74(4). 695.
Barsalou, Lawrence W. 1992a. *Cognitive psychology. An overview for cognitive sciences.* Hillsdale, NJ: Lawrence Erlbaum Associates.
Barsalou, Lawrence W. 1992b. *Frames, concepts, and conceptual fields.* Hillsdale, NJ: Lawrence Erlbaum Associates.
Bauer, Laurie, Rochelle Lieber & Ingo Plag. 2013. *Oxford reference guide to English morphology.* Oxford: Oxford University Press.
Bonami, Olivier & Berthold Crysmann. 2016. The role of morphology in constraint-based lexicalist grammars. In Andrew Hippisley & Gregory T. Stump (eds.), *Cambridge handbook of morphology*, 609–656. Cambridge: Cambridge University Press.
Bonami, Olivier & Matías Guzmán Naranjo. 2023. Distributional evidence for derivational paradigms. In Sven Kotowski & Ingo Plag (eds.), *The semantics of derivational morphology. Theory, methods, evidence*, 219–259. Berlin and Boston: De Gruyter.
Booij, Geert E. 2010. *Construction morphology.* Oxford: Oxford University Press.
Borer, Hagit. 2013. *Structuring sense. vol. 3: Taking form.* Oxford: Oxford University Press.
Bram, Barli. 2011. *Major total conversion in english.* Wellington: Victoria University dissertation.
Davies, Mark. 2004. British National Corpus (from Oxford University Press). https://www.english-corpora.org/bnc.

Davies, Mark. 2008-. The Corpus of Contemporary American English (COCA): 520 million words, 1990-present. http://www.americancorpus.org/.
Gamerschlag, Thomas, Doris Gerland, Rainer Osswald & Wiebke Petersen. 2014. General introduction. In Thomas Gamerschlag (ed.), *Frames and concept types*, 3–21. Cham: Springer.
Grimshaw, Jane Barbara. 1990. *Argument structure*. Cambridge, MA: MIT Press.
Haspelmath, M. 2001. Word classes and parts of speech. In Neil J. Smelser & Paul B. Baltes (eds.), *International encyclopedia of the social & behavioral sciences*, 16538–16545. Amsterdam: Elsevier.
Kawaletz, Lea. 2023. *The semantics of English -ment nominalizations*. Berlin: Language Science Press.
Kawaletz, Lea & Ingo Plag. 2015. Predicting the semantics of English nominalizations: A frame-based analysis of *-ment* suffixation. In Laurie Bauer, Lívia Körtvélyessy & Pavol Štekauer (eds.), *Semantics of complex words*, 289–319. Dordrecht: Springer.
Koenig, Jean-Pierre. 1999. *Lexical relations*. Stanford, CA: CSLI Publications.
Larson, Richard K. 1998. Events and modification in nominals. *Semantics and Linguistic Theory* 8. 145–168.
Lieber, Rochelle. 2004. *Morphology and lexical semantics*. Cambridge: Cambridge University Press.
Lieber, Rochelle. 2016. *English nouns: The ecology of nominalization*, vol. 150. Cambridge: Cambridge University Press.
Lieber, Rochelle. 2017. Nominalization: General overview and theoretical issues. In Mark Aronoff (ed.), *Oxford research encyclopedias*, Oxford: Oxford University Press. https://doi.org/10.1093/acrefore/9780199384655.013.501.
Löbner, Sebastian. 2013. *Understanding semantics, 2nd ed.* London: Routledge.
Löbner, Sebastian. 2014. Evidence for frames from human language. In Thomas Gamerschlag (ed.), *Frames and concept types*, vol. 94, 23–67. Cham: Springer.
Moltmann, Friederike. 2019. Natural language and its ontology. In Alvin I. Goldman & Brian P. McLaughlin (eds.), *Metaphysics and cognitive science*, 206–232. New York, NY, USA: Oxford University Press.
Mühleisen, Susanne. 2010. *Heterogeneity in word-formation patterns: A corpus-based analysis of suffixation with -ee and its productivity in english*. Amsterdam and Philadelphia: John Benjamins.
OED. 2021. *Oxford English Dictionary Online*. Oxford: Oxford University Press. https://www.oed.com/.
Petersen, Wiebke. 2007. Representation of concepts as frames. In Jurgis Skilters, Fiorenza Toccafondi & Gerhard Stemberger (eds.), *Complex cognition and qualitative science: A legacy of oswald kulpe (the baltic international yearbook of cognition, logic and communication 2)*, vol. 2, 151–170. Riga: University of Latvia.
Plag, Ingo. 1999. *Morphological productivity: structural constraints in English derivation*. Berlin: De Gruyter.
Plag, Ingo. 2004. Syntactic category information and the semantics of derivational morphological rules. *Folia Linguistica* 38(3-4). 193–225.
Plag, Ingo. 2018. *Word-formation in English, 2nd ed.* Cambridge, UK and New York, NY: Cambridge University Press.
Plag, Ingo, Marios Andreou & Lea Kawaletz. 2018. A frame-semantic approach to polysemy in affixation. In Olivier Bonami, Gilles Boyé, Georgette Dal, Hélène Giraudo & Fiammetta

Namer (eds.), *The lexeme in descriptive and theoretical morphology*, 467–486. Berlin and Boston: Language Science Press.

Pollard, Carl & Ivan A. Sag. 1994. *Head-driven phrase structure grammar*. Chicago, IL: University of Chicago Press.

Pustejovsky, James. 1996. *The generative lexicon, 2nd ed.* Cambridge, MA: MIT Press.

Riehemann, Susanne Z. 1998. Type-based derivational morphology. *Journal of Comparative Germanic Linguistics* 2(1). 49–77.

Szabó, Zoltán Gendler. 2015. Major parts of speech. *Erkenntnis* 80(S1). 3–29.

Van Valin, Robert D. & Randy J. LaPolla. 1997/2002. *Syntax: Structure, meaning and function*. Cambridge: Cambridge University Press.

Winter, Yoad & Joost Zwarts. 2012. On the event semantics of nominals and adjectives - the one-argument hypothesis. *Proceedings of Sinn und Bedeutung* 16(2). 639–647.

Verginica Barbu Mititelu, Gianina Iordăchioaia, Svetlozara Leseva & Ivelina Stoyanova
The meaning of zero nouns and zero verbs

Abstract: We carry out a large-scale study of noun-verb zero derivation pairs in English in order to identify possible semantic contrasts between the two derivational directions: V-to-N (zero nouns) and N-to-V (zero verbs). We compile a dataset of 4,879 N-V word sense pairs from the Princeton WordNet, which are annotated for noun and verb semantic classes and are assigned a morphosemantic relation. These sense pairs are labelled with a derivational direction from the Oxford English Dictionary. This makes it possible to investigate, on the one hand, the morphosemantic relations and, on the other hand, the noun and verb semantic classes that typically associate with each direction of zero derivation with the aim of offering a better understanding of the semantics involved in this morphological process.

Keywords: zero derivation, lexical semantics, derivational direction

1 Introduction

In this paper we are concerned with zero-derived noun-verb pairs in English as in (1), which we call *zero formations*, given the null marking of the categorial change undergone by the base.

(1)   a.   to climb > the climb   (Zero nouns: V-to-N direction)
        b.   the bottle > to bottle   (Zero verbs: N-to-V direction)

The choice of terminology depends on the theoretical view that linguists take on formations as in (1). While some consider these to instantiate a subtype of derivation which lacks morphological marking and call this process *zero derivation*, others consider them as representative of an independent word formation process which they call *conversion* to keep it separate from derivation (Valera 2014).

    The goal of our study is to determine possible semantic differences between zero formations as in (1) depending on the direction in which they are built: i.e., from V to N as in (1-a) or from N to V as in (1-b). We work with a dataset of 4,879

Verginica Barbu Mititelu, Gianina Iordăchioaia, Svetlozara Leseva & Ivelina Stoyanova, VBM, Romanian Academy Research Institute for Artificial Intelligence, Bucharest; GI, Humboldt-Universität Berlin; SL & IS, Bulgarian Academy of Sciences, Sofia, email of corresponding author: vergi@racai.ro

∂ Open Access. © 2023 the author(s), published by De Gruyter. [CC BY-ND] This work is licensed under the Creative Commons Attribution-NoDerivatives 4.0 International License.
https://doi.org/10.1515/9783111074917-004

N-V word sense pairs extracted from the Princeton WordNet standoff file containing pairs of morphosemantically related noun and verb senses (Fellbaum 1998; Fellbaum et al. 2009). For these pairs, we use the derivational direction provided by the Oxford English Dictionary (OED) (see §3.3) as a fixed predictor variable that will inform us on direction-specific semantic properties of zero formations. We investigate the semantic differences between zero nouns and zero verbs in terms of the semantic classes (or 'primes') of nouns (such as noun.artifact, noun.act, etc.) and verbs (verb.change, verb.motion, etc.) postulated by Miller et al. (1990) and the 14 morphosemantic relations (such as Event, Agent, Result) assigned to the N-V pairs in Fellbaum et al. (2009) (see §3.1). We undertake: (i) to seek whether such a large-scale study may reveal semantic properties typical of zero nouns and zero verbs and (ii) to check how our findings fare in relation to previous literature on the apparent differences between the two formations.

We address the following research questions:
1. Do the individual morphosemantic relations particularly associate with one derivational direction or the other? That is, do we find relations that primarily involve zero nouns or zero verbs?
2. Do the noun/verb semantic classes (or combinations thereof) particularly associate with either of the two directions in our dataset?
3. What do the apparent tendencies tell us about the semantics of zero nouns and zero verbs in view of previous theoretical studies?

A positive answer to the first two questions would allow an improvement of the current understanding of nouns and verbs as the output of zero derivation and, implicitly, of this morphological process so hotly debated in the linguistic literature. A qualitative (and quantitative) advantage of our approach is that it relies on a dataset compiled from large-scale resources available independently of our study, namely, the Princeton WordNet and the OED.

A close inspection of the morphosemantic relations and of the semantic classes ('primes') in our dataset allows us to identify some general semantic tendencies with respect to the derivational direction. On the one hand, we find that the morphosemantic relation Event favours zero nouns, relations such as Agent, Instrument, Location and others favour zero verbs, while relations such as State and Property are balanced between zero nouns and zero verbs. On the other hand, the majority of zero nouns instantiate the relation Event, while zero verbs are more evenly distributed between several such relations, indicating a more restricted pool of interpretations for zero nouns than for zero verbs. Moreover, within most relations, zero verbs exhibit more semantic classes than their base nouns, while zero nouns mostly show fewer or a similar number of semantic classes as their base verbs. This indicates that zero verbs expand the semantic range introduced by the base, while zero nouns reduce it, pointing to a clear contrast between the two formations which also resonates with previous observations in the literature that we describe in Section §2.

We start with the theoretical background on zero nouns and zero verbs in Section §2. In Section §3 we present the lexical resources we used as well as the methodology for compiling our dataset of 4,879 zero-derived N-V word sense pairs and their analysis. Section §3.2 summarises our results, which we interpret in Section §5 in relation to our research questions and the previous literature. In Section §7 we conclude on our findings.

2 Theoretical background

In this section we briefly summarise the previous literature on zero nouns and zero verbs as a background against which we can evaluate our empirical findings. To our knowledge, the theoretical literature has not directly compared the two directions so far. However, an overview of the independent studies dedicated to each of the two formations, which we present in §2.1 and §2.2, suggests a contrast between the two derivational directions to the extent that zero nouns behave as expected of overt derivations by systematically restricting the semantics of the base, while zero verbs do not conform to this expectation. This contrast is confirmed by the computational study in Kisselew et al. (2016), which we summarise in §2.3.

2.1 Zero nouns in theoretical literature

Over the past few decades zero nouns have not received much attention in the literature, but they used to be more thoroughly investigated especially in the late 1960s (Kastovsky 1968; Marchand 1969; Irmer 1972). Marchand (1969) and Irmer (1972) analyse zero nouns as nominalisations by means of a zero suffix, and especially their semantics is described along the same patterns found with suffixed nominalisations: as action- and participant-denoting (see Plag et al. 2023) for a case study on the polysemy of *-ment* nominalisations).

Cetnarowska (1993) closely investigates the morphosyntactic and semantic behaviour of zero nouns and argues that they behave like deverbal nominalisations by means of suffixes such as *-ing*, *-ation*, *-ment*, *-al*, *-ance*. She argues that, like suffixed nominalisations, they are primarily action-denoting (e.g. *a jump, a pull*), while participant readings may appear more frequently than for suffixed nominals, but correspond to the same general patterns justified by meaning shifts:

result entities (e.g. *a cut, a rip*; cf. *a building, an establishment*), affected objects (e.g. *a find, a catch*; cf. *a borrowing, an inheritance*), and causers (e.g. *a bother*; cf. *a distraction, an embarrassment, a reminder*). For agents and instruments, zero nouns are in competition with the *-er* suffix (see *a guide / a guider, a sweep / a sweeper*), but typical action nouns may also form collective agents such as *administration*. For recent studies on affix competition in deverbal nominalisations see Plag et al. (2023) for English and Huyghe et al. (2023) for French.

Lieber (2016) also shows that zero nouns present semantic and morphosyntactic behaviour similar to that of suffixed nominals. Lieber (2016, 112) relies on her previous analysis of conversion as a conceptual process of lexical coinage, in which words are relisted with a different category (Lieber 1992). From this perspective, Lieber does not make any predictions about possible differences between zero nouns and zero verbs, even though she assumes directionality. However, she highlights important semantic parallelisms between zero nouns and suffixed nominalisations: see her parallel skeletons for zero and suffixed nominals (Lieber 2016, 111) and also her paper in this volume (Lieber 2023). Thus, Lieber's conclusions on zero nouns partially support their behaviour like overt derivations in relation to the base verbs.

This theoretical discussion indicates that zero nouns display substantial similarities to nominalisations derived with overt suffixes, as their semantics relies on systematic patterns defined in relation to their base verbs similar to those of suffixed nominals. Borer (2013, ch. 7) partially argues against such a similarity, although she does not address the polysemy of zero and suffixed nominals as Cetnarowska (1993) and Lieber (2016) do. Borer discusses argument structure, which she claims zero nouns fail to inherit from their base verbs, in contrast to suffixed nominals. However, her arguments have been seriously challenged by Lieber (2016) and Iordăchioaia (2020).

2.2 Zero verbs in theoretical literature

Zero verbs have been more at the centre of theoretical research. Clark & Clark (1979) insightfully show how spontaneous and productive denominal zero verb formation is and how these verbs may acquire a whole array of context-dependent and pragmatically-motivated meanings, which could not be predicted from the meaning of the base noun alone (see *He wristed the ball over the net*, stated by a tennis commentator). This finding cannot be accounted for by a directional derivational approach, which makes the centre of Lieber's (1981; 1992) proposal that zero verbs cannot be the output of a zero derivation process but must be a case of lexical coinage and relisting. Kiparsky (1982) and Hale & Keyser (2002) attempt to identify regular patterns in the behaviour of zero verbs depending on the meanings of their base nouns. Kiparsky argues that some zero verbs incorporate the meanings of their base nouns as arguments in their event structure, while others do not. He distinguishes between instrumental verbs like *to hammer* and *to tape* as to whether they allow an adjunct PP that introduces an instrument different from that expressed by their base nouns, as in (2):

(2)   a.   Lola hammered the metal (with her shoe).
       b.   Lola taped pictures to the wall (*with pushpins).

From (2) Kiparsky concludes that *hammer*-type verbs are not derived from the base nouns, and their meanings are not tied to these, given that other instruments are possible in (2-a). *Tape* verbs, however, must be derived from their base nouns, since no other instruments are possible in (2-b) (see also Arad 2005).

Harley & Haugen (2007) challenge Kiparsky's contrast and argue that even *tape* verbs allow different instrument PPs to the extent that they involve the same manner of action, as illustrated in (3). The difference between band-aids and pushpins is that they involve different manners of action. Harley and Haugen conclude that not even verbs like *tape* encode the instrument of their base nouns in their meaning; the base nouns loosely specify the manner of action the zero verbs denote.

(3)   Lola taped the poster to the wall with band-aids / mailing-labels.

Rimell (2012) provides extensive support for this conclusion on the basis of corpus data. In simple terms, she argues that denominal zero verbs cannot be viewed as regularly derived from their base nouns, since the meaning of the noun is not encoded in that of the verb; the base noun is interpreted as a predicate of events and not as an argument of the verb (cf. Hale & Keyser 2002).

Additional observations compatible with this observation are provided by Plag (1999) and Lieber (2004). While rejecting a treatment of zero verbs as the output of a zero derivation process, Plag argues that the semantics of a purported zero suffix for such verbs is too polysemous to instantiate one unitary suffix. For instance, he finds that of the 488 recent zero verbs in his dataset only 79 express meanings that are also associated with overt verbalising suffixes such as *-ise*, *-ify* or *-ate*. Plag concludes that a zero verbalising suffix would have no corresponding overt analogue (Sanders 1988) and is thus untenable.

From this theoretical overview we conclude that the meaning patterns that zero nouns acquire in relation to their base verbs represent a well-defined set similar to those of overtly derived nominalisations. By contrast, the meaning patterns that zero verbs receive are richer than those of overt verbalising derivations and do not establish a systematic semantic relationship with the base such as that between a predicate and its argument. The meaning of the base only loosely contributes to some pragmatically and contextually determined manner specification on the event of the output zero verb. This indicates that the meaning of zero nouns is more restricted in relation to that of the base than the meaning of zero verbs is, a conclusion that is also reached by the computational study in Kisselew et al. (2016), which we summarise below.

2.3 Computational insights on zero nouns vs. zero verbs

For a manually created dataset of N-V pairs, Kisselew et al. (2016) use historical precedence as a proxy for the derivational direction and test the reliability of frequency and semantic specificity in this respect. To the extent that more directionality tests converge, this enforces the direction and shows that such N-V pairs are well-behaved. Semantic specificity refers to the observation that the output of overt derivation is semantically more complex and more specific than its base (see Koontz-Garboden's 2007 Monotonicity Hypothesis for derivation). If zero derivation is similar to overt derivation, zero verbs and zero nouns are expected to be semantically more specific than their base nouns and verbs.

Kisselew et al. apply measures of information content to distributional representations to estimate semantic specificity. For overt derivation, these measures yield 90% accuracy (Padó et al. 2015), confirming the validity of semantic specificity in this morphological process. While Kisselew et al.'s best model for zero derivation combines semantic specificity with frequency, semantic specificity alone yields almost as good results for zero nouns and drops to chance level for zero verbs. This means that semantic specificity successfully predicts zero nouns (like in the case of overt derivations) but fails with zero verbs. Kisselew et al. take this result to indicate that zero nouns are semantically more specific than their bases and consistent with a derivational approach, while zero verbs are semantically more irregular and compatible with a non-derivational approach (see overview on approaches to zero derivation in Darby (2015, §1.4).

While the theoretical studies in §2.1 and §2.2 have not directly addressed semantic specificity as used in Koontz-Garboden (2007) and Kisselew et al. (2016), their independent insights on the semantics of zero nouns and zero verbs converge with those in Kisselew et al. (2016) and support the contrast the latter observe. In §4.3 we will have a look at the semantic classes that nouns and verbs show in our dataset when they represent the base or the output of zero derivation and we will see that our PWN data provide some support for this contrast between zero nouns and zero verbs, as well.

3 Resources and methodology

Below we briefly describe the resources we used in our analysis. The Princeton WordNet provides the initial set of noun-verb sense pairs annotated with morphosemantic relations and the semantic class each word sense belongs to. From the OED we draw information about the direction of zero derivation. To serve our objectives, the two resources were aligned with respect to the data under focus.

3.1 Princeton WordNet

Princeton WordNet (PWN) was conceived as a network of English word senses: its nodes are represented by synonym sets (called synsets) of words of the same part of speech, be they nouns, verbs, adjectives or adverbs. A word may occur in the network several times, equal to its number of senses, be it polysemous or homograph. Synsets are interlinked by means of a number of semantic relations: within the classes of nouns and verbs these relations are mainly hierarchical: hypo-/hyperonymy, holo-/meronymy, troponymy. Each verb or noun synset is assigned a semantic prime (Miller et al. 1990), which shows its membership to a relevant semantic category; hence a prime assigns a noun or a verb to a relevant semantic class. Table 1 shows in boldface the semantic primes for nouns and verbs. Each semantic class is organised into one or more trees in PWN. Although the distinction among primes is not straightforward, and the meaning of a synset might share semantics with more than one semantic class, we take the data as they are provided, i.e., each synset is assigned one prime.[1] This approach might not reflect all the semantic distinctions of a synset's meaning, but it is informative enough in terms of the semantics of (zero) derivation. Further considerations on the representativeness of the data are given in §3.4.

Besides the conceptual relations between synsets (e.g. hypo-/hyperonymy), there are also lexical relations between words from different synsets in PWN. Derivational relations are instances of such lexical relations. For example, the noun *cost:1* with the gloss "the total spent for goods or services including money and time and labor" is derivationally related to the verb *cost:1* with the gloss "be priced at". Note, however, that, as implemented in the PWN, these relations do not show the direction of the derivation, but only the lexical items involved. In our

---

[1] The PWN lexicographic files are downloadable from https://wordnet.princeton.edu/download.

Tab. 1: The 25 semantic primes for nouns and 15 semantic primes for verbs in PWN.

Noun primes		Verb primes
noun.act: acts or actions	noun.phenomenon: natural phenomena	verb.body: verbs of grooming, dressing and bodily care
noun.animal: animals	noun.plant: plants	verb.change: verbs of size, temperature change, intensifying, etc.
noun.artifact: man-made objects	noun.possession: (transfer of) possession	verb.cognition: verbs of thinking, judging, analysing, doubting
noun.attribute: attributes of people/objects	noun.process: natural processes	verb.communication: verbs of telling, asking, ordering, singing
noun.body: body parts	noun.quantity: quantities and units of measure	verb.competition: verbs of fighting, athletic activities
noun.cognition: cognitive processes and contents		
noun.communication: communicative processes and contents	noun.relation: relations b/n people/things/ideas	verb.consumption: verbs of eating and drinking
noun.event: natural events	noun.shape: two and three dimensional shapes	verb.contact: verbs of touching, hitting, tying, digging
noun.feeling: feelings and emotions		verb.creation: verbs of sewing, baking, painting, performing
noun.food: foods and drinks	noun.state: stable states of affairs	verb.emotion: verbs of feeling
noun.group: groupings of people or objects	noun.substance: substances	verb.motion: verbs of walking, flying, swimming
noun.location: spatial position	noun.time: time and temporal relations	verb.perception: verbs of seeing, hearing, feeling
noun.motive: goals		verb.possession: verbs of buying, selling, owning
noun.object: natural objects (not man-made)		verb.social: verbs of political and social activities and events
noun.person: people		verb.stative: verbs of being, having, spatial relations
		verb.weather: verbs of raining, snowing, thawing, thundering

endeavour, labelling the direction has necessitated the additional employment of the OED (see §3.2).

Fellbaum et al. (2009) enriched these derivational relations with semantic information leading to a set of 14 morphosemantic relations: Agent, Body-part, By-means-of, Destination, Event, Instrument, Location, Material, Property, Result, State, Undergoer, Uses, Vehicle. These morphosemantic relations were designed following previous lexical semantic literature (see the Cases proposed in Fillmore 1968, the frame elements of FrameNet in Ruppenhofer et al. 2002 and the semantic roles in Gildea & Jurafsky 2000) and we used them to annotate a set of 17,739 noun-verb pairs (irrespective of the direction of the derivational process) made available as a standoff file. Table 2 lists these relations together with a brief description of their semantics and examples from PWN.

Tab. 2: The 14 morphosemantic relations used in the PWN standoff file.

Relation	Description	Example
Agent	an entity that acts volitionally so as to bring about a result	ruin – ruiner, bully$_N$ – bully$_V$
Body-part	a part of the body (e.g. of an Agent) involved in the situation	extend – extensor, finger$_N$ – finger$_V$
By-means-of	something that causes, facilitates, enables the occurrence of	float – floater, smelly – smell$_N$
Destination	a recipient, an addressee or a goal	patent – patentee, tee$_N$ – tee$_V$
Event	something that happens at a given place and time	beatify – beatification, chat$_V$ – chat$_N$
Instrument	an object (rarely abstract) acting under the control of an Agent	instill – instillator, microwave$_N$ – microwave$_V$
Location	a concrete or an abstract place involved in the situation	bifurcate – bifurcation, chamber$_N$ – chamber$_V$
Material	a substance or material used to obtain a certain effect or result	sweeten – sweetener, plaster$_N$ – plaster$_V$
Property	an attribute or a quality	magnetise – magnetisation, overlap$_V$ – overlap$_N$
Result	the outcome of the situation described by the verb	syllabify – syllable, ash$_N$ – ashy$_V$
State	an abstract entity, such as a feeling, a cognitive state, etc.	demoralise – demoralisation, pother$_N$ – pother$_V$
Undergoer	an entity affected by the situation described by the verb	invite – invitee, harvest$_N$ – harvest$_V$
Uses	a function an entity has or a purpose it serves	attest – attestation, brine$_N$ – brine$_V$
Vehicle	an artifact serving as a means of transportation	cruise – cruiser, sled$_N$ – sled$_V$

In the PWN standoff file, a pair of two words can occur several times, each time at least one of the words having a different sense number. For example, the relation between the noun *cost*:1 and the verb *cost*:1 is Event.[2] Other senses of the two

---

[2] The examples use the following notation: word followed by its sense number (for the respective part of speech in the case of homographs) from PWN version 3.1, which is available for querying at http://wordnetweb.princeton.edu/perl/webwn.

words are also considered derivationally related, and an appropriate morphosemantic relation is attached to them, as shown in Table 3.

Tab. 3: morphosemantic relations attached to derivational relations.

Verb gloss	Verb	morphosemantic relation	Noun	Noun gloss
"be priced at"	cost:1	Event	cost:1	"the total spent for goods or services including money and time and labor"
"be priced at"	cost:1	Property	cost:2	"the property of having material worth (often indicated by the amount of money something would bring if sold)"
"require to lose, suffer, or sacrifice"	cost:3	Result	cost:3	"value measured by what must be given or done or undergone to obtain something"

As many morphosemantic relations are grounded in well-established generalisations of semantic roles, they are liable to the same line of criticism. One of the concerns raised, which we are well aware of, is that the grounds for the selection of this inventory are not clear. In particular, some relations may cover distinct meanings, and not all relations seem to be equally justified or of the same level of granularity. An analysis of the morphosemantic relations with proposed definitions and semantic restrictions (couched in terms of noun and verb primes) is presented in Koeva et al. (2016). A concise critical overview in light of further observations on the relations is dealt with in Mititelu et al. (2021). Our understanding is that the differences among morphosemantic relations are inherent to and stem from the varying granularity of prominent semantic components even if some of them may be redundant for our task. Therefore, we take the data as given and try to make sense of the generalisations underlying the distinctions made in the resource, where relevant.

3.2 Oxford English Dictionary

The OED contains 600,000 words from over 1,000 years of history of the English language. For each word in our dataset, we used the OED API to obtain the list of lemmas (separate OED entries) with the part of speech and the list of senses with definitions.

In addition, we have applied two special resources derived from OED:[3]
- a list of 2,830 pairs of verb and noun OED lexical entries labeled as V-to-N zero derivation;
- a list of 5,921 pairs of verb and noun OED lexical entries labeled as N-to-V zero derivation.

These were processed into 2,660 **unique** word pairs V-to-N, 5,521 **unique** word pairs N-to-V and 347 **unique** word pairs that show both directions of derivation in some of their senses.

3.3 Dataset compilation

Our data initially comprised the overall dataset of verb – noun pairs from the PWN that are labeled with a morphosemantic relation (see §3.1). For each pair we assigned the direction of derivation if known from the OED (V-to-N, N-to-V or both). We discarded pairs if (i) there are homonym entries in OED for some of which a direction is not assigned (so we do not know whether our WordNet senses correspond to any of the relevant OED senses and whether the derivational direction stands), or if (ii) two different directions are assigned to different senses of the verb and noun, so no clear direction can be established between the two.

We also make sure that the WordNet gloss is similar to one or more of the OED senses in order to confirm the reliability of the directionality information transferred from the OED onto the WordNet entries. The verification was initially performed by measuring text similarity automatically (based on the number of overlapping meaningful words, including their synonyms, in the OED definition and the WordNet gloss) and the results were manually validated.

The compiled dataset comprises 4,879 verb – noun **word sense pairs** with confirmed direction of derivation: 2,917 (60%) of them are zero verbs (N-to-V) and 1,962 (40%) are zero nouns (V-to-N). The bias towards zero verbs is expected, given that they are in general more productive than zero nouns. In what follows we often refer to these pairs as 'N-V pairs', by which we mean 'N-V word sense pairs'.

---

[3] We thank James McCracken and Emily Hoyland (from the OED team) for providing us with the lists of zero nouns and zero verbs, as well as the API access.

3.4 Further remarks on methodology

In this section we briefly describe the features and the steps followed for the analysis of V-to-N and N-to-V zero derivation. Our observations are solely based on the N-V pairs derived from WordNet and labeled as morphosemantically related (cf. §3.1).

It is worth mentioning some limitations on the WordNet data:
(a) morphosemantic relations in Princeton WordNet are not comprehensive.
(b) Some morphosemantic relations are not clearly distinctive and overlap in semantics (e.g., By-means-of and Uses).
(c) Some verbs share the semantics of more than one semantic class (labeled by the semantic prime it is assigned).
(d) Some nouns share the semantics of more than one semantic class.
(e) WordNet has limited coverage.
(f) The frequency data presented here and the statistics show the distribution of the cases within the lexical-semantic network and not the frequency of their usage in text.

A further limitation occurs in the process of selecting the relevant N-V pairs:
(g) We only take those pairs for which directionality is present in the OED data (see §3.2). This excludes homonymous or other border-case examples for which the direction in the current senses of the verb and/or noun cannot be confirmed. These are the examples which are likely to exhibit non-typical features or behaviour, and introduce more variety in the data. The analysis of these examples falls among the tasks for future work.

Brief manual verification confirmed the validity of the alignment between the OED senses and the WordNet synset entries, which justifies the assignment of the direction of derivation from OED onto WordNet verb-noun pairs.

A last possible limitation concerns the reliability of the derivational direction established in the OED for zero N-V pairs. To determine this, OED lexicographers have reportedly considered the full history of each word, including date of attestation, early frequency of use, but also linguistic and etymological factors such as the behavior of cognate words, the donor in case of loanwords, and semantic properties to the extent that the more basic meaning would be associated with the base word (Philip Durkin, p. c.). These complex considerations ensure a high reliability of the derivational direction for the zero N-V pairs employed in our study (cf. directionality criteria in Plag 2003, §5.1.1.).

The results presented in §3.2 rely on simple statistical analysis of frequencies of occurrence of zero verbs and zero nouns. We apply Pearson's Chi-squared test (Manning & Schütze 1999) to check whether the direction of derivation is independent of the morphosemantic relation, as well as of the verb and noun primes. The chi-square tests are followed by a post-hoc analysis, which observes the standardised residuals and the relative contribution of each cell to the overall chi-square statistic (Beasley & Schumacker 1995). The standardised residuals are expressed as a ratio of the difference between the observed and the expected value and the standard deviation of the expected value. They provide a measure of how significant the cells are to the chi-square value and can be used for comparing the relative contribution between cells to draw conclusions on the significance of certain classes.

In each case we first set the chi-square null hypothesis H_0 of independence and we aim at significance level of $p = 0.01$. The calculation of the chi-square values and the post-hoc analysis are carried out in RStudio using the chisq.test and the chisq.posthoc.test package.[4] The p-values reported in the analysis represent the probability that a certain value registered in the data can occur by chance. We look for the cells with higher standardised residuals, thus stronger contribution to the overall chi-square statistic, but also associated with low values of p corresponding to the set significant level.

The in-depth analysis of zero formations is focused on the semantic features of the verb-noun pair as expressed through the morphosemantic relations between them, as well as the verb primes and the noun primes representative for each relation. The relations are grouped based on the semantic diversity they exhibit with respect to the number of prime pairs and their compatibility. The analysis aims at providing evidence for answering the research questions proposed in §1.

4 Results

Below we first offer the overall results on the distribution of zero nouns and zero verbs for each of the 14 morphosemantic relations (§4.1), followed by an overview of the verb and noun prime distribution (§4.2). Then, in §4.3, we present the most frequent combinations of semantic primes for each relation and each direction of zero derivation, while in §4.4 we look into the possibility of having pairs of semantic primes specific to each of the two derivational directions. An interpretation of these results is offered in §5.

---

[4] https://CRAN.R-project.org/package=chisq.posthoc.test

4.1 morphosemantic relations

An overview of the frequency of zero nouns and zero verbs for each of the 14 morphosemantic relations is given in Figure 1: in dark grey we see the numbers of zero nouns and in light grey those of zero verbs. Table 4 shows the total number of N-V word sense pairs for each relation and the corresponding percentages of zero nouns (V-to-N direction) and zero verbs (N-to-V direction) among them.

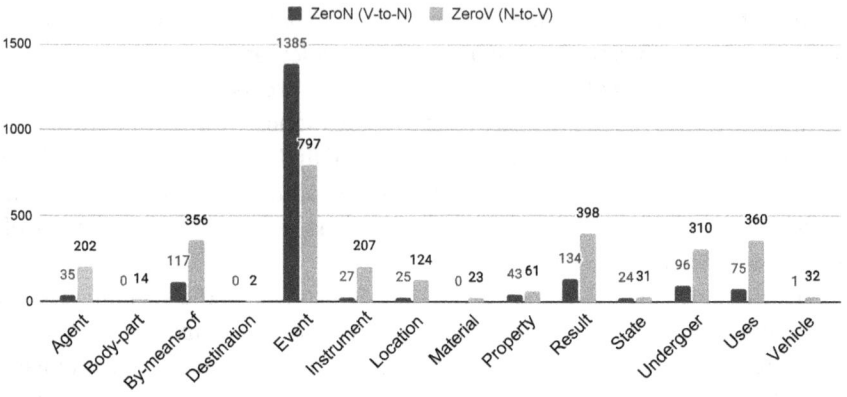

Fig. 1: Distribution of zero nouns and zero verbs per morphosemantic relation.

The Event relation is by far the most frequent with a total of 2,182 N-V pairs. In contrast, the relations Body-part, Destination, Material and Vehicle are very rare, exhibiting between 2 and 33 N-V pairs. The next most frequent relations are Result (532 N-V pairs), By-means-of (473 pairs), Uses (435 pairs), Undergoer (406 pairs), Instrument (238 pairs) and Agent (237 pairs).

The distribution of the two directions V-to-N and N-to-V within these morphosemantic relations shows some clear tendencies (see Table 4). The relations Body-part, Destination, Material and Vehicle appear (almost) exclusively with zero verbs, but they are quite infrequent in comparison with the other relations. The most frequent relation Event shows a preference for zero nouns (63.5%), while Agent, By-means-of, Instrument, Location, Result, Uses and Undergoer associate mainly with zero verbs (74.9% to 88.5%). The relations Property and State do not particularly associate with either direction: their distribution roughly corresponds to the overall distribution of zero nouns and zero verbs in the full dataset.

We apply the chi-square test to check the hypothesis of independence between the direction of derivation and the morphosemantic relations. The calcu-

Tab. 4: Distribution of zero nouns and zero verbs per morphosemantic relation, standardised residuals and p-values for morphosemantic relations. Light grey shading indicates relevant significant values for zero verbs and dark grey shading for zero nouns.

Relation	Agent	Body-part	By-means-of	Destination	Event	Instrument	Location
Total pairs	237	14	473	2	2,182	234	149
V-to-N	35 (14.8%)	–	117 (24.7%)	–	1,385 (63.5%)	27 (11.5%)	25 (16.8%)
N-to-V	202 (85.2%)	14 (100%)	356 (75.3%)	2 (100%)	797 (36.5%)	207 (88.5%)	124 (83.2%)
Chi² std. residuals ZeroN	-8.19	-3.07	-7.22	-1.16	29.80	-9.16	-5.92
Chi² std. residuals ZeroV	8.19	3.07	7.22	1.16	-29.80	9.16	5.92
Chi² p-value	0.00	0.059	1.4e-11	1.00	0.00	0.00	8.74e-08

Relation	Material	Property	Result	State	Uses	Undergoer	Vehicle
Total pairs	23	104	532	55	435	406	33
V-to-N	–	43 (41.3%)	134 (25.1%)	24 (43.6%)	75 (17.2%)	96 (23.6%)	1 (3%)
N-to-V	23 (100%)	61 (58.7%)	398 (74.9%)	31 (56.7%)	360 (82.8%)	310 (76.4%)	32 (97%)
Chi² std. residuals ZeroN	-3.94	0.24	-7.49	0.52	-7.11	-10.24	-4.37
Chi² std. residuals ZeroV	3.94	-0.24	7.49	-0.52	7.11	10.24	4.37
Chi² p-value	0.0023	1.00	2.00e-12	1.00	3.20e-11	0.00	0.00034

lated chi-square value of 953.39 ($N = 4,879$, $df = 13$, $p < 2.2e-16$) firmly rejects the hypothesis of independence.

As expected, the relations Agent, By-means-of, Instrument, Location, Result, Uses and Undergoer significantly associate with zero verbs, while Event associates with zero nouns. All these contribute significantly to the chi-value, as opposed to Property and State (among the richer relations), which show no significant association with either direction.[5]

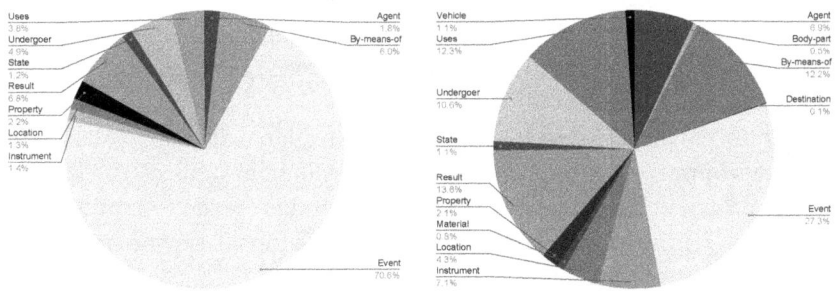

(a) Zero nouns (total of 1,962) (b) Zero verbs (total of 2,917)

Fig. 2: Distribution of the morphosemantic relations within zero nouns and zero verbs.

---

5 Although we keep Body-Part, Destination, Material and Vehicle in the data, many researchers exclude categories where an expected value is less than 5. The inclusion of a small number of such cases is permissible and does not influence the quality of the overall results.

The distribution of the 14 relations within zero nouns and zero verbs is given in Figure 2. The Event relation contains the majority of zero nouns: i.e. a proportion of 70.6% of the 1,962 V-to-N pairs. Implicitly, all the other relations are quite infrequent with zero nouns: only By-means-of and Result come closer to the expected even distribution of 7.1%, given the 14 relations. By contrast, zero verbs exhibit a much more balanced distribution. The Event relation is still best represented, but it covers only 27.3% of the 2,917 N-to-V pairs. Six further relations such as Agent, By-means-of, Instrument, Result, Uses and Undergoer appear with around 7% or more of the N-to-V pairs each. These results show that zero nouns primarily denote events, while zero verbs are semantically more diverse, an observation we will interpret in §5.2 in light of the overview in §2.

4.2 Verb and noun prime distribution

In this section we report on how noun/verb semantic classes may associate with a derivational direction irrespective of the morphosemantic relation. These observations will be informative for the subsequent analysis of verb prime – noun prime combinations in §4.3.

We apply chi-square tests of independence for the direction of derivation and the noun and verb primes. The hypothesis of independence between the direction and the noun prime is rejected with high confidence level as the chi-square value is 937.38 ($N = 4,879, df = 24, p < 2.2e - 16$). Significant contributors to the chi-value and thus, to rejecting the hypothesis of independence, are the noun primes with shaded values for the relevant direction in Table 5: noun.act, noun.animal, noun.artifact, noun.body etc.

The hypothesis of independence between the derivational direction and the verb primes is also firmly rejected although with a smaller chi-value of 189.16 ($N = 4,879, df = 14, p < 2.2e - 16$). Significant contributors are the verb primes with shaded values for the relevant direction in Table 6: verb.motion, verb.perception, verb.creation and verb.possession.

The statistical data indicate strong correlations between noun and verb semantic primes and the direction of derivation. These results are discussed in the beginning of Section §5. In order to delve deeper into the correspondences between zero derivation and semantics, a next step is to look at the distribution of noun and verb prime pairs within each relation and how those are reflected in the direction of derivation. The results of this analysis are presented in §4.3.

Tab. 5: Distribution of zero nouns and zero verbs, standardised residuals and p-values for noun primes. Shading highlights the positive residuals indicating the relevant derivational direction (4th and 5th column) for the corresponding significant p-values (6th column).

	ZeroN (%)	ZeroV (%)	ZeroN std. res.	ZeroV std. res.	p-value
noun.act	722 (67.5%)	347 (32.5%)	20.62	-20.62	0.00
noun.animal	2 (4.7%)	41 (95.3%)	-4.78	4.78	8.9e-5
noun.artifact	146 (16.8%)	725 (83.2%)	-15.57	15.57	0.00
noun.attribute	114 (47.1%)	128 (52.9%)	2.24	-2.24	1.00
noun.body	10 (14.3%)	60 (85.7%)	-4.46	4.46	4.2e-4
noun.cognition	76 (38.6%)	121 (61.4%)	-0.48	0.48	1.00
noun.communication	218 (38.8%)	344 (61.2%)	-0.73	0.73	1.00
noun.event	260 (73.2%)	95 (26.8%)	13.18	-13.18	0.00
noun.feeling	24 (46.2%)	28 (53.8%)	0.88	-0.88	1.00
noun.food	23 (25.0%)	69 (75.0%)	-3.00	3.00	0.13
noun.group	22 (19.1%)	93 (80.9%)	-4.67	4.67	1.5e-4
noun.location	24 (26.1%)	68 (73.9%)	-2.79	2.79	0.26
noun.motive	0 (0.0%)	1 (100.0%)	-0.82	0.82	1.00
noun.object	30 (30.0%)	70 (70.0%)	-2.1	2.1	1.00
noun.person	34 (14.5%)	200 (85.5%)	-8.21	8.21	0.00
noun.phenomenon	27 (42.9%)	36 (57.1%)	0.43	-0.43	1.00
noun.plant	5 (10.2%)	44 (89.8%)	-4.31	4.31	8.3e-4
noun.possession	27 (30.3%)	62 (69.7%)	-1.92	1.92	1.00
noun.process	21 (56.8%)	16 (43.2%)	2.06	-2.06	1.00
noun.quantity	10 (21.7%)	36 (78.3%)	-2.57	2.57	0.52
noun.relation	2 (20.0%)	8 (80.0%)	-1.3	1.3	1.00
noun.shape	38 (40.0%)	57 (60.0%)	-0.04	0.04	1.00
noun.state	88 (46.3%)	102 (53.7%)	1.75	-1.75	1.00
noun.substance	18 (11.7%)	136 (88.3%)	-7.34	7.34	1.10e-11
noun.time	21 (41.2%)	30 (58.8%)	0.14	-0.14	1.00

4.3 Semantic classes involved in N-V pairs

In this section, we analyse the predominant pairs of semantic primes involved in both the N-to-V and the V-to-N direction for each relation.[6] This provides an overview of the semantic diversity of zero nouns and zero verbs in comparison to their bases.

For each relation and each direction, all combinations of N and V primes were extracted and filtered according to their frequency. We ignored those with poor representation and kept only the most frequent prime pairs for each direction covering around 70% of the prime pairs for each relation. The data show three types

---

[6] We discard the relations Body-part, Destination, Material and Vehicle due to data parsimony.

Tab. 6: Distribution of zero nouns and zero verbs, standardised residuals and p-values for verb primes. Shading highlights the positive residuals indicating the relevant derivational direction (4th and 5th column) for the corresponding significant p-values (6th column).

	ZeroN (%)	ZeroV (%)	ZeroN std. res.	ZeroV std. res.	p-value
verb.body	121 (49.0%)	126 (51.0%)	2.88	-2.88	0.12
verb.change	197 (39.4%)	303 (60.6%)	-0.39	0.39	1.00
verb.cognition	61 (33.5%)	121 (66.5%)	-1.88	1.88	1.00
verb.communication	244 (40.3%)	362 (59.7%)	0.027	-0.027	1.00
verb.competition	53 (29.1%)	129 (70.9%)	-3.11	3.11	0.56
verb.consumption	35 (47.3%)	39 (52.7%)	1.25	-1.25	1.00
verb.contact	416 (38.3%)	669 (61.7%)	-1.43	1.43	1.00
verb.creation	59 (21.6%)	214 (78.4%)	-6.45	6.45	3.0e-9
verb.emotion	41 (45.6%)	49 (54.4%)	1.04	-1.04	1.00
verb.motion	329 (55.8%)	261 (44.2%)	8.22	-8.22	0.00
verb.perception	137 (58.8%)	96 (41.2%)	5.93	-5.93	9.1e-8
verb.possession	73 (26.4%)	203 (73.6%)	-4.8	4.8	4.7e-5
verb.social	98 (31.8%)	210 (68.2%)	-3.10	3.10	0.06
verb.stative	84 (43.5%)	109 (56.5%)	0.96	-0.96	1.00
verb.weather	14 (35.0%)	26 (65.0%)	-0.68	0.68	1.00

of situations with respect to the number of semantic classes (or primes) characterising the N-V pairs (see Table 7):

- the number of V primes is greater that that of the N primes, thus showing greater variety in terms of verb semantics (the dark grey cells in Table 7);
- the number of N primes is greater than that of the V primes, showing greater variety in terms of noun semantics (the white cells in Table 7);
- the number of N primes is approximately equal to that of the V primes (the light grey cells in Table 7).

Tab. 7: Overview of the comparison between the number of primes of zero formations and their bases: dark grey indicates a higher number of V primes than of N primes; white indicates a higher number of N primes; light grey indicates equal numbers of N and V primes.

	Agent	By-means-of	Event	Instrument	Location	Property	Result	State	Undergoer	Uses
N-to-V										
V-to-N										

The prime combinations yield four groups of morphosemantic relations:

- relations for which the number of V primes is higher than that of N primes, irrespective of the direction (in Table 7 both cells of these relations are in dark grey): Agent, Event, and Property (subsection §4.3.1);
- relations for which the number of N primes is higher than that of V primes, irrespective of the direction (in Table 7 both cells are white): Result and Undergoer (subsection §4.3.2);
- a relation for which the number of primes for zero verbs is higher than that of their base nouns, while for zero nouns, the number of primes of the base verbs is a little smaller than that of the primes of the zero nouns (in Table 7 the cell for N-to-V is dark grey and the one for V-to-N is white): By-means-of (subsection §4.3.3);
- relations for which the number of primes for zero verbs is higher than that of their base nouns, while for zero nouns, the number of primes of the base verbs is equal to that of the primes of the zero nouns (in Table 7 the cell for N-to-V is dark grey and the one for V-to-N is light grey): Instrument, Location, State and Uses (subsection §4.3.4).

The rest of the subsection presents the data for all the discussed relations grouped according to the tendencies outlined above. Each subsection begins with a table showing the number of N and V primes involved in each derivation direction for each morphosemantic relation and continues with a brief discussion of the data and examples of the most frequent prime pairs. A detailed representation of the N and V prime combinations for each relation is included in the appendix.

4.3.1 Verb primes prevailing for both directions

The relations Agent, Event and Property (Table 8) demonstrate a greater diversity of verb primes both as bases and as results.

Tab. 8: The number of N and V primes for the relations Agent, Event and Property.

	N-to-V		V-to-N	
	# N primes	# V primes	# V primes	# N primes
Agent	1	9	6	1
Event	11	14	11	4
Property	5	6	5	3

Agent. The relation is characterised by a single noun prime (noun.person) and many verb primes. The unique noun prime attests to the specificity of the relation. Examples of the most frequent prime pairs for N-to-V direction include:
- n.person_v.social: *clerk – to clerk*;
- n.person_v.communication: *cipher – to cipher*;
- n.person_v.creation: *cook – to cook*;
- n.person_v.competition: *jockey – to jockey*;
- n.person_v.possession: *hog – to hog*;
- n.person_v.cognition: *pioneer – to pioneer*.

Some examples of the most frequent prime pairs for V-to-N direction include:
- v.social_n.person: *to affiliate – affiliate*;
- v.communication_n.person: *to flirt – flirt*;
- v.motion_n.person: *to sneak – sneak*.

Event. This relation is characterised by a diversity of verb and noun semantic primes. Slightly more semantic verb classes are involved when zero verbs are created than in the case of zero nouns (see 14 vs. 11 in Table 8). Examples for the most represented combinations of primes for zero verbs include:
- n.communication_v.communication: *cheer – to cheer*;
- n.act_v.motion: *curvet – to curvet*;
- n.act_v.contact: *contact – to contact*;
- n.act_v.social: *crusade – to crusade*;
- n.act_v.possession: *finance – to finance*;
- n.event_v.motion: *progress – to progress*.

The most frequent combinations of primes for creating zero noun Events include:
- v.motion_n.act: *to prowl – prowl*;
- v.motion_n.event: *to quake – quake*;
- v.contact_n.act: *to pull – pull*;
- v.communication_n.communication: *to boast – boast*;
- v.change_n.act: *to purge – purge*.

A very neat distribution is observed with respect to the noun primes involved in the relation: although the base noun and the zero verb classes are quite diverse (11 noun primes and 14 verb primes), the most frequent noun primes (both in terms of the number of pairs and the diversity of the primes of the resulting verbs) serving as bases for verbs from various primes are in fact only two: n.act and n.event (see the shaded rows in the N-to-V part of Table 14 in the appendix). The same holds in the opposite direction: 11 verb primes are bases for only 4 noun primes, of which noun.act and noun.event are by far the most frequent (the shaded columns in the V-to-N part of Table 14).

Property. At first glance the data on N-to-V derivation with this relation do not show greater variety of verb primes: the resulting verbs of the 5 base noun primes belong to 6 verb primes; however, the majority of derivations and the greatest diversity of resulting verb primes are concentrated in the most productive noun prime (noun.attribute) (the shaded row in the N-to-V part of Table 15 in the appendix). Here are several examples to illustrate the most frequent N-V pairs:
- n.attribute_v.communication: *glamour – to glamour*;
- n.attribute_v.change: *silence – to silence*;
- n.attribute_v.cognition: *order – to order*;
- n.attribute_v.contact: *grade – to grade*;
- n.attribute_v.social: *disadvantage – to disadvantage*.

As compared with the base verbs (5 primes), zero nouns involve a more restricted number of primes (3). At a closer look, we also find that various base verb primes (the shaded column in the V-to-N part of Table 15 in the appendix) result in semantically uniform nouns denoting properties and attributes (noun.attribute). The only exception with respect to the noun primes is verb.stative, which results in location and relation nouns, too:
- v.perception_n.attribute: *to feel – feel*;
- v.contact_n.attribute: *to polish – polish*;
- v.stative_n.attribute: *to overlap – overlap*;
- v.stative_n.location: *to reach – reach*;
- v.stative_n.relation: *to trim – trim*;
- v.motion_n.attribute: *to slope – slope*;
- v.change_n.attribute: *to simmer – simmer*.

In addition, the diversity of verb primes with Property is much more limited than the one attested with relations such as Event or Agent. This, along with the fact that attributes are both the best represented bases and results, points to the conclusion that this relation is more specialised than, for instance, Event.

4.3.2 Noun primes prevailing for both directions

The relations Result and Undergoer (Table 9) are characterised by a greater diversity of noun primes both as bases and as results of the derivation. We should note, however, that base nouns are only slightly more diverse than the resulting zero verbs.

Tab. 9: The number of N and V primes for the relations Result and Undergoer.

	N-to-V		V-to-N	
	# N primes	# V primes	# V primes	# N primes
Result	13	11	7	13
Undergoer	12	11	10	13

Result. At first sight, the number of base noun primes (13) exceeds the number of resulting verb primes (11) by only a little. However, if we consider the variety of base noun primes in light of the concentration of the resulting verb primes, it is obvious that 3 of the latter, verb.contact, verb.creation and verb.change, are more frequent (as shown by the shaded cells in Table 16 in the appendix). Below are examples of the most frequent N-to-V prime pairs:
- n.artifact_v.contact: *knot – to knot*;
- n.shape_v.contact: *groove – to groove*;
- n.object_v.contact: *segment – to segment*;
- n.artifact_v.creation: *fresco – to fresco*;
- n.communication_v.creation: *film – to film*;
- n.object_v.change: *splinter – to splinter*;
- n.food_v.change: *stew – to stew*;
- n.attribute_v.change: *bleach – to bleach*;
- n.substance_v.change: *rust – to rust*.

With respect to the zero nouns, their number of primes (13) is substantially greater than that of the verbs (7).[7] The best represented base verb primes, v.contact, v.creation and v.change, are the same as the resulting verb primes in the N-to-V derivation (see the shaded cells in Table 16 in the appendix). Below are given a few examples of the patterns found in the data:
- v.contact_n.shape: *to scratch – scratch*;
- v.contact_n.state: *to scrape – scrape*;
- v.contact_n.object: *to slice – slice*;
- v.change_n.shape: *to crease – crease*;
- v.change_n.attribute: *to tinge – tinge*;
- v.change_n.object: *to split – split*;
- v.creation_n.artifact: *to knit – knit*;
- v.creation_n.communication: *to reissue – reissue*.

---

[7] The data for the relation Result are estimated for 80-81% of the prime pairs (not 70% as for the others) because of the large number of pairs with the same number of attestations.

The productivity of verb.contact, verb.change and verb.creation as both bases and results of the derivation resonates well with the semantics of the relation. In the V-to-N direction, change verbs and creation verbs are naturally related to results denoting the entity that is formed or undergoes a change (*to curl – a curl*) or comes into existence (*to produce – produce*) or is affected (*to scrape – a scrape*) as a result of the verb's event. Many of the base nouns in the N-to-V direction are concrete entities, with primes such as noun.object, noun.artifact, noun.food, noun.substance.

Undergoer. For the N-to-V direction the number of noun primes involved exceeds the verb primes only by a little. Although we find 12 base noun primes, only two of them, i.e. noun.communication and noun.artifact, produce verbs from various primes (see the first 2 shaded rows in the N-to-V part of Table 17 in the appendix). The remaining ones yield verbs that are concentrated in a limited number of primes, most favoured being verb.contact and verb.change (see the shaded columns in the N-to-V part of Table 17). Here are some examples of the most frequent prime pairs:
- n.communication_v.communication: *decree – to decree*;
- n.communication_v.creation: *solo – to solo* '= perform a solo';
- n.artifact_v.contact: *freight – to freight*;
- n.artifact_v.creation: *microfilm – to microfilm*;
- n.possession_v.possession: *allowance – to allowance*.

In the V-to-N direction we find 10 base verb primes and 13 zero noun primes. Even so, we should note that there is a marked tendency for verbs from diverse primes to form nouns denoting artifacts (the shaded column in the V-to-N direction in Table 17), with most of the verb primes producing nouns from only 3 primes. The resulting nouns are quite scattered across primes although there is logic to this distribution: verbs of communication form nouns of communication, verbs of consumption – nouns denoting food, etc. This goes in line with the default assumption that the resulting zero nouns are the natural affected entities (undergoers) of the respective predicates:
- v.possession_n.possession: *to refund – refund*;
- v.contact_n.artifact: *to cover – cover*;
- v.communication_n.communication: *to rehash – rehash*;
- v.consumption_n.food: *to feed – feed*;
- v.body_n.body: *to slobber – slobber*.

4.3.3 Zero verbs – semantically more diverse than their base nouns; zero nouns – semantically slightly more diverse than their base verbs

Tab. 10: The number of N and V primes for the relation By-means-of.

	N-to-V		V-to-N	
	# N primes	# V primes	# V primes	# N primes
By-means-of	8	11	10	11

By-means-of. This relation is characterised by great diversity with respect to the semantic classes to which the verbs and nouns involved (either as bases or as results of zero derivation) belong. Table 10 shows that 8 noun primes are bases for 11 zero verb primes. However, a closer inspection reveals that two semantic classes of nouns (n.artifact and n.communication) are bases for a wide spectrum of verb classes (see the shaded lines in Table 18 in the appendix). Some examples from the most representative pairs of primes include:
- n.artifact_v.contact: *border – to border*;
- n.artifact_v.motion: *fan – to fan*;
- n.communication_v.communication: *certificate – to certificate.*

For zero nouns, although 10 verb primes are involved as bases for deriving nouns belonging to 11 primes, most of the created nouns tend to belong to the semantic classes noun.artifact and noun.attribute, while their base verbs cover a wide semantic range for this direction of derivation too (see the shaded columns in Table 18). Some examples of the prevailing primes combinations are:
- v.contact_n.artifact: *to cover – cover*;
- v.social_n.attribute: *to control – control.*

Tab. 11: The number of N and V primes for the relations Instrument, Location, State and Uses.

	N-to-V		V-to-N	
	# N primes	# V primes	# V primes	# N primes
Instrument	1	5	1	1
Location	3	6	3	3
State	4	6	3	3
Uses	8	9	6	6

4.3.4 Zero verbs – semantically more diverse than their base nouns; zero nouns – as semantically diverse as their base verbs

Instrument. Just like Agent, this relation involves only one noun prime, i.e. noun.artifact, irrespective of the derivation direction, and various verb semantic classes (see Table 19 in the appendix). Examples of these combinations are:
- n.artifact_v.contact: *hammer – to hammer*;
- n.artifact_v.creation: *pencil – to pencil*;
- n.artifact_v.motion: *pedal – to pedal*;
- n.artifact_v.body: *splint – to splint*;
- n.artifact_v.change: *hose – to hose*.

For zero nouns only one combination of primes occurs for the majority of pairs: v.contact – n.artifact (e.g., *lift – to lift*).

Location. The semantic diversity of zero verbs is greater than that of the base nouns. Some of the most representative combinations are:
- n.artifact_v.contact: *barrel – to barrel*;
- n.artifact_v.motion: *dock – to dock*;
- n.location_v.motion: *corner – to corner*;
- n.object_v.motion: *puddle – to puddle*.

The zero nouns of type Location display only a few pairs of semantic classes for 3 verb and 3 noun primes (see Table 20 in the appendix). We give below examples for these combinations:
- v.contact_n.location: *to scour – scour*;
- v.change_n.attribute: *to burn – burn*;
- v.motion_n.location: *to stop – stop*;
- v.motion_n.artifact: *to walk – walk*.

State. The N-to-V direction of derivation for State shows 4 noun primes and 6 verb primes. The prime noun.state is best represented, and the rest – noun.feeling, noun.quantity and noun.attribute – are clearly stative in nature, too. The resulting verbs belong to various primes (see Table 21 in the appendix). Below are some examples of the prime pairs:
- n.state_v.contact: *contact – to contact*;
- n.state_v.emotion: *miff – to miff*;
- n.state_v.change: *mess – to mess*;
- n.feeling_v.emotion: *pity – to pity*;

The zero nouns involve 3 base verb primes and 3 resulting noun primes. However, as the data further show (Table 21), most of the zero nouns are states and the remaining ones have stative semantics, like for zero verbs. As the number of prime pairs considered is small, below we list examples for all of them:
- v.emotion_n.state: *to glow – glow*;
- v.emotion_n.feeling: *to dread – dread*;
- v.change_n.state: *to polish – polish*;
- v.change_n.attribute: *to temper – temper*;
- v.body_n.state: *to frazzle – frazzle*.

Uses. In the N-to-V direction of derivation for this relation there are 8 noun primes and 9 verb primes. The most productive base prime, noun.artifact, produces verbs from various primes (see Table 22 in the appendix). Nouns of the classes noun.substance and noun.communication, which are also productive, are bases for verbs belonging to the most numerous semantic primes occurring with this relation.

The remaining noun primes yield a modest number of verbs from different primes. In fact, we note that nouns from various primes tend to produce verbs primarily with the primes verb.contact and verb.possession. Examples of the most productive primes pairs are:
- n.artifact_v.contact: *canopy – to canopy*;
- n.artifact_v.possession: *armour – to armour* 'equip with armour';
- n.artifact_v.body: *powder – to powder*;
- n.substance_v.contact: *copper – to copper*;
- n.communication_v.communication: *autograph – to autograph*.

The V-to-N direction of derivation involves an even number of 6 primes for both nouns and verbs; in addition, the most productive prime verb.contact yields nouns from various primes, with the higher number of noun.artifact,

n.communication and n.substance (see Table 22). Below are examples of the productive patterns:
- v.contact_n.artifact: *to paint – paint*;
- v.contact_n.communication: *to stamp – stamp*;
- v.contact_n.substance: *to daub – daub*;
- v.body_n.artifact: *to attire – attire*;
- v.creation_n.artifact: *to trim – trim*.

4.4 Prime combinations and the direction of zero derivation

In this section we consider the possibility of having prime pairs that manifest the tendency of occurring with zero derivations of a certain direction.

The 25 noun primes and the 15 verb primes are found in 263 combinations in our dataset, 40 of which are hapax legomena and 23 have more than 50 occurrences. We present here the results of the investigation we made for establishing their specificity to a certain direction of zero derivation.[8] The first remark is that most prime combinations (163 pairs) are found with both directions, 24 are specific to zero nouns formation, while 76 are specific to zero verbs formation.

From the prime combinations that are specific to one direction of derivation, we highlight here the more frequent ones: for zero nouns, only one combination, namely v.stative – n.event (11 occurrences) is specific, while several pairs are specific to zero verb formation:
- v.creation – n.person (17 occurrences) – specific to Agent only,
- v.contact – n.animal (16 occurrences),
- v.contact – n.group (15 occurrences),
- v.competition – n.person (14 occurrences) – specific to Agent only,
- v.competition – n.group (12 occurrences),
- v.body – n.person (12 occurrences),
- v.contact – n.plant (11 occurrences),
- v.body – n.animal (11 occurrences),
- v.change – n.cognition (10 occurrences),
- v.perception – n.person (10 occurrences) – specific to Agent only.

We subjected to a closer inspection 23 pairs of primes combinations that (i) occur more than 50 times in the dataset and (ii) display a frequency of occurrence for a

---

8 There is only one example of zero derivation for each of the hapax legomena in the dataset.

derivational direction higher than expected.[9] The data showed that some of these prime pairs are specific to a certain direction when occurring with a certain morphosemantic relation. This happens mostly with zero verbs of creation, as shown in Table 12.[10]

Tab. 12: Semantic primes specific to certain relations for zero verbs creation: the number shows how many zero derivations exist for the respective primes combination and relation; frequency is calculated with respect to the whole number of derivations of the respective direction for all relations.

Primes pair	Relation	#occur.	Freq.	Examples
n.artifact_v.creation	Instrument	12	14%	$chalk_N$ - $chalk_V$, $charcoal_N$ - $charcoal_V$, $pencil_N$ - $pencil_V$
n.artifact_v.creation	Undergoer	11	13%	$bead_N$ - $bead_V$, $drum_N$ - $drum_V$, $microfilm_N$ - $microfilm_V$
n.substance_v.contact	By-means-of	9	12%	$cement_N$ - $cement_V$, $glue_N$ - $glue_V$, $grout_N$ - $grout_V$
n.substance_v.contact	Material	10	13%	$copper_N$ - $copper_V$, $metal_N$ - $metal_V$, $silver_N$ - $silver_V$
n.artifact_v.possession	Location	9	18%	$bank_N$ - $bank_V$, $garage_N$ - $garage_V$, $shop_N$ - $shop_V$
n.communication_v.creation	Undergoer	11	26%	$madrigal_N$ - $madrigal_V$, $hymn_N$ - $hymn_V$, $paragraph_N$ - $paragraph_V$

5 Interpretation of the results

We now proceed to interpret the results presented above from the perspective of our initial research questions and the literature overview in §2. Our first aim was to check whether the 14 morphosemantic relations annotated in the PWN standoff file and the PWN noun/verb primes show any correlations with the direction of derivation in our dataset of N-V word sense pairs. The second aim was to interpret these findings in the context of the previous literature.

---

9 The expected frequency is the representation of V-to-N and N-to-V forms in the overall dataset, i.e., 40% and 60%, respectively (see §3.3). The thresholds we established, higher than these frequencies, are 60% for zero nouns and 75% for zero verbs.
10 We left aside those cases when the occurrences represent less than 10% of the whole number of derivations for the respective direction.

To begin with, the results in §4.1 and §4.2 allow us to state that we do find strong correlations with the derivational direction both for the morphosemantic relations and the noun/verb primes. Table 4 in §4.1 reveals statistically significant correlations for most of the morphosemantic relations and one direction of derivation, which we discuss in more detail in §5.1 below.

Section §4.2 (see Tables 5 and 6) shows that 9 of the 25 noun primes and 4 of the 15 verb primes establish statistically significant correlations with one direction or the other. Nouns of the classes noun.act and noun.event associate with zero nouns, while noun.animal, noun.artifact, noun.body, noun.group, noun.person, noun.plant and noun.substance associate with zero verbs. Ontologically speaking, these results conform to our expectations about lexical categories. Verbs ontologically denote acts and events, while nouns mostly refer to objects (Baker & Croft 2017). Consequently, nouns that denote acts and events will be the output of deverbal derivation (see *transfer, escape, ambush, beat* for acts and *twinkle, twist, drip* for events derived from verbs), while nouns referring to animals, artifacts, persons, plants, substances will represent the input to denominal verbs (see *lamb, cub, kitten* for noun.animal, *bandage, chain, buckle* for noun.artifact, *chair, champion, doctor* for noun.person, *fruit, mushroom, seed* for noun.plant and *cement, glue, metal, paper* for noun.substance as input to zero verbs).

For the verb primes in Table 6, we see that verb.motion and verb.perception associate with zero nouns (see *to march, to limp, to ride, to sail* for verb.motion and *to smell, to sound, to scent, to knock* for verb.perception, as input to zero nouns), while verb.creation and verb.possession associate with zero verbs (see *to hammer, to ornament, to instrument, to garden* for verb.creation and *to loan, to profit, to sacrifice, to fund* for verb.possession, as zero verbs derived from nouns). This suggests that verbs of motion and of perception are more likely to form the input to zero nouns than to be derived from lexical nouns, while verbs of creation and verbs of possession are more likely derived from nouns.

5.1 Interpretation of the morphosemantic relations

In §4.1, we saw that the Event relation is the most frequent one in the dataset and substantially more frequent with zero nouns (63.5%) than with zero verbs (36.5%), if we keep in mind that the overall dataset is biased towards zero verbs (60%). The relation Event between nouns and verbs is expected to be frequent, given the primarily eventive meaning of verbs (Koontz-Garboden 2005; Baker & Croft 2017). Its higher frequency with zero nouns, however, also confirms the intuition that, to create an Event relation, the input category must be that of the verb, whose primary ontological meaning is eventive. The noun is the output category, as events are not typical denotations in the ontology of nouns (pace some exceptions like *trip, movie*).

Unlike Event, relations such as Agent, By-means-of, Instrument, Location, Result, Undergoer and Uses are substantially more frequent with zero verbs, which represent 75% or more of the corresponding pairs.[11] These relations are relatively frequent in our dataset and represent typical morphosemantic relations that appear between morphologically related N-V pairs, to the extent that the noun loosely corresponds to some semantic argument in the event structure of the related verb. From this perspective, it is natural for them to appear more frequently with zero verbs, as the meaning of the verb is construed around a semantic argument instantiated by the base noun (but see §2.2 for more subtle observations on this).

An interesting case is that of the Property and State relations, which are not very frequent in our dataset, nor do they show any tendency towards one direction or the other. From the literature on the semantics of lexical categories we know that in English properties and states are typically categorised as adjectives, and not as verbs or nouns (Dixon 1982; Koontz-Garboden 2005, 2007; Baker & Croft 2017; Koontz-Garboden & Francez 2017). This explains the smaller number of N-V pairs for these relations to begin with but also their indeterminacy with respect to a derivational direction, since neither the verb nor the noun represents a default base category for zero formations that denote properties and states (in contrast with Event, Agent, Instrument, etc. above).

From the perspective of how zero nouns and zero verbs are distributed across the different relations in Figure 2, §4.1, we can also make some insightful observations, which support previous claims in the literature. Namely, the figure shows that zero nouns are primarily formed to denote events: 70.3% of them appear in this relation, indicating a clear morphosemantic relation to the base from which they inherit an eventive meaning. Other relations are much more rarely attested with zero nouns: only By-means-of and Result come close to what would be expected from a by-chance distribution (i.e. 7.1%). This picture confirms Cetnarowska's (1993) conclusion that zero nouns primarily denote events, and participant readings are the result of metonymic shifts and only limitedly available. For zero verb formation, however, we find a broader spectrum of morphosemantic relations, indicating more indeterminacy about their semantics in relation to the base: Agent, By-means-of, Event, Instrument, Result, Undergoer and Uses include between 6.9% and 27.3% of the zero verbs. This contrast be-

---

[11] The dataset is indeed biased for zero verbs, which make 60% of it, but these relations show a considerably higher proportion than this baseline (see statistical results in §4.1).

tween zero nouns and zero verbs supports the observation from the literature overview in §2 and the results from Kisselew et al. (2016) according to which the semantic relationship between zero nouns and their base is more systematic and predictable with information content measures than that between zero verbs and their base.

5.2 Interpretation of the noun and verb prime distribution

Zero nouns have been argued to be well-behaved and exhibit meanings similar to those of overt nominalisations (Cetnarowska 1993), which are semantically more specific and restricted than the meaning of the base (Kisselew et al. 2016). Zero verbs, however, have been argued not to receive more specific meanings than the base (Kisselew et al. 2016) and to show a broader range of meanings than overt derivations, whereby they do not establish systematic relations to the meaning of their base as in an argument-predicate relation (see Harley & Haugen 2007; Rimell 2012). The question is whether our dataset allows us to draw any conclusions with respect to these observations.

More evidence on the greater semantic diversity of zero verbs compared to zero nouns in support of these previous findings appears when we interpret the results from §4.3 on the prime pairs (i.e. semantic verb and noun classes) involved in each such relation. For many relations, a small set of base noun primes results in verbs of many more primes, while in zero noun derivation the opposite holds: a broad range of base verb primes yields nouns grouped in only 1 or 2 noun primes. This contrast is particularly surprising, if we take into account that the pool of noun primes is much larger than that of verb primes in our dataset (see 25 noun primes vs. 15 verb primes in §3.1 and §4.2) and implicitly provides stronger support for the previous observation that zero verbs are semantically more diverse (in relation to their base and by comparison to overtly derived verbs) than zero nouns are.

Looking closely at this contrast, we notice that for the N-to-V direction, the extent of the phenomenon is quite vast (see Table 7), manifesting for 8 out of the 10 relations analysed. For zero nouns it is more moderate: three relations (Agent, Event and Property) clearly manifest this, two (By-means-of and State) manifest it for the most frequent prime combinations, while others (Result and Undergoer) seem not to confirm it, and still others (Instrument, Location and Uses) contain insufficient data for drawing any conclusion.

With respect to the correlation between prime combinations and the direction of zero derivation (§4.4), we noticed that most of the primes combinations occur with both directions, so there are only a few such correlations, and most of them concern zero verbs, which is again suggestive of their more diverse semantics.

6 Conclusions and future work

In this paper we investigated whether morphosemantic relations and noun/verb semantic classes (primes) from the PWN show any correlations with the OED direction of derivation in a dataset of 4,879 zero-related N-V word sense pairs. We aimed to capture possible semantic differences between nouns and verbs formed by zero derivation for a better understanding of this morphological process.

We found statistically significant correlations with the derivational direction both for the morphosemantic relations and the semantic classes. First, we have shown that most of the morphosemantic relations associate with one direction or the other: Event appears most often with zero nouns created from verbs, while Agent, By-means-of, Instrument, Location, Result, Undergoer, Uses appear most often with zero verbs created from nouns. The relations Property and State appear with similar proportions of zero nouns and zero verbs. We explained this peculiar behaviour by the fact that properties and states are unusual denotations for verbs and nouns in English. Consequently, we expect them to show no particular tendency towards one direction or the other, and we also expect many noun-verb pairs belonging to this relation to be undetermined in terms of derivational direction. The latter is something to investigate in future research on the basis of zero pairs whose directionality is not known.

Second, we have shown that, for most relations, irrespective of the derivational direction, zero verbs are characterised by greater diversity than zero nouns. This means that within the relations we discussed, zero nouns usually show fewer or just as many primes as the corresponding base verbs, while zero verbs often show more primes than the corresponding base nouns, despite the fact that there are more noun primes than verb primes in the PWN ontology. This picture supports observations from the previous literature, according to which zero nouns are semantically more restricted in relation to the base than zero verbs are.

One important aspect of our dataset is that it contains N-V word *sense* pairs. At this point, the OED does not provide a derivational direction for individual senses. However, Plank (2010) convincingly argues that zero-derived pairs of polysemous words may show both derivational directions for different senses. In English the word *taxi* offers such an example: the verb *taxi* with the sense 'to travel in a taxi' is derived from the noun with the sense 'taxicab', but the noun with the sense 'an act or instance of taxiing' is derived from the zero verb's new sense '(of an aeroplane) to travel slowly along the ground before take-off or after landing'. Our current dataset includes only the senses available with the N-to-V derivation (the zero verb), but we believe that a larger study of this kind would be able to distinguish between different senses associated with the same lexeme but with different derivational directions.

Zero derivation affects not only the lexical category, but also the meaning of new formations. Our employment of general lexical resources with large sets of data (the OED and the WordNet) to investigate semantic parameters available in N-V zero pairs promises a better understanding of whether the formation of zero nouns follows similar rules as the formation of zero verbs. This has further implications for their modeling and for a more refined view on this word formation process in general.

A possible application of the results obtained (and to be further elaborated) is the implementation of linguistically-informed computational models for predicting the direction of derivation for pairs of senses for which such information is not available yet, whether they prove to be directional or not (see Darby 2015; Darby & Lahiri 2016). Our dataset is a good point of departure for developing methods to predict the morphosemantic relation of previously unattested pairs, based on the distribution of the derivational direction across semantic primes and morphosemantic relations observed here. The research presented here also opens the way to similar endeavours for languages other than English, provided that similar lexical resources are available.

Acknowledgments

We thank the two reviewers and the editors for their thought-provoking feedback to previous versions of this paper. Iordăchioaia's contribution was funded by the Deutsche Forschungsgemeinschaft (DFG, German Research Foundation) – 404208593.

Bibliography

Arad, Maya. 2005. *Roots and patterns: Hebrew morpho-syntax*. Dordrecht: Springer.
Baker, Mark & William Croft. 2017. Lexical categories: Legacy, lacuna, and opportunity for functionalists and formalists. *The Annual Review of Linguistics* 3. 179–197.

Beasley, Mark & Randall Schumacker. 1995. Multiple regression approach to analyzing contingency tables: Post hoc and planned comparison procedures. *Journal of Experimental Education* 64. 79–93.

Borer, Hagit. 2013. *Taking form*. Oxford: Oxford University Press.

Cetnarowska, Bożena. 1993. *The syntax, semantics and derivation of bare nominalisations in English*. Katowice: Uniwersytet Śląski.

Clark, Eve V. & Herbert H. Clark. 1979. When nouns surface as verbs. *Language* 55(4). 767–811.

Darby, Jeannique. 2015. *The processing of conversion in English: Morphological complexity and underspecification*. Oxford: University of Oxford dissertation.

Darby, Jeannique & Aditi Lahiri. 2016. Covert morphological structure and the processing of zero-derived words. *The Mental Lexicon* 11.2. 186–215.

Dixon, Robert M. W. 1982. *Where have all the adjectives gone?* Berlin: De Gruyter.

Fellbaum, Christiane (ed.). 1998. *WordNet: An electronic lexical database*. Cambridge, MA: MIT Press.

Fellbaum, Christiane, Anne Osherson & Peter E. Clark. 2009. Putting semantics into WordNet's 'morphosemantic' links. In Z. Vetulani & H. Uszkoreit (eds.), *Human language technology. challenges of the information society. ltc 2007*, 350–358. Berlin, Heidelberg: Springer.

Fillmore, Charles J. 1968. The case for case. In Emmon Bach & Robert T. Harms (eds.), *Universals in linguistic theory*, 1–88. New York: Holt, Rinehart, and Winston.

Gildea, Daniel & Daniel Jurafsky. 2000. Automatic labeling of semantic roles. In Anna Braasch & Claus Povlsen (eds.), *Proceedings of the ACL 2000*, 512–520. Hong Kong: Association for Computational Linguistics.

Hale, Ken & Jay Keyser. 2002. *Prolegomenon to a theory of argument structure*. Cambridge, MA: MIT Press.

Harley, Heidi & Jason D. Haugen. 2007. Are there really two different classes of instrumental denominal verbs in english? *Snippets* 16. 9–10.

Huyghe, Richard, Alizée Lombard, Justine Salvadori & Sandra Schwab. 2023. Semantic rivalry between French deverbal neologisms in *-age*, *-ion* and *-ment*. In Sven Kotowski & Ingo Plag (eds.), *The semantics of derivational morphology. Theory, methods, evidence*, 143–175. Berlin/Boston: De Gruyter.

Iordăchioaia, Gianina. 2020. Categorization and nominalization in zero nominals. In Artemis Alexiadou & Hagit Borer (eds.), *Nominalization: 50 Years on from Chomsky's Remarks*, 231–253. Oxford: Oxford University Press.

Irmer, Roland. 1972. *Die mit Nullmorphem abgeleiteten deverbalen Substantive des heutigen Englisch*. Tübingen: University of Tübingen dissertation.

Kastovsky, Dieter. 1968. *Old English deverbal substantives derived by means of a zero morpheme*. Esslingen am Neckar: Langer.

Kiparsky, Paul. 1982. From cyclic phonology to lexical phonology. In Harry van der Hulst & Norval Smith (eds.), *The structure of phonological representations*, 131–175. Dordrecht: Foris.

Kisselew, Max, Laura Rimell, Alexis Palmer & Sebastian Padó. 2016. Predicting the direction of derivation in English conversion. In *Proceedings of the ACL SIG-MORPHON workshop*, 93–98. Berlin: Association for Computational Linguistics. https://aclanthology.org/W16-2015.

Koeva, Svetla, Svetlozara Leseva, Ivelina Stoyanova, Tsvetana Dimitrova & Maria Todorova. 2016. Automatic prediction of morphosemantic relations. In *Proceedings of the 8th global*

WordNet conference (gwc), 169–177. Bucharest, Romania: Global Wordnet Association. https://aclanthology.org/2016.gwc-1.26.
Koontz-Garboden, Andrew. 2005. On the typology of state/change of state alternations. In Geert Booij & Jaap van Marle (eds.), *Yearbook of Morphology 2005*, 83–117. Dordrecht: Springer.
Koontz-Garboden, Andrew. 2007. *States, changes of state, and the monotonicity hypothesis*. Stanford, CA: Stanford University dissertation.
Koontz-Garboden, Andrew & Itamar Francez. 2017. *Semantic and morphosyntactic variation: Qualities and the grammar of property concepts*. Oxford: Oxford University Press.
Lieber, Rochelle. 1981. *On the organization of the lexicon*. Bloomington, OH: Indiana University Linguistics Club.
Lieber, Rochelle. 1992. *Deconstructing morphology. Word formation in syntactic theory*. Chicago: University of Chicago Press.
Lieber, Rochelle. 2004. *Morphology and lexical semantics*. Cambridge: Cambridge University Press.
Lieber, Rochelle. 2016. *English nouns. The ecology of nominalization*. Cambridge: Cambridge University Press.
Lieber, Rochelle. 2023. Ghost aspect and double plurality. In Sven Kotowski & Ingo Plag (eds.), *The semantics of derivational morphology. Theory, methods, evidence*, 15–35. Berlin/Boston: De Gruyter.
Manning, Chris & Hinrich Schütze. 1999. *Foundations of statistical natural language processing*. Cambridge, MA: MIT Press.
Marchand, Hans. 1969. *The categories and types of present-day English word-formation: A synchronic-diachronic approach*. 2nd ed. München: Beck.
Miller, George A., Richard Beckwith, Christiane Fellbaum, Derek Gross & Katherine Miller. 1990. Introduction to WordNet: An online lexical database. *International Journal of Lexicography* 3(4). 235–244.
Mititelu, Verginica Barbu, Svetlozara Leseva & Ivelina Stoyanova. 2021. Semantic Analysis of Verb-Noun Derivation in Princeton WordNet. In *Proceedings of the Global WordNet Conference 2021*, 108–117. Pretoria.
Padó, Sebastian, Alexis Palmer, Max Kisselew & Jan Šnajder. 2015. Measuring semantic content to assess asymmetry in derivation. In *Proceedings of the IWCS workshop on advances in distributional semantics*, London. https://www.nlpado.de/~sebastian/pub/papers/iwcs15_pado.pdf.
Plag, Ingo. 1999. *Morphological productivity: Structural constraints in English derivation*. Berlin and New York: De Gruyter.
Plag, Ingo. 2003. *Word-formation in English*. Cambridge: Cambridge University Press.
Plag, Ingo, Lea Kawaletz, Sabine Arndt-Lappe & Rochelle Lieber. 2023. Analogical modeling of derivational semantics. Two case studies. In Sven Kotowski & Ingo Plag (eds.), *The semantics of derivational morphology. Theory, methods, evidence*, 103–141. Berlin/Boston: De Gruyter.
Plank, Frans. 2010. Variable direction in zero-derivation and the unity of polysemous lexical items. *Word Structure* 3.1. 82–97.
Rimell, Laura. 2012. *Nominal roots as event predicates in English denominal conversion verbs*: University of New York dissertation.

Ruppenhofer, Josef, Colin F. Baker & Charles J. Fillmore. 2002. The FrameNet database and software tools. In Anna Braasch & Claus Povlsen (eds.), *Proceedings of the tenth EURALEX international congress*, 371–375. Copenhagen: EURALEX.

Sanders, Gerald. 1988. Zero derivation and the overt analogue criterion. In Michael Hammond & Michael Noonan (eds.), *Theoretical morphology. approaches in modern linguistics*, 155–175. San Diego: Academic Press.

Valera, Salvador. 2014. Conversion. In Rochelle Lieber & Pavol Štekauer (eds.), *The Oxford handbook of derivational morphology*, 154–168. Oxford: Oxford University Press.

Appendix

Below we present a detailed overview of the N and V prime combinations for each relation and direction: the numbers and percentages are calculated with respect to the total number of N-V pairs across the observed pairs of prime combination within each relation and direction.

Tab. 13: The combination of semantic primes to express the relation Agent. The grey cells show that only one noun prime (n.person) combines with various verb primes in the data.

N-to-V	v.social	v.communication	v.creation	v.competition	v.possession	v.cognition	v.body	v.state	v.motion
n.person	53 (26%)	20 (10%)	17 (8%)	14 (7%)	13 (6%)	12 (6%)	11 (5%)	11 (5%)	11 (5%)
V-to-N	n.person								
v.social	7 (20%)								
v.commun	6 (17%)								
v.motion	4 (11%)								
v.poss	2 (6%)								
v.consum	2 (6%)								
v.emotion	2 (6%)								

Tab. 14: The combination of semantic primes to express the relation Event. The grey cells highlight the prime combinations in which 2 noun primes (n.act and n.event) are paired with a larger variety of verb primes.

N-to-V	v.communication	v.motion	v.contact	v.social	v.possession	v.change	v.creation	v.body	v.perception	v.emotion	v.cognition	v.weather	v.consumption	v.stative
n.communication	88 (11%)							8 (1%)			8 (1%)			
n.act	23 (3%)	52 (7%)	51 (6%)	44 (6%)	33 (4%)	23 (3%)	19 (2%)	17 (2%)	5 (1%)		11 (1%)			6 (1%)
n.event	8 (1%)	22 (3%)	9 (1%)			14 (2%)			17 (2%)					
n.feeling										17 (2%)				
n.state				7 (1%)		7 (1%)		13 (2%)						
n.cognition				7 (1%)							10 (1%)			
n.possession					10 (1%)									
n.process						8 (1%)					9 (1%)			
n.phenomenon						6 (1%)						7 (1%)		
n.food													6 (1%)	
n.time						6 (1%)								

V-to-N	n.communication	n.event	n.act	n.cognition
v.contact		39 (3%)	184 (13%)	
v.motion		53 (4%)	194 (14%)	
v.communication	106 (8%)	41 (3%)	39 (3%)	
v.change		36 (3%)	55 (4%)	
v.body	23 (2%)		48 (3%)	
v.perception		43 (3%)	22 (2%)	16 (1%)
v.social			42 (3%)	
v.competition			36 (3%)	
v.stative			26 (2%)	
v.possession			26 (2%)	
v.cognition				19 (1%)

Tab. 15: The combination of semantic primes to express the relation Property. The grey cells show that only one noun prime (n.attribute) can be the base for more verb primes in the N-to-V direction and different verb primes are base to create zero nominalisations of mostly one semantic class (also n.attribute).

N-to-V	v.communication	v.change	v.cognition	v.contact	v.social	v.emotion
n.attribute	9 (15%)	8 (13%)	6 (10%)	3 (5%)	3 (5%)	
n.communication	4 (7%)					
n.cognition			4 (7%)			2 (3%)
n.state			2 (3%)			
n.quantity	2 (3%)					

V-to-N	n.attribute	n.location	n.relation
v.perception	7 (16%)		
v.contact	7 (16%)		
v.stative	3 (7%)	5 (12%)	2 (5%)
v.motion	5 (12%)		
v.change	3 (7%)		

Tab. 16: The combination of semantic primes to express the relation Result. The grey cells show the three verb primes (v.contact, v.creation and v.change) are combined with more diverse noun primes to account for most of the data.

N-to-V	v.contact	v.creation	v.change	v.communication	v.motion	v.body	v.cognition	v.competition	v.possession	v.social	v.stative
n.artifact	33 (8%)	32 (8%)	5 (1%)	6 (1.5%)	3 (1%)						
n.object	11 (3%)	3 (1%)	17 (4%)								
n.communication		15 (4%)		14 (3.5%)							
n.shape	14 (3.5%)	3 (1%)	9 (2%)		5 (1%)					3 (1%)	
n.food	6 (1.5%)		11 (3%)								
n.attribute	3 (1%)	4 (1%)	10 (2.5%)								
n.substance	3 (1%)		10 (2.5%)			3 (1%)					
n.group	8 (2%)		5 (1%)		9 (2%)		5 (1%)	5 (1%)		3 (1%)	
n.plant			7 (2%)			3 (1%)					
n.animal						7 (2%)					
n.cognition		5 (1%)	3 (1%)				7 (2%)				
n.body	4 (1%)		5 (1%)								
n.possession							3 (1%)		4 (1%)		
V-to-N	**n.shape**	**n.artifact**	**n.state**	**n.communication**	**n.object**	**n.attribute**	**n.food**	**n.cognition**	**n.location**	**n.plant**	**n.act**	**n.body**	**n.group**
v.contact	13 (10%)	6 (4%)	9 (7%)		7 (5%)	4 (3%)	3 (2%)	2 (1%)	2 (1%)			2 (1%)	
v.communication		2 (1%)		6 (4%)									
v.change	5 (4%)		2 (1%)			4 (3%)	5 (4%)	3 (2%)		2 (1%)			
v.creation		9 (7%)		4 (3%)				2 (1%)	2 (1%)				
v.perception			3 (2%)										2 (1%)
v.motion	5 (4%)			2 (1%)							2 (1%)		
v.stative								2 (1%)					

Tab. 17: The combination of semantic primes to express the relation Undergoer. The grey cells show that for the N-to-V direction two noun primes (n.communication and n.artifact) account for most of the data, while for the V-to-N direction there is one noun prime (n.artifact) occurring with almost all verb primes in the data.

N-to-V	v.communication	v.contact	v.possession	v.creation	v.change	v.competition	v.motion	v.cognition	v.consumption	v.perception	v.social
n.communication	23 (10%)	3 (1%)	3 (1%)	11 (5%)	4 (2%)		5 (2%)			3 (1%)	3 (1%)
n.artifact		19 (8%)	3 (1%)	11 (5%)		4 (2%)		6 (3%)		3 (1%)	
n.possession			18 (8%)			3 (1%)					
n.plant		5 (2%)		8 (4%)							
n.animal		8 (4%)		3 (1%)		7 (3%)					
n.food		8 (4%)		4 (2%)		3 (1%)			3 (1%)		
n.substance		7 (3%)	4 (2%)	6 (3%)							
n.group		7 (3%)									
n.person		6 (3%)									
n.quantity		5 (2%)		3 (1%)							
n.attribute	5 (2%)			3 (1%)							
n.body		4 (2%)									
V-to-N	**n.communication**	**n.artifact**	**n.possession**	**n.food**	**n.body**	**n.substance**	**n.object**	**n.quantity**	**n.group**	**n.person**	**n.cognition**	**n.attribute**	**n.event**
v.possession		2 (2%)	9 (9%)										
v.contact		8 (8%)		2 (2%)				3 (3%)					
v.communication	4 (4%)									2 (2%)	2 (2%)		
v.consumption				(4%)									
v.body		2 (2%)			4 (4%)	3 (3%)							
v.motion		2 (2%)							3 (3%)				
v.competition		2 (2%)											2 (2%)
v.cognition	2 (2%)	2 (2%)									2 (2%)		
v.stative												2 (2%)	
v.social								2 (2%)					

Tab. 18: The combination of semantic primes to express the relation By-means-of. The grey cells show that only two noun primes (n.artifact and n.communication) are more frequent in the prime combinations, irrespective of the zero derivation direction, whereas the number of verb primes is much higher.

N-to-V	v.contact	v.communication	v.motion	v.creation	v.change	v.social	v.stative	v.perception	v.cognition	v.body	v.possession
n.artifact	67 (19%)	11 (3%)	14 (4%)	12 (3%)	11 (3%)		6 (2%)	4 (1%)		3 (1%)	
n.communication	3 (1%)	47 (13%)	3 (1%)	5 (1%)		7 (2%)			3 (1%)		3 (1%)
n.body	11 (3%)		4 (1%)								
n.substance	9 (3%)				4 (1%)						
n.cognition		4 (1%)				5 (1%)		4 (1%)	4 (1%)		
n.attribute		4 (1%)				3 (1%)					
n.relation	3 (1%)										
n.state						3 (1%)					

V-to-N	n.artifact	n.attribute	n.communication	n.possession	n.cognition	n.phenomenon	n.quantity	n.object	n.substance	n.state	n.shape
v.contact	19 (16%)	3 (3%)				3 (3%)		2 (2%)			2 (2%)
v.social		6 (5%)			2 (2%)						
v.communication		4 (3%)	5 (4%)						2 (2%)		
v.possession			3 (3%)	4 (3%)							
v.change	2 (2%)	4 (3%)						2 (2%)	2 (2%)		
v.emotion					4 (3%)						
v.creation	3 (3%)										
v.perception	2 (2%)	3 (3%)									
v.motion	2 (2%)						2 (2%)	2 (2%)			
v.stative	2 (2%)										

Tab. 19: The combination of semantic primes to express the relation Instrument. We notice that the noun prime n.artifact is basis for all verb primes and is the only prime to which zero nominalisations belong.

N-to-V	v.contact	v.creation	v.motion	v.body	v.change
n.artifact	131 (63%)	12 (6%)	9 (4%)	9 (4%)	9 (4%)

V-to-N	n.artifact
v.contact	131 (75%)

Tab. 20: The combination of semantic primes to express the relation Location. We show by means of the grey cells that two noun primes (n.artifact and n.location) prevail in combining with a higher number of verb primes (for N-to-V) or with the same number of verb primes (for V-to-N).

N-to-V	v.contact	v.emotion	v.stative	v.possession	v.social	v.creation
n.artifact	17 (14%)	11 (9%)	7 (6%)	9 (7%)	5 (4%)	5 (4%)
n.location	8 (6%)	13 (10%)	9 (7%)		6 (5%)	
n.object		10 (8%)				

V-to-N	n.location	n.attribute	n.artifact
v.contact	7 (25%)		
v.change		3 (12%)	
v.motion	3 (12%)		3 (12%)

Tab. 21: The combination of semantic primes to express the relation State. The grey cells show one noun prime (n.state) is more frequently combined with various verb primes, for each direction of the zero derivation.

N-to-V	v.contact	v.communication	v.emotion	v.change	v.stative	v.social
n.state	4 (13%)		3 (10%)	3 (10%)	2 (6%)	2 (6%)
n.quantity		3 (10%)				
n.feeling			3 (10%)			
n.attribute		2 (6%)				

V-to-N	n.state	n.attribute	n.feeling
v.emotion	7 (29%)		2 (8%)
v.change	3 (12.5%)	3 (12.5%)	
v.body	2 (8%)		

Tab. 22: The combination of semantic primes to express the relation Uses. The grey cells show, for N-to-V direction, the higher number of two noun primes (n.artifact and n.communication) and of two verb primes (v.contact and v.possession), while for the V-to-N direction one verb prime (v.contact) and one noun prime (n.artifact) prevail.

N-to-V	v.contact	v.possession	v.communication	v.body	v.change	v.creation	v.cognition	v.competition	v.stative
n.artifact	49 (40%)	36 (29.5%)		20 (16%)	6 (5%)	10 (8%)		6 (5%)	5 (4%)
n.substance	42 (34%)			11 (9%)					
n.communication	9 (7%)	5 (4%)	26 (21%)						
n.possession		9 (7%)							
n.time							8 (7%)		
n.attribute					6 (5%)				
n.food	6 (5%)				5 (4%)				
n.plant	5 (4%)								

V-to-N	n.artifact	n.communication	n.substance	n.shape	n.attribute	n.possession
v.contact	13 (17%)	5 (7%)	4 (5%)	3 (4%)	2 (3%)	
v.body	7 (9%)					
v.creation	5 (7%)					
v.possession					2 (3%)	2 (3%)
v.weather					2 (3%)	
v.change	2 (3%)					

Ingo Plag, Lea Kawaletz, Sabine Arndt-Lappe, Rochelle Lieber
Analogical modeling of derivational semantics: Two case studies

Abstract: This paper addresses two fundamental problems of derivational semantics. The first one is that one meaning or concept may be expressed by more than one form ('affix competition'), the second one is that one affix may give rise to different meanings ('affix polysemy'). In one case study for each of the two problems, we explore a particular theoretical approach to morphology, analogy, using a computational analogical model, the AML algorithm (Skousen et al. 2013; Arndt-Lappe et al. 2018). We use that algorithm to test how an analogy-based mechanism can tackle the two problems. It is the first study to implement analogical modeling in the study of the semantics of complex words, instead of formal properties of complex words (e.g. Eddington 2002, Plag et al. 2007, Arndt-Lappe 2011, Arndt-Lappe 2014). In the first study we model the choice between English *-ing* and conversion to derive deverbal nouns, in the second we model the choice of different interpretations for English *-ment* derivatives. The two studies show that both the influence of semantics on affix competition and affix polysemy can be successfully modeled using analogy. The models are not only quite accurate in their predictions. Closer inspection also reveals that important generalizations of different grain size fall out automatically in AML. The article demonstrates that analogy is a computationally tractable and cognitively plausible mechanism also in the domain of derivational semantics.

Keywords: derivation, semantics, affix competition, affix polysemy, analogical modeling

1 Introduction

Although derivational semantics has gained more attention over the years (e.g. Bauer et al. 2015), fundamental questions remain under debate. This article deals with two of them, affix competition and affix polysemy. 'Affix competition' refers to the common phenomenon that different affixes often encode the same meaning. For instance, *-ity* and *-ness* in English are taken to derive abstract nouns with no clear difference in meaning between the two morphological categories (see Bauer

Ingo Plag, Lea Kawaletz, Sabine Arndt-Lappe, Rochelle Lieber, IP and LK: Heinrich-Heine-Universität Düsseldorf; SA-L: Universität Trier; RL: University of New Hampshire, email of corresponding author: ingo.plag@uni-duesseldorf.de

∂ Open Access. © 2023 the author(s), published by De Gruyter. [CC BY-ND] This work is licensed under the Creative Commons Attribution-NoDerivatives 4.0 International License.
https://doi.org/10.1515/9783111074917-005

et al. 2013, 257f). Another case is the formation of deverbal nominalizations by -*ing* and conversion (as in *the betting* vs. *the bet*). 'Affix polysemy' refers to the fact that the derivatives of a particular morphological category can have different interpretations. For instance, English -*ment* derivatives have been shown to exhibit change-of-state readings, stimulus readings, result-state readings and a few others (e.g. Bauer et al. 2013; Kawaletz & Plag 2015; Plag et al. 2018; Kawaletz 2023). A note on terminology is in order here. For ease of reference we have used the term 'affix' here in a loose sense, including non-affixational morphological processes like conversion or truncation. The expressions 'competition of morphological forms' and 'polysemy of a morphological category' would be more appropriate ways of speaking about these two phenomena.

Recent studies using modern empirical methods have shown that many generalizations in the theoretically-oriented literature concerning these two problems (some of them long-cherished) are wrong (e.g. Lieber 2016; Lieber & Andreou 2018; Lieber & Plag 2022; Schirakowski 2021). In particular, the received wisdom is being challenged by increasing evidence for the under-specification of derivational semantics and the importance of contextual and world knowledge (see, for instance, Alexiadou 2019).

These new findings present both theoretical and methodological challenges. At the theoretical level, we have to concede that categorical approaches are not able to cope with the variability attested in the data, and that these theories must either be seriously revised, or alternative theories must be developed and tested. At the empirical level, tractable statistical and computational models are needed to account for how complex words mean. The present article explores a particular, and very traditional, theoretical approach to morphology, analogy (see Arndt-Lappe 2015 for an overview). Specifically, we will use a computational analogical model, the AML algorithm (Skousen et al. 2013; Arndt-Lappe et al. 2018), to test how an analogy-based mechanism can tackle the two problems introduced above.

Analogical modeling is conceptualized here as an exemplar-based approach in which storage of individual occurrences of expressions plays a prominent role. More specifically, analogical models are computational algorithms that work on the basis of a lexicon in which forms are stored together with their properties, including the property in question ('outcome'), for instance the kind of morphological form or the interpretation they exhibit. Based on the similarity of a given form with the forms stored in the lexicon, the given form is assigned a probability of a particular outcome (for instance, 'conversion' as the morphological form, or 'result-state' as its interpretation). So far, the semantics of complex words has played only a marginal role in the analogical modeling of morphology, which has mainly focused on formal properties of simplex and complex words (e.g. their phonological structure) to predict, for example, stress (Eddington 2000), inflectional forms (e.g. Skousen 1989; Keuleers et al. 2007), morpho-phonological alternations (e.g. stress assignment to compounds, Plag et al. 2007; Arndt-Lappe 2011) or affix selection in situations of competition (e.g. Eddington 2002; Arndt-Lappe 2014).

We propose to implement analogical models in which we predict outcomes on the basis of semantic features, addressing the two fundamental problems above. Our focus will be on the analogical mechanism. By contrast, the semantic representations on which we set this mechanism to operate will comprise features that are well-established across different theoretical linguistic frameworks in the literature, and that have been validated in recent empirical work.

In our first case study we tackle the form competition problem by modeling the choice between -*ing* and conversion based on, first, the meaning that is to be expressed with the derived noun and, second, the aspectual class of the base verb. The data set for this study consists of almost 1500 nominalization tokens from COCA (Davies, 2008-) that were used in Lieber & Plag (2022). It will be shown that the analogical model can quite accurately predict the choice between the two morphological forms.

In our second case study we investigate how particular readings are selected for a given -*ment* derivative. For this, we make use of a data set of 40 -*ment* neologisms used in Kawaletz (2023). The nominalizations in the data set are polysemous, exhibiting up to seven different readings per type. This range of readings is systematically related to semantic properties of the base verb as well as to selectional restrictions of -*ment*. We will show that, by providing AML with a well-founded set of features pertaining to the base verbs' semantics, the algorithm does an excellent job of predicting the emergent patterns in the nominalizations' possible readings.

2 Modeling derivational semantics

There are a number of approaches that try to go beyond assigning impressionistic semantic labels to morphological categories. In those approaches an attempt is made to understand in more detail how meanings are generated based on the properties of base, affix and other available information. We will briefly lay out three prominent architectures before we turn to analogical modeling: syntactic approaches, Lieber's Lexical Semantic Framework, and distributional semantics. The purpose of this overview is to situate the analogical approach in the landscape of a rather wide range of competing approaches. We will do this with a special emphasis on how these approaches can deal with the variability that recent studies have found in the data obtained in studies of actual language use.

A family of important approaches to the treatment of the semantics of nominalization are syntactic approaches, among them Distributed Morphology (Alexiadou 2001; Harley 2009), Borer's (2013) Exoskeletal model, and Nanosyntax (Baunaz et al. 2018). In these frameworks a particular reading for a derived word is attributed to a difference in syntactic structure, for instance, the location of particular entities in the array of functional projections above or below the affix.

Such an analysis works best if the range of readings is highly restricted, and clearly tied to particular categories that behave in clearly distinct ways. Broader empirical studies have shown that quite often a different situation holds, with an unexpected degree of variability in interpretation. The nominalizations in -*ing* and conversion are a case in point, as shown in Lieber & Andreou (2018) and Lieber & Plag (2022).

Another approach to modeling of the behavior of derived words is Lieber's Lexical Semantic Framework (LSF, Lieber 2004, 2016). In LSF, interpretation works on the basis of the semantic representations of base and affix. Both representations are composed using particular mechanisms, including underspecification. In LSF, polysemous semantic representations can be easily derived and are part and parcel of the system, but any combination of semantic attributes with morphological form is as likely as any other. Predictions about possible tendencies cannot be derived based on this framework.

Yet another perspective on meaning is taken by distributional semantics. In this framework, meanings are determined by the contexts in which words occur. Vectors are used as meaning representations that record the contexts in which a given item occurs in the corpus. The closer to each other the vectors are, the closer in meaning are the words represented by those vectors. As shown by some of the contributions in this volume (Kotowski & Schäfer 2023; Bonami & Guzmán Naranjo 2023; Schäfer 2023), this approach can also be implemented for various purposes when investigating complex words (see also, for example, Marelli & Baroni 2015; Varvara 2017; Lapesa et al. 2018; Wauquier 2020; Huyghe & Wauquier 2020; Missud & Villoing 2021). Although the distributional semantics framework is consistent with semantic patternings of complex words that are neither categorical nor random, and therefore might be able to handle the data we present, we will not explore this framework here. Instead, we turn to a fourth approach that has the potential to handle probabilistic data, namely analogical modeling.

3 Analogical Modeling

The term 'analogical modeling' is a cover term for a variety of computational approaches which all hold that linguistic generalization emerges through similarities in the lexicon. Four prominent ones are 'Analogical Modeling of Language (AML)' (e.g. Skousen 1989; Skousen et al. 2002; Skousen & Stanford 2007; Skousen et al. 2013 et seq.), 'Tilburg Memory-based Learner (TiMBL)' (e.g. Daelemans 2002; Daelemans & van den Bosch 2005; Daelemans et al. 2007), the 'Generalized Context Model (GCM)' (Nosofsky 1986) and the 'Minimal Generalization Learner (MGL)' (Albright & Hayes 2003; Albright 2009).

Appeal to analogy has generally had a long tradition especially in the fields of morphology and language change, but it has often been criticized, especially from a generative perspective, for a lack of rigor and restrictions. The computational analogical models mentioned above address this criticism, as they provide a tractable analysis and can generate falsifiable hypotheses that can be tested in various ways, e.g. by experiments or corpus data.

In the present paper we will use the AML algorithm, and the rest of this section is devoted to introducing the reader to the specifics of this model. An analogical model basically performs a classification task. For each item that is given to the algorithm as a test item, the algorithm decides between different outcomes (e.g. *-ing* nominalization or conversion) on the basis of the distribution of similar items in the lexicon. The similarities between lexical items is computed over the properties of these items (so-called 'features') that are listed in the lexicon (i.e. coded for the data set in question). For instance, in Arndt-Lappe (2014) the choice between the rival suffixes *-ity* and *-ness* was modeled based on features that coded the syntactic category information and certain phonological properties of pertinent words.

One interesting property of analogical models is that they can address a long-standing problem in morphology, the nature of rules. Traditional, especially generative, approaches often assume the existence of rules accompanied by lexically listed exceptions, as witnessed in the classic 'words and rules' debate (e.g. Pinker 1999). In analogical models, by contrast, generalizations of different grain sizes emerge as a natural consequence of the analogical architecture.

This article presents two different semantic tasks. In the first task (see section 4) we model the choice between two forms, *-ing* nominalization or conversion nominalization, based on semantic features. In the other task (see section 5) we model the choice between different interpretations of *-ment* derivatives based on the semantic properties of the base verb.

Figure 1 illustrates the architecture of the analogical model, using the choice between *-ing* and conversion as an example. The central component of the system is the lexicon, i.e. the set of stored exemplars. In this lexicon each item is represented as a set of features. In figure 1, for each item the four features 'base', 'aktionsart', 'quantification' and 'eventivity' are coded. On the basis of these features, the fifth feature ('nominalization') is to be predicted. 'Aktionsart' encodes the aktionsart of the base, 'quantification' encodes whether the derivative is interpreted as mass or count, and 'eventivity' encodes whether the derived noun is eventive or referential in its interpretation. The outcome feature 'nominalization' encodes the morphological form of the nominalization (-*ing* or conversion).

	item	base	aktionsart	quantification	eventivity	nominalization
Lexicon	ACCOUNT	account	activity	count	referential	conversion
	ASSIST	assist	activity	count	referential	conversion
	ASSIST	assist	activity	mass	referential	ing
	BEND	bend	accomplishment	mass	eventive	ing
	BLEND	blend	accomplishment	count	referential	conversion
	BLEND	blend	accomplishment	mass	eventive	ing
	BLEND	blend	accomplishment	count	eventive	conversion
	BLINK	blink	semelfactive	count	eventive	conversion
	BLINK	blink	semelfactive	count	eventive	conversion
	BLINK	blink	semelfactive	count	eventive	conversion
	BREAK	break	achievement	count	eventive	conversion
	BREAK	break	achievement	count	eventive	ing
	BREAK	break	achievement	count	eventive	ing
	BURN	burn	accomplishment	count	referential	conversion
	BURN	burn	accomplishment	mass	eventive	ing
	BURST	burst	achievement	mass	eventive	conversion
	CATCH	catch	achievement	mass	eventive	conversion
	FINISH	finish	achievement	mass	eventive	conversion

	item	base	aktionsart	quantification	eventivity	nominalization
Analogical set	BREAK	break	achievement	count	eventive	conversion
	BREAK	break	achievement	count	eventive	ing
	BREAK	break	achievement	count	eventive	ing
	BURST	burst	achievement	mass	eventive	conversion

	item	base	aktionsart	quantification	eventivity	nominalization
New item: BURST	BURST	burst	achievement	count	eventive	conversion

Fig. 1: The architecture of an analogical model.

The model can be set up to deal with tokens (case study 1), or with types (case study 2). In exemplar-based models, even individual tokens of a lexeme can be stored. For instance, a given token of a particular lexeme may occur in a given discourse with a particular reading, and this token may then be stored with this reading. The next occurrence of the same lemma may instantiate a different reading and this new token may now be stored with this different reading. In our first case study, we have a data set with multiple tokens of the same lexemes, and our analysis will be token-based. Having a lexicon with token representations means that the lexicon may already contain nominalizations for the same type, i.e. different instances in which a speaker has experienced pertinent words with a particular meaning before. In the toy example in figure 1, the new item to be classified is a new token of BURST. This word is already part of the lexicon with a particular nominalization (see the third row from the bottom in the box labeled 'Lexicon'). We assume, in accordance with the observed facts, that, in general, for each verb both morphological forms are available to form a nominalization (even if one may not find both forms attested for each verb in a given corpus). If a new token of BURST is to be classified for the morphological form of its nominalization, the system extracts from the lexicon a group of exemplars which are similar to the new item. This group is called 'analogical set'. The exemplars in the analogical set serve as analogues on the basis of which the morphological form of the nominalization will be assigned to the new item. Abstracting away from various further intricacies to be discussed below, the new item will be classified like the majority of items in the analogical set.

In figure 1, all exemplars in the analogical set share three features with the new item. The nominalization for BURST is then selected on the basis of the distribution of the nominalizations in the analogical set. In the toy example, -ing would be chosen in half of the cases, or with a probability of 50 percent. The algorithm gives the probability of each possible value being assigned, based on the distribution of these values amongst exemplars in the analogical set. In calculating these probabilities, AML takes into account the degree of similarity between an exemplar and the new item, as well as the number of exemplars with a particular set of features. The more similar an exemplar is to the new item, the more weight it receives, and the more exemplars that share a particular set of features, the greater the weight that is assigned to each of them. The latter procedure is particularly important in cases where a feature constellation is particularly frequent in the lexicon. In a classification task where exemplars sharing that feature constellation are part of the analogical set, they may outweigh exemplars that are more similar to the target word, but that are smaller in number.

Returning to our example in figure 1, the reader may have noticed that the set of features also includes 'base', which means that different exemplars with the same base may be listed in the lexicon. This is desirable since the same base may have more than one nominalization, with different quantification and eventivity readings in different contexts.

The crucial question is of course how the system determines which exemplars end up in the analogical set. As one can see in figure 1, the analogical set in our toy example contains two different types of exemplars. In the parlance of AML, the set of all exemplars sharing a particular feature constellation is called a 'gang'. The idea behind this terminology is that the words that instantiate a particular feature constellation 'gang up' in analogical sets to influence the outcome. In our example, one gang, comprising three instances of BREAK, shares the three semantic features 'aktionsart', 'quantification', and 'eventivity' with our new item BURST. The other gang consists of only one exemplar, an instance of BURST, which differs semantically from the new item in that it has a mass reading, but shares the features 'base', 'aktionsart', and 'eventivity' with the new item. What both gangs in the analogical set have in common is that they share a total of three features with the new item. This raises the question, however, why AML does not also include less similar exemplars. Consider, for example, the two items CATCH and FINISH from the lexicon, which share two features with the new item, 'aktionsart' ('achievement') and 'eventivity' ('eventive'). In AML, the degree of similarity that is relevant for exemplars to be included in the analogical set is decided for each new item individually. The rationale of this procedure is that, on the one hand, the model will always incorporate maximally similar items, but, on the other hand, items with lower degrees of similarity will be incorporated only if that incorporation does not lead to greater uncertainty with respect to the classification task. In our example, the reason why AML does not include all eventive achievement nouns is that the gangs of exemplars sharing these two features do not behave in the same way as the gangs sharing these two features plus one more feature with the new item, i.e. the items in the analogical set. As we have seen, the items in our analogical set testify to both -*ing* and conversion outcomes. By contrast, the two eventive achievement nouns CATCH and FINISH, which have a 'mass' reading, provide evidence for conversion only. They are therefore not included in the analogical set.[1] On a conceptual level, AML's way of constraining analogical sets provides a transparent and interpretable way of operationalizing a fundamental idea in analogy-based linguistic theories, i.e. that certain exemplars are privileged in analogical reasoning (cf. e.g. Arndt-Lappe 2015 for an overview of the literature). Exemplars that are both highly similar to a target and informative with regard to a particular task are more important than exemplars that are not.

As mentioned above, for each item to be classified, AML computes probabilities for the different outcomes. For instance, for a given item, the outcome -*ing* might have the probability of 73 percent, and the outcome *conversion* the probability of 27 percent. AML then selects randomly from analogical sets, which means that in 73 percent of the cases -*ing* will be selected. The percentages can of course also be turned into classification decisions (reflecting assignment to discrete categories) by way of categorizing percentages at a particular threshold. For instance,

---

[1] A similar case are the second BLEND item and the three exemplars of BLINK. These items also share two features with the new item ('count' and 'eventive'), but they also have a uniform outcome, i.e. conversion. Readers interested in more details of how analogical sets are computed are referred e.g. to Skousen (2005).

with a binary decision between two classes A and B, a percentage below 50 percent means assignment to class A, a percentage of 50+ means assignment to class B.

AML can compute probabilities for binary outcomes, but also for multinomial outcomes. In the next two sections we will first see an example of a binary outcome. This will be followed in section 5 with an example of a model with multiple possible outcomes.

4 One meaning - more than one form: *-ing* and conversion nominalizations

4.1 The problem

In English, verbs can be nominalized in various ways, with *-ing* suffixation and conversion both being very productive. In a broad empirical study, Lieber & Plag (2022) examine the extent to which these two types of nominalizations in English can be quantified as either count or mass, can express either eventive or referential readings, and can be based on verbs of particular aspectual classes (state, activity, accomplishment, achievement, semelfactive). The examples in (1) illustrate count and mass readings.[2] Lieber & Plag applied the usual tests to categorize the derived nouns as either count or mass (e.g. the presence of the determiner *a*, or of quantifiers indicating one or the other category, such as *many* or *much*).

The examples in (2) illustrate eventive and referential readings. Various tests were employed to determine whether a nominalization referred to an eventuality (e.g. modification with a temporal adverbial), or to an entity (e.g. coreference with another noun in the context that is clearly concrete in its interpretation). For a discussion of the details of the coding of the data the reader is referred to Lieber & Plag (2022).

(1) a. conversion count reading
   Accent on Living 1992: And if enough people tell you you're no good, you end up believing it and become what they say you are. A CHANGE has to come.
   b. conversion mass reading
   Independent School 2006: Overall, then, the single greatest obstacle to

---

[2] The examples in (1) and (2) are taken from Lieber & Plag (2022) (their examples (3), (7a) and (8a)). Example (2c) is taken directly from COCA.

implementing curricular CHANGE and, over time, establishing a culture that values continuous reflection and improvement in a school, is the general predisposition of educators to resist change itself.
    c. *-ing* count reading
BNC 1992: ...tiny phosphorescent sparks around its hands, small ripples in the stone beneath its feet, a gentle breeze around its head, a sudden dampness and DRIPPING of water from the stones of the walls around it.
    d. *-ing* mass reading
BNC 1978: Listen to the rain. Compare slow DRIPPING, fast gushing, trickling, etc.

(2) a. *-ing* and conversion eventive readings
Massachusetts Review 1995: ...a muffled BANGING began, a thumping, not rapid but steady, like the DRIP of water on a slab, a noise as though someone above was stamping one foot, heavily booted, on a bare board floor.
    b. *-ing* referential reading
Mag. Inc. 1995: "Today," says Holman, "employees in the cleaning department, for example, know not to work on the easiest-to-clean CASTING or on the one that happens to be on the top of the pile."
    c. conversion referential reading
Cosmopolitan 2006: The one downside: Skin in this category tends to have a greenish CAST.

Aspectual class (also known as aktionsart, Vendler class, lexical aspect, or inner aspect) was coded as default lexical aspect without considering surrounding syntactic context. An overview of the aspectual classes of the base verbs in Lieber & Plag (2021) is given in table 1. For certain analyses, these authors recoded the aspectual classes using the three aspectual features [dynamic], [durative], and [implied endpoint] (or [endpoint] for short), as shown in table 2. In the AML models below, we have used the binary features. (Lieber & Plag, 2022, 318) used standard definitions of the five classes, and coded the binary feature values for the three aspectual features as follows: "A verb was coded as [+dynamic] if it implied an input of energy, [-dynamic] if not (Comrie 1976). Verbs of change of state, directed change of position, or verbs which otherwise implied an outcome or product were coded as [+implied endpoint]. Other verbs were coded as [-implied endpoint]. Verbs which implied a passage of time were coded as [+durative] and verbs that implied a punctual event were coded as [-durative]."

Based on corpus attestations, it is safe to say that both nominalizations can be used to express the same readings. The authors present statistical evidence that

Tab. 1: Verbs and their aspectual classes.

Aspectual class	Verbs
Accomplishment/achievement	bet, cast, cut, divide, draw, exit, grant, hire, offer, order, pay, return, shift
Accomplishment	bend, blend, burn, change, cover, display, fall, fix, form, heat, melt, mix, repair, report, rise, spread, strip, surround, take, transfer, wash
Achievement	break, burst, catch, chop, find, finish, fracture, kill reach, reveal, slam, split, win
Activity/achievement	pass
Activity/state	smell, taste
Activity	account, assist, chat, climb, dance, design, drink, drive, embrace, float, gurgle, hold, hurt, kiss, leak, play, push, rest, ride, run, sail, spin, stay, step, stir, stretch, stumble, swim, wait
Semelfactive/achievement	pop, strike
Semelfactive/activity	beat, shake, shove
Semelfactive	blink, cough, drip, flash, hit, jump, kick, knock, poke, punch, spring, tap
State	concern, desire, doubt, fear, hate, hope, lack, love, stink, worry

Tab. 2: Aspectual class and aspectual features.

Aspectual class	Example	Dynamic	Durative	Endpoint
state	*know, love*	-	+	-
activity	*push, float*	+	+	-
accomplishment	*cook, cover*	+	+	+
achievement	*arrive, find*	+	-	+
semelfactive	*blink, knock*	+	-	-

the relationship between morphological form, type of quantification, and aspectual class of base verb is neither categorical, as the syntactic models suggest, nor completely free, as Lieber's framework predicts, but rather is probabilistic.

For investigating the effect of quantification, eventivity and the three aspectual features ([dynamic], [durative], and [implied endpoint]) on the choice of morphological form in a multivariate analysis, Lieber and Plag used conditional inference trees, which is a particular type of classification and regression analysis. Conditional inference trees partition the data into subsets that share particular constellations of feature values and behave significantly differently from other subsets concerning the predicted outcome. The tree shown in figure 2 gives the result of that analysis. The nodes of the tree are numbered for reference. Each terminal node gives the total number of observations in this subset and a stacked bar chart showing the distribution of the dependent variable for the respective constellation of features.

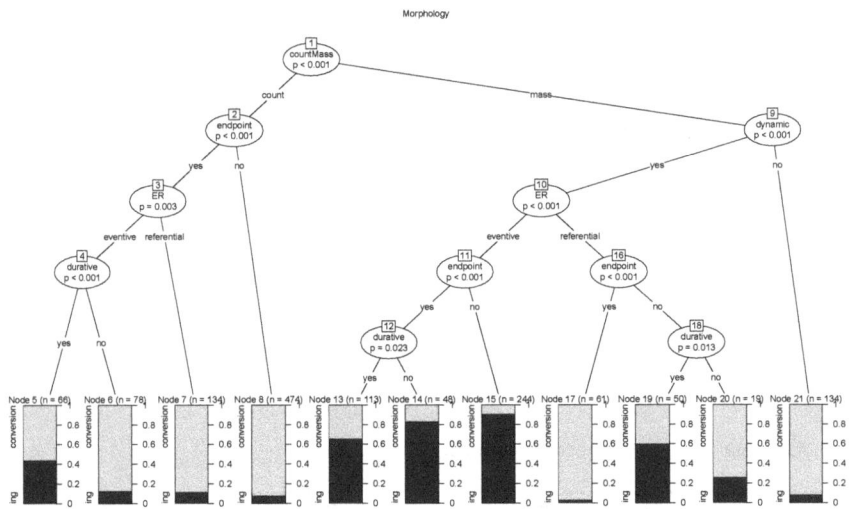

Fig. 2: Conditional inference tree modeling the choice of morphological form (taken from Lieber & Plag 2022).

Figure 2 shows that all variables have a say. The model is able to predict the correct morphological category for 86 percent of all cases. When the derivative has a count interpretation, conversion is the clear majority choice (see nodes 5 through 8). Among the count nominalizations, [implied endpoint], eventivity and [durative] also play a role, and do so in particular subsets. With mass nominalizations, things are more complicated. If based on state verbs ([dynamic]: no), conversion is prevalent (node 21), but if based on dynamic verbs ([dynamic]: yes), further distinctions are necessary. Eventive nominals favor -*ing* (nodes 13 through 15), but this preference depends on the presence or absence of the features [implied endpoint] and [durative]. For the referential nominals, the choice depends on the features [implied endpoint] and [durative] (nodes 17, 19, 20). To summarize, the relationship among the variables of morphological form, eventivity, quantification and aspect is rather complex. Tendencies sometimes go in the direction suggested by past literature (e.g. -*ing* forms tend to be eventive), but sometimes contradict past predictions (conversion also tends to be eventive).

A distributional analysis showed that at least for some base verbs there is a strong tendency towards one of the two morphological forms. A mixed-effects regression analysis by Lieber and Plag supported this finding. In predicting the morphological form (in the presence of the predictors QUANTIFICATION and EVENTIVITY), the base verb plays a significant, even if quite moderate role.

The variability of the data raises the question which kind of linguistic model can account for the distribution of the two morphological forms based on the intended semantics and the aspectual properties and the identity of the base. The conditional inference tree analysis makes good predictions and can therefore serve as a reference point. However, a conditional inference tree does not seem to be a cognitively plausible model of how speakers choose a morphological form. Analogy, in contrast, is a plausible cognitive mechanism, and an analogical model, if successful, would therefore be a step forward in understanding competition between morphological forms.

4.2 Setting up the analogical model

For this study we used the same data set that was analyzed statistically in Lieber & Plag (2022). In particular, we employed the subset of the data for which all three semantic categories (eventivity, quantification and aspectual features) were coded unambiguously. This data set consists of 1421 tokens of nominalization, with 150 types based on 84 base verbs.[3] In addition, to test the possibility that phonological properties might also play a role in the choice between -*ing* and conversion,

---

[3] We refer the reader to Lieber & Plag (2022, section 3) for a detailed description of the generation of the data set and the coding procedures.

we also coded the segmental and syllabic structure of all items in the same way as in Arndt-Lappe's (2014) study of the competition between *-ity* and *-ness*.[4]

The model was implemented using the 'Transparent Analogical Modeling of Language (TraML)' package (Arndt-Lappe et al. 2018), which provides rather convenient access to the model output. The algorithm was set up in such a way that the data set was used both as the lexicon file and as the test file. Specifically, for each word in the file, the morphological form is predicted on the basis of all other words in the file. In AML, this is implemented by the parameter setting 'exclude given'. In general, this kind of method is also known as 'leave-one-out' (see, for example, Daelemans & van den Bosch 2005). This simulates that a speaker decides on the form of the nominalization for a given verb on the basis of their knowledge of (potentially all) the words that are in the lexicon.[5] In our explorations of the analogical model we largely follow the rationale and procedures laid out in Arndt-Lappe (2021). In trying to get a better understanding of the analogical model, we first investigate how successful the model is in its predictions, and how certain particular predictions are. Then we will inspect how similar forms behave and why they do so. We use R (R Core Team 2019) for the statistical analysis.

4.3 Results

4.3.1 Accuracy

The model that includes phonological features on top of the base and the semantic features performs worse than the model without the phonological features. Only 58 percent of the nominalization forms are predicted correctly, and *-ing* is predicted correctly only in one third of the cases. It thus seems that similarities in the phonological make-up do not help to decide whether speakers choose conversion or *-ing*.[6]

The model that includes only the base and the semantic information as features is quite successful in choosing the right morphological form. Of the 1421 forms, 84 percent are predicted correctly. This is very similar to the accuracy of

---

[4] Six features were introduced to represent the phonemic makeup of the last two syllables. Each feature represents a syllabic constituent (onset, nucleus, and coda). See Arndt-Lappe (2014, 521) for details and exemplification.
[5] Another parameter setting concerns the way the relations between gangs are computed. We used the default setting 'linear' (instead of 'squared').
[6] This null effect for phonological features may be due to problems of feature coding or feature weighting. This issue is left for future studies to explore.

the conditional inference tree analysis (86 percent), in spite of the fact that the latter analysis did not use a leave-one-out design, hence did not classify unseen items.

The output of the analogical model allows us to investigate in more detail the quality of the predictions. Figure 3 shows the certainty of predictions separately for conversion and -*ing* nominals. For each of the 945 conversion cases and 476 -*ing* nominals in the data set, the y-axis plots the probability with which the model predicts conversion (left panel) and -*ing* (right panel). We can see that the probabilities in the left panel are generally higher, and that percentages below 50 percent (which means wrong prediction if we dichotomized the probabilities at the 50 percent level), are quite rare for conversion nouns. Dichotomizing these probabilities, we end up with only 11 percent wrong predictions of conversion and 27 percent wrongly predicted -*ing* derivatives. Again this is in the same ballpark as the predictions of the tree analysis, in which 10 percent conversions and 23 percent of all -*ing* nouns were wrongly predicted. In sum, the accuracy of the analogical model is highly satisfactory.

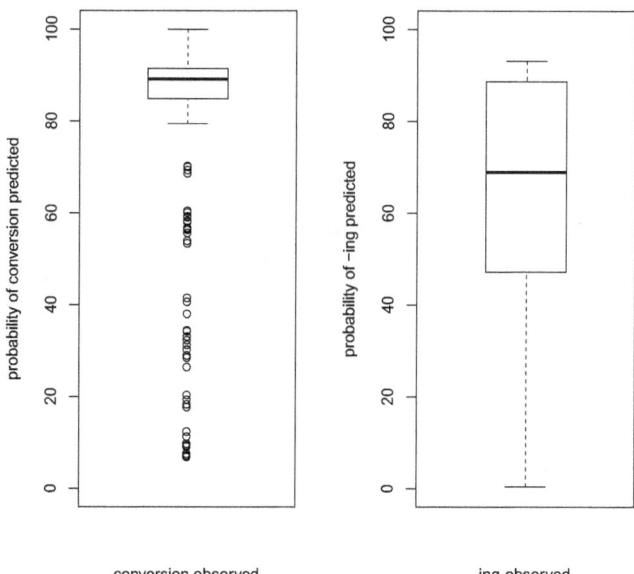

Fig. 3: Certainty of predictions for conversion vs. -*ing*.

Tab. 3: Feature constellations. Empty cells indicate features not shared with the target item.

Item	Base	Quantification	Eventuality	Dynamic	Durative	Endpoint
BEND		count	eventive	yes	yes	yes
BEND	bend	count		yes		yes
BEND	bend		eventive	yes	yes	yes

The distribution of the percentages as shown in figure 3 also means that AML predicts speakers to be generally very certain and less variable when choosing conversion: On average, the probability of conversion within analogical sets is somewhere near 90 percent, and the variance is rather low. This is different when -*ing* is predicted. Here, the average probability is only around 70 percent, and there is greater item-by-item variance. This means that speakers will be less certain about choosing -*ing*.

4.3.2 Gangs: How similar forms behave

The output of the AML model also allows us to have a closer look at how similar forms behave. This is interesting from a theoretical perspective as this behavior can demonstrate how rather clear generalizations can emerge in an analogical system. For these kinds of analysis it is useful to inspect specific feature constellations. In the case of our toy example shown in figure 1, the words in the analogical set all share the same feature constellation (i.e. [break; achievement; count; eventive]).[7] However, this is not necessarily the case in all analogical sets. For instance, for one of the tokens of the conversion noun *bend* in our data set, the words in its analogical set instantiate three different feature constellations as shown in table 3. Nominalization tokens of the following verbs instantiate these constellations: *bend, burn, change, display, fall, fix, form, heat, melt, mix, repair, rise, spread, strip, take, transfer, wash*.

The target token has the feature constellation [bend; count; eventive; yes; yes; yes]. All three constellations are equally similar to the constellation of the target item in that they all lack one of the target item's features. Our target token thus has three gangs in its analogical set (instantiated by the nominalization tokens of the 17 verbs mentioned above). Depending on how many words instantiate a particular feature constellation, and depending on how uniformly this feature

---

[7] We use a different font-type and semicolons between feature values to indicate feature constellations.

constellation behaves concerning the outcome, a gang is more or less influential, and contributes more or less to the probability of a particular choice of outcome (Skousen et al. 2002; Skousen 2002).

To see emergent generalizations, we can now inspect the relation between particular kinds of gangs and particular outcomes by using the output files of TraML. In our first analysis we included all gangs that were most influential in their analogical set (i.e. that had the greatest say in the vote for the outcome) and that had outcome probabilities for either conversion or *-ing* of more than 80 percent. The threshold of 80 percent means that those gangs can be taken to behave in an almost uniform way. Table 4 shows these gangs and the outcomes with which they are associated, first for conversion nouns, then for *-ing* nominalizations.

Tab. 4: Highly predictive feature constellations and their outcomes.

Base	Quantification	Referentiality	Dynamic	Durative	Endpoint	Tokens
conversion						
	count	eventive	yes	no	no	122
	count	eventive	yes	no	yes	49
	count	eventive	yes	yes	no	237
	count	referential	no	yes	no	3
	count	referential	yes	no	yes	7
	count	referential	yes	yes	no	58
	count	referential	yes	yes	yes	79
	mass	eventive	no	yes	no	130
	mass	referential	yes	yes	yes	23
fear		eventive	no	yes	no	1
love		eventive	no	yes	no	2
-ing						
	mass	eventive	yes	no	no	1
	mass	eventive	yes	no	yes	9
	mass	eventive	yes	yes	no	177
drive	mass		yes	yes	no	2

The highly predictive gangs are in line with the tendencies or generalizations proposed in the literature, in that count readings are often associated with conversion, and mass readings with *-ing* nominalization. In AML these tendencies find an explanation as emerging from the similarities of target words with the words in the lexicon. Also, the analogical model provides a cognitively plausible explanation for why these generalizations are not absolute, but tendencies. First, table 4 shows that the influence of individual base words is also evident, but naturally holds only for small numbers of items. Second, we have to bear in mind that the gangs represented are only the subset of particularly predictive gangs. While exemplars sharing these features and sharing a nominalization strategy are numerous in the lexicon, hence exerting strong pressure on classification of novel items, they are by far not the only exemplars influencing classification. How important a 'highly predictive gang' is for the classification of a novel item, will crucially depend on what other exemplars there are in the lexicon that are similar to that item.

Finally, we can inspect the relation between feature constellations and observed versus predicted outcomes. We take the same gangs as before (i.e. the highly predictive ones) and plot two networks that visualize these relations. Figure 4 shows the network of the gangs that lead to a conversion prediction, figure 5 shows the network for the predicted *-ing* nouns.[8] Recall that these predictions are at a probability level of 80 percent or more. In the center of each cloud the feature constellation is given in small letters. The actual target forms sharing this feature constellation are given in capital letters. They are connected with arcs to the feature constellation that they instantiate.

---

8 We used the igraph package (Csardi & Nepusz 2006) in R (R Core Team 2019) to produce the graphs in figures 4 and 5.

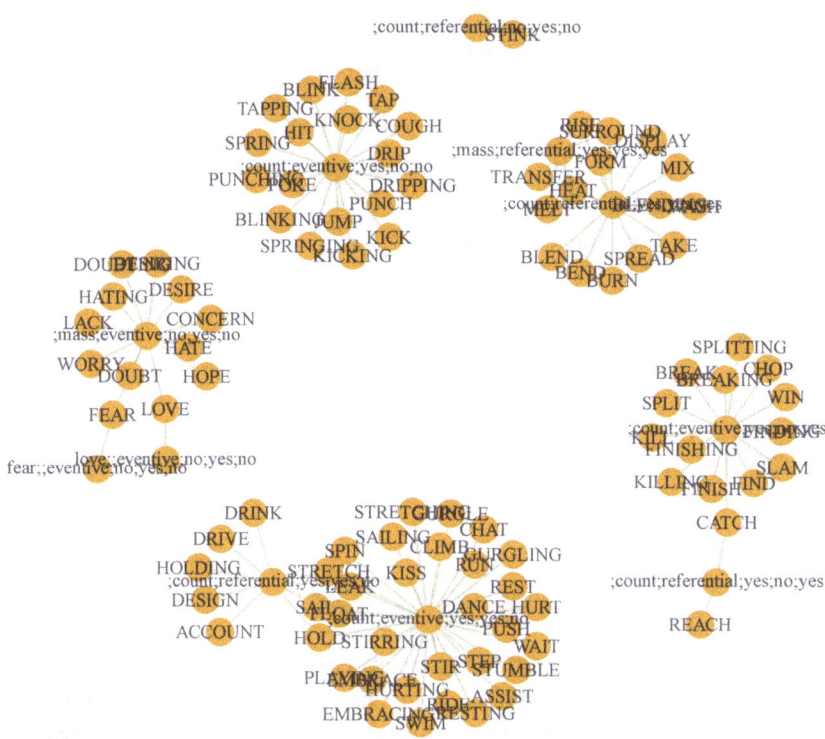

Fig. 4: Network of gangs for conversion items.

We can see that, as expected, in the conversion network most observed forms are conversion nouns, and in the *-ing* network most observed forms are *-ing* nominalizations. We can also see that the same forms may participate in more than one gang. For instance, LOVE (in the leftmost network in figure 4) participates in two gangs, with complementary and overlapping features ([love; -; eventive; no; yes; no] and [-; mass; eventive; no; yes; no]). Another case of the same forms participating in more than one gang is SPIN, STRETCH, LEAK, SAIL, FLOAT, HOLD (in the bottom-most network in figure 4). With these items we see two feature constellations ([-; count; eventive; yes; yes; no] and [-; count; referential; yes; yes; no]) that have opposing features (eventive vs. referential), but also overlapping features ([count; yes; yes; no]). The presence of

Fig. 5: Network of gangs for *-ing* items.

opposing semantic features for different tokens of the same type means that these words are polysemous. The conversion nouns just mentioned (like many others) have both an eventive and a referential interpretation. As this kind of polysemy is wide-spread it necessarily introduces variability and uncertainty also into the construction of the analogical sets, and thus into the decisions. At the conceptual level, this variability and uncertainty is part and parcel of analogical reasoning, and not an unwelcome disturbance of an otherwise neat categorical system. Recall in this context that classification accuracy is typically measured in terms of a majority vote among exemplars in the analogical sets. However, this majority vote is a generalizing simplification of what the algorithm computes as a probabilistic outcome for each individual test word.

Another important observation is that a given feature constellation may be instantiated by different target forms derived from the same verbal base. This can be most clearly seen in the rightmost network in figure 5, which includes FINISH and FINISHING, both of which share the feature constellation [-; mass; eventive; yes; no; yes]. Similar cases are PLAY and PLAYING, or CHAT and CHATTING, in the bottom left network of figure 5. Again, this kind of situation is a source of variability and uncertainty that the analogical system deals with straightforwardly.

4.4 Summary: One meaning – more than one form

In this case study we have modeled a data set in which the competition between two morphological forms is determined by semantics, but in a non-categorical and highly complex fashion. The traditional statistical analysis provided by Lieber and Plag had revealed the intricate interaction of different features.

We have shown that the analogical model is able to cope successfully with the challenges of this data set at a similar level of accuracy as a conditional inference tree model. However, the conditional inference tree has several conceptual disadvantages. First, it does not include the influence of the individual base although there is evidence that this is a relevant predictor. Second, wrong predictions are to be treated as unexplained exceptions to some rule. Third, the interaction of predictors is taken into account, but the nature and cause of these interactions is unclear. Fourth, the statistical algorithm cannot easily map onto plausible cognitive mechanisms (but see section 5 for discussion of this point).

In contrast, the analogical model has several advantages. It is based on a cognitively plausible mechanism, it is rather accurate in its predictions, and what is conceptualized as the interaction of variables in a regression model emerges naturally on the basis of similarities in these properties between lexical items. Furthermore, the model makes satisfactory generalizations at different levels of granularity, and the notion of 'exception to the rule' becomes obsolete. Finally, the role of the base is straightforwardly included in an analogical model alongside other properties of the words involved.

In summary, although analogy has hitherto been applied mainly on the basis of formal properties, analogy also proves to be a very promising approach when it comes to semantic properties. Semantic properties can be used equally well (and successfully) to understand the choice between two morphological forms. We may now turn to the second general problem in derivational semantics, affix polysemy.

5 One form – many meanings: *-ment*

5.1 The problem

We speak of affix polysemy when one affix is able to generate several possible and related readings. This is wide-spread in English: Lieber (2016) investigates a total of 27 nominalizing suffixes and shows that 19 of these are able to produce more than one reading (p. 60f). The suffix that we will focus on in this part of the paper, *-ment*, can be considered highly polysemous, as is illustrated in (3) with examples from the literature (Gadde 1910; Marchand 1969; Bauer et al. 2013; Lieber 2016; the actual semantic labels partly differ between authors).

(3)   a.   EVENT: *ceasement*
       b.   ACTION: *repayment*
       c.   STATE/CONDITION: *contentment*
       d.   RESULT: *improvement*
       e.   PRODUCT: *pavement*
       f.   INSTRUMENT/MEANS: *refreshment*
       g.   inanimate PATIENT/THEME: *investment*
       h.   LOCATION: *establishment*

In addition, it is often the case that several readings are possible even for one and the same derivative. For example, according to the OED (2021), *refreshment* can denote "a means of refreshment" as well as the "action of refreshing a person or thing." That is, *refreshment* can not only exhibit reading (3-f), but also reading (3-a). At the same time, a given derivative will most likely not exhibit the full range of readings that its affix can potentially produce. For example, the **?** does not list *refreshment* as 'something which has been refreshed' or as 'the place of refreshing' (readings (3-g) and (3-h)).

It has been observed that the readings which are possible for a given derivative are often predictable. For example, INSTRUMENT nominalizations derive from verbs that denote actions requiring an INSTRUMENT participant (e.g. *season > seasoning, equip > equipment*; Bauer et al. 2013, 213-4). For deverbal *-ment* neologisms, Kawaletz (2023) has shown that their full range of readings can be predicted, given a detailed enough decomposition of their bases' semantics. The base offers an array of semantic elements, and the suffix selects from this array in a systematic way, producing a polysemous *-ment* derivative. Kawaletz (2023) models the semantics of both the verbal input and its derived output with frames, which are recursive typed feature–value structures that formalize the semantic representations.

A crucial question, however, remains unanswered in Kawaletz's work: By means of what mechanism do speakers determine for a given derivative which readings are possible, given a base verb with particular semantic properties? In this section, we test analogy as a possible mechanism, using Kawaletz's data set and a translation of her frame formalizations into an AML-readable feature matrix.

5.2 Setting up the analogical model

In the analogical model, we want to predict the readings that are possible for a *-ment* derivative, given the semantic properties of its base. For this, we use Kawaletz's (2023) data set of 40 *-ment* neologisms. For each derivative, a number of readings are available in context, which were assessed with a study of several hundred attestations extracted from various corpora. Each derivative enters the data base for the present study, i.e. our AML lexicon, with as many entries as there are attested readings for this type. The base verbs belong to two semantic classes (see Levin 1993; Kipper Schuler 2005): change-of-state verbs (e.g. *embrittle, discolor, unfold*; henceforth COS verbs) and verbs of psychological state (e.g. *enrapture, reassure, stagger*; henceforth psych verbs). Kawaletz (2023) proposes seven distinct frames, representing semantically slightly different subgroups of verbs within these two classes.

As explained above, for AML, a feature matrix is needed that encodes the properties of the exemplars of the lexicon. This poses a challenge because the semantic properties of the words in Kawaletz's data set are coded in a very different format, i.e. with hierarchical, recursive attribute–value matrices (called 'frames', see Barsalou 1992a,b; Löbner 2013), similar to those used in other frameworks (such as HPSG or Sign-based Construction Grammar; see Pollard & Sag 1994; Sag 2012). To serve as input for AML these frames must be transformed into a two-dimensional table (i.e. feature matrix). In order to illustrate the problem, let us have a look at the frame in figure 6, which is a semantic representation of the possible readings of COS verbs in the form of a lexeme formation rule (see Plag et al. 2018). The derivative *embrittlement*, for example, would be an instantiation of this rule.

The lexeme-formation rule includes phonological information (PHON), syntactic information (CAT), semantic information (SEM), and possible readings (REF), both for the derivative (first column) and for its base (second column, introduced by M-BASE). Small numbered boxes are used for (co-)indexation. The *change-of-state causation ∧ come-into-being causation* event denoted by the base verb is a complex event with two subevents (CAUSE and EFFECT). This complex event has four participants, ACTOR, PATIENT, INSTRUMENT and PRODUCT (nodes [1] to [4]), and the complex event structure given in nodes [5] and [6]. The first subevent, CAUSE, is underspecified; it can be any kind of event with any kind of participant. The second subevent, EFFECT, is specified as a *change-of-state ∧ come-into-being*, during which the PATIENT attains a *state*, and the PRODUCT comes into existence. The labels used in the frames are hierarchically related to one another, which is formalized in a 'type hierarchy.' For example, *change-of-state causation ∧ come-into-*

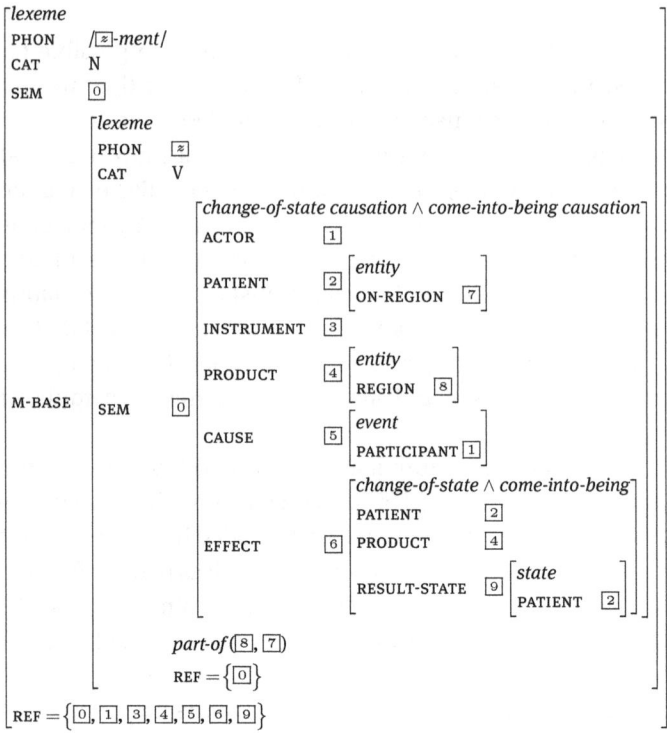

Fig. 6: Lexical rule for the possible readings of -*ment* derivatives derived on the basis of COS verbs like *embrittle*, adapted from Kawaletz (2023, Figure 4.18).

being causation is a subtype of *event*, and a PRODUCT is a special kind of RESULT (see Kawaletz 2023, figure 4.23 for details).

In the frame-based approach, the semantics of an affix is describable as its potential to perform a referential shift on the frames of its bases (see also Plag et al. 2018). The set of possible readings for a given derivative is specified as "REF = {[0], [1], [3], [4], [5], [6], [9]}". This notation signifies that these seven nodes represent possible interpretations of the derived noun (e.g. *embrittlement*), reflecting the polysemy of the derivative. According to Kawaletz (2023), the derivative can refer to the whole, complex event ([0]), to either event participant except for PATIENT ([1], [3], [4]), to one of the two subevents ([5] or [6]), or to the RESULT-STATE ([9]).

We translated the frames into a feature matrix using the coding strategies illustrated in table 5. It includes two exemplary types, with two readings of *embrittlement* (items 1 and 2) and one reading of *approvement* (item 3). We chose

Tab. 5: Partial lexicon for the *-ment* data: bases *embrittle* and *approve of*. Attributes are given in small caps, values in regular type font. Abbreviations: att = attribute, cib = come into being, cos = change of state, eff = effect, ent = entity, evt = event, exp = experiencer, instr = instrument, part = participant, pat = patient, psy = psych, refnode = reference node, rs = result state, st = state, stim = stimulus, und = undergoer, val = value (see Kawaletz 2023 for details).

Feature	Item 1	Item 2	Item 3
1. item	embrittlement	embrittlement	approvement
2. base	embrittle	embrittle	approve_of
3. ACTOR+1	AGENT/CAUSER	AGENT/CAUSER	CAUSER
4. ACTOR+2			STIM
5. INSTR	INSTR	INSTR	
6. PAT+1			EXP
7. RESULT	RESULT	RESULT	
8. RESULT+1	PRODUCT	PRODUCT	
9. CAUSE:val	CAUSE:evt	CAUSE:evt	
10. EFF:val	EFF:COS	EFF:COS	
11. EFF:val+1	EFF:cos&cib	EFF:cos&cib	
12. st+1	st	st	psy-st
13. cos	cos&cib	cos&cib	
14. refnode	causation	causation	state
15. ..._ST	UND:ent_ST	UND:ent_ST	UND:ent_ST
16. ..._ST+1	PAT:ent_ST	PAT:ent_ST	EXP:ent_PSY-ST
17. CAUSE:val_ATT	CAUSE:evt_PART	CAUSE:evt_PART	
18. EFF:val_ATT	EFF:COS_RS	EFF:COS_RS	
19. EFF:val_ATT+1	EFF:COS_RS	EFF:COS_RS	
20. EFF:val_ATT:val	EFF:COS_RS:st	EFF:COS_RS:st	
21. EFF:val_ATT:val+1	EFF:COS_RS:st	EFF:COS_RS:st	
22. INSTR/STIM			
23. reading	transposition	instrument	transposition

these two derivatives as their base verbs come from two different verb classes, COS verbs (*embrittlement*) and psych verbs (*approvement*). The information in row one ('item') functions as an identifier. For each item, 21 features are coded. On the basis of these, the feature in row 23 ('reading') is to be predicted.

As the first feature we took the base. All other features encode semantic properties of the base verbs. The next set of features encoded whether a given frame element (e.g. the attribute PRODUCT or the node *state* in figure 6) occurs in the frame (features 3 to 13). We then coded at which level of embedding the element occurs (features 14 to 21). Finally, we included a feature that encoded the presence of co-indexation (feature 22). We only included features that were distinctive between verbs.

With regard to the presence or absence of particular semantic elements, consider features five and eight by way of example. For *embrittlement,* the presence of the two attributes INSTRUMENT and PRODUCT in the frame is encoded. The frame for verbs like *approve of,* on the other hand, has neither of the two, which is why the corresponding cells in rows five and eight are left empty. Given that the absence of a feature is a meaningful bit of information, AML was instructed to treat empty cells not as missing information, but as valid feature values. This is encapsulated in the parameter setting 'include nulls'.

The hierarchical information, i.e. the degree of embedding of a frame element in the type hierarchy, is coded by the tags '+1' or '+2.' For example, ACTOR+1 (feature 3) is embedded one level below its parent node, coding for its daughters (here AGENT and CAUSER). ACTOR+2 (feature 4), is further embedded by one level, where we find STIMULUS – a category which is only relevant for psych verbs.

We further addressed the recursive frame structure by spelling out attribute paths, showing where and how deeply a frame element is embedded in the given frame (features 14 to 21). For example, the value *state* is deeply embedded in the *embrittle*-frame, and can be reached via the attribute path 'EFFECT:COS_RESULT-STATE:state' (feature 20; note also how the path builds up in features ten and 18). Verbs like *approve of,* on the other hand, denote psych states, which is why their reference node is labeled *state* (feature 14) or, on a finer level of granularity, *psych-state* (feature 12).

The last frame property encoded in the feature matrix is the presence or absence of co-indexed nodes. Feature 22 contains explicit information with regard to co-indexation, namely whether or not the values of the attributes INSTRUMENT and STIMULUS are co-indexed. This feature sets apart two subgroups of psych verb from the remaining data set. Other co-indexed nodes are not distinctive and are therefore not included in the model.

The resulting feature matrix contained one column for each reading of a given type. We see this illustrated in table 5 for the noun *embrittlement,* for which the table shows two entries, each with a different reading. Obviously, for a given nominalization, the semantic structure of its base verb is always the same, hence the features 1 to 22 are identical. The two entries only differ in their reading, that is, in feature 23. Overall, the lexicon contains 194 items, i.e. combinations of a particular derivative and a particular reading. Using the resulting feature matrix as input, the model was set up using the parameter settings 'exclude given', 'linear' (see section 4) and 'include nulls' (see above).

5.3 Results

In this section we will present different aspects of the analogical model we implemented to predict possible readings of *-ment* derivatives. We will begin with an analysis of the predictions to see how successful the model is. This will be followed by an investigation of other aspects of the model in order to gain further insights into the nature of the model and its architecture.

5.3.1 Predictions: The polysemy of *-ment*

In this section we want to answer the question of whether the analogical model is capable of correctly determining which readings are available for a given derivative, given a base verb with particular semantic properties and a lexicon containing derivatives of the same morphological category.

Figures 7 and 8 give a visual impression of the predictions made by AML. For each derivative, a stacked bar gives the different readings that were predicted and the probability of their being selected. Readings not shown ended up with a probability of zero, i.e. they were not predicted to be available readings. For example, the bar labeled *abridgement* (to the very left in figure 7) shows that AML predicts seven different readings for this derivative. The probability of a given combination of noun and reading is color-coded, with shades of blue representing predicted eventive readings and shades of orange representing predicted participant readings.[9]

Overall, we see that AML predicts (with variable, non-zero percentages) four or more readings for all derivatives. This means that *-ment* is predicted by the algorithm to produce highly polysemous derivatives. This corresponds to Kawaletz's (2023) findings. Moreover, the readings that AML predicts largely correspond to those that are attested: In Kawaletz's data base, 194 combinations of derivative and reading are attested, of which AML predicts 189 (i.e. 97 percent). The probabilities of the different readings are mostly quite evenly distributed for a given derivative, with no clear majority decisions (but one, (*musement*, see below for further discussion). With some verbs, certain readings are not very likely (e.g. 'implicit product' for *congealment* and *debauchment*), which is indicated by the low percentage of that reading.

---

[9] Each bar subsumes all predictions for a given derivative, with each derivative being represented by a set of items. For example, *abridgement* is represented by six items in the lexicon because it is attested in six different readings. Since the coding of the features 1 to 22 is the same for these six items, the predictions for feature 23 (the reading) are also the same.

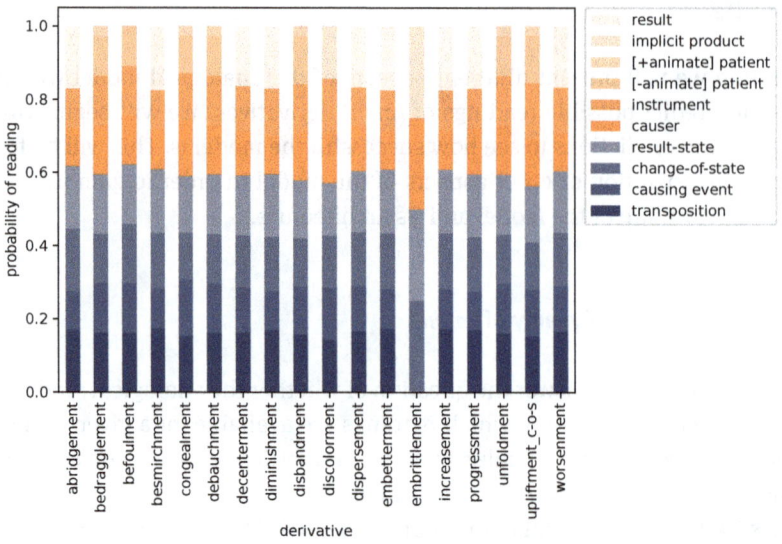

Fig. 7: Predictions of readings for derivatives in the change-of-state subset of the data.

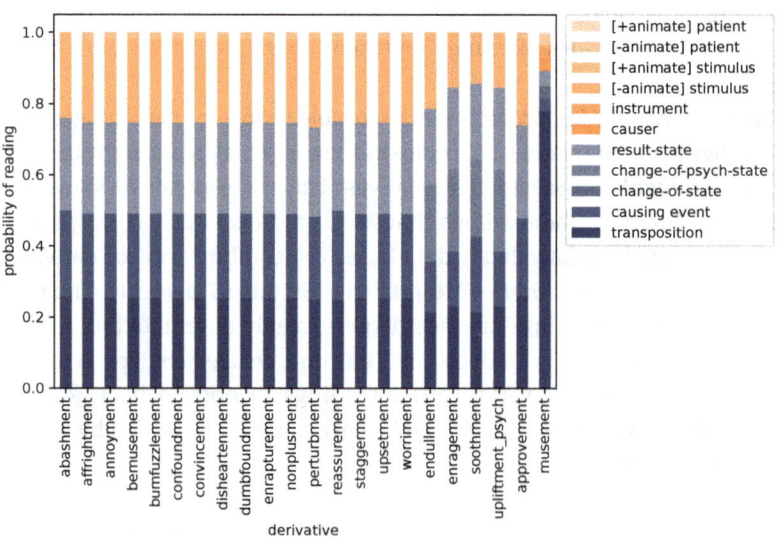

Fig. 8: Predictions of readings for derivatives in the psych subset of the data.

Let us examine a number of predictions more closely to see what motivated them and what this teaches us about the model. We start with two readings for which AML does very well: CHANGE-OF-PSYCH-STATE and TRANSPOSITION. CHANGE-OF-PSYCH-STATE is a reading that is specific to a subgroup of psych nouns, namely those that are based on verbs with a *change-of-psych-state* subevent (as opposed to just a *psych-state* subevent or to no complex event structure at all; see also table 5 on page 127). AML predicts this reading precisely for those nouns for which it is attested, namely *endullment, enragement, soothment* and *upliftment* (towards the right in figure 8). TRANSPOSITION is a reading that is available for all productively formed *-ment* derivatives. AML predicts this reading across the board, as shown by the very dark blue portions of the bars in figures 7 and 8.

The only derivative for which TRANSPOSITION is not predicted is *embrittlement*. In fact, Kawaletz (2023) finds the derivative attested in seven different readings, but AML only predicts four of these. *Embrittlement* is thus predicted to be less polysemous than the other COS derivatives (see figure 7). Where does this exceptional behavior originate? A look into the analogical sets reveals that these predictions are based on only one other derivative, *discolorment* (see also figure 9 below). The attestations for *discolorment*, in turn, are patchy: Based on the frame for the base *discolor*, the readings TRANSPOSITION, INSTRUMENT and CAUSING-EVENT should be possible, but Kawaletz (2023) does not find them attested for this derivative. Since the AML lexicon does not contain items representing *discolorment* in these readings, then, they are not predicted for *embrittlement* either. In section 5.3.3 we will come back to the issue of such gaps in the lexicon data.

Two further derivatives for which AML's predictions stand out are the psych nouns *approvement* and *musement* (see the two rightmost bars in figure 8). We have already mentioned that, for some reason, *musement* is the only derivative for which AML makes a clear majority decision (0.78 probability of a TRANSPOSITION reading). *Approvement*, on the other hand, is predicted to have four different readings, two of which (CAUSING-EVENT and RESULT-STATE) should not be possible, based on its base verb frame. An additional four such unexpected readings surface with a very low probability of 0.02 percent.

These odd predictions are made because *approvement* and *musement* are odd as well: Both have unique base verbs in the data set, sharing their semantic representation with no other base verbs. What is more, their frames model simple events (psych-state and psych-action, respectively) and therefore differ substantially from the other five frames, which all model complex events. AML is thus confronted with two feature constellations that are very different from all the others in the lexicon. An inspection of the derivative's gangs tells us how the model dealt with this: It resorted to calculating *approvement*'s and *musement*'s analogical set members on the basis of very few gang features. For example, one of *approve-*

ment's gangs contains only the feature value 'UNDERGOER:entity_STATE,' which it shares with all bases except for *muse over*. Because both *approvement* and *musement* are unique within the data set, AML had to resort to such an underspecified feature constellation. As we have seen above, this results in wrong predictions for these two nominalizations.

Another interesting observation is that the model predicts the readings [+animate] STIMULUS and [+animate] PATIENT. According to the literature, *-ment* does not produce [+animate] readings (see Kawaletz & Plag 2015; Lieber 2016; Kawaletz 2023). There are, however, exceptions to this rule: In Kawaletz's (2023) data set, *befoulment* is attested in an [+animate] PATIENT reading and *abashment* is attested in an [+animate] STIMULUS reading. These exceptional items in the lexicon lead to AML predicting such readings, albeit with a very low probability, for those nouns which have *befoulment* and/or *abashment* in their analogical set (for instance *bedragglement*; see figure 6 above). For these derivatives, the probabilities range from 2.56 percent to 2.7 percent for an [+animate] PATIENT reading and from 1.45 percent to 1.7 percent for an [+animate] STIMULUS reading. Note that *befoulment* and *abashment* themselves are not predicted to exhibit [+animate] readings due to the leave-one-out method. Although these predictions do not match the attested readings, they do reflect linguistic reality: [+animate] readings are not entirely impossible for speakers, but merely very unlikely.

5.3.2 Analogical sets: Emergent base verb classes

Kawaletz (2023) builds on the common assumption that there is a systematic relationship between the semantics of the base and the semantics of the derivatives of a particular morphological category. In her approach, verbs of a particular semantic class (e.g. psych verbs) produce derivatives that are systematically different from derivatives of other classes in terms of their possible interpretations. In an analogical approach, verb classes such as those used by Kawaletz do not play a role as analytical entities that are given a priori. Using an analogical algorithm, such a class would emerge bottom up as a set of verbs that share a particular feature constellation. And if these feature constellations are really influential in choosing possible interpretations, they should emerge as analogical sets in the analogical model. If Kawaletz's analysis is on the right track, and at the same time AML can successfully model her data, the analogical sets emerging in the AML model should reflect the verb classes that feature prominently in Kawaletz's approach.

Figure 9 visualizes the analogical sets that the AML algorithm has used to classify the test items.[10] This offers us an insight as to which sets of base verbs are similar to each other, and at the same time influential for the task. Each node represents a derivative, and the two semantic classes of base verb are indicated by color: derivatives with psych verbs as bases ('psych items' for short) are blue, while derivatives with COS verbs as bases ('COS items' for short) are yellow. An arrow between two words is drawn if a given word ('word 1') is part of the analogical set that is used for the prediction of the interpretation of the other word ('word 2'). Quite often, word 1 is in the analogical set of word 2, and word 2 is also in the analogical set of word 1. In such cases, we get arrows pointing in two directions. If many words are in each others' analogical sets, we see the emergence of rather large clouds. A cloud can thus be interpreted as a set of words that are similar to each other and mutually predictive for the decision to be taken.

The first observation that can be made upon inspecting figure 9 is that the items that AML deems similar form five clouds. This means that five classes of base verb emerge in the model. We can also see that the blue nodes (i.e. the psych items) and the yellow nodes (i.e. the COS items) largely keep to themselves, with few interconnections between blue and yellow clouds. This signifies that, by and large, psych items tend to be like psych items, while COS items tend to be like COS items.

Let us look at individual clouds. The very small cloud with only two yellow nodes at the right edge indicates that the algorithm has used *embrittlement* to classify only one other nominalization, i.e. *discolorment*, and vice versa. The nodes representing the psych items form two clusters, one in the bottom left and one in the top middle. The nodes representing COS items, on the other hand, form three clusters, one in the bottom right, one in the mid-right, and one in the top left. We can thus say that two subclasses of psych verbs and three subclasses of COS verbs emerge from the model.

These subclasses largely match Kawaletz's (2023) semantic classification of base verbs. Kawaletz distinguishes two types of psych causation event, namely those with a caused psych-state and those with a caused change-of-psych-state. The corresponding items can be found in the bottom left cluster and in the top middle cluster, respectively. For the COS verbs, Kawaletz distinguishes whether or not they lexicalize a RESULT, that is, whether or not their frame representation contains a RESULT attribute. There are three corresponding subclasses of COS verb in her study: those that do not lexicalize a RESULT (here: items in the top left clus-

---

10 We used the tool Flourish (available at https://app.flourish.studio) to produce the graph in figure 9.

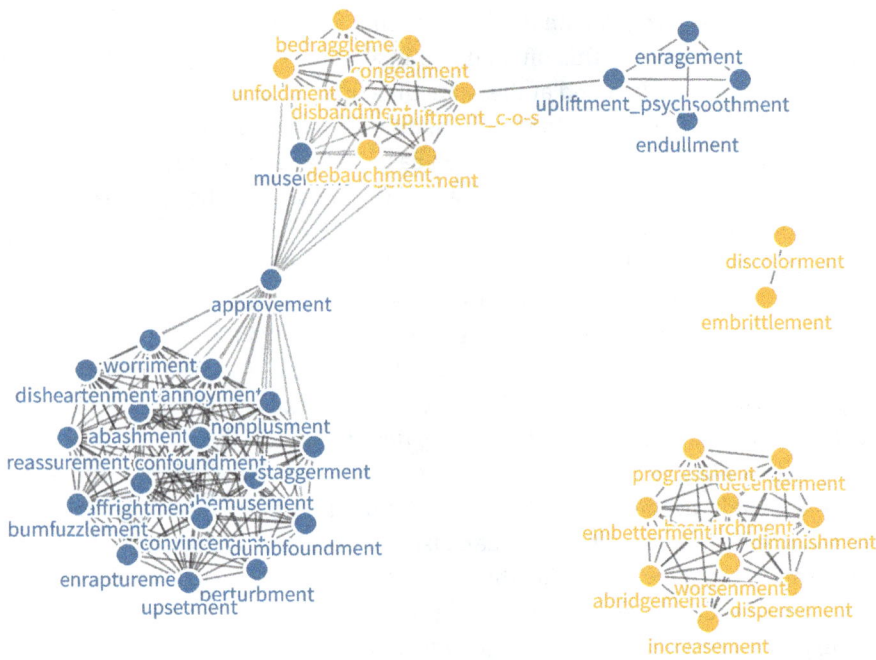

Fig. 9: Analogical sets of the *-ment* derivatives. The verb classes of the derivatives are indicated by color (blue = psych items, yellow = COS items). The source node of an arrow represents an item which is in the analogical set of its target.

ter), those that do (items in the bottom right cluster), and those that lexicalize a PRODUCT – a hyponym of RESULT (mid-right cluster).

Two of Kawaletz's base verb classes, however, do not emerge in the model. The first is psych verbs that denote a simple psych-state, the second is psych verbs that denote a psych-action. This result is not surprising since these are the classes that have only one member each, *approve of* and *muse over*, respectively. As already discussed in section 5.3.1, this scarcity of information poses a problem for AML. In the figure, we see that the nodes representing *approvement* (between the top left and the bottom left cluster) and *musement* (within the top left cluster) have arrows coming in not only from other psych items, but from COS items as well. This means that, due to the underspecified gang feature constellations we observed earlier, AML has also used COS items to classify *approvement* and *musement*.

Another connection between two clouds is visible at the top of the figure, where we see a two-way arrow between the nodes representing *upliftment_cos* and *upliftment_psych*. An inspection of the two derivatives' gangs reveals that this mutual influence between a COS item and a psych item takes place because of the shared polysemous base verb *uplift*: One of their gangs contains the feature 'base,' which is specified for both derivatives as *uplift*. This gang is only marginally influential, but it leads to the two derivatives appearing in each other's analogical sets.

5.3.3 Gaps: Missing readings

Generally speaking, a gap is a reading that can in principle be produced by *-ment*, but that is not attested for a given derivative. Such gaps are interesting as they can serve as a litmus test for the reliability of the algorithm. There are two kinds of gaps, which we will call 'accidental' and 'systematic' gaps. We will discuss each of these in turn.

Accidental gaps are readings that should be possible for a given derivative, but are not attested. For example, *-ment* can produce CHANGE-OF-STATE readings, and *abridgement* has a *change-of-state* node in its base verb frame. *Abridgement* should therefore be attested in a CHANGE-OF-STATE reading – but it is not (at least not in Kawaletz's data set). Accidental gaps can be attributed to scarcity of data in combination with potential partial blocking effects (see Kawaletz 2023, section 6.1). Therefore, our analogical model would ideally fill in those gaps, predicting all readings that can be expected based on the base verb frame. That is, it should predict CHANGE-OF-STATE for *abridgement*.

Above, we saw for the example of *embrittlement* that accidental gaps in the training data can lead to unwelcome predictions if the analogical set for a given item is very small. Mostly, however, it can be observed that the gaps in the data are ironed out by AML: There are 28 accidental gaps in the lexicon, and AML predicts 26 of these readings. For example, AML does predict CHANGE-OF-STATE for *abridgement* because the reading is attested for all members of the derivative's analogical set .

Let us turn to the systematic gaps. These are readings that should not be possible for a given derivative, and that indeed are not attested. For example, *-ment* can produce STIMULUS readings, but *abridgement* does not have a STIMULUS participant in its base verb frame. *Abridgement* should therefore not be attested in a STIMULUS reading – and it indeed is not. Here, our model should *not* fill in the gaps, predicting only readings that are expected based on the base verb frame, and not predicting those that are not. That is, it should not predict STIMULUS for *abridgement*.

Here, the model also does well. There are 299 combinations of reading and derivative which should not be possible given the base verb frames, and AML correctly predicts that 258 of these should not be possible. For example, STIMULUS is not predicted for *abridgement* because none of the members of the derivative's analogical set has this reading attested.

In sum, the model does well with regard to both accidental and systematic gaps. But why is it not 100 percent successful? There are two reasons for this. First, the training data is not entirely categorical. As described in section 5.3.1, in the data set there are two exceptional combinations of derivative and reading (i.e. [+animate] PATIENT for *befoulment* and [+animate] STIMULUS for *abashment*). Second, scarcity of data led to two unique feature constellations (i.e. the items representing *approvement* and *musement*, respectively). When these four exceptional items figure in the analogical set of a given derivative, this results in predictions that do not match the attested readings. For example, the item representing *befoulment* in an [+animate] PATIENT reading leads to this reading being predicted for seven derivatives, albeit with very low probability (2.56 percent to 2.7 percent).

Interestingly, these predictions, which at first glance may appear wrong or at least odd, do not present unwelcome results. Rather, they reflect linguistic reality: First, the existence of [+animate] readings for *befoulment* and *abashment* shows that speakers may use other derivatives in this reading as well – this usage is just so unlikely that Kawaletz did not find it attested in the corpora, although it might appear with further data. Second, scarcity of data is not something that only the model is confronted with, but speakers as well. Very rare items will therefore also pose a challenge to speakers, the only (but essential) difference being that a speaker can resort to disambiguation by context.

5.4 Summary: One form – many meanings

In this study of the polysemy of *-ment*, we have seen that AML does an excellent job in predicting the patterns in the nominalizations' possible readings. First, the semantic classes of base verbs asserted by Kawaletz (2023) emerge in the form of analogical sets. The different sets nicely instantiate the distinction between COS verbs and psych verbs, and even capture the more fine-grained distinctions between different subclasses of COS verbs and psych verbs proposed in the literature, respectively. Second, the readings which AML predicts for the derivatives largely correspond to the predictions that can be made on the basis of the base verb frames. Finally, with regard to gaps in the training data, we have seen that systematic gaps largely remain unpredicted by the algorithm. In contrast, the accidental gaps ('accidental' in terms of the available data in Kawaletz 2021) come out as truly accidental because the algorithm predicts the possible existence of these words. This works as expected, however, only if enough data are available. In general, unexpected or uninterpretable results only occur when the training data is insufficient, so that AML does not have enough data points to go by. In such cases, the presence of accidental gaps or of unique base verbs (*approve of* and *muse over* in our data set) leads to out-of-band connections between analogical set clouds, which in turn produce wrong predictions.

6 Discussion and conclusion

In this paper, we have investigated two fundamental problems of derivational semantics, affix competition and affix polysemy. It has been the first attempt to implement analogy as a mechanism to solve essentially semantic, as against formal, selection problems. We have seen that analogy is indeed able to capture the gradient nature of the pertinent empirical data in an adequate manner. Generalizations emerge as a natural consequence of analogy at different levels of generality, depending on the degree of similarity between lexical entries.

With regard to affix competition, our test case has demonstrated that an analogical algorithm is as good at predicting the right morphological form as regression analysis (in the form of conditional inference trees). The crucial difference between the two is conceptual. While analogy works on the basis of a plausible cognitive mechanism, it is unclear what cognitive correlates might be evoked for conditional inference trees, unless one interprets regression itself as a kind of analogical model. As argued, for example, by Guzmán Naranjo (2020, 225), both models (and indeed many kinds of neural networks) are conceptually very similar because they "capture the same basic intuition: items that are similar belong to the same class". Still, the underlying statistical computations may differ quite a bit, to the effect that the predictions for individual words may also differ, and to the effect that certain factors are more, or less, important across algorithms. A case in point is the influence of the individual base verb, which cannot be meaningfully taken into account in the tree analysis.

With regard to affix polysemy, we have shown that AML can be successfully employed to model the choice between different interpretations for English *-ment* derivatives. The resulting model has many properties that are most welcome at the theoretical and empirical level. The predictions are highly accurate, lexical classes emerge as a by-product of the similarities between words (and need not be stated as indispensable separate entities), and systematic gaps are detected. Even the occasional failures of the system are an indication of the high quality of the model: Too few data lead to insecurities and wrong predictions.

Overall, the two case studies have demonstrated that derivational semantics can be fruitfully analyzed using analogical modeling.

Bibliography

Albright, Adam. 2009. Modeling analogy as probabilistic grammar. In James P. Blevins & Juliette Blevins (eds.), *Analogy in grammar*, 185–213. Oxford: OUP.
Albright, Adam & Bruce Hayes. 2003. Rules vs. analogy in English past tenses: A computational/experimental study. *Cognition* 90. 119–161.
Alexiadou, Artemis. 2001. *Functional structure in nominals: Nominalization and ergativity*, vol. 42 Linguistik Aktuell/Linguistics Today. Amsterdam/Philadelphia: John Benjamins.
Alexiadou, Artemis. 2019. Review of R. Lieber, English nouns: The ecology of nominalization. *English Language and Linguistics* 23(3). 735–739.
Arndt-Lappe, Sabine. 2011. Towards an exemplar-based model of stress in English noun-noun compounds. *Journal of Linguistics* 47(11). 549–585.
Arndt-Lappe, Sabine. 2014. Analogy in suffix rivalry. The case of English *-ity* and *-ness*. *English Language and Linguistics* 18(03). 497–548.
Arndt-Lappe, Sabine. 2015. Word-formation and analogy. In Peter O. Müller, Ingeborg Ohnheiser, Susan Olsen & Franz Rainer (eds.), *Word-formation - an international handbook of the languages of Europe*, 822–841. Berlin: De Gruyter.
Arndt-Lappe, Sabine. 2021. Different lexicons make different rivals. http://dx.doi.org/10.23668/psycharchives.5083.
Arndt-Lappe, Sabine, Ingo Plag, Kai Koch & Mikalai Krott. 2018. Transparent Analogical Modeling of Language (TrAML). Software package. https://github.com/SabineArndtLappe/TrAML.
Barsalou, Lawrence W. 1992a. *Cognitive psychology: An overview for cognitive sciences*. Hillsdale: Lawrence Erlbaum Associates.
Barsalou, Lawrence W. 1992b. Frames, concepts, and conceptual fields. In Adrienne Lehrer & Eva Feder Kittay (eds.), *Frames, fields and contrasts*, 21–74. Hillsdale: Lawrence Erlbaum Associates.
Bauer, Laurie, Lívia Körtvélyessy & Pavol Štekauer (eds.). 2015. *Semantics of complex words*. Cham: Springer.
Bauer, Laurie, Rochelle Lieber & Ingo Plag. 2013. *The Oxford reference guide to English morphology*. Oxford: Oxford University Press.
Baunaz, Lena, Eric Lander, Karen De Clercq & Liliane Haegeman. 2018. Nanosyntax: The basics. In Lena Baunaz, Liliane Haegeman, Karen De Clercq & Eric Lander (eds.), *Exploring nanosyntax*, 3–56. Oxford: Oxford University Press.
Bonami, Olivier & Matías Guzmán Naranjo. 2023. Distributional evidence for derivational paradigms. In Sven Kotowski & Ingo Plag (eds.), *The semantics of derivational morphology. Theory, methods, evidence*, 219–259. Berlin and Boston: De Gruyter.
Borer, Hagit. 2013. *Structuring sense. Volume iii: Taking form*. Oxford University Press.
Comrie, Bernard. 1976. *Aspect*. Cambridge: Cambridge University Press.
Csardi, Gabor & Tamas Nepusz. 2006. The igraph software package for complex network research. *InterJournal* Vol. Complex Systems. 1695. https://igraph.org.
Daelemans, Walter. 2002. A comparison of analogical modeling of language to memory-based language processing. In Royal Skousen, Deryle Lonsdale & Dilworth B. Parkinson (eds.), *Analogical modeling: An exemplar-based approach to language*, 157–179. Amsterdam: John Benjamins.

Daelemans, Walter & Antal van den Bosch. 2005. *Memory-based language processing*. Cambridge: Cambridge University Press.

Daelemans, Walter, Jakub Zavrel, Ko van der Sloot & Antal van den Bosch. 2007. Timbl. tilburg memory based learner, version 6.0, reference guide. ilk technical report 07-03.

Davies, Mark. 2008-. The Corpus of Contemporary American English: 450 million words, 1990-present. http://www.americancorpus.org/.

Eddington, David. 2000. Spanish stress assignment within the analogical modeling of language. *Language* 76(1). 92–109.

Eddington, David. 2002. A comparison of two analogical models: Tilburg Memory-Based Learner versus Analogical Modeling. In Royal Skousen, Deryle Lonsdale & Dilworth B. Parkinson (eds.), *Analogical modeling*, 141–156. Amsterdam/Philadelphia: John Benjamins.

Gadde, Fredrik. 1910. *On the history and use of the suffixes -ery (-ry), -age and -ment in English*. Lund: Berlingska Boktryckeriet.

Guzmán Naranjo, Matías. 2020. Analogy, complexity and predictability in the Russian nominal inflection system. *Morphology* 30(3). 219–262.

Harley, Heidi. 2009. Compounding and distributed morphology. In Rochelle Lieber & Pavol Štekauer (eds.), *The Oxford handbook of compounding* Oxford Handbooks in linguistics, 129–144. Oxford, New York: Oxford University Press.

Huyghe, Richard & Marine Wauquier. 2020. What's in an agent? *Morphology* 30(3). 185–218.

Kawaletz, Lea. 2023. *The semantics of English -ment nominalizations*. Berlin: Language Science Press.

Kawaletz, Lea & Ingo Plag. 2015. Predicting the semantics of English nominalizations: A frame-based analysis of -*ment* suffixation. In Laurie Bauer, Pavol Stekauer & Livia Kortvelyessy (eds.), *Semantics of complex words*, 289–319. Cham: Springer.

Keuleers, E., D. Sandra, W. Daelemans, S. Gillis, G. Durieux & E. Martens. 2007. Dutch plural inflection: The exception that proves the analogy. *Cognitive Psychology* 54. 283–318.

Kipper Schuler, Karin. 2005. *Verbnet: A broad-coverage, comprehensive verb lexicon*. Philadelphia: University of Pennsylvania dissertation.

Kotowski, Sven & Martin Schäfer. 2023. Quantifying semantic relatedness across base verbs and derivatives. english *out*-prefixation. In Sven Kotowski & Ingo Plag (eds.), *The semantics of derivational morphology. Theory, methods, evidence*, 177–217. Berlin and Boston: De Gruyter.

Lapesa, Gabriella, Lea Kawaletz, Ingo Plag, Marios Andreou, Max Kisselew & Sebastian Padó. 2018. Disambiguation of newly derived nominalizations in context: A distributional semantics approach. *Word Structure* 11(3). 277–312.

Levin, Beth. 1993. *English verb classes and alternations: A preliminary investigation*. Chicago: University of Chicago Press.

Lieber, Rochelle. 2004. *Morphology and lexical semantics*. Cambridge: Cambridge University Press.

Lieber, Rochelle. 2016. *English nouns: The ecology of nominalization*. Cambridge: Cambridge University Press.

Lieber, Rochelle & Marios Andreou. 2018. Aspect and modality in the interpretation of deverbal -*er* nominals in English. *Morphology* 28(3). 187–217.

Lieber, Rochelle & Ingo Plag. 2022. The semantics of conversion nouns and -*ing* nominalizations: A quantitative and theoretical perspective. *Journal of Linguistics* 58(2). 307–343.

Löbner, Sebastian. 2013. *Understanding semantics*. 2nd edn. London: Routledge.

Marchand, Hans. 1969. *The categories and types of present-day English word-formation.* 2nd ed. Munich: Beck.
Marelli, Marco & Marco Baroni. 2015. Affixation in semantic space: Modeling morpheme meanings with compositional distributional semantics. *Psychological review* 122(3). 485–515.
Missud, Alice & Florence Villoing. 2021. Investigating the distributional properties of rival *-age* suffixation and verb-to-noun conversion in French. *Verbum* XLIII(1).
Nosofsky, Robert M. 1986. Attention, similarity, and the identification-categorization relationship. *Journal of Experimental Psychology: General* 115. 39F–57.
OED. 2021. *Oxford English Dictionary online.* https://www.oed.com/ *(January 21, 2021).* Oxford: Oxford University Press.
Pinker, Steven. 1999. *Words and rules: The ingredients of language.* London: Weidenfeld and Nicolson.
Plag, Ingo, Marios Andreou & Lea Kawaletz. 2018. A frame-semantic approach to polysemy in affixation. In Olivier Bonami, Gilles Boyé, Georgette Dal, Hélène Giraudo & Fiammetta Namer (eds.), *The lexeme in descriptive and theoretical morphology,* 546–568. Berlin: Language Science Press.
Plag, Ingo, Gero Kunter & Sabine Lappe. 2007. Testing hypotheses about compound stress assignment in English: A corpus-based investigation. *Corpus Linguistics and Linguistic Theory* 3. 199–232.
Pollard, Carl & Ivan A. Sag. 1994. *Head-driven phrase structure grammar.* Chicago: University of Chicago Press.
R Core Team. 2019. *R: A language and environment for statistical computing.* R Foundation for Statistical Computing Vienna, Austria. https://www.R-project.org/.
Sag, Ivan A. 2012. Sign-based construction grammar: An informal synopsis. In Hans Boas & Ivan A. Sag (eds.), *Sign-based construction grammar,* 69–202. Stanford: CSLI publications.
Schäfer, Martin. 2023. Splitting -ly's. using word embeddings to distinguish derivation and inflection. In Sven Kotowski & Ingo Plag (eds.), *The semantics of derivational morphology. Theory, methods, evidence,* 261–296. Berlin and Boston: De Gruyter.
Schirakowski, Barbara. 2021. *Nominalisierte infinitive im Spanischen.* Berlin/Boston: De Gruyter.
Skousen, Royal. 1989. *Analogical modeling of language.* Dordrecht: Kluwer Academic.
Skousen, Royal. 2002. Issues in Analogical Modeling. In Royal Skousen, Deryle Lonsdale & Dilworth B. Parkinson (eds.), *Analogical Modeling,* 27–48. Amsterdam/Philadelphia: John Benjamins.
Skousen, Royal. 2005. Analogical Modeling (49). In Reinhard Köhler, Gabriel Altmann & Rajmund G. Piotrowski (eds.), *Quantitative Linguistik. Ein internationales Handbuch = Quantitative linguistics* (Handbücher Zur Sprach- Und Kommunikationswissenschaft = Handbooks of linguistics and communication science = Manuels de linguistique et des sciences de communication / mitbegr. von Gerold Ungeheuer. Hrsg. von Armin Burkhardt ... ; Bd. 27), 705–716. Berlin: de Gruyter.
Skousen, Royal, Deryle Lonsdale & Dilworth B. Parkinson (eds.). 2002. *Analogical modeling: An exemplar-based approach to language.* Amsterdam: John Benjamins.
Skousen, Royal & Thereon Stanford. 2007. *AM::Parallel.* http://humanities.byu.edu/am.
Skousen, Royal, Thereon Stanford & Nathan Glenn. 2013. *Algorithm::AM.* https://github.com/garfieldnate/Algorithm-AM.

Varvara, Rossella. 2017. *Verbs as nouns: Empirical investigations on event-denoting nominalizations*: University of Trento dissertation.
Wauquier, Marine. 2020. *Confrontation des procédés dérivationnels et des catégories sémantiques dans les modèles distributionnels.* Toulouse: Université Toulouse 2 - Jean Jaurès Phd dissertation.

Richard Huyghe, Alizée Lombard, Justine Salvadori, and Sandra Schwab

Semantic rivalry between French deverbal neologisms in *-age*, *-ion* and *-ment*

Abstract: This study investigates the semantic aspects of the rivalry between French nominalizing suffixes *-age*, *-ion* and *-ment*. To control for lexicalization effects on derivational semantics, a sample of neologisms ending with the three suffixes is examined. A detailed systematic description of base verbs and derived nouns is provided, taking into account their lexical ambiguity. A total of 501 verb-noun pairs are described with respect to lexical aspect, semantic role assignment properties, and nominal semantic type. Different statistical methods are used to evaluate the relative influence of these properties on suffix selection, the predictability of suffix distribution, and the gradient nature of the rivalry between the three suffixes. Results reveal the importance of discriminative properties such as the referential type of the noun and the ability for event-denoting verbs and nouns to have a result state interpretation. Different degrees of distinctiveness and rivalry can be identified between the three suffixes. It appears that *-age* and *-ment* compete more with each other than they do with *-ion*.

Keywords: derivation, semantics, affix rivalry, neologism, nominalization

1 Introduction

The suffixes *-age*, *-ion* and *-ment* are arguably the most productive suffixes used to form eventuality-denoting deverbal nouns in French. Their semantic rivalry[1] has attracted a lot of attention in the last decades, but no consensus has yet emerged

---

[1] Affix rivalry is understood here in a broad sense, based on the similarity of derivational patterns (Aronoff 1976; Baayen et al. 2013; Arndt-Lappe 2014; Schulte 2015; Bonami & Thuilier 2019; Dressler et al. 2019; Naccarato 2019; Varvara 2020; Huyghe & Wauquier 2021; a.o.). Two or more affixes are regarded as rivals if, in at least one of their patterns, they apply to base words from the same lexical class, and derive words from the same lexical class and with the same coarse-grained meaning. For a theoretical and historical overview of morphological competition, see Gardani et al. (2019).

Richard Huyghe, Alizée Lombard, Justine Salvadori, Sandra Schwab, Université de Fribourg, email of corresponding author: richard.huyghe@unifr.ch

as to whether these suffixes are equivalent forms or not, and what their distinctive properties could be. Some authors have claimed that there is no systematic difference between *-age*, *-ion* and/or *-ment* and that these suffixes are related to the same derivation type, as morphological exponents of the same word-formation rule or as possible allomorphs of a single affix expressing 'action' (Zwanenburg, 1984; Debaty-Luca, 1986; Dal et al., 2018). Others argue that different constraints apply to the three suffixes, but diverge on the constraints or focus on different aspects of the morphosemantic patterns associated with the suffixes. For instance, Dubois (1962) and Lüdtke (1978) suggest that *-age* contrasts with *-ment* in that it preferentially selects transitive verbal bases, whereas Kelling (2001) considers that the essential difference between *-age* and *-ment* is not the transitivity of the base verb, but the degree of agentivity of its subjects (*-age* selecting more agentive base verbs than *-ment*). Martin (2010) advocates a multifactorial analysis, involving agentivity, but also the length of the eventive chain (including more subevents for *-age* than for *-ment*), the incremental relation between events and themes (observable in the case of *-age* but not of *-ion* and *-ment*), and processive ontology (nouns in *-age* denoting physical processes more frequently than nouns in *-ment* and *-ion*). Fradin (2016, 2019) defends the idea that *-age* selects base verbs which denote more controlled or more concrete events than *-ment*, and that nominalizations in *-ment* denote states more frequently than nominalizations in *-age*. Finally, Wauquier (2020) argues that *-age* is preferentially used in technical domains and is therefore more specialized than *-ion* and *-ment*.

A limitation of existing studies is that they rarely provide quantitative information about the differences observed between the nominalizing suffixes, which hinders the possibility of generalization. Moreover, studies usually focus on lexicalized words, especially on morphological doublets (i.e. lexemes based on the same verbal input but ending with different suffixes). Although not infrequent, doublets remain the exception.[2] They may not reveal all differences between competing affixes and when lexicalized, they could exhibit idiosyncratic properties. More generally, lexicalized derivatives integrate all sorts of variations due to diachronic evolution, onomasiological needs, lexical competition, etc. (Corbin, 1987; Plag, 1999; Kawaletz & Plag, 2015). They do not directly allow for an exploration of derivational semantics (i.e. semantic correlates of morphological processes) as opposed to lexical semantics (i.e. semantic properties of estab-

---

[2] As an indication, the Démonette database, which is a large morphological resource for French (Hathout & Namer, 2014), contains 404 cases of doublets in *-age* and *-ment* (13.9% and 16.5% of the nouns in the database ending in *-age* and *-ment*, respectively), 35 cases of doublets in *-ion* and *-ment* (1.2% and 1.4% of the nouns ending in *-ion* and *-ment*, respectively), and 26 cases of doublets in *-age* and *-ion* (0.9% of the nouns in both cases).

lished words in the lexicon), if one assumes that lexical semantics is based on derivational semantics but can further specify word meaning.

Our goal in this paper is to contribute to the study of the semantic rivalry between -*age*, -*ion* and -*ment* by investigating non-lexicalized derivatives in contemporary French. We will examine a sample of neologisms ending in -*age*, -*ion*, -*ment* in a quantitative approach and provide a detailed systematic description of both base verbs and derived nouns, taking into account their lexical ambiguity. It will be asked whether significant semantic differences can be observed between the three suffixes, and to what extent they could explain suffix distribution. In addition, considering affix rivalry as a gradient phenomenon, we will discuss whether different degrees of rivalry can be identified between the competing suffixes.

The article is structured as follows. In Section 2, we present the method used to sample and describe the semantic properties of French neologisms ending in -*age*, -*ion* and -*ment*. In Section 3, we report the results of the semantic description and present some differences observed between the three suffixes. In Section 4, we investigate the relative importance of the semantic properties and examine how they combine to predict suffix distribution. Finally, in Section 5, we discuss the gradient nature of the rivalry between the three suffixes. It will be concluded that -*age*, -*ion* and -*ment* are tendentially associated with different semantic operations, especially with respect to the type of entities or eventualities denoted by suffixed nouns. However, differences between the three suffixes are neutralized in many cases. The semantic overlap is particularly important in the case of -*age* and -*ment*, which compete with each other more than they do with -*ion*.

2 Method

Our study is based on the analysis of a sample of 300 French deverbal neologisms ending in -*age*, -*ion* and -*ment* (100 nouns per suffix). In this section, we present the method used to collect the neologisms, the semantic properties described for each verb-noun pair, and the annotation protocol we followed.

2.1 Data sampling

Neologisms in -*age*, -*ion* and -*ment* were extracted from the FRCOW16A corpus, which is a large French web corpus containing 10.8 billion tokens (Schäfer & Bildhauer, 2012; Schäfer, 2015). Words from the corpus ending in -*age(s)*, -*ion(s)*, and -*ment(s)* were filtered automatically using large lists of existing word forms taken from the *Lexique* (New et al., 2004) and *Lefff* (Sagot, 2010) resources. Filtered data were abundant and noisy, due among other things to many misspellings and irrelevant forms. As a consequence, we randomly ordered candidate words and for each suffix selected the first 100 nouns that would satisfy the conditions C1-C3 below.

C1: The noun is morphosemantically related to a verb present either in lexicographic resources (*Le Petit Robert*, *Wiktionnaire*) or in the reference corpus (FR-COW16A). At least one meaning of the noun can be analyzed in relation to one meaning of the verb, whether the noun denotes the same eventuality as the verb or a participant in that eventuality. A noun such as *barillage* 'putting into barrels' was thus excluded because we could not find any attestation of the verb *bariller* with the meaning of 'put into barrels'.

C2: The noun is not analyzable as derived both from a verb and from an existing noun in *-age*, *-ion* or *-ment*. Possible nominal compounds or prefixed denominal nouns are discarded, on the assumption that existing nouns in *-age*, *-ion* and *-ment* may influence by analogy the form of neologisms. Accordingly, nouns such as *coenseignement* 'co-teaching' and *photocoagulation* 'photocoagulation' were excluded from the sample, as they can be analyzed as derived from *coenseigner* 'co-teach' and *photocoaguler* 'photocoagulate' or from *enseignement* 'teaching' and *coagulation* 'coagulation'.[3]

C3: The noun is not strictly a technical term. Although unknown to most speakers, technical terms may be lexicalized in specialized languages and there-

---

3 We excluded candidate nouns with the prefixes *dé-* and *re-* that are formally a prefixed version of an existing noun ending in *-age*, *-ion* or *-ment*. *Dé-* and *re-* are mostly deverbal prefixes, and it is uncertain whether they can select nominal bases or not. However, even deverbal *déXsuff* and *reXsuff* nouns might be formed by analogy with an existing *Xsuff* noun. To test this possibility, we selected 100 prefixed verbs in FRCOW16A for which there was an attested nominalization in *-age*, *-ion* or *-ment*: half of the verbs prefixed with *re-*, the rest prefixed with *dé-*. For each nominalization, we then checked in FRCOW16A whether there was a competing noun with the same prefix and one of the two other suffixes. We also searched for non-prefixed nominalizations corresponding to the three prefixed nominalizations. For example, for *débureaucratiser* 'debureaucratize' and *débureaucratisation* 'debureaucratization', we found that *bureaucratisation* 'bureaucratization' was also attested in the corpus, but that *débureaucratisage*, *débureaucratisement*, *bureaucratisage* and *bureaucratisement* were not. Finally, we performed a logistic regression analysis on the collected data. The fitted regression model was: $Prob\_Exist\_prefXsuff = -3.61 + 4.19 \times Exist\_Xsuff$. Likelihood ratio-tests showed a significant effect ($p < 2.2e{-}16$). The probability that a nominalization in *-age*, *-ion* or *-ment* prefixed with *re-* or *dé-* exists is strongly influenced by the existence of a corresponding non-prefixed nominalization. In other words, there is an important formal attractiveness between prefixed nominalizations and their non-prefixed equivalents. Such formal analogies may bias the analysis of the relationship between suffix selection and semantic properties of verb-noun pairs, hence the exclusion of the words concerned.

fore not be neologisms. Technical terms absent from standard lexicographic resources can be identified through their corpus occurrences, when these clearly relate to specialized discourse. For example, listed candidates such as *abergeage* 'feodal contract', *carassonage* 'vineyard trellis repair', *chanfreinage* 'bevelling', *enzymage* 'enzyming', *trancanage* 'crosswinding', and *panotage* 'panning' were excluded from the sample. During the selection, it appeared that technical terms were much more frequently found among *-age* candidates than among *-ion* and *-ment* candidates. Although we did not precisely quantify the difference, this seems to confirm previous claims made by Dubois (1962), Fleischman (1980), Uth (2010) and Wauquier (2020) about the technicality of *-age*.

Examples of neologisms in *-age*, *-ion* and *-ment* satisfying C1-C3 and included in the sample are given in (1).

(1) a. affolage 'panic', brancardage 'stretcher bearing', corbeillage 'trashing', dandinage 'swaying', implorage 'imploring', militage 'campaining', oubliage 'forgetting', pixelisage 'pixelization', suspectage 'suspecting', visitage 'visit'
   b. alternation 'alternating', christification 'christification', colmatation 'filling-in', confortation 'comfort', expulsation 'expulsion', foiration 'screwing up', poutinisation 'putinization', romanticisation 'romanticization', rutilation 'shine', semestrialisation 'semesterization'
   c. absorbement 'absorption', atténuement 'softening', bedonnement 'paunch', cernement 'encirclement', ficellement 'tying up', ignorement 'ignoring', malaxement 'kneading', résiliement 'termination', subissement 'putting up with', trompement 'cheating'

2.2 Annotated properties

A number of syntactic and semantic properties are mentioned in the literature as possible discriminating factors between *-age*, *-ion* and *-ment*, including:
- the transitivity of the base verb;
- the semantic type of the derived noun;
- the lexical aspect of both verbs and nouns;
- the semantic roles assigned by verbs and nouns to their arguments.

In this study, we propose a systematic analysis of these properties. For each verb-noun pair included in the sample, we annotated a series of features related to the above-mentioned properties, while also taking into account the lexical ambiguity of both the verb and the noun. The description was based on controlled manual annotation and precise definitions of the annotated features. The general principles and linguistic tests used to analyze the properties of verbs and nouns are detailed in an annotation guide available in the supplementary material of the paper.

We analyzed the semantic type of the nouns by distinguishing between their ontological and relational descriptive properties, each noun being doubly classified. Ontological types relate to the nature of the referents, whereas relational types depend on the semantic relation with the base. Existing classifications of nominalizations often assimilate the two kinds of properties, possibly leading to confusion in semantic descriptions. Ontological and relational types belong to different taxonomies since, as illustrated in (2) and (3), an ontological type can be related to different relational types and conversely.

(2)   a.   bâtir 'build' → bâtiment 'building'   [ARTEFACT-RESULT]
      b.   fixer 'fasten' → fixation 'fastener'   [ARTEFACT-INSTRUMENT]
      c.   garer 'park' → garage 'garage'   [ARTEFACT-LOCATION]

(3)   a.   bâtir 'build' → bâtiment 'building'   [ARTEFACT-RESULT]
      b.   énerver 'irritate' → énervement 'irritation'   [STATE-RESULT]
      c.   traduire 'translate' → traduction 'translation'   [COGNITIVE-RESULT]

Thirteen ontological simple types are distinguished based on distributional tests taken from the literature on French nominal semantics (Godard & Jayez, 1996; Flaux & Van de Velde, 2000; Huyghe, 2015; Haas et al., 2022). Some of them combine to form complex types, in which case characteristic predicates of different simple types are contextually compatible (Copestake & Briscoe, 1995; Cruse, 1995; Pustejovsky, 1995; Kleiber, 1999; Asher, 2011; Dölling, 2020; a.o.). For example, the noun *déclaration* 'statement' in (4) instantiates a complex type of event and cognitive object. The eventive facet is selected by *effectuer* 'perform' and the cognitive facet by *selon lequel P* 'according to which P'.

(4)   L'hôpital Legouest de Metz a effectué une déclaration selon laquelle il venait d'accueillir deux victimes blessées par balles. (web)
        'The Legouest Hospital in Metz made a statement according to which they had just received two victims with gunshot wounds'

Relational types are based on the semantic roles used to analyze arguments, complemented with a transpositional type for nouns that denote roughly the same kind of eventualities as their base verb (i.e. with respect to the event/state distinction). We defined a set of 17 semantic roles adapted from *Verbnet* (Kipper-Schuler, 2005) and *Lirics* (Petukhova & Bunt, 2008). Since distributional tests cannot be used to differentiate semantic roles, we relied on explicit definitions to identify the roles assigned to the arguments of verbs and nouns.

Lexical aspect was decomposed into four basic features (dynamicity, durativity, telicity, and post-phase) and analyzed using linguistic tests proposed in the literature (Vendler, 1967; Dowty, 1979; Rothstein, 2004; Haas et al., 2008; Filip, 2012; a.o.). telicity was encoded by default with a delimited internal argument, and annotated as variable for degree achievements (Abusch, 1986; Bertinetto & Squartini, 1995; Hay et al., 1999; Rothstein, 2008; a.o.). Other aspectual features are binary. We labelled as 'post-phase' the possibility for a dynamic eventuality to include a durative result state, as illustrated in (5) with *partir* 'leave' vs. *arriver* 'arrive' (Piñón, 1997, 1999; Apothéloz, 2008; Fradin, 2011; Haas & Jugnet, 2013).

(5) Julie {est partie/?est arrivée} pendant deux jours.
'Julie {left/arrived} for two days'

The possibility of being interpreted as a result state when combined with temporal complements or with the verb *durer* 'last', as in (6), was used as a criterion for the identification of nominal post-phase.

(6) L'exclusion a duré six jours, avant que les services éducatifs régionaux n'ordonnent sa réintégration. (web)
'The exclusion lasted six days before regional educational services ordered his reinstatement'

To account for the polysemy of nominalizations, the different meanings of each verb and noun were carefully distinguished and systematically paired. Ambiguous nouns were assigned one entry per meaning in the database. The lexical ambiguity of a given form was identified through the variation of at least one annotated property. Verbal and nominal lexemes were paired based on the principle of closest semantic correspondence: If a verb or a noun is ambiguous, the verbal and nominal lexemes that share the most aspectual and role-assigning properties are paired together. For instance, two eventive meanings were found for the noun *croquement* 'crunching/sketching', illustrated by occurrences such as *le croquement des glaçons* 'the crunching of ice cubes' and *le croquement des tatouages* 'the sketching of tattoos'. These two meanings are, respectively, punctual and durative, and associated with the subcategorization of a patient and a result argument. They were paired with two different verbs (*croquer* 'crunch' and *croquer* 'sketch') exhibiting the same distinctive features as the two nominal lexemes, and were annotated in both cases as instantiating a transpositional relational type. Two meanings were also found for the noun *retouchement* 'retouching/modification': an event and an artefact meaning (*opérer un retouchement des paupières* 'perform an eyelid retouching' vs. *des retouchements blancs sur graphite* 'white modifications on graphite'). But in this case both meanings are related to the same meaning of the verb *retoucher* 'retouch', i.e. a transitive accomplishment verb subcategorizing an agent and a patient. *Retouchement* was then assigned two entries linked to the same base verb, analyzed respectively as a transpositional and a resultative relational type.

2.3 Annotation protocol

Verb-noun pairs included in the sample were annotated in a double-blind process and adjudicated with the help of a third annotator. The different meanings of each noun were identified through the occurrences in FRCOW16A, complemented with examples taken from the web. Ten nouns per suffix were used for joint training and refinement of the annotation guidelines; then, two annotation sessions of 45 nouns per suffix were conducted. Inter-annotator agreement scores over the two sessions were calculated using Cohen's kappa, as well as prevalence-adjusted and bias-adjusted kappa (PABAK). The latter compensates for the overvaluation of disagreement cases with Cohen's kappa when categories are highly unbalanced in value distribution (Byrt et al., 1993). Agreement scores for each annotated verbal and nominal property are presented in Table 1. They indicate an overall substantial inter-annotator agreement[4] and can be regarded as evidence of the operationality of the linguistic categories we used to describe the properties of verbs and nouns.

The 300 nouns in the sample were finally associated with 501 meanings (162 for *-age*, 168 for *-ion*, 171 for *-ment*), ranging from 1 to 4 meanings per noun, with an average of 1.67. These 501 meanings are related to 418 distinct verbal meanings (123 for *-age*, 153 for *-ion*, 142 for *-ment*). In 107 cases of ambiguity (59.1%), multiple nominal meanings associated with the same form are derived from multiple verbal

---

[4] Various scales have been proposed to interpret kappa values. According to the reference scale defined by Landis & Koch (1977), the agreement is "substantial" when kappa scores range from 0.61 to 0.80 and "almost perfect" when they range from 0.81 to 1.00. In the alternate scale introduced by McHugh (2012), the agreement is said to be "moderate" between 0.60 and 0.79, "strong" between 0.80 and 0.90, and "almost perfect" between 0.90 and 1.00. Beyond the inevitable arbitrariness of those evaluation scales, inter-annotator agreement should be interpreted with regard to the specific nature of each annotation task and the inherent fuzziness of the phenomena described.

Tab. 1: Inter-annotator agreement per property.

	Observed agreement	Kappa	PABAK
V transitivity	0.96	0.92	0.93
V Dynamicity	0.98	0.56	0.96
V durativity	0.86	0.59	0.72
V telicity	0.82	0.72	0.73
V Post-phase	0.78	0.65	0.67
V Role of subject	0.79	0.71	0.76
V Role of object	0.83	0.78	0.82
V Role of oblique	0.90	0.61	0.90
N Ontological type	0.83	0.77	0.82
N Relational type	0.93	0.78	0.92
N Dynamicity	0.95	0.85	0.92
N durativity	0.87	0.71	0.80
N telicity	0.85	0.79	0.77
N Post-phase	0.83	0.73	0.74
N Role of 1st arg.	0.78	0.72	0.77
N Role of 2nd arg.	0.80	0.71	0.78
N Role of 3rd arg.	0.95	0.60	0.93
Average	0.87	0.72	0.82

meanings, following the pattern in (7). In 74 cases of ambiguity (40.9%), they are derived from the same verbal meaning, following the pattern in (8).[5]

(7) Multibase ambiguity
    V1 → N1
    V2 → N2

(8) Single-base ambiguity
    V1 → N1
    V1 → N2

---

[5] It is uncertain whether N2s in single-base ambiguities result from a derivational operation or from a lexical figure such as metonymy (see Ferret & Villoing 2015 for a related discussion on the formation of instrument-denoting nouns in -age). Evidence in favor of the morphological or figurative construction is difficult to provide. For a given N1/N2 type, the existence of derived N2s without a corresponding N1 in the lexicon shows the existence of a morphological pattern, but does not imply that any N2 with the semantic type considered results from derivation. Conversely, the existence in the lexicon of metonymically-related underived N1s and N2s shows the existence of a figurative pattern, but does not imply that any N2 results from metonymy. It could also be hypothesized that the two types of patterns are not necessarily exclusive of each other, and that morphological and figurative derivations actually combine to favor the formation of ambiguous words (Huyghe, 2021).

The 501 verb-noun pairs vary with respect to annotated properties, and it can be asked whether these variations depend on the suffix used to form deverbal nouns.

3 Observed differences

In this section, we describe the distribution between *-age*, *-ion*, *-ment* according to the different properties we analyzed, as a first approach to suffix similarity and distinctiveness. Due to space limitations, we present only a subset of the results.[6] Some properties of our sampled verb-noun pairs deserve special attention, either because they have been much debated in the literature, or because they show important variation between neologisms formed with the three suffixes. We focus on six properties: (i) three verbal properties frequently discussed in studies on *-age*, *-ion* and *-ment*, and (ii) three nominal properties distributed across the suffixes with particularly salient differences—and that will prove in further analyses to have a major influence on suffix selection (see Section 4).

3.1 Verb transitivity

As shown in Figure 1, the three suffixes mostly select transitive base verbs, but the preference is more pronounced for *-age* (76.4% of transitive base verbs) than for *-ion* and *-ment* (58.8% and 59.9% of transitive base verbs, respectively).[7] To some extent, this result supports the observations of Dubois (1962) and Lüdtke (1978) who state that *-age* tends to select transitive bases and *-ment* intransitive bases. Counterexamples mentioned by Kelling (2001) and Martin (2010) do not seem to affect the general tendency towards a more frequent selection of transitive bases with *-age*. Nevertheless, the tendency only holds true in the perspective of suffix comparison. The suffix *-age* does not privilege transitive over intransitive base verbs with regard to the distribution of transitive and intransitive verbs in

---

[6] The complete description of the 17 verbal and nominal properties is available in the supplementary material of the paper.
[7] The quantitative results in Sections 3.1, 3.2 and 3.3 are based on the number of distinct verbal lexemes in the dataset, as opposed to their frequency as a base in the dataset. Verbal lexemes present in multiple entries, i.e. associated with different nominal lexemes in single-base ambiguity configuration, were counted only once in the statistics. This counting is appropriate for a discussion of previous claims about the rivalry between *-age*, *-ion* and *-ment*, given that existing studies do not take into account nominal ambiguity in the comparison of the base verbs selected by the different suffixes.

the lexicon. As a comparison, the lexical resource *Les Verbes Français* (Dubois & Dubois-Charlier, 1997) contains 19580 transitive and 6029 intransitive verbal lexemes (in the sense intended here). That distribution is not significantly different from that of verbs deriving *-age* nouns in our sample (χ^2 (1, N = 25732) = 0.0001, p = .99). By contrast, the distribution between transitive and intransitive is clearly unbalanced in favor of intransitive verbs with *-ment*, even if *-ment* selects mostly transitive bases (χ^2 (1, N = 25751) = 21.56, p = 3.4e-06).

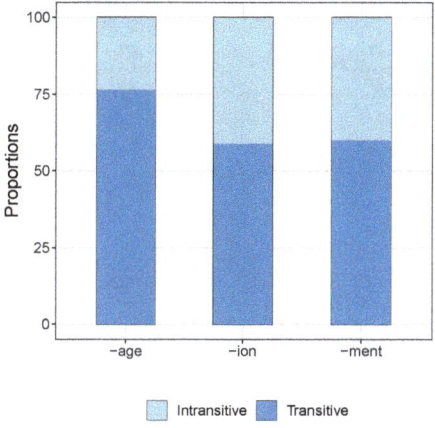

Fig. 1: Transitive and intransitive base verbs per suffix (%).

3.2 Semantic role of verb subjects

Important differences can be observed between *-age*, *-ion* and *-ment* with respect to semantic roles assigned to their base verb subjects. As illustrated in Figure 2, *-age* has a strong predilection for base verbs subcategorizing agent subjects, whereas *-ion* prefers base verbs with cause or patient subjects (especially verbs allowing for the causative-anticausative alternation). The suffix *-ment* is more similar to *-age* than to *-ion*, but it selects less agentive and more patientive verbs than *-age*, as well as verbs assigning more diverse roles to their subjects (with higher proportions of theme, stimulus, pivot subjects than the two other suffixes). This specificity echoes Kelling's statement that "the French suffix *-age* combines with verb stems whose first argument is proto-agentive, whereas the French suffix *-(e)ment* combines with verb stems whose first argument is less proto-agentive" (Kelling, 2001, 155). However, this contrast should only be regarded as a tendency, since prototypical agentive base verbs regularly combine with -*ment* to form neologisms (e.g. *déblatèrement* 'badmouthing', *mitraillement* 'machine-gunning', *retapement* 'refurbishment').

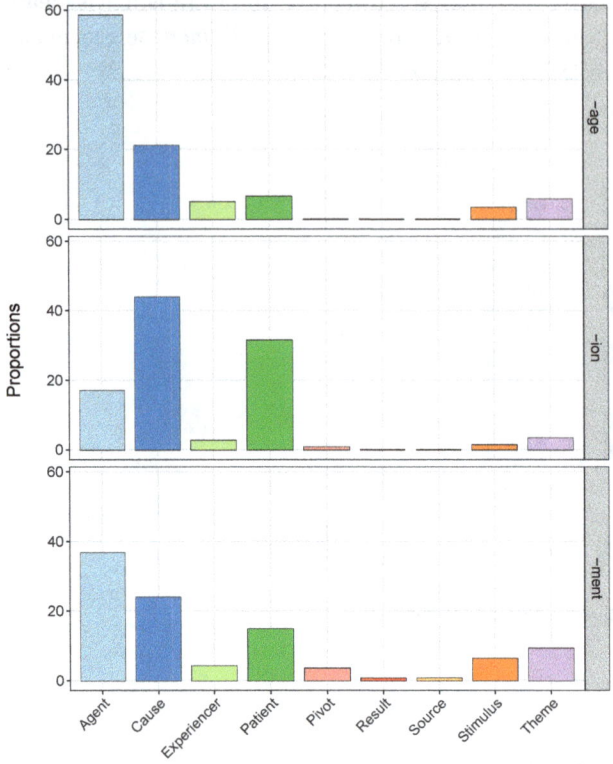

Fig. 2: Semantic roles assigned to base verb subjects per suffix (%).

3.3 Verb telicity

The data we collected do not show any significant difference between -*age* and -*ment* with respect to base verb telicity (χ^2 (1, N = 265) = 3.43, *p* = .18). In both cases, about half of the base verbs are telic, less than half atelic, and a minority of verbs with variable telicity can be observed (see Figure 3). There is a clear contrast with -*ion*, which shows a strong preference for verbs with variable telicity

(66.0% of the base verbs). These results contradict the findings of Martin (2010), who argues that the selection between -*age*, -*ment* and -*ion* is not correlated with the aspectual properties of base verbs. The fact that Martin focuses on psychological verbs and their nominalizations, and does not encode variable telicity as a distinct feature could explain this difference. It can also be noted that in our data, most verbs with variable telicity and deriving -*ion* nouns are suffixed with -*iser* (84.2%)—and reciprocally, that most verbs ending in -*iser* are nominalized with -*ion* and have variable telicity (81.7%). Not only does -*ion* select more -*iser* verbs than the two other suffixes (see Table 2), but most -*iser* verbs are also verbs with variable telicity in our sample (see Table 3).⁸ The fact that verbs in -*iser* preferentially form neologisms ending in -*ion* rather than -*age* and -*ment* confirms the morphological tendency reported by Missud & Villoing (2020). The semantic counterpart of that morphological tendency appears to be the predilection for verbs with variable telicity.

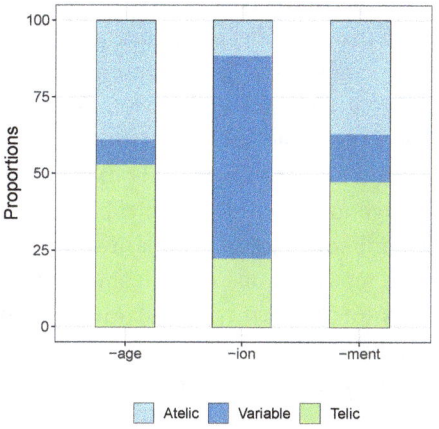

Fig. 3: Telicity of base verbs per suffix (%).

---

8 It can be asked whether -*isation* should be analyzed as a suffix in contemporary French, given its productivity and the fact that some nouns in -*isation* do not have a corresponding verb in -*iser* (Lignon et al., 2014; Dal & Namer, 2015; Cartier, 2018; Missud & Villoing, 2020). Our sample only includes nouns in -*isation* for which an existing verb in -*iser* is attested, to ensure at least the possibility of analyzing neologisms in -*isation* as derived from verbs.

Tab. 2: Number of base verbs ending or not in -*iser* per suffix (percentages by row).

	V ending in -*iser*	V not ending in -*iser*
-*age*	1 (0.8%)	122 (99.2%)
-*ion*	103 (67.3%)	50 (32.7%)
-*ment*	0 (0%)	142 (100%)

Tab. 3: Number of base verbs with or without variable telicity ending or not in -*iser* (percentages by row).

	V with variable telicity	V without variable telicity
V ending in -*iser*	86 (82.7%)	18 (17.3%)
V not ending in -*iser*	47 (15%)	267 (85%)

3.4 Nominal ontological type

The semantic type of derived nouns is one of the most discriminative properties between -*age*, -*ion* and -*ment*. The most contrasted properties pertain to ontological types, as opposed to relational types. Since -*age*, -*ion* and -*ment* are mostly transpositional suffixes, differences between the three suffixes with respect to relational types are only marginal—the main difference observed is the propensity of -*ment* to denote more results than -*age* and -*ion*.[9] Ontological types are more diverse, as can be seen in Figure 4, and some suffix peculiarities can be observed. A specificity of -*ion* is that it forms mostly nouns with a complex type combining eventive and stative descriptions (66.7% of the nouns). Most neologisms in -*ion* denote dynamic eventualities that involve a salient state, which is also strongly correlated with the variable telicity of the nouns inherited from the base verbs: 90.2% of the -*ion* nouns with a complex event-state type have variable telicity (e.g. *compaction* 'compacting', *turquification* 'turkification', *verdurisation* 'greenification'). In other words, -*ion* clearly privileges the derivation of nouns that denote a progressive change of state. Neologisms in -*ion* also denote events (in 20.8% of the cases), but other ontological types are poorly represented. Unlike -*ion*, the suffixes -*age* and -*ment* form mostly event nouns (52.5% and 38.0% of the nouns respectively) and are more likely to derive nouns that denote artefacts (8.0% and 7.6% of the nouns) and complex entities combining events and cogni-

---

[9] Chi-squared statistics for the distribution between resultative and non-resultative nominal types indicate a significant distinction in the case of -*age*/-*ment* (χ^2 (1, N = 333) = 9.600, p = .0019) and -*ion*/-*ment* (χ^2 (1, N = 339) = 18.086, p = 2.1e-05), but not in the case of -*age*/-*ion* (χ^2 (1, N = 330) = 1.4367, p = .2306).

tive objects (8.0% and 5.3% of the nouns). The suffix -*ment* forms less strictly eventive nouns than -*age*, but more nouns with a complex event-state type (e.g. *crispement* 'clenching') and more nouns denoting states (e.g. *déconcertement* 'confusion'). The specificity of -*age*, besides the fact that it is the suffix that forms the most event nouns, is that it is the only one in our data to derive domain-denoting nouns—domains being defined as non-occurrential activities, i.e. dynamic eventualities that do not 'take place' as spatio-temporally individuated events (e.g. *marketage* 'marketing', *aquarellage* 'watercoloring', *militage* 'campaining'). We identified 20 domain-denoting neologisms, all of which are suffixed with -*age*, which reflects the affinity between -*age* and domain description.

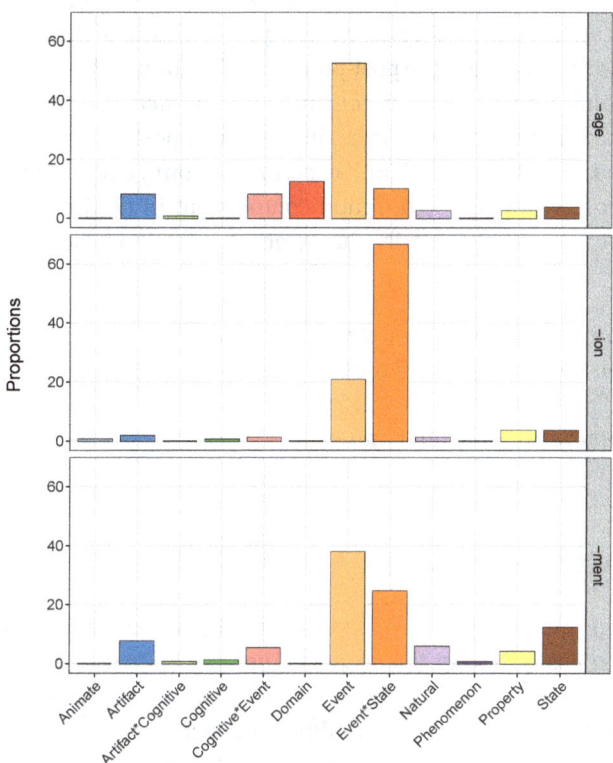

Fig. 4: Semantic type of derived nouns per suffix (%).

3.5 Nominal post-phase

Another property that varies considerably across nominalizations in -*age*, -*ion* and -*ment* is the ability to denote eventualities with a post-phase and to be interpreted as the result state of an event (see Figure 5). The suffix -*ion* contrasts with -*age* and -*ment* in that it forms mostly nouns that can have a post-phase interpretation, which is directly related to the predilection of -*ion* for complex event-state eventualities. Many nouns denoting a gradable change of state can be contextually interpreted as denoting the state that results from the changing process.

The suffixes -*age* and -*ment* derive mostly nouns that denote eventualities without post-phase, but this tendency is more prominent in the case of -*age* (77.2% of the derived nouns) than in the case of -*ment* (59.1% of the derived nouns). Transpositional nouns in -*age* can frequently change the post-phase feature of the base verb: 19.1% of those nouns do not inherit the post-phase specification of their base verb, while that proportion is only of 3.3% for -*ion* and 4.1% for -*ment*.[10] Changes observed between verbs and nouns always consist in the loss of post-phase interpretation. For example, *sortage* 'taking out', unlike *sortir* 'take out', cannot have a post-phase interpretation. Whereas the duration complement in (9-a) can be related to a result locative state, it necessarily characterizes a motion process in (9-b).

(9) a. Il a sorti son appareil photo pendant dix minutes.
 'He took out his camera for ten minutes'
 b. Le sortage de l'appareil photo a duré dix minutes.
 'Taking the camera out took ten minutes'

3.6 Nominal durativity

durativity as an aspectual property applies only to nouns that denote eventualities and is comparable to post-phase in this respect. The specificity of nominal durativity is that it distinguishes -*ment* from both -*age* and -*ion*. The suffix -*ment* forms more nouns that denote punctual eventualities, i.e. achievements, than its rivals (e.g. *démissionnement* 'resignation', *trinquement* 'clinking of glasses', *heurtement* 'knock'). durative eventualities are denoted by 74.7%, 81.0%, and 55.6% of the neologisms suffixed with -*age*, -*ion*, and -*ment*, respectively. By con-

---

10 The difference observed with respect to preservation of verbal post-phase is significant between -*age* and -*ion* (χ^2 (1, N = 317) = 14.7637, p = 1.22e-04), between -*age* and -*ment* (χ^2 (1, N = 289) = 10.9067, p = 9.58e-04), but not between -*ion* and -*ment* (χ^2 (1, N = 282) = 0.1032, p = .7480).

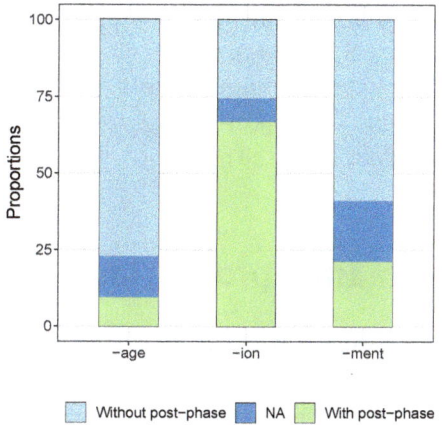

Fig. 5: Post-phase of derived nouns per suffix (%).

trast, non-durative eventualities are denoted by 11.7%, 11.3%, and 24.6% of the neologisms suffixed with *-age*, *-ion*, and *-ment*, respectively (see Figure 6). Overall, 52.5% of the nouns that denote achievements in our sample are suffixed with *-ment*.

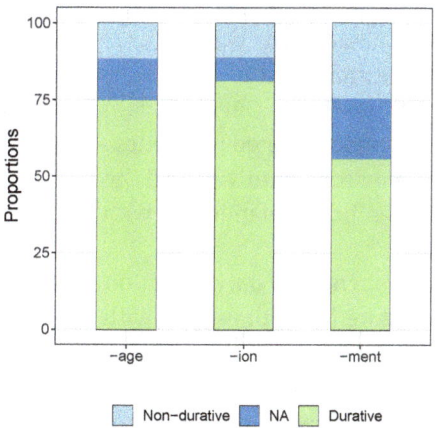

Fig. 6: Durativity of derived nouns per suffix (%)

Verbal durativity is more frequently preserved through nominalization than verbal post-phase, and the punctual aspect of derivatives in *-ment* is inherited from their base verb. Only 1.3% and 2.2% of the eventuality-denoting nouns in *-ion* and

-*ment* differ from their base with respect to durativity, whereas the proportion is 9.3% in the case of -*age*.[11] The change of aspect with -*age* can be observed for nouns derived from achievement verbs and denoting durative events (e.g. *déposer* 'drop off' vs. *déposage* 'dropping off'). As in the case of post-phase, -*age* appears to be the suffix that least preserves the lexical aspect of the base.

4 Combined influence of semantic properties

Semantic properties of verbs and nouns jointly influence the selection of -*age*, -*ion* and -*ment*. It can be asked how these properties combine to determine the distribution of the three suffixes, which properties are the most influential, and how much of the suffix distribution they can explain. In this section, we first examine correlations between the semantic properties we encoded, then use a random forest analysis to assess their relative importance and the predictability of suffix selection.

4.1 Correlations between properties

As a preliminary to statistical analysis of joint influence, we estimated pairwise correlations between the 17 annotated properties. The correlations were first evaluated using Pearson's chi-squared tests, with simulated p-value based on 2000 replicates for categories with expected counts less than 5. Out of 136 pairs, 98 show a significant relationship at $p < .05$. The most uncorrelated properties are the semantic role of the third nominal argument, nominal durativity, and the semantic role of the verb oblique, which have a non-significant relationship with 10, 9 and 8 other properties, respectively.

We used Cramér's V tests to evaluate the strength of the correlation for significant associations. Results are reported in Figure 7. The properties with the greatest number of strong correlations are the semantic role of the first nominal argument, verbal telicity, and nominal telicity, which are correlated respectively with 12, 9, and 9 other properties at Cramér's V > 0.5. Special attention can be paid to semantic properties present both in the verbal and nominal domains, such as aspectual properties and argument roles. These appear to be strongly but not fully

---

11 The difference observed with respect to preservation of verbal durativity is significant between -*age* and -*ion* (χ^2 (1, N = 295) = 9.7434, p = .0114), between -*age* and -*ment* (χ^2 (1, N = 277) = 6.406, p = .0018), but not between -*ion* and -*ment* (χ^2 (1, N = 292) = 0.3496, p = .5544).

correlated, which suggests that the preservation of semantic features across categories is not necessarily observed (even in the case of eventuality-denoting nominalizations), as already noted in Sections 3.5 and 3.6. Among aspectual features, dynamicity is subject to important variation (Cramér's V = 0.40), with possible aspectual shifts from dynamic verbs to stative nouns, as in the case of nominal result state reading. The correlation is stronger for telicity (Cramér's V = 0.94), durativity (Cramér's V = 0.88), and post-phase (Cramér's V = 0.83), but with differences that indicate the possibility of cross-categorial variation, especially in the case of post-phase.

The preservation of argument structure cannot be assessed as directly as that of lexical aspect, because of syntactic differences between verbal and nominal arguments, and of the possible variation in nominal argument position. However, high correlations can be observed between semantic roles of verbal objects and first nominal arguments (Cramér's V = 0.93), and semantic roles of verbal obliques and second nominal arguments (Cramér's V = 0.91), presumably because of semantic preservation. The correlation between verb subjects and nominal arguments is somewhat weaker, since the highest correlation coefficient observed between their semantic roles is 0.84, which indicates a possible alteration of the subject argument in nominalization.

The considerable amount of correlations observed in our data requires the use of an adapted statistical method to analyze the combined and relative influence of semantic properties on suffix selection.

4.2 Relative importance of properties

We used a random forest algorithm to determine how verbal and nominal properties can jointly predict the distribution of -*age*, -*ion* and -*ment*, and individually contribute to the prediction. random forests are an ensemble method designed to predict a response variable with respect to a set of possible explanatory variables (Breiman, 2001; Tagliamonte & Baayen, 2012; Levshina, 2020). They operate by averaging predictions from a large number of conditional inference trees, themselves resulting from binary recursive partitioning of data according to predictors. random forests are based on the randomization of both the data subsamples used as training sets in decision trees and the subset of predictors tested at each node of each tree. They provide reliable information about predictive accuracy and can be used to assess the relative importance of predictor variables. Being non-parametric and able to handle high dimensional data with correlated and interacting variables, random forests are well adapted to the analysis of our data,

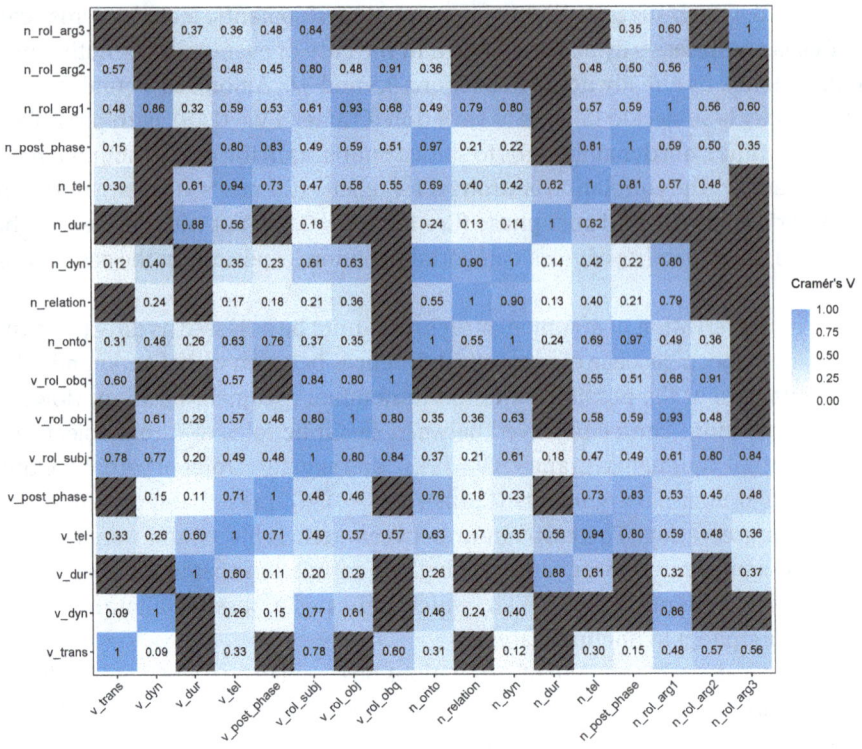

Fig. 7: Correlations between nominal and verbal properties based on Cramér's V tests. Coefficients are not computed for non-significant associations.

given its sparseness (i.e. the small number of observations with respect to the number of predictors) and the correlations observed between semantic properties.

We conducted a random forest analysis based on 3000 conditional inference trees, with random samples of 5 predictor variables at each tree node.[12] The developed model shows an accuracy of 62.3%. The important proportion of wrongly predicted cases can be interpreted as the effect of semantic indistinguishability between the three suffixes. A closer look at the discrepancies between observed and predicted data reveals important differences between the three suffixes (see Table 4). The most predictable suffix is -*ion*, followed by -*age* and then -*ment*. The discrepancy between observed and predicted suffixes varies according to suffix

---

12 The random forest analysis was performed using the party (Hothorn et al., 2006; Strobl et al., 2007, 2008) and permimp (Debeer & Strobl, 2020) packages in R.

pairs. The suffixes -*age* and -*ment* are more frequently confused with each other than they are both with -*ion*: 68.0% of the wrongly predicted cases for -*age* are mistaken for -*ment*, whereas 60.3% of the wrongly predicted cases for -*ment* are mistaken for -*age*. As for -*ion*, it is more frequently confused with -*ment* than with -*age*, since 66.7% of the wrongly predicted cases for -*ion* are mistaken for -*ment*. This result suggests the existence of degrees of rivalry between the three suffixes, -*age* and -*ment* competing more with each other (as being more confusable and therefore more similar) than they both compete with -*ion*, and -*ion* competing more with -*ment* than with -*age*. The gradient aspects of rivalry will be further explored in the next section.

Tab. 4: Classification of deverbal neologisms in random forest model according to their suffix. Percentages indicate the proportion of reference items predicted as -*age*, -*ion* or -*ment* (in columns). The most abundant items in each predicted group are indicated in bold.

		Reference		
		-*age*	-*ion*	-*ment*
Prediction	-*age*	**103 (63.6%)**	24 (14.3%)	51 (29.8%)
	-*ion*	12 (7.4%)	**113 (67.3%)**	24 (14.1%)
	-*ment*	47 (29.0%)	31 (18.4%)	**96 (56.1%)**

We analyzed the contribution of each semantic property to the random forest prediction by using a conditional computation of variable importance that takes into account predictor correlations (Debeer & Strobl, 2020).[13] The outcome of the analysis is presented in Figure 8. Results indicate an alternation of nominal and verbal properties in variable ranking, with some predominance of the former, three nominal properties being found among the four most important variables. Almost all properties contribute to the prediction of suffix distribution (with the exception of verb dynamicity and role of third nominal argument), which confirms both the rel-

---

[13] As noted by Debeer & Strobl (2020), there is no consensus on the exact nature of variable importance. It can be defined in a more or less marginal or partial perspective, depending on whether the impact of a predictor is evaluated independently or conditionally upon other predictors. When predicting the distribution of -*age*, -*ion* and -*ment*, the main difference between conditional and unconditional computations of variable importance concerns nominal and verbal telicity (ranked 14th and 15th in conditional estimation, but 3rd and 4th in unconditional estimation). This difference can be explained by the fact that (i) telicity in itself is an important discriminative factor between the three suffixes, and is therefore important in a marginal perspective, but (ii) telicity is one of the most correlated predictors, presumably highly redundant, and therefore minor in a partial perspective.

evance of the selected predictors and the semantic complexity of the distinction between -*age*, -*ion* and -*ment*. The most influential property is the semantic ontological type of the noun, whose impact on suffix selection is described in Section 3.4. The discriminative capacity of ontological type as opposed to relational type is not unexpected since the three suffixes compete in having mostly the same relational output. Nevertheless, the major importance of ontological type compared to all encoded properties shows that derivational semantics determines not only relations, but also referential descriptions.

Among the aspectual properties of verb-noun pairs, post-phase appears to be the most important variable. Post-phase properties of related nouns and verbs may diverge in some cases, with significant differences between the three suffixes, which explains why both are highly ranked. Verbal post-phase notably influences the distribution between -*ion* on the one hand (which selects mostly verbs with post-phase) and -*age* and -*ment* on the other (which select mostly verbs without post-phase). Nominal post-phase further distinguishes -*age* from -*ment*, as described in Section 3.5. Nominal durativity is another important aspectual variable in that it contributes to the distinction of -*ment*, which tends to form more achievement nouns than -*age* and -*ion*, as indicated in Section 3.6.

The semantic role of verbal oblique arguments is ranked as the most influential role assignment property, partly because it is one of the most uncorrelated features in the dataset. Its contribution concerns mainly locative roles, indicating predilections for base verbs that assign the roles of location (-*age*), theme (-*ment*), source (-*ion*), and destination (-*age* and -*ment*) to their oblique arguments. The semantic role of the verb subject plays an important role as well, following the preferences presented in Section 3.2 and related to the salient agentivity of -*age* base verbs, and the important causativity and patientivity of -*ion* base verbs. The role of the second argument of the noun (ranked as 3rd role assignment property) varies between -*age* and -*ion*, which select agentive and causative arguments, respectively. However, the distinctive contribution of that property concerns -*ment*. Nouns suffixed with -*ment* exhibit a relative preference for monovalent structure (in which case the second argument is absent) or for theme external arguments (especially in co-theme configuration, as in *le convergement de X avec Y* 'the converging of X with Y').

5 Gradient rivalry

As argued by Huyghe & Wauquier (2021), affix rivalry can be considered a gradient phenomenon. Affixes can be seen as more or less rivaling depending on the se-

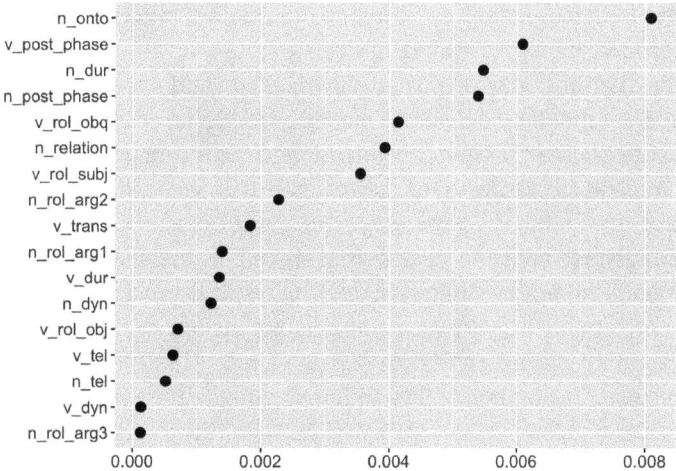

Fig. 8: Conditional importance of predictor variables for suffix selection.

mantic granularity with which morphological competition is evaluated. Furthermore, given that many affixes are polyfunctional, affix rivalry can vary according to (i) the proportion of semantic functions shared between affixes, and (ii) the frequency of lexical realization of these functions. Rivalry between -*age*, -*ion* and -*ment* is usually inferred from the fact that these suffixes can form event nouns. However, finer semantic distinctions can be made, and both the proportion of specific semantic functions the three suffixes have in common and the frequency with which they instantiate these functions may be variable. Results from Sections 3 and 4 suggest the existence of different degrees of rivalry between -*age*, -*ion* and -*ment*. In this section, we further investigate suffix similarity and gradient rivalry by using unsupervised methods, based on cluster analysis and dimensional reduction of our semantic dataset.

5.1 Cluster analysis

A way to approach gradient rivalry is to perform a cluster analysis of words with competing affixes, based on their distinctive properties. Clustering consists in grouping together similar objects of a dataset, so that objects in the same cluster are more similar than objects in different clusters.ABiding the sample of neologisms into clusters based on semantic properties and examining the distribution of the three suffixes in these clusters can provide information about their degree of similarity or dissimilarity, and therefore of rivalry.

To examine the distribution of neologisms in *-age*, *-ion* and *-ment* in semantically similar groups, we first built a distance matrix based on our dataset, using a dissimilarity measure that can handle categorical data (Gower distance).[14] Then we applied a hierarchical clustering to the matrix using a linkage method that creates clusters in such a way that the variance of the merged clusters is minimized (Ward linkage). Finally, we split the dataset into three clusters to be compared with the distribution between the three suffixes. The result is presented in Table 5. No one-to-one correspondence between suffixes and clusters can be observed, but clustering and suffix distribution are not independent (χ^2 (4, N = 501) = 145.83, $p < 2.2e\text{-}16$). Each cluster is dominated by a different suffix, although with important differences in cluster size: 59.7%, 13.8% and 26.5% of the items are grouped in the first, second and third clusters, respectively. Almost four-fifths of the *-age* items fall into the same cluster, whereas *-ion* is characterized by the existence of a cohesive distinctive subgroup containing three-fifths of its items. The specificity of *-ment* is to be mostly represented in a group in which it is not dominant (Cluster 1).

The clustering reveals similarity differences between the three suffixes. It shows the distinctiveness of *-ion* and the close rivalry of *-age* and *-ment*. Cluster 3 contains 76.1% of *-ion* items, whereas Clusters 1 and 2 include, respectively, 44.1% of *-age* and 38.1% of *-ment*, and 32.9% of *-age* and 48.1% of *-ment* —all rates being weighted by the proportion of *-age*, *-ion* and *-ment* verb-noun pairs in the sample. This result confirms that *-age* and *-ment* compete more with each other than they both do with *-ion*. More marginally, *-ion* seems to be more similar to *-ment* than to *-age*, since Cluster 3 contains more of the former than of the latter, which is in line with the prediction analysis reported in Table 4. These observations support the existence of degrees of rivalry between pairs of suffixes, *-age* and *-ment* being by far the closest rivals, followed by *-ion* and *-ment*, and then by *-age* and *-ion*.

5.2 Dimensional reduction

We used a dimensionality reduction method to visualize neighborhood relationships between items in our dataset and evaluate the degree of similarity between the three suffixes based on the encoded semantic properties. The method we used is the t-distributed stochastic neighbor embedding (t-SNE), which is based on a

---

14 The cluster analysis was performed using the cluster package in R (Maechler et al., 2021).

Tab. 5: Distribution of deverbal neologisms in clusters based on 17 properties. Percentages indicate the proportion of items per cluster for each suffix (in columns). The most abundant items in each cluster are indicated in bold.

Cluster	-age	-ion	-ment
1	**127 (78.4%)**	54 (32.2%)	116 (67.8%)
2	22 (13.6%)	13 (7.7%)	**34 (19.9%)**
3	13 (8.0%)	**101 (60.1%)**	21 (12.3%)

probabilistic interpretation of similarities between objects and aims to preserve neighborhood relationships between data points in a high-dimensional space, when reducing it to a two- or three-dimensional space (Maaten & Hinton, 2008). Two objects with a high probability of being neighbors in the high-dimensional space are expected to also have a high probability of being neighbors in the reduced dimensional space. We applied the t-SNE algorithm to our dataset,[15] and then mapped the three suffixes onto the resulting two-dimensional t-SNE plot, in order to examine the correspondence between semantically consistent groups of items and suffix distribution. The result of this operation is presented in Figure 9.

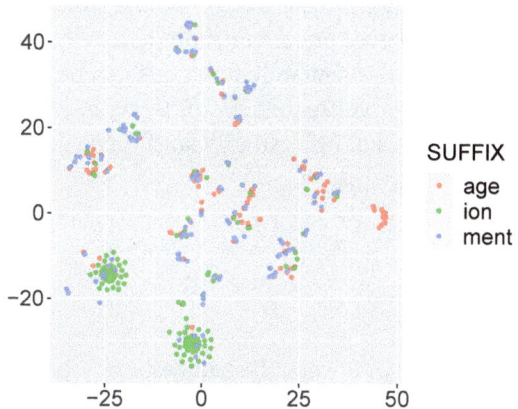

Fig. 9: t-SNE reduction of the dataset (501 deverbal neologisms analyzed for 17 properties) with suffix mapping. Each dot represents a neologism.

Two large and dense clusters including a vast majority of *-ion* items can be observed at the bottom left of the figure, showing the distinctiveness of *-ion*. A

---

[15] The t-SNE analysis was performed using the Rtsne package in R (Krijthe, 2015).

detailed analysis of these clusters reveals that they comprise nouns with variable telicity, denoting events with a stative facet, and derived from verbs that allow post-phase reading. The base verbs are transitive verbs with causative subjects in one cluster, and intransitive verbs with patient subjects in the other. The two clusters thus distinguish nominalizations in *-ion* derived from causative and anticausative constructions. The rest of the data is more scattered in the two-dimensional space and less homogeneous with respect to suffix distribution. Although *-ion* is not absent, *-age* and *-ment* are the most represented suffixes in these areas. The most indistinguishable items are nouns with non-variable telicity that denote events, possibly with a cognitive facet, and to a lesser extent artefacts, animates, cognitive objects, natural objects, phenomena, and properties. Small isolated groups can be identified, such as the ones in ([25,35],[0,10])[16] and in ([-35,-25],[10,15]), which are equally populated with *-age* and *-ment* items, corroborating the semantic proximity between the two suffixes. Two groups exclusively or almost exclusively include one suffix. A cluster of *-age* can be observed in ([40,45],[-5,5]), and a cluster of *-ment* in ([-10,0],[35,45]). When mapped onto nominal ontological types, these two groups appear to be constituted of domain-denoting and state-denoting nouns, respectively. They reveal marginal distinctive uses of each suffix.

Overall, the analysis of the dimensionally reduced dataset confirms that *-age*, *-ion* and *-ment* cannot be fully distinguished based on semantic properties of bases and derivatives. It also suggests that distinctive semantic functions can be identified for rival suffixes, but with highly variable frequencies in terms of lexical realization, which results in different degrees of dissimilarity, and conversely of rivalry, between suffixes.

6 Conclusion

In this paper, we have investigated the rivalry between the suffixes *-age*, *-ion* and *-ment* in the formation of deverbal nouns in French. We focused on the semantic aspects of the rivalry in a quantitative approach and, to control for lexicalization effects on derivational semantics, examined a sample of neologisms ending with the three suffixes.

Some suffix preferences can be observed with respect to semantic properties of base verbs and derived nouns. Different discriminative properties combine with

---

16 The numbers between commas in square brackets denote intervals, whereas the numbers between commas in parentheses denote x and y coordinates.

a variable influence on suffix selection. The most important are the semantic ontological type of the noun, the ability to have a result state interpretation for both verbs and nouns, the nominal features of durativity and telicity, and the semantic role assigned to base verb subjects and obliques. Our results support some existing claims in the literature, but also demonstrate the importance of previously unconsidered properties. In addition, the quantitative approach allowed us to evaluate discriminative properties as tendencies rather than as categorical distinctions and to estimate their respective effect on suffix selection.

The main differences observed between the three suffixes are the following. The suffix -*age* is the most oriented towards the expression of dynamicity. Nouns in -*age* mostly refer to strictly dynamic eventualities, with a distinctive ability to denote domains of activities. They tend to block result state interpretation, and -*age* is able to modify the lexical aspect of base verbs with respect to post-phase and durativity. It also selects more transitive and agentive verbs than the two other suffixes. Neologisms ending in -*ion* have a preference for the denotation of gradable changes of state. They combine eventive and stative facets, have variable telicity and possible post-phase reading. They correspond to causative and patientive verbal constructions, selecting verbs that allow for the causative-anticausative alternation. The predilection of -*ion* for change-of-state denotation is related morphologically to its affinity for verbs ending in -*iser* and to the productivity of -*isation* in contemporary French. The suffix -*ment* is the one with the least salient distinctive properties and consequently appears as the least predictable of the three suffixes. It is nevertheless characterized by the formation of more state-denoting nouns than -*age* and -*ion* and by the selection of less dynamic verbs. In addition, -*ment* selects verbs with more stimulus and theme subjects than the two other suffixes and derives more achievement nouns.

Despite these preferences, the three suffixes are not always distinguishable semantically. Considering semantic properties of bases and derivatives, it is often difficult to predict which suffix will be selected. In a number of cases, preferences are neutralized, i.e. the same kinds of verbs and nouns are involved in the derivational process, and the suffixes seem to be interchangeable. However, the neutralization capacity is not the same for all pairs of suffixes and various degrees of rivalry can be identified. In particular, our observations indicate that -*age* and -*ment* compete more with each other than they both do with -*ion*.

The fact that the properties we examined do not allow a complete differentiation of -*age*, -*ion* and -*ment* leads to various hypotheses. Other factors than those considered here could play a role in the resolution of the rivalry. Additional semantic properties could be investigated, such as the type of polysemy associated with derivational patterns, with respect to ambiguity configuration and meaning specifications. Non-semantic (e.g. phonological, morphological, stylistic, diachronic) characteristics can also be considered (Uth, 2010; Missud & Villoing, 2020). An investigation of the combined effects of these factors is necessary to provide a full account of the rivalry between the three suffixes. Nevertheless, it can also be hypothesized that affix rivalry is not ruled by fine-grained discrete discrimination, and that competing affixes have an inherent element of indistinction. Productive rival suffixes such as *-age*, *-ion* and *-ment* in French may overlap in distribution. Their coexistence in the morphological system is accompanied by semantic preferences and could ultimately favor the creation of niches (Lindsay & Aronoff, 2013; Aronoff, 2016). Due to the limited size of the sample of derivatives studied here, the preferences we observed for *-age*, *-ion*, *-ment* may not be exhaustive. Other niches than those addressed in the study could appear by taking into account larger sets of nouns (e.g. sound denotation in the case of *-ment* derivatives, such as *bruissement* 'rustling', *chuintement* 'hissing', *couinement* 'squealing', *craquement* 'crack', *crépitement* 'crackling', *crissement* 'grating', *grincement* 'grinding').

Acknowledgments

This research was supported by the Swiss National Science Foundation under grant 10001F_188782 ('The semantics of deverbal nouns in French'). We are grateful to the two anonymous reviewers and to the editors for their helpful comments on an earlier version of this paper. All remaining errors are our own.

Supplementary material

The annotation guidelines, dataset, statistical scripts and descriptive results used in this study are available online at the following URL: https://github.com/neologisms-annotation/deverbal-nouns-rivalry

Bibliography

Abusch, Dorit. 1986. *Verbs of change, causation and time*. Stanford: CSLI report.
Apothéloz, Denis. 2008. *Entrer quelques instants* vs *arriver quelques instants*: Le problème de la spécification de la durée de l'état résultant. *Verbum* 30. 199–219.
Arndt-Lappe, Sabine. 2014. Analogy in suffix rivalry: The case of English *-ity* and *-ness*. *English Language & Linguistics* 18(3). 497–548.
Aronoff, Mark. 1976. *Word formation in generative grammar*. Cambridge, MA: The MIT Press.

Aronoff, Mark. 2016. Competition and the lexicon. In Annibale Elia, Claudio Iacobini & Miriam Voghera (eds.), *Livelli di analisi e fenomeni di interfaccia. Atti del XLVII Congresso Internazionale di Studi della Società di Linguistica Italiana (Fasciano, Salerno 26-28 settembre 2013)*, 39–51. Roma: Bulzoni Editore.

Asher, Nicholas. 2011. *Lexical meaning in context: A web of words*. Cambridge: Cambridge University Press.

Baayen, R Harald, Anna Endresen, Laura A Janda, Anastasia Makarova & Tore Nesset. 2013. Making choices in Russian: Pros and cons of statistical methods for rival forms. *Russian Linguistics* 37(3). 253–291.

Bertinetto, Pier Marco & Mario Squartini. 1995. An attempt at defining the class of gradual completion verbs. In Pier Marco Bertinetto, Valentina Bianchi, James Higginbotham & Mario Squartini (eds.), *Temporal reference aspect and actionality 1: Semantics and syntactic perspectives*, 11–26. Torino: Rosenberg and Sellier.

Bonami, Olivier & Juliette Thuilier. 2019. A statistical approach to rivalry in lexeme formation. French *-iser* and *-ifier*. *Word structure* 12(1). 4–41.

Breiman, Leo. 2001. Random forests. *Machine Learning* 45(1). 5–32.

Byrt, Ted, Janet Bishop & John B Carlin. 1993. Bias, prevalence and kappa. *Journal of Clinical Epidemiology* 46(5). 423–429.

Cartier, Emmanuel. 2018. *De l'extraction d'information à la représentation sémantique*. Paris: Université Paris 13 Habilitation dissertation.

Copestake, Ann & Ted Briscoe. 1995. Semi-productive polysemy and sense extension. *Journal of Semantics* 12(1). 15–67.

Corbin, Danielle. 1987. *Morphologie dérivationnelle et structuration du lexique*. Tübingen: Max Niemeyer Verlag.

Cruse, D. Alan. 1995. Polysemy and related phenomena from a cognitive linguistic viewpoint. In Patrick St Dizier & Evelyne Viegas (eds.), *Computational lexical semantics*, 33–49. Cambridge: Cambridge University Press.

Dal, Georgette, Nabil Hathout, Stéphanie Lignon, Fiammetta Namer & Ludovic Tanguy. 2018. Toile *versus* dictionnaires: Les nominalisations du français en *-age* et en *-ment*. In Franck Neveu, Bernard Harmegnies, Linda Hriba & Sophie Prévost (eds.), *Congrès Mondial de Linguistique Française - CMLF 2018*, Paris: Institut de Linguistique Française. https://doi.org/10.1051/shsconf/20184608003.

Dal, Georgette & Fiammetta Namer. 2015. La fréquence en morphologie: Pour quels usages? *Langages* 197(1). 47–68.

Debaty-Luca, Thierry. 1986. *Théorie fonctionnelle de la suffixation (appliquée principalement au français et au wallon du centre)*. Genève: Librairie Droz.

Debeer, Dries & Carolin Strobl. 2020. Conditional permutation importance revisited. *BMC Bioinformatics* 21(1). 1–30.

Dowty, David R. 1979. *Word meaning and Montague grammar: The semantics of verbs and times in generative semantics and in Montague's PTQ*. Dordrecht: D. Reidel Publishing Company.

Dressler, Wolfgang U, Lavinia Merlini Barbaresi, Sonja Schwaiger, Jutta Ransmayr, Sabine Sommer-Lolei & Katharina Korecky-Kröll. 2019. Rivalry and lack of blocking among italian and german diminutives in adult and child language. In Franz Rainer, Francesco Gardani, Wolfgang U. Dressler & Hans Christian Luschützky (eds.), *Competition in inflection and word-formation*, 123–143. Cham: Springer.

Dubois, Jean. 1962. *Étude sur la dérivation suffixale en français moderne et contemporain: Essai d'interprétation des mouvements observés dans le domaine de la morphologie des mots construits*. Paris: Larousse.

Dubois, Jean & Françoise Dubois-Charlier. 1997. *Les verbes français*. Paris: Larousse.

Dölling, Johannes. 2020. Systematic polysemy. In Daniel Gutzmann, Lisa Matthewson, Cécile Meier, Hotze Rullmann & Thomas Ede Zimmermann (eds.), *The Wiley Blackwell companion to semantics*, 1–27. Hoboken, NJ: John Wiley & Sons.

Ferret, Karen & Florence Villoing. 2015. French N-*age* instrumentals: Semantic properties of the base verb. *Morphology* 25. 473–496.

Filip, Hana. 2012. Lexical aspect. In Robert I. Binnick (ed.), *The Oxford handbook of tense and aspect*, 721–751. Oxford: Oxford University Press.

Flaux, Nelly & Danièle Van de Velde. 2000. *Les noms en français: Esquisse de classement*. Paris: Editions Ophrys.

Fleischman, Suzanne. 1980. *The French suffix -age: Its genesis, internal growth, and diffusion*. Ann Arbor, MI: University Microfilms International.

Fradin, Bernard. 2011. Remarks on state-denoting nominalizations. *Recherches Linguistiques de Vincennes* 40. 73–99.

Fradin, Bernard. 2016. L'interprétation des nominalisations en N-*age* et N-*ment* en français. In Franz Rainer, Michela Russo & Fernando Sánchez Miret (eds.), *Actes du XXVIIe Congrès International de Linguistique et Philologie Romanes*, 53–66. Nancy: ATILF.

Fradin, Bernard. 2019. Competition in derivation: What can we learn from French doublets in -*age* and -*ment*? In Franz Rainer, Francesco Gardani, Wolfgang U. Dressler & Hans Christian Luschützky (eds.), *Competition in inflection and word-formation*, 67–93. Berlin: Springer.

Gardani, Francesco, Franz Rainer & Hans Christian Luschützky. 2019. Competition in morphology: A historical outline. In Franz Rainer, Francesco Gardani, Wolfgang U. Dressler & Hans Christian Luschützky (eds.), *Competition in inflection and word-formation*, 3–36. Cham: Springer.

Godard, Danièle & Jacques Jayez. 1996. Types nominaux et anaphores: Le cas des objets et des événements. *Cahiers Chronos* 1. 41–58.

Haas, Pauline, Lucie Barque, Richard Huyghe & Delphine Tribout. 2022. Pour une classification sémantique des noms en français appuyée sur des tests linguistiques. *Journal of French Language Studies* 1–30.

Haas, Pauline, Richard Huyghe & Rafael Marín. 2008. Du verbe au nom: Calques et décalages aspectuels. In Jacques Durand, Benoît Habert & Bernard Laks (eds.), *Congrès Mondial de Linguistique Française - CMLF 2008*, 2051–2065. Paris: Institut de Linguistique Française.

Haas, Pauline & Anne Jugnet. 2013. De l'existence des prédicats d'achèvements. *Lingvisticæ Investigationes* 36(1). 56–89.

Hathout, Nabil & Fiammetta Namer. 2014. Démonette, a French derivational morpho-semantic network. *Linguistic Issues in Language Technology* 11(5). 208–219.

Hay, Jennifer, Christopher Kennedy & Beth Levin. 1999. Scalar structure underlies telicity in 'degree achievements'. In Tanya Matthews & Devon Strolovitch (eds.), *Proceedings of SALT 9*, 127–144. Ithaca, NY: CLC Publications.

Hothorn, Torsten, Peter Buehlmann, Sandrine Dudoit, Annette Molinaro & Mark Van Der Laan. 2006. Survival ensembles. *Biostatistics* 7(3). 355–373.

Huyghe, Richard. 2015. Les typologies nominales: présentation. *Langue Française* (1). 5–27.

Huyghe, Richard. 2021. Building a lexical database to investigate the semantics of French deverbal nouns. *Resources and Tools for Derivational Morphology (DeriMo 2021)* 21.

Huyghe, Richard & Marine Wauquier. 2021. Distributional semantics insights on agentive suffix rivalry in French. *Word Structure* 14(3). 354–391.

Kawaletz, Lea & Ingo Plag. 2015. Predicting the semantics of English nominalizations: A frame-based analysis of *-ment* suffixation. In Laurie Bauer, Lívia Körtvélyessy & Pavol Štekauer (eds.), *Semantics of complex words*, 289–319. Berlin: Springer.

Kelling, Carmen. 2001. Agentivity and suffix selection. In Miriam Butt & Tracy H. King (eds.), *Proceedings LFG 2001*, 147–162. Stanford, CA: CSLI Publications.

Kipper-Schuler, Karin. 2005. *Verbnet: A broad-coverage, comprehensive verb lexicon*. Philadelphia, PA: University of Pennsylvania dissertation.

Kleiber, Georges. 1999. *Problèmes de sémantique: La polysémie en question(s)*. Villeneuve d'Ascq: Presses Universitaires du Septentrion.

Krijthe, Jesse H. 2015. *Rtsne: T-distributed stochastic neighbor embedding using barnes-hut implementation*. https://github.com/jkrijthe/Rtsne. R package version 0.15.

Landis, J Richard & Gary G Koch. 1977. The measurement of observer agreement for categorical data. *Biometrics* 33(1). 159–174.

Levshina, Natalia. 2020. Conditional inference trees and random forests. In Magali Paquot & Stefan Th. Gries (eds.), *A practical handbook of corpus linguistics*, 611–643. Berlin: Springer.

Lignon, Stéphanie, Fiammetta Namer & Florence Villoing. 2014. De l'agglutination à la triangulation ou comment expliquer certaines séries morphologiques. In Franck Neveu, Peter Blumenthal, Linda Hriba, Annette Gerstenberg, Judith Meinschaefer & Sophie Prévost (eds.), *Congrès Mondial de Linguistique Française - CMLF 2014*, 1813–1835. Paris: Institut de Linguistique Française.

Lindsay, Mark & Mark Aronoff. 2013. Natural selection in self-organizing morphological systems. In Nabil Hathout, Fabio Montermini & Jesse Tseng (eds.), *Morphology in Toulouse: Selected proceedings of Décembrettes 7*, 133–153. München: LINCOM Europe.

Lüdtke, Jens. 1978. *Prädikative Nominalisierungen mit Suffixen im Katalanischen, Spanischen und Französischen*. Tübingen: Niemeyer.

Maaten, Laurens van der & Geoffrey Hinton. 2008. Visualizing data using t-SNE. *Journal of Machine Learning Research* 9(11). 2579–2605.

Maechler, Martin, Peter Rousseeuw, Anja Struyf, Mia Hubert & Kurt Hornik. 2021. *cluster: Cluster analysis basics and extensions*. https://CRAN.R-project.org/package=cluster. R package version 2.1.2.

Martin, Fabienne. 2010. The semantics of eventive suffixes in French. In Monika Rathert & Artemis Alexiadou (eds.), *The semantics of nominalizations across languages and frameworks*, 109–141. Berlin: De Gruyter.

McHugh, Mary L. 2012. Interrater reliability: The kappa statistic. *Biochemia Medica* 22(3). 276–282.

Missud, Alice & Florence Villoing. 2020. The morphology of rival *-ion*, *-age* and *-ment* selected verbal bases. *Lexique* 26. 29–52.

Naccarato, Chiara. 2019. Agentive (para)synthetic compounds in Russian: A quantitative study of rival constructions. *Morphology* 29(1). 1–30.

New, Boris, Christophe Pallier, Marc Brysbaert & Ludovic Ferrand. 2004. Lexique 2: A new French lexical database. *Behavior Research Methods, Instruments, & Computers* 36(3). 516–524.

Petukhova, Volhaand & Harry Bunt. 2008. LIRICS semantic role annotation: Design and evaluation of a set of data categories. In Nicoletta Calzolari, Khalid Choukri, Bente Maegaard,

Joseph Mariani, Jan Odijk, Stelios Piperidis & Daniel Tapias (eds.), *Proceedings of the Sixth International Conference on Language Resources and Evaluation (LREC'08)*, 39–45. Marrakech, Morocco: European Language Resources Association (ELRA).
Piñón, Christopher. 1997. Achievements in an event semantics. In Aaron Lawson & Eun Cho (eds.), *Proceedings of SALT 7*, 273–296. Ithaca, NY: CLC Publications.
Piñón, Christopher. 1999. Durative adverbials for result states. In Sonya Bird, Andrew Carnie, Jason D. Haugen & Peter Norquest (eds.), *WCCFL18: Proceedings of the 18th West Coast Conference on Formal Linguistics*, 420–433. Somerville, MA: Cascadilla Press.
Plag, Ingo. 1999. *Morphological productivity: Structural constraints in English derivation*. Berlin: De Gruyter.
Pustejovsky, James. 1995. *The generative lexicon*. Cambridge, MA: MIT Press.
Rothstein, Susan. 2004. *Structuring events: A study in the semantics of lexical aspect*. Oxford: Blackwell Publishing.
Rothstein, Susan. 2008. Two puzzles for a theory of lexical aspect: Semelfactives and degree achievements. In Johannes Dölling, Tatjana Heyde-Zybatow & Martin Shäfer (eds.), *Event structures in linguistic form and interpretation*, 175–198. Berlin: De Gruyter.
Sagot, Benoît. 2010. The Lefff, a freely available and large-coverage morphological and syntactic lexicon for French. In Nicoletta Calzolari, Khalid Choukri, Bente Maegaard, Joseph Mariani, Jan Odijk, Stelios Piperidis, Mike Rosner & Daniel Tapias (eds.), *Proceedings of the seventh international conference on language resources and evaluation (LREC'10)*, Valletta, Malta: European Language Resources Association (ELRA).
Schulte, Marion. 2015. Polysemy and synonymy in derivational affixation: A case study of the English suffixes -*age* and -*ery*. *Morphology* 25(4). 371–390.
Schäfer, Roland. 2015. Processing and querying large web corpora with the COW14 architecture. In Piotr Bański, Hanno Biber, Evelyn Breiteneder, Marc Kupietz, Harald Lüngen & Andreas Witt (eds.), *Proceedings of Challenges in the Management of Large Corpora 3 (CMLC-3)*, Lancaster: IDS.
Schäfer, Roland & Felix Bildhauer. 2012. Building large corpora from the web using a new efficient tool chain. In Nicoletta Calzolari, Khalid Choukri, Thierry Declerck, Mehmet Ugur Dogan, Bente Maegaard, Joseph Mariani, Jan Odijk & Stelios Piperidis (eds.), *Proceedings of the Eight International Conference on Language Resources and Evaluation (LREC'12)*, 486–493. Istanbul, Turkey: European Language Resources Association (ELRA).
Strobl, Carolin, Anne-Laure Boulesteix, Thomas Kneib, Thomas Augustin & Achim Zeileis. 2008. Conditional variable importance for random forests. *BMC Bioinformatics* 9(1). 1–11.
Strobl, Carolin, Anne-Laure Boulesteix, Achim Zeileis & Torsten Hothorn. 2007. Bias in random forest variable importance measures: Illustrations, sources and a solution. *BMC Bioinformatics* 8(25). 1–21.
Tagliamonte, Sali A & R Harald Baayen. 2012. Models, forests, and trees of York English: *Was/were* variation as a case study for statistical practice. *Language Variation and Change* 24(2). 135–78.
Uth, Melanie. 2010. The rivalry of French -*ment* and -*age* from a diachronic perspective. In Monika Rathert & Artemis Alexiadou (eds.), *The semantics of nominalizations across languages and frameworks*, 215–244. Berlin: De Gruyter.
Varvara, Rossella. 2020. Constraints on nominalizations: Investigating the productivity domain of Italian -*mento* and -*zione*. *Zeitschrift für Wortbildung/Journal of Word Formation* 4(2). 78–99.
Vendler, Zeno. 1967. *Linguistics in philosophy*. Ithaca, NY: Cornell University Press.

Wauquier, Marine. 2020. *Confrontation des procédés dérivationnels et des catégories sémantiques dans les modèles distributionnels*. Toulouse: Université Toulouse Jean Jaurès dissertation.

Zwanenburg, Wiecher. 1984. Word formation and meaning. *Quaderni di Semantica* 5(1). 130–142.

Sven Kotowski & Martin Schäfer
Quantifying semantic relatedness across base verbs and derivatives: English *out*-prefixation

Abstract: Most authors on derivational semantics agree that the meaning of complex words builds on components contributed by the base, components contributed by the word formation process, as well as contextual knowledge components. There is far less agreement on how these components interact or on their relative contributions. In this paper, we approach the question of relative contributions by looking at relatedness between bases, between derivatives, as well as between bases and derivatives. We use the English scalar-comparative verb prefix *out-* as a test case. We show that classes of bases serve as predictors for the resolution of systematically underspecified parts of the semantics of *out-*derivatives. By means of distributional similarity measures, we also show that the word formation process's derivatives exhibit a high degree of uniformity relative to the similarities between other components of the process. Finally, distributional measures for four further prefixes suggest that this rich contribution of the affix is peculiar to scalar-comparative *out-* rather than a characteristic of prefixation in general.

Keywords: verb semantics, English prefixation, distributional measures, quantitative semantics

1 Introduction

This article deals with the relative importance of base semantics and affix semantics in English *out*-prefixation. All accounts of derivational semantics agree that the meaning of complex words is in some way derived via an interplay of the meaning of the base, the meaning introduced by the word formation process, and contextual or extra-linguistic information (see e.g. Rainer et al. 2014, Lieber 2004). Also, it is common ground in the literature that the derivatives of any productive derivational process share a semantic core, as can be seen for example in the notions of 'semantic coherence' (Aronoff 1976), 'systematic form-meaning correspondences' (Haspelmath & Sims 2013), or 'lexical relatedness' (Spencer 2013). However, lexical relatedness can come in various guises, and so can the prominence of the semantic contribution of different word formation processes relative to the contribution of their bases.

As argued by Spencer (2010a; 2010b; 2013), lexical relatedness is a continuum. It ranges from closely related word forms with minimal morphosyntactic differences ('canonical inflection' such as agreement morphology on verbs; *to draw → draws*) to more distantly related lexemes with differences in form, syntactic category, and semantic make-up ('canonical derivation', as in *to draw → drawable*).

In between these poles, we find less clear-cut categories. These include transpositional operations, i.e. syntactic category change with little or no semantic contribution (such as action nominalizations of the kind *to arrive → arrival*, as well as semantic shifts without formal marking (such as conversion phenomena of the kind *to dump → a dump*). In the following, we will focus on semantic relatedness in the realm of processes that are clearly derivational.

The general perspective on lexical relations just sketched is obviously process-related, i.e. it primarily looks at the relatedness of a given base and its derivative. However, the notion can also be extended to the relatedness between bases of a given morphological process or between its derivatives. The idea that the products of a derivational process are semantically related is a truism. If there was no discernible meaning shared by a set of derivatives, and if this meaning could not be attributed to the derivational process, we would not speak of such a process in the first place. Consider, for example, the commonalities between deverbal *-ible/-able*-adjectives in English. The vast majority of these adjectives indicate the capacity of the base verb's PATIENT/THEME argument to undergo the process denoted by that verb (e.g. *downloadable, searchable*). Quite evidently, the shared modal meaning component is a fairly specific product of *-ible/-able*-suffixation, rather than of the bases. At the same time, for this output to show such coherence, *-ible/-able* imposes the restriction that its base verbs license PATIENT/THEME arguments (see Plag 2003, 94f.; Bauer et al. 2013, 307f.).

However, morphological processes differ with respect to how specific and how uniform their meaning contributions are (see e.g. Koefoed & van Marle 2000; Wauquier 2020, ch.8). For example, the English person/participant-deriving suffix *-er* gives rise to various semantic categories, such as AGENT, EXPERIENCER, STIMULUS, INSTRUMENT, LOCATION, MEASURE etc. As a consequence of this multiplicity of meaning, the semantics of *-er* is difficult to pin down, rather underspecified, and highly dependent on the meaning of the base (Bauer et al. 2013, ch.11; Plag 2003, 89; Rappaport Hovav & Levin 1992). As shown in several studies on derivational polysemy, semantic classes of bases often predict or narrow down the possible readings of derivatives (see e.g. Aronoff & Cho 2001; Kawaletz 2021; Lieber 2016; Plag et al. 2018; Plag et al. 2023).

In this article, we build on the notion of relatedness and investigate the semantics of the English verbal comparative prefix *out-*, as in *to outsing s.o.* (i.e., roughly, to defeat s.o. by singing better/louder/more frequently etc.). We present four studies that quantitatively approach semantic relatedness between derivatives, between bases, and between bases and derivatives of this word formation process. First, we make use of traditional corpus studies that tap into the role of the base in the resolution of systematically underspecified elements of meaning in derivatives. Second, we employ distributional semantic measures and operationalize relatedness as distributional similarity across bases, between bases and derivatives, and across derivatives. Finally, we contrast the distribution of *out-* to that of several other English prefixes. The picture emerging from these studies is that comparative *out-* is fairly rich in semantic content and that derivatives show a relatively high degree of semantic relatedness to each other, both in comparison to the relatedness to their bases and in comparison to other prefixes. At the same time, we also provide quantitative evidence for base–derivative relatedness and show that both base lemmas as well as base verb classes are informative for spelling out underspecified meaning components.

The following section introduces the main characteristics of *out*-prefixation, motivates the studies, and provides an outline of the paper.

2 Background and objectives

2.1 Characteristics of comparative *out*-prefixation

A number of studies deal with comparative *out*-verbs, partly disagreeing on fundamental questions (see in particular Ahn 2022; Kotowski 2021; Talmy 2000; Tolskaya 2014). This section largely confines itself to uncontroversial properties of the word formation process. It shows why comparative *out-* is a highly interesting testing ground for exploring the questions of semantic relatedness, and thereby motivates the studies to follow.

Synchronically, comparative *out-* is among the most productive locative prefixes in English (see Schröder 2011), and all claims on base restrictions for this process have been shown to be far too restrictive (Kotowski 2021). Although there seems to be a preponderance of activity and semelfactive base verbs (as in *to outrun s.o.* and *to outfart s.o.*, respectively), verbs from all aspectual classes are attested as bases, such as stative verbs (e.g. *to outweigh s.o.*), achievements (e.g. *to outspot s.o.*), or change-of-state/accomplishment verbs (e.g. *to outcrush s.o.*). Comparative *out-* is also one of the few clearly category-changing prefixes in English and regularly occurs with nominal (e.g. *to outtechnology s.o.*) and adjectival bases (e.g. *to outabsurd s.o.*). At least prima facie, *out-*'s bases thus do not seem to show systematic lexical relatedness.

In contrast, all derivatives exhibit a number of strikingly homogeneous features, irrespective of the respective base. First, all derivatives have a comparative meaning component. (1-a) is a fairly typical attestation, and the context clearly indicates the relevant scalar meaning component for *outsing*: the subject argument singing louder than the object argument, i.e. the lead vocalist. Interrelated with their comparative semantics, *out*-verbs are syntactically invariably transitive and, passive sentences aside, occur in frames of the kind [NP$_{subject}$–*out*-X–NP$_{object}$]. (1-b) shows the oddness of *out*-forms in intransitive contexts.

(1)   a.   Good vocal control is essential, a backing singer must not try to **'outsing' the lead vocalist** [...] it is important for singers who have strong voices to remember to back off the microphone a bit (iWeb)
       b.   ??He outsang.

Second, this syntactic configuration is a clear reflex of argument structural effects (see Haspelmath & Sims 2013, ch.11; Wunderlich 2012 on morphology inducing changes of argument structure). For example, the lemma SING occurs either as a one-place verb (e.g. *He sang*), or as a two-place verb with a THEME-argument that denotes some form of song or tune (e.g. *He sang a song*). (2-a) is odd, however, as a vocalist cannot easily be construed as the THEME of a singing-event. In contrast, the derived lemma OUTSING does not readily allow *a song* as direct object, in particular not as the THEME of a singing event, as indicated by (2-b).

(2)   a. ??He sang the lead vocalist.
       b. ??He outsang a song.

The example in (3-a) shows *out-* to have the same argument structural effect on a causative change-of-state (and thus necessarily transitive) base verb such as *to crush sth.*, as the object argument is not interpreted as the PATIENT of a crushing-event. Further, the denominal example in (3-b) illustrates that argument structure is also created in the case of base forms that do not readily support arguments on their own, such as *technology*.

(3)   a.   ...that woman has toes that could **outcrush a boa constrictor**![1]
       b.   Global big data competitors can **out-technology you** [...] (iWeb)

---

[1] Bishop, David. 2006. Honour be Damned. Black Flame Publishing. Retrieved from http.//books.google.com, n.p.

Thus, comparative *out-* creates its own argument structure. It is applicative in the sense that it adds an object-argument or induces a change of thematic role of this argument. However, the specific nature of the introduced argument structure is contested. Let us very briefly sketch the two alternative analyses in the literature with the help of example (1-a). The first analysis would treat *outsing the lead vocalist* as a pure comparison between two distinct singing events (see e.g. Ahn 2022, Tolskaya 2014). Thus, *the lead vocalist* functions as the mere threshold surpassed by the subject argument regarding some event property (in this case, the loudness of singing events). The second kind of analysis understands *out-*prefixation as a competition construction that introduces a causative macro-event (see Kotowski 2021; Marchand 1969; McIntyre 2003). On this treatment, subject arguments are CAUSERS, i.e. *out-* introduces a further change in argument structure, while object arguments such as the *the lead vocalist* are licensed by a resultative sub-event. Conceptually, these object-arguments 'lose out' or are surpassed in a contest described by the morphological base (in the case of (1-a), by singing less loudly).

Either way, *out-*derivatives have an event structure that differs from the structure of the event denoted by the base. Simplified schematic semantic templates for the purely comparative approach and for the causative approach are given in (4) and (5), respectively.

(4) $\text{SCALAR PROPERTY}(\text{EVENT}_1(\text{PARTICIPANT}_1)) \xrightarrow{\text{exceed}}$
$\text{SCALAR PROPERTY}(\text{EVENT}_2(\text{PARTICIPANT}_2))$

(5) $[\text{SCALAR PROPERTY}(\text{EVENT}_1(\text{PARTICIPANT}_1)) \xrightarrow{\text{exceed}}$
$\text{SCALAR PROPERTY}(\text{EVENT}_2(\text{PARTICIPANT}_2))] \xrightarrow{\text{cause}}$
$\text{DEFEATED/SURPASSED}(\text{PARTICIPANT}_2)$

On either of these decompositional analyses, comparative *out-* can be regarded as a semantically rich word formation process, whose derivatives denote events of ontologically different types than the events denoted by their respective bases. This can be illustrated via a comparison to the far less productive spatial sense of *out-*.[2] Consider the derivative OUTHAUL, which is attested with both senses. In the comparative sense in (6-a), two eventualities or properties are compared (roughly, ships regarding their load capacities), and the object argument (*indus-*

---

2 Terminologically, we will always refer to the comparative sense unless indicated otherwise, i.e. we will always use 'spatial *out-*' when referring to the spatial sense. We will not deal with the historical relationship between spatial and comparative *out-* in this article and will remain agnostic regarding the question of whether they are analyzed best as two senses of one prefix or as two divergent word-formation processes; see Bauer et al. (2013, 347) for some discussion.

trial ships) is not interpreted as the THEME of a hauling-event. Rather, either of the two interpretations just sketched applies, i.e. analyses as an exceeding event or as a causation event. In contrast, the spatial prefix sense in (6-b) modifies the motion event encoded by the base by bounding its path, and the derivative still denotes a hauling-event (see e.g. Rappaport Hovav & Levin 2001, 780ff.; Zwarts 2008 on directed motion and event complexity). Unsurprisingly then, as in (6-c), the verbal base allows for the same argument structure as the form prefixed with spatial *out-*.

(6) a. With a great base cargohold and four low slots, it easily **outhauls all other racial Tech I industrial ships** at Industrial IV... (iWeb)
   b. "haulback" means the cable used to **outhaul the rigging** or grapple when yarding... (iWeb)
   c. I can vividly recall helping him on Sunday mornings to **haul the rope** that rang the church bell (iWeb)

In total, comparative *out*-prefixation thus seems semantically both rich and uniform: it introduces fairly predictable argument and event structures, and contributes comparative semantics. This latter component, however, remains systematically underspecified, as the scalar dimensions required for any form of comparison are not fixed on the lexical level (see Kennedy & McNally 2005; Solt 2015 for overviews of scalarity). Unlike in (1-a), for example, singing-events in (7) are compared along the dimension of QUALITY rather than LOUDNESS, as can be gathered from the underlined explication.

(7) ...you can't deny [LBT's] vocal abilities [...] nobody out there can **outsing them** from a technical standpoint. (iWeb)

The ambiguity of *out*-derivatives is not accidental, as the majority of verbs do not encode a single dimension (arguably, degree achievements such as *to heat* or *to widen* do; see Kennedy & Levin 2008). This does not mean that derivatives are systematically polysemous in the narrow sense. Rather, the morphological process introduces comparison but typically leaves underspecified the domain to which said comparison is applied. The ambiguity at hand is thus a matter of indeterminacy or vagueness (on indeterminacy, see Maienborn 2019; see also Mititelu et al. 2023).

At the same time, there is a strong intuition that an anything-goes approach to comparison in *out*-attestations is misguided. An immediate question that arises concerns the extent to which bases nevertheless determine, constrain, or help to identify possible scalar dimensions (see in particular Ahn 2019). The idea that the semantics of the base is crucial for dimension resolution is backed up by asymmetric comparisons. Consider the item in (8), which clearly suggests a contest between an eagle that is flying and Mr. Paxton who is running. The example thus nicely illustrates that there are always at least two distinct sub-events in *out*-prefixation contexts. In (8), however, and unlike in the examples above, we deal with events of different kinds, which nonetheless allow for comparison (while the scalar dimension, possibly SPEED or DISTANCE, remains undetermined).

(8) "I wasn't going to run," Mr. Paxton said later after the game. "I figured I'm not going to **outrun an eagle**, so we might as well just see what happens." (forbes.com)

As argued by Kotowski (2021), it is the common conceptual nature of, or similarity between, items from the same lexical or ontological class that allows for asymmetric comparisons in the first place. Building on the example in (8), the reasoning can be summarized as follows: events of motion in space can be measured out along several parameters, some of which are salient, such as SPEED or DISTANCE (see e.g. Herweg 2020). Both running- and flying-events are subkinds of motion events. Given this shared property, they can be compared in general, and they also suggest salient dimensions for comparison (such as SPEED or DISTANCE). In contrast, we would not expect *out*-attestations to give rise to comparisons between, say, running- and singing-events.

2.2 Outline and objectives of studies

The objective of this paper is to empirically test several of the predictions derived from the characteristics of comparative *out*-prefixation just sketched. The four studies we present below aim at quantifying the contributions of the morphological base as well as the contributions of the word-formation process to the semantics of *out*-derivatives. Our approach across all of these studies is grounded in measures of semantic relatedness. Both the data and their coding (for Studies 1 & 2) as well as the code used in the distributional studies (Studies 3 & 4) are available at https://doi.org/10.6084/m9.figshare.20367735.v1.

In our first study, we are interested in a specific aspect of semantic relatedness of base and derivative. We quantify the role of different semantic classes of base verbs for resolving the underspecification of scalar dimensions in *out*-derivatives. To this end, we cull data from iWeb (Davies 2018) for all base lemmas from seven different VerbNet classes (Kipper et al. 2008), i.e. from classes whose respective members share semantic and conceptual structure. We annotate the data for contextual cues in order to find out whether base classes predict dominant scalar dimensions or distinct dimension profiles in derivatives.

The second study is very similar in nature to the first one, but focuses on individual base lemmas rather than classes of lemmas. We investigate the role of the individual lemma for resolving dimensional ambiguity in *out*-derivatives. Again using iWeb, a total of roughly 1,000 tokens from 12 base verb lemmas are annotated in their sentential contexts in order to investigate whether the class-based behavior established in Study 1 is reflected on the level of individual base verbs. In Study 2, we also take into consideration dimensionally unspecified tokens and thus quantify non-resolved underspecification of derivatives. By doing so, we address the question of how prominent specific interpretations of comparison are in the first place.

Our third study takes a more holistic approach to relatedness and analyzes the semantic coherence of *out*-derivatives relative to the semantic coherence of bases as well as relative to the relatedness of bases and derivatives. We make use of the ukWaC web corpus (Baroni et al. 2009), expanded by using derivatives from iWeb, and employ distributional semantic measures (see Boleda 2020) for the same verbs that we used in Study 2. We operationalize coherence as cosine similarities between the vectors of different components of the morphological process. Building on the hypothesis that *out-* is a semantically rich word-formation process with a fairly uniform output, we assume that creating argument/event structure and adding comparative semantics are reflected in distributional measures. We therefore expect relatively high degrees of similarity between *out*-derivatives when compared to the similarities between bases or between bases and derivatives.

Finally, our fourth study establishes whether the patterns of similarity found for *out-* are peculiar in the grander scheme of English prefixation, or whether these are a common feature of verb-to-verb derivation in English. To this end, we compare the distributional behavior of *out-* established in Study 3 with similarity measures for four further prefixes (spatial senses of *over-* and *out-*, reversative *un-*, and iterative *re-*). All of these additional processes presumably differ from *out*-prefixation regarding how rich their respective semantic contributions are: derivatives (mostly) encode the same event types as their bases and show no or weaker argument structural effects than *out-*. We therefore hypothesize that *out*-derivatives show more pronounced semantic coherence than the derivatives of the other prefixes investigated.

Tab. 1: Properties of the seven VerbNet classes used in Study 1 (see Kipper et al. 2008).

VerbNet-class	Description	No. of members (examples)
RUN	manner of movement	159 (*crawl, creep, run* etc.)
PERFORMANCE	performance as effected object	29 (*chant, play, dance* etc.)
EXIST	existence at some location	26 (*dwell, exist, live* etc.)
CARRY	caused accompanied motion	20 (*carry, drag, draw* etc.)
HIT	bringing an entity into contact with another entity	40 (*bang, hit, jab* etc.)
SPRAY	covering of surfaces	48 (*baste, sprinkle, splash* etc.)
SOUND EMISSION	emission of sound	129 (*babble, cry, rap* etc.)

3 Study 1: Predicting scalar dimensions via base verb classes

3.1 Rationale

In this study, we are interested in quantifying the role of the base verb class for the resolution of underspecification in derivatives. We probe the connection between base verb classes and the specific scalar dimensions encoded in *out*-derivatives:

Research question 1a (RQ1a): Do semantic classes of base verbs show preferences for specific (sets of) scalar dimensions in the *out*-derivatives based on members of this class? Can we predict unique distributions or profiles via class membership?

In order to answer RQ1a, we culled a large sample of *out*-formations from iWeb with bases from members of seven VerbNet classes. VerbNet is a lexical data base that categorizes verbs into semantic classes based on their compatibility with syntactic frames and semantic argument specifications. VerbNet classes have been successfully employed as partial predictors for polysemy patterns in English nominalizations (see Plag et al. 2018; Kawaletz 2021; Plag et al. 2023). In this study, we use the classes introduced in Table 1.

The classes in Table 1 were chosen for three reasons. First, all the classes needed to be large enough (at least 20 and up to 159 members). Second, previous corpus searches had shown that several of their members are attested as bases to *out*-derivatives. Third, we wanted the classes to be conceptually fairly different and therefore made sure that no two classes are from the same superordinate class. This ensured that the events the respective members of our classes encode differ in salient properties.

Ambiguity of verbs in VerbNet, including both homonymy and polysemy, is characterized by multiple class membership. For example, SING is cross-listed in three classes, as shown in Table 2. As different verbs show different degrees of ambiguity, VerbNet classes also encode different levels of ambiguity once we generalize over their respective sets of members. In order to assess the influence of ambiguity on the dimensions encoded in *out*-contexts, we therefore also investigate multiple class membership of base forms along the lines of RQ1b.

Tab. 2: The different VerbNet classes in which *to sing* is listed.

Example	VerbNet-class	Syntax/argument structure
Susan sang to the children.	MANNER-SPEAKING	AGENT V {+$_{DIRECT}$} RECIPIENT
Sandy sang a song.	PERFORMANCE	AGENT V THEME
The street sang with horns.	SOUND EMISSION	LOCATION V {with} THEME

RQ1b: Does the degree of ambiguity of the members of a base class predict how informative this class is regarding the scalar dimensions encoded in *out*-derivatives?

3.2 Methodology

All attestations used in Study 1 were culled from iWeb via its web interface (see https://www.english-corpora.org/iweb/). Queries were performed individually for all potential base verbs. An example query string for the base lemma RUN is provided in (9) and returns (among nonpertinent hits) all possible word forms of the lemma OUTRUN, both with and without hyphens, i.e.: *outrun, out-run, outruns, out-runs, outran, out-ran, outrunning,* and *out-running.* Mutatis mutandis, this search was performed for all verbs from the VerbNet classes described in Table 1 above.

(9) outrun*|out-run*|outran|out-ran

A total of 451 searches were performed (corresponding to the total number of verbs in all seven classes), which yielded 104 different *out*-verb types, i.e. 104 different base verbs as input to *out-*. We did not distinguish between hyphenated and non-hyphenated examples. For example, *outrunning* and *out-running* were counted as tokens of the same lemma OUTRUN. For lemmas with more than 100 pertinent hits, we selected the first 100 hits and included different word forms for a given lemma relative to their frequencies.[3] For lemmas with fewer than 100 hits, all tokens with explicit information on dimensions were included in the preliminary data set.

Subsequently, we used iWeb's expanded context menu and coded the data for explicit information on the specific dimensions on which the comparisons were based. The data in (10) illustrate our procedure for the lemma OUTRUN. On the basis of the underlined material, we classified SPEED as the target dimension for the context in (10-a) and coded the item as the lemma–dimension combination OUTRUN-SPEED. In contrast, the item in (10-b), again based on the underlined material, was coded as the combination OUTRUN-DISTANCE. Finally, items such as (10-c) were discarded from the data, because their contexts do not resolve dimension ambiguity. As this study looks at the predictive power of verb classes rather than lemmas, all lemma–dimension combinations, such as OUTRUN–SPEED for (10-a), were counted only once. All other combinations of OUTRUN and SPEED were discarded from the data. This method resulted in a total of 148 lemma–dimension combinations.

(10) a. He immediately ran away before I could get there myself and **outran me** (I didn't pick up the elven swiftness skill, usually if I want speed I just mount a beast so running isn't my characters forte).
 b. Arsenal have been **outran by all of the Premier League opponents**. [...] Arsenal players have clocked in less kilometres than their rivals...
 c. Jacquelyn Sertic [...] retired Oklahoma in order in the bottom of the ninth. That included an over-the-shoulder catch from DeCamp, who **outran the ball** into left center to make the catch.

Coding for the variable 'dimension' is not always straightforward. This holds in particular as there is no predefined list of possible values, i.e. dimensions, and as it is impossible to a priori define what constitutes specific contextual information on a dimension for any case imaginable. We used the following strategy: The annotations were carried out by the first author. In order to establish both the difficulty and the reliability of the task, a second annotator went through the whole data set

---

[3] That is, if for the lemma OUTRUN there were 900 tokens of word form *outruns* and 100 tokens of word form *out-ran*, we would have kept the first 90 *outruns* tokens and the first 10 *out-ran* tokens from iWeb's context menu on the web interface. We discarded obviously corrupted corpus attestations and, if possible, topped up the data with further attestations in their stead. To keep our procedure as reproducible as possible, we did not randomize the hits. That is, later iWeb searches will return the same order of hits for a word form. We think this procedure is all the more reasonable, as whatever ordering iWeb uses internally, this will be used across all items.

used in Study 2 ($N = 948$), which is a subset of the data that we looked at in Study 1. The two annotators agreed in 64% of all cases, using a total of eleven different values (Cohen's Kappa for two raters: 0.394, $z = 22.4$, $p = 0$). Although this amounts to only fair to moderate agreement (see e.g. McHugh 2012), we decided to include all data from the first author's original annotation for the following reasons: First, the percentage of cases agreed upon is comparable to annotator agreement in similar semantic tasks (see e.g Maguire et al. 2007 with 68% for two raters on compound relations). Second, and more importantly, disagreement between the two annotators concerns almost exclusively the question of whether an item is contextually specified for a dimension or not. There are only five cases for which the annotators disagreed regarding a specified dimension (for example, an item which one rater classified as OUTSWIM–STAMINA, and the other rater as OUTSWIM–DISTANCE). Reporting only those items both annotators agreed on thus primarily leads to higher relative percentages of unspecified cases and the loss of a substantial amount of data. We therefore decided to keep all items in the data set.

In order to address the ambiguity problem (see RQ1b), we operationalized multiple class membership in VerbNet as a measure of uncertainty. We quantified how ambiguous the members of a given class are on average by, first, counting the number of VerbNet classes each base lemma in the data set is listed in. For example, the lemma SING occurs in three classes in total (PERFORMANCE, SOUND-EMISSION, and MANNER-SPEAKING; see Table 2). We therefore assigned SING a cross-listing score of 2, i.e. besides being a member of the class under investigation, it is listed as a member of two further classes. Second, we calculated the mean of the individual base verb scores for each class in our study and used this as the cross-listing score for the respective classes. This value can then be understood as a measure of uncertainty: the higher a class's cross-listing score, the less sure we can be that the *out*-formation's base is in fact from this class.

The classes' cross-listing scores were set in relation to values assessing dimensional variability. First, higher percentages for a dominant dimension for a given class are taken as indicators of the class's homogeneity. In contrast, higher absolute numbers of different dimensions and a higher dimension entropy for a class are taken as indicators for heterogeneity. Dimension entropy is a measure of the overall level of uncertainty about the dimensions that are associated with a class. We calculated it via probabilities derived from the dimension distribution for each class. The more dimensions with similar frequencies there are for a class, i.e. the more difficult it is to predict which dimensions are linked to a verb type, the higher the entropy. The fewer dimensions we find for a class, and the more frequent one dimension is compared to others, the lower the entropy. The entropy is at zero if there is only one dimension.

Tab. 3: Dimension distribution in % over 7 VerbNet-classes (N = 148; percentages are rounded; percentage of majority dimension per class underlined; EMISSION is short for SOUND EMISSION).

	PERFORMANCE	RUN	EXIST	SPRAY	EMISSION	CARRY	HIT
QUALITY	<u>48</u>	14	/	33	15	5	20
SPEED	5	<u>51</u>	/	7	4	<u>32</u>	<u>27</u>
DURATION	14	/	<u>67</u>	/	8	/	/
QUANTITY	5	/	/	<u>60</u>	4	21	/
LOUDNESS	14	/	/	/	<u>50</u>	/	20
DISTANCE	/	21	/	/	/	16	/
FREQUENCY	/	5	/	/	12	5	20
IMPACT	/	/	22	/	/	5	/
other	14	9	11	/	8	16	13

3.3 Results

The distribution of lemma–dimension combinations over the seven VerbNet classes is shown in Table 3. Base verb classes are represented in table columns and dimensions in lines.[4] The respective majority dimension for each class is indicated by underlined percentages. For example, read top-down, the column for the PERFORMANCE base class (leftmost) encodes the following information: 48% of lemma-dimension combinations co-occur with the majority dimension QUALITY, 5% with SPEED, 14% with DURATION, 5% with QUANTITY, 14% with LOUDNESS, and 14% with further dimensions (i.e. category 'other').

All classes include different dimensions and for five out of the seven classes, there is a clearly dominant, class-specific dimension that approaches or exceeds 50% of all type-dimension combinations of this class. Only the CARRY and HIT classes behave differently in this respect, with SPEED as the most dominant category in both cases (32% and 27%, respectively). The dimension profiles are unique to all base classes, i.e. no two classes co-occur with the same dimensions.

Several values are necessary for assessing how the ambiguity of a class's members influences the variability and the distribution of dimensions. Information on the dominant dimensions per class can be retrieved from Table 3. In Table 4, the first row shows the cross-listing scores for the base classes, dimension entropy is displayed in the second row, and the third row shows the number of different dimensions per class.

---

4 The category 'other' exists for reasons of readability and includes various low frequency dimensions. Only dimensions that made up more than 10% for at least one base class were included in the table as individual dimensions.

Tab. 4: The cross-listing scores (CL score), the dimension entropies (Entropy), and the number of different dimensions (Dimensions) for the 7 VerbNet-classes (EMISSION is short for SOUND EMISSION).

	PERFORMANCE	RUN	EXIST	SPRAY	EMISSION	CARRY	HIT
CL score	3.1	1.0	1.1	0.7	2.2	3.0	3.3
Entropy	2.13	1.89	1.22	1.24	2.23	2.49	2.29
Dimensions	8	7	3	3	8	8	6

We tested for correlations between the classes' cross-listing scores and the three variability values. Our data show that the more ambiguous the members of a class are, the more different and the more diverse scalar dimensions we find encoded in *out*-forms based on these members. As depicted in Figure 1, the higher its cross-listing score, the weaker a class's potential for predicting a dimension profile. First, the cross-listing score is strongly negatively correlated with dominant dimensions: the lower the cross-listing score, the higher the percentage of the dominant dimension (Pearson's r: -0.83, p = 0.022). Second, the negative correlation is even stronger, and more significant, for cross-listing score and dimension entropy (Pearson's r: 0.85, p = 0.016). Last, the absolute number of dimensions per class also correlates negatively with the cross-listing score, but this correlation is not significant(Pearson's r: 0.67, p = 0.09).

3.4 Discussion

Study 1 set out to investigate the extent to which semantic classes of base verbs predict the scalar dimensions of the comparative meaning component of *out*-derivatives. The results clearly show lexical semantic relatedness between verb classes and derivatives. The base classes we investigated are associated with different dimension profiles in *out*-formations and we find clearly dominant dimensions for five out of the seven classes. With respect to RQ1a, these findings suggest that VerbNet classes serve as suitable vantage points for predicting the intended interpretations of *out*-derivatives.

For example, our results suggest that the preference for the dimension SPEED for *out*-lemmas based on RUN-class bases, as opposed to, for example, PERFORMANCE-class bases, is no coincidence. This finding is in line with the assumption in section 2.1 that the word-formation process remains underspecified for scalar dimensions, and reliant on its bases in this regard (see Ahn 2022; Kotowski 2021). Therefore, it appears reasonable to assume that the respective dominant dimen-

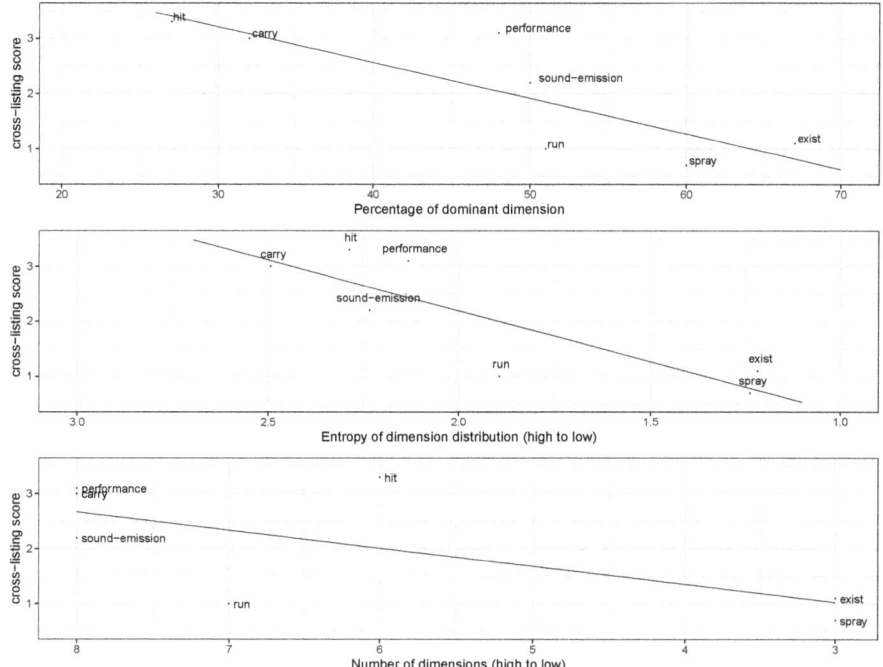

Fig. 1: From top to bottom: correlation dominant dimension–cross-listing score, Pearson's *r*: -0.83, *p* = 0.02), correlation dimension entropy–cross-listing score, Pearson's *r*: 0.85, *p* = 0.016, and correlation of number of dimensions–cross-listing score; Pearson's *r*: 0.67, *p* = 0.09. The lines show the corresponding linear regression lines.

sions are salient properties of the events denoted by the verbs from classes with unambiguous dimension profiles, such as SPEED for RUN-verbs.

However, all classes have the potential to give rise to a number of dimensions (between 3 and 8) and two classes, HIT and CARRY, do not exhibit dominant dimensions. Regarding the question of the influence of ambiguity on a class's predictive potential (see RQ1b), two different correlations are insightful: the degree of ambiguity of a VerbNet class's members, quantified as a class's cross-listing score, is strongly negatively correlated with both the class's dominant dimension and the entropy of the dimension distribution. If we take multiple membership as an indicator of polysemy (or partly homonymy), dimension profiles thus partially depend on how ambiguous a class is: the more polysemous a given VerbNet class's members are overall, the more difficult it is to predict a dominant dimension based on this class.

Building on these class-based findings, let us now move on to the closely related lemma-based investigation in Study 2.

4 Study 2: Predicting scalar dimensions via base verb lemmas

4.1 Rationale

This study investigates the role of different base lemmas as predictors of scalar dimensions in *out*-formations. Unlike Study 1, it does not count types of lemma–dimension combinations, but looks at the frequencies of token–dimension combinations:

Research question 2a (RQ2a): To what extent do tokens of individual verbs reflect the dimension profiles of their respective verb class?

In this study, we are also interested in how frequently ambiguity is in fact explicitly resolved in context. Recall that neither of the analyses introduced in section 2.1 doubt that *out-* includes a comparative core. However, large numbers of tokens in which dimensional ambiguity remains unresolved would possibly cast doubt on comparison as the word formation process's sole semantic contribution, and would make causative analyses that do not rely on the prominence of comparison more plausible:

RQ2b: How frequently is dimensional underspecification resolved and is such resolution the default case?

In order to answer RQ2a and RQ2b, we used large samples of tokens from twelve *out*-lemmas based on three of the VerbNet classes used in Study 1.

4.2 Methodology

Methodologically, Study 2 is very similar to Study 1. All attestations were culled from iWeb via its web interface. We used the same search format as above (see the search string in example (9)), but performed searches for twelve base verbs. These verbs and their respective VerbNet classes are shown in (11). If available, 100 attestations were culled from iWeb. For lemmas with less than 100 hits, we included all items. For lemmas with more than 100 hits, we used the first 100 hits and included different word forms of a given lemma relative to their frequencies (see footnote 3 for the procedure). Upon discarding hits based on obvious corpus corruptions (e.g., *Hardly anything comes outWritten*), we ended up with a data set of 949 tokens; the number of tokens per lemma is given in parentheses in (11):

(11)   PERFORMANCE: outdance (51), outrap (21), outwrite (32), outsing (100)
       RUN: outrun (100), outfly (100), outswim (100), outsprint (100)
       EXIST: outlive (100), outstay (100), outwait (100), outsurvive (45)

For any individual token, we annotated a specific dimension in case concrete contextual information was available in iWeb's expanded context menu.

Unlike in Study 1, we kept items without explicit dimension information. Examples such as (10-c) were coded as "unspecified" regarding their dimension. The data set created for Study 2 further contrasts with the data set used in Study 1 as multiple occurrences of a particular *out*-lemma and a particular dimension were counted, e.g. multiple tokens of OUTRUN specified for the SPEED-dimension.

4.3 Results

The distribution of dimensions across tokens of the twelve *out*-lemmas are shown as horizontally stacked bars grouped by base verb class in Figure 2. Each bar represents all tokens of one *out*-lemma. The topmost row in Figure 2-a), for example, encodes all 100 attestations of the lemma OUTSPRINT. Bar sections indicate the percentages of attestations co-occurring with a scalar dimension as well as with unspecified dimensions (black sections). For OUTSPRINT, the bar shows the following distribution: 32% of the tokens are unspecified regarding a scalar dimension and 68% explicitly refer to SPEED.[5]

For nearly all lemmas, we find a general pattern of a relatively high proportion of unspecified tokens (on average, 52% of a lemma's total) and a clear majority dimension among the specified cases (on average, 42% of a lemma's total). Moreover, we find a clear pattern of intra-class homogeneity, i.e. lemmas from a class behave similarly, and the preferred dimensions are the same ones we find for the class-based investigation (see Table 3). For example, just as the EXIST-class itself,

---

[5] The category 'other' exists for reasons of readability and includes various low frequency dimensions. Only dimensions that make up more than 5% of dimensions for at least one verb of a base class were included in the table as individual dimensions.

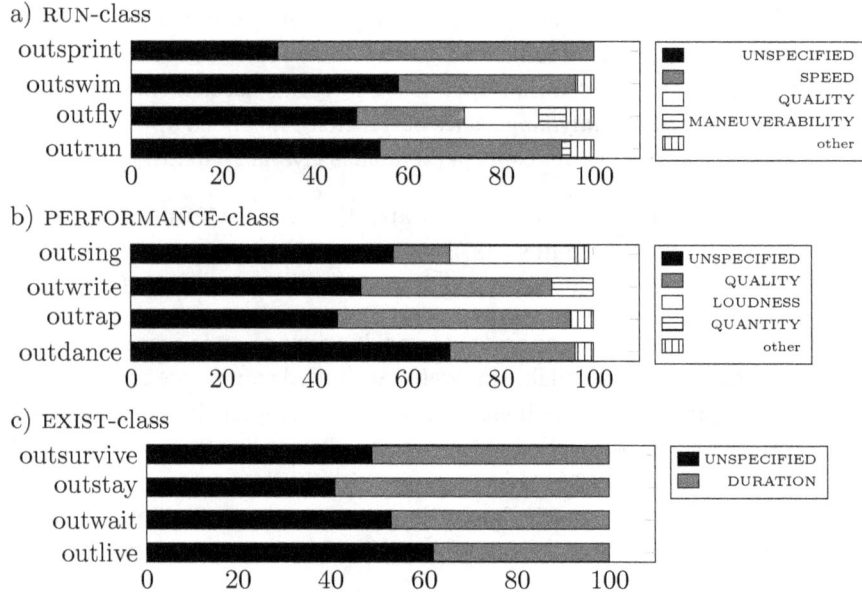

Fig. 2: Distribution in % of scalar dimensions in *out*-forms for lemmas based on VerbNet's a) RUN-class, b) PERFORMANCE-class, and c) EXIST-class; N = 949.

the tokens of all four *out*-lemmas based on EXIST-verbs have a preference for the dimension DURATION.

Only one lemma does not follow this overall pattern. The verb OUTSING from the PERFORMANCE-class is attested most with LOUDNESS (27%). Given the results of Study 1 as well as the behavior of other PERFORMANCE-verbs, one would expect QUALITY to feature as the verb's majority dimension, for which we only find 12% of attestations. To a lesser degree, OUTFLY stands out as well, as it shows a less clear preference for SPEED compared to the other RUN-lemmas.

4.4 Discussion

Regarding RQ2a, the class-based findings from Study 1 are clearly reflected in the results of the token-based investigation. In other words, the investigated lemmas cluster by class with respect to their preferred dimensions, and these dimensions are the same ones that are preferred by the respective classes. Leaving aside 'unspecified' cases, all four RUN-lemmas occur most often with SPEED, all four EXIST-lemmas with DURATION, and three out of four PERFORMANCE-lemmas with QUAL-

ITY. More generally speaking, the results thus indicate base–derivative relatedness regarding salient event properties.

Only the lemmas OUTSING and, to a lesser degree, OUTFLY deviate from the behavior their class membership would suggest. A plausible explanation for these two lemmas' preferences can be found in the ambiguity of their respective base forms. For example, SING is cross-listed in VerbNet as a PERFORMANCE, a MANNER-OF-SPEAKING, and a SOUND-EMISSION verb (see Table 2). The reason that OUTSING-contexts are mostly measured out along the scale of LOUDNESS (27%), rather than along the scale of the expected dimension QUALITY, appears to be that *out*- preferentially takes the verb's SOUND-EMISSION sense as base. As shown in section 3.1, members of the SOUND-EMISSION class productively serve as base to *out*-prefixation and LOUDNESS is this class's preferred dimension for comparisons.[6]

With respect to RQ2b, we find a large proportion of unspecified cases for all lemmas, i.e. attestations without explicit contextual clues on scalar dimensions. For eight of the twelve lemmas, these unspecified cases constitute the majority among the tokens and their nature is in need of comment. Importantly, having been coded as 'unspecified' does not mean that an item does not suggest a dimension. Consider, for example, the attestations in (12) (all from iWeb):

(12) a. When was the last time we <u>made more noise</u> than the away support (we've been **outsung** by fewer supporters than Wrexham brought)? [coded as LOUDNESS]
 b. I thought our fans were terrific. They showed the world that when they fill any stadium they will not get **outsung**. [coded as UNSPECIFIED]
 c. The most memorable scene of unadulterated Allied jingoism occurs when free-French patrons of Ricks Place (sic) **out-sing** the Nazi patrons in a battle of national anthems. [coded as UNSPECIFIED]

Based on the underlined material (*make more noise*), the dimension for the item in (12-a) was coded as LOUDNESS, while the item in (12-b) was coded as 'unspecified'. However, like example (12-a), very many OUTSING-examples refer to football supporters competing in some form of singing contest whose primary goal is to sing louder than, and thereby defeat, a rival group of supporters at some football ground. Arguably, it is such pieces of world knowledge that lead to the inference

---

6 We do not have any numbers available for VerbNet's DRIVE class. However, it seems likely that OUTFLY's behavior finds a similar explanation via FLY's membership in this class. As the DRIVE class's members typically specify the means or vehicle used in motion events, they arguably suggest quality-judgements of the operation of a vehicle.

that examples such as (12-b) are also based on LOUDNESS and thus follow the pattern of the specified majority dimensions of the lemma.

At the same time, for quite a number of examples the available linguistic context does not allow for resolving dimensional ambiguity, as in (12-c). Recall from section 2.1 that two competing theories on *out-*'s semantics analyze the comparative component as either the macro-event itself (Ahn 2022; Tolskaya 2014) or as embedded as a sub-event in a causative macro-event (Kotowski 2021; McIntyre 2003). On the fairly uncontroversial assumption that dimensions are indispensable in scalar constructions (see Solt 2015), the existence of a fair amount of unclear examples at least casts doubt on comparison as the only semantic component of *out-* as a word formation process. Albeit tentatively, we regard this finding as an argument in favor of causative analyses that rely less on the prominence of comparison.

We will now move on to Study 3 and the investigation of distributional similarity measures.

5 Study 3: Distributional similarities – *out-* across VerbNet classes

5.1 Rationale

In Study 3, we operationalize semantic relatedness using distributional similarity measures and apply these to both the *out-*lemmas used in Study 2 as well as to their bases. The objective is to tease apart the relative contributions of the base and of the word formation process to the semantics of *out-*derivatives. To this end, we look at distributional similarities between bases, between derivatives, and between bases and derivatives.

Distributional semantic approaches have been used successfully in investigating a variety of morphological phenomena. A number of studies tries to model derivation by isolating a distributional representation of an affix and combining it with the vector representation of the base. For example, Marelli & Baroni (2015) model affixes as matrices that are multiplied with base vectors, while Padó et al. (2016) and Kisselew et al. (2015) test various models on their predictive power depending on the base forms' properties. A similar strain of research explores whether different types of affixation show different distributional reflexes. For example, Bonami & Paperno (2018) investigate distributional differences between inflected and derived forms, Varvara (2017) looks at different German event nominalizations, while Bonami & Guzmán Naranjo (2023) explore distributional evidence for paradigmatic processes of derivational categories. Finally, some studies have looked at more fine-grained aspects of derivation. Lapesa et al. (2017) show that when using valence as a tertium comparationis, the same German derivational suffixes have different effects depending on lexical properties of the bases, while Lapesa et al. (2018) use distributional semantics to disambiguate the meanings of new English -*ment* derivations. Similarly, Wauquier (2020) uses the vectors of different semantic and morphological classes of words to investigate the uniformity of these classes, and Schäfer (2023) investigates the alleged derivation–inflection dichotomy by looking at the distribution of -*ly*-adverbs based on different semantic base classes.

Our approach differs from the first strain since we are not interested in modeling derivation as composition or subtraction. It differs from the second strain in that we only consider a single prefix and its base-dependent internal variation. There are conceptual similarities with the last strain, as we are interested in specific aspects of a single word formation process, and in the possible influence of different semantic classes of bases.

The first measure we are interested in concerns similarities between bases and derivatives. We compare pairwise similarities, i.e. similarities between base and derivative (e.g. between the lemmas RUN and OUTRUN), with similarities across pairs, i.e. similarities between non-pairs of bases and derivatives in the data (e.g. between RUN and OUTSWIM). If properties of the base are preserved in *out*-derivatives, as strongly suggested by Studies 1 and 2 above, we expect base-derivative pairs to be more similar to each other than non-pairs are to each other. This measure can also be taken as a proof of concept for Study 3, as the assumptions reflect that, lexicalized forms aside, we expect the semantics of base words to feature in the corresponding derivative semantics:

Research question 3a (RQ3a) Do distributional measures show a higher degree of similarity between base-derivative pairs than between non-pairs?

The argument structural and event structural properties and the comparison-adding nature of *out*-prefixation clearly suggest a generally rather homogeneous semantic make-up of *out*-derivatives (see Section 2.1). We therefore also investigate similarities that hold between derivatives (e.g. between OUTRUN and OUTSWIM) and how these derivative-derivative similarities compare with both base-base similarities (e.g. between RUN and SWIM) and with similarities of base-derivative pairs:

RQ3b Do derivative-derivative similarities differ from base-base similarities and base-derivative similarities?

5.2 Methodology

Most *out*-derivatives have low token frequencies in corpora and are therefore typically not included in pretrained collections of distributional vectors. For example, the semantic space that produces the best empirical results in Baroni et al. (2014) only contains vectors for three of the *out*-lemmas from Study 2: OUTLIVE, OUTRUN, and OUTSTAY. We therefore decided to calculate our own vectors, opting for a classic distributional semantics approach strictly based on co-occurrence counts.

5.2.1 Corpus

We used a combination of two corpora for our measures. To create our vectors, we used the ukWaC corpus, a web-derived 2 billion word corpus of English (see Baroni et al. 2009). The version we used is part-of-speech-tagged and lemmatized with TreeTagger.[7] As the absolute frequencies of most of our target items are still low in ukWaC, we expanded the corpus by adding all sentences containing the *out*-lemmas from the iWeb corpus (14 billion words).

In order to be able to use the iWeb data as an expansion of the tagged ukWaC corpus, we first extracted all sentences containing any wordform of our target lemmata. We then tagged and lemmatized the sentences using Python's NLTK library (see Bird et al. 2009) and adjusted the tags to the tree tagger conventions used in the tagged ukWaC.[8]

Table 5 provides the absolute numbers of occurrences of *out*-formations that we extracted from iWeb.

---

[7] https://www.cis.uni-muenchen.de/~schmid/tools/TreeTagger/
[8] One reviewer remarks that ukWac is a corpus of British English, while iWeb is a multi-variety corpus. While we acknowledge this difference, we are not aware of any differences in the usage of *out*- depending on the variety of English. We therefore cannot comment on whether this may bear on our results.

Tab. 5: *out*-derivatives in iWeb: absolute number of occurrences.

EXIST-verb	occurrences	PERFORMANCE-verb	occurrences	RUN-verb	occurrences
outlive	12389	outdance	51	outfly	134
outstay	830	outrap	21	outrun	11291
outsurvive	46	outsing	166	outsprint	545
outwait	134	outwrite	62	outswim	104

5.2.2 Creation of distributional vectors

We created vectors strictly based on co-occurrence counts, that is, no machine learning was involved. We proceeded as follows:
1. Co-occurrence counts were collected for the top 10,000 content words (nouns, verbs, adjectives, and adverbs) in ukWaC, resulting in raw vectors with 10,000 dimensions for our target lemmata.
2. For further parameter setting, we explored different window sizes (sentence, and ranges of 2 to 4 words to the left and right of the target word) and transformations (pointwise mutual information and log-likelihood, both with and without logarithm) by comparing the correlation of the resulting cosine similarity measures between pairs of verbs with the human similarity and association scores in the SimLex-999 dataset described in Hill et al. (2014).
3. We chose the combination of window size and transformation that correlated best with both the similarity and the association scores: a three-word window, and a transformation of the raw counts to pointwise mutual information (with logarithm). This setting has also been shown to perform best for adjective similarities in the SimLex-999 dataset (see Schäfer 2020).

Keeping our procedure as simple and transparent as possible, we did not reduce the dimensionality of the resulting vectors (note also that Baroni et al. 2014a found that within the count models they considered those using no compression at all worked best).

5.2.3 Accomodating differences in overall frequencies

The similarities we are interested in are between vectors that are based on hugely diverging numbers of absolute occurrences. These differences are tied to major differences in the expected range of co-occurring other lexical items. Take our least frequent lemma, OUTRAP, as an example: it occurs 21 times in total. Given that we used a three-word window to the left and right of our target words, the theoretically maximally possible number of different content words that could occur here are only 6x21=126 content words, necessarily resulting in a very sparse vector. Even its base, RAP, the base with the lowest frequency, occurs only 1589 times, yielding maximally 6*1589 = 9534 content words, still less than the dimensions of our vectors. This is very different from our most frequent base, WRITE, which occurs 837,319 times. In order to address this issue, we used vectors created from smaller samples of co-occurrences.

Specifically, per lemma, we drew 10 random samples of 100 contexts each from the set of all contexts of that lemma. We then created 10 sets of vectors based on these 10 random samples for each of these lemmas. The size of 100 contexts per sample makes the resulting vectors very similar in terms of the expected overall sparsity to the vectors of the rare items. Using 10 random samples each safeguards against the possibility that a single randomly drawn set of 100 contexts might in fact not be very representative of the contexts of the target verbs. Four verb lemmas occur in less than 100 sentences and were therefore not downsampled (i.e. OUTWRITE (62 tokens), OUTRAP (21), OUTSURVIVE (46), OUTDANCE (51)).

To calculate cosine similarities, we used average values across all ten samples. That is, the similarity between the rare item OUTWRITE and the most frequent base WRITE is calculated by taking the mean of the ten cosine similarities between the vector for OUTWRITE on the one hand and each of the 10 vectors based on the 10 downsampled contexts randomly drawn from all WRITE sentences on the other hand. Thus, we report the average of 10 similarity values. In contrast, the similarity between RUN and OUTRUN, both occurring more than 100 times, is based on the average similarity between 10 vectors each, created from 10 random samples of 100 contexts for both of these lemmas. In this case, we report the average of 100 similarity values. Note that one result of our approach is, relatively speaking, low similarity values. For example, the mean similarity across all the base-derivative pairs with *out-* is at just 0.06. For validation of our approach, we compare these values against the values of the full data, i.e. pre-downsampling, and against values from word embeddings in the next section.

5.2.4 Comparison to word embeddings

Most current distributional studies use machine-learned word embeddings (cf. the two other studies using distributional semantics in this volume, Bonami & Guzmán Naranjo 2023 and Schäfer 2023). While Baroni et al. (2014a) argue against using count vectors, subsequent studies comparing the two apppproaches paint a more nuanced picture, see Varvara et al. (2021). Most importantly, by using count vectors, we keep our approach transparent and lightweight. It is transparent, because neither machine-learning nor dimension reduction is involved, and we know exactly how every single value in the vectors was created. It is lightweight, because our method only requires the sentences with our target verbs and the already available frequency list for all words in the corpus. Furthermore, we believe that our method of accounting for frequency effects by both some transformation (in our case, pointwise mutual information with logarithm) and our downsampling procedure can lead to new insights into how frequency differences are best dealt with.

For comparability to word embedding approaches, we compared our vectors in their full (pre-downsampling) and downsampled versions against the best performing vector space in Baroni et al. (2014a), available via Baroni et al. (2014b).[9]

The Baroni vectorspace is not lemmatized. For our comparison, we used the base form vectors. Since only three of our *out*-derivatives in their base forms are included, we compared not only against the pairs used in Study 3 but also against the additional pairs used in Study 4.

For the resulting 13 base–derivative pairs, we calculated three sets of cosine similarities, using i) the Baroni vectors, ii) our pre-downsampling vectors, and iii) our downsampled vectors. Table 6 summarizes the range of the similarities observed in the three vectorspaces.

Tab. 6: Overview of the distribution of cosine similarities based on three different sets of vectors.

vectors	Min	Max	Mean	Median
a. Baroni	0.05	0.51	0.22	0.20
b. Pre-downsampling	-0.06	0.50	0.17	0.15
c. Downsampled	0.03	0.15	0.06	0.05

Mean and median are relatively close to each other in all three datasets, with the mean always slightly higher, reflecting a right skew in all three datasets. Both the pre-downsampling and the Baroni vectors are overall similar to a normal distribution, while the downsampled vectors are clearly different (Shapiro-Wilk normality test, $W = 0.76$, p-value = 0.003). The cosine similarities based on the downsampled vectors occupy a much smaller range than both the full and the Baroni-based similarities. This should be kept in mind when interpreting the results. Also, the mean

---

[9] Many thanks to Ingo Plag for not only suggesting this comparison but also for running it on a previous version of our data.

and median values based on the Baroni vectors are highest within this set, but still relatively low when compared to e.g. Lazaridou et al. (2013, 1522), who find mean cosine similarity values of 0.47 for base-derivative pairs in English. In other words, the absolute value of cosine similarities is not meaningfully comparable across methods and corpora. This contrasts with the correlations between the similarities across items, which allow us a direct comparison of the three vectorsets. We calculated the correlations between the cosine similarities from the three different sets, and also between these values and absolute frequencies of the bases and derivatives in our corpus. Only three correlations turn out to be significant. The downsampled vectors are positively correlated with the pre-downsampling vectors (Pearson's $r=0.66$, $p = .015$), and the pre-downsampling vectors are negatively correlated with the absolute number of occurrences of the bases ($r=-0.67$, $p = .011$). Most importantly, there is a very strong and highly significant positive correlation between the similarities based on the downsampled vectors and the similarities based on the Baroni vector space ($r = 0.88$, $p = 6.675e-05$).

We take this as clear evidence for the success of our downsampling method to eliminate the influence of differences in absolute frequency, and for the overall validity of our approach.

5.2.5 Statistical analysis

As described in Section 5.1, we compare cosine similarities involving four conditions: To answer RQ3a, we compared the cosine similarities between the conditions base-derivative pairwise and base-derivative across pairs. To answer RQ3b, we compared the derivative-derivative similarities to a) the base-base similarities and b) the base-derivative pairwise similarities. We used the Shapiro-Wilk test of normality on all our grouped similarity values. As not all of them are normally distributed, we used the non-parametric two-sample Wilcoxon test to compare the similarities across conditions. Note that this does not create a problem of multiple comparisons: For any constellation we are interested in, we consistently only make one comparison, namely comparison of cosine similarities.

For all comparisons, we are primarily interested in generalizing over the measures for all twelve lemmas we investigated, although we are using the same lemmas from the same three VerbNet classes that we used in Study 2. However, these classes are represented by only four lemmas each, which makes generalizations over specific classes difficult. While we will focus on all items, we will also report both the numbers and the significant patterns per verb class.

5.3 Results

The similarity values of interest are reported in Table 7 as two columns each for all items and per VerbNet class, the first column showing the mean cosine similarities, the second one the standard deviations within the similarities. The first two rows of pairings show the average similarities between bases and derivatives. The first row, base-derivative pairwise, only considers base-derivative pairs (e.g. SPRINT-OUTSPRINT) and quantifies the extent to which the meaning of the base is related to that of the derived form. The second row, base-derivative across pairs, quantifies the similarities of all bases and derivatives in the data except for base-derivative pairs (e.g. for RUN-OUTSPRINT). The last two rows show the base-base and derivative-derivative similarity measures.

Tab. 7: Cosine similarity measures across 12 *out*-lemmas from VerbNet's RUN, EXIST, and PERFORMANCE classes.

Pairings	All items		RUN		EXIST		PERFORMANCE	
	SIM	SD	SIM	SD	SIM	SD	SIM	SD
base-base	0.03	0.01	0.04	0.01	0.04	0.01	0.05	0.03
base-derivative across pairs	0.04	0.01	0.05	0.01	0.04	0.01	0.03	0.02
base-derivative pairwise	0.06	0.02	0.08	0.02	0.05	0.00	0.05	0.02
derivative-derivative	0.07	0.03	0.10	0.02	0.06	0.01	0.06	0.02

Figure 3 represents the results graphically by indicating via brackets the three comparisons between the conditions of interest here. The brackets are labeled with the p-values of the respective comparison.

As shown in the left panel, across all items base-derivative pairwise similarities are significantly higher than base-derivative across pairs (w=200, p = 1.907e-05). Although the measures for the individual VerbNet classes pull in the same direction, the difference is significant only for the RUN class (W = 44, p = .01319).

Across all items, derivative-derivative similarities are significantly more similar to each other than the bases are to each other (w = 536, p = 7.976e-14). These differences are also significant for the RUN and EXIST classes (W = 0, p = .002 and W = 3, p = .015, respectively).

Finally, across all items and within each individual class, derivative-derivative similarities are descriptively slightly higher than the similarities of base-derivative pairs, both in their means as well as their medians. However, this difference does not reach significance, neither across classes nor within any class.

5.4 Discussion

Our RQ3a asked whether base-derivative pairs are more similar to each other than the non-pairs. In line with our expectations, this turned out to be the case, and is reflected in higher cosine similarities for the base-derivative pairs in comparison to base-derivative pairless similarities.

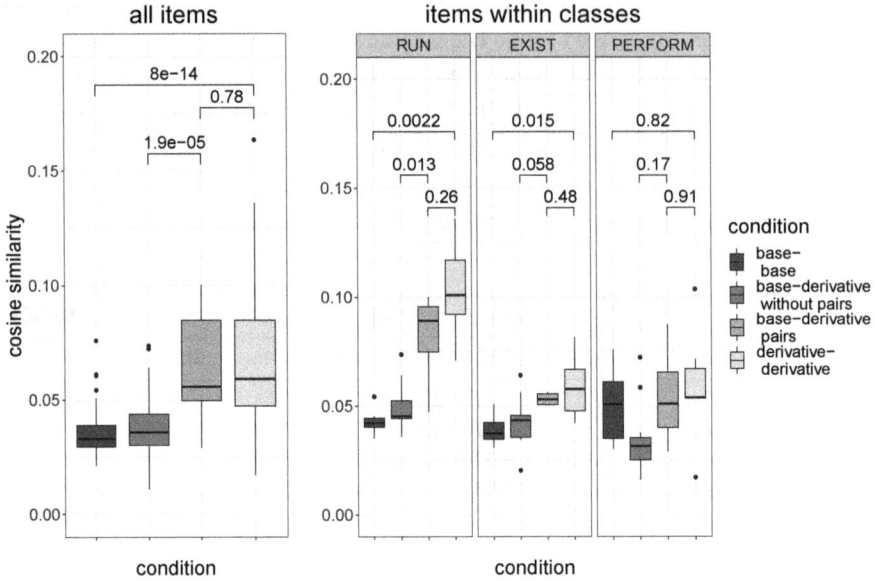

Fig. 3: Cosine similarities across all items and by semantic class in the four different conditions. The p-values for the target comparisons are given across the braces for the respective comparisons.

Turning to RQ3b, exploring differences between derivative-derivative, base-base, and base-derivative similarities, we find the overall highest similarities between derivatives. The derivatives are more similar to each other than the bases are to each other. Furthermore, descriptively, derivatives are more similar to each other than bases are to (their) derivatives. On the assumption that relatively high derivative-derivative similarities indicate a high degree of semantic coherence of the products of the word-formation process, this is strong support for the view that *out*-prefixation itself imposes a uniform semantics. Importantly, these findings are not evidence that derivatives do not inherit any features from their bases outside (sets of) suggested scalar dimensions (pace Ahn 2022). The way we set up our investigation does not allow any such conjecture.

One caveat is in place concerning the interpretation of our findings in terms of a relatively high degree of semantic coherence between derivatives: Recall that we did not distinguish between different senses of bases in either study presented here. This also holds for all vector representations of bases in Study 3. Thus, while we used random example sentences for all bases, their vectors represent generalizations over all senses. We cannot exclude the possibility that the word-formation process is selective with respect to the senses of a particular base form. In other words, a given *out*-lemma may inherit only a subset of the senses its base lemma encodes. This possibility is in line with post-hoc comparisons of the standard deviations of the similarity measures in Table 7 and the average cross-listing scores for the lemmas of the three classes (see Section 3.3). The PERFORMANCE-class has the highest cross-listing score (3.5), and the pertinent sample shows consistently high standard deviations. One reason for these consistently high deviations, relative to the other two classes, could lie in the a priori higher number of different senses the derivatives are based on.

As we saw in Studies 1 and 2, the members from different VerbNet classes differ in their preferred scalar dimensions when serving as bases to *out*-. The low number of lemmas per VerbNet class in Study 3 makes claims on class-specific distributional characteristics difficult. While the patterns that we find hold, at least descriptively, per individual verb class, they also hold upon comparing derivatives across classes, e.g. OUTRUN-OUTLIVE. In other words, the distributional similarities in this study do not point to a privileged status of the verb classes under consideration, but to a pronounced effect of the word formation process.

In summary, similarity measures show that *out*-prefixation has a relatively large distributional effect, in that *out*-derivatives show a relatively high degree of uniformity. While Studies 1 and 2 have shown that *out*-formations can be distinguished by base verb classes, Study 3 has shown that all three classes show similar distributional characteristics. However, it is unclear from this investigation whether this behavior is peculiar to *out*-verbs. The last study will address this question by gathering distributional data on four further English prefixes, including the spatial prefix *out*-.

6 Study 4: Distributional similarities – comparative *out-* contrasted with other prefixes

6.1 Rationale

In order to establish whether the relatively high similarity among derivatives is peculiar to comparative *out-*prefixation, we extended our investigation of distributional similarity measures to four further prefixes. We compare the patterns observed for comparative *out-* i) to a second prefix with bases from the same verb class (i.e. spatial *over-* and the RUN-class), ii) to spatial *out-*, and iii) to two different prefixes with bases from a different VerbNet class (reversative *un-*, iterative *re-*, and the TAPE-class). We chose these prefixes for comparison as they all show clearly weaker argument structural and event structural effects than comparative *out-* and thus presumably are more similar to their respective bases distributionally. Recall from Section 2.1 that comparative *out-*derivatives systematically license direct object arguments that are not licensed by their respective base verbs and systematically differ in event structure from their bases (for example ??*Mary sang John* vs. *Mary outsang John*).

As illustrated by means of the (base) verb *to fly* in (13) (both from iWeb), spatial *over-* (see Lieber 2004, ch.4) shows a pattern of preposition incorporation. The realization as a prefixed verb with a direct object in (13-b) is semantically identical to a base form with a PP-object as in (13-a), with the internal PP-argument corresponding to the direct object (see Wunderlich 2012). This constitutes a weaker form of argument structural effect than the one we observe for comparative *out-*. Overflying-events are still flying-events, and both of these events allow for the same type of locative argument, i.e., roughly, physical objects with some dimensional extension in space.

(13) a. Today, cotton growers hire companies with airplanes to **fly over the field**...
      b. For airports with no AWOS or ASOS, **overfly the field** at or above pattern altitude and check the windsock.

Spatial *out-* behaves in similar ways to spatial *over-* with respect to argument structural effects. The examples in (14-a,b) with the (base) verb *to haul*, partly repeated here from section 2.1, illustrate that *out-* as a spatial prefix has a similar distribution as the synonymous spatial particle *out*, and licenses the same kinds of argument. Moreover, as shown in (14-c), *haul* also behaves similarly without any locative argument and all verbs in (14) denote hauling-events (all from iWeb):

(14) a. "haulback" means the cable used to **outhaul the rigging** or grapple when yarding...
b. They used a cable system to **haul out the ore**.
c. another driver has a job as a second truck had **to haul the extra freight**.

Reversative *un-* (cf. Bauer et al. 2013, 371ff.) and iterative *re-* (cf. Bauer et al. 2013, 419f.; Lieber 2004) do not display any clear effects on argument structure and license the same argument types as their respective bases. This is shown for both prefixes and the (base) verb *to seal* in (15) (all from iWeb). In terms of semantic type, resealing-events are clearly sealing-events, while the negation semantics of reversative *un-* always changes the base's event type.

(15) a. I recently did use white teflon tape to **seal a fuel pressure tester joint** [...]
b. [...] **unsealing a pressure tube** with very high reliability is necessary each time a fuel bundle is added or taken away.
c. Its only an hours work to **reseal a swing cylinder** if everything goes ok [...]

In this study, we thus compare different deverbal prefixed verbs, which differ regarding the strength of argument structural effects as well as the change in semantic type of the respective bases. To our knowledge, this kind of comparison has not been addressed in work on distributional semantics before. Primarily, we are interested in the following question:

Research question 4 (RQ4) Compared to comparative *out-*, are the presumably weaker semantic contributions and the relative lack of induced argument structural effects of the prefixes *over–*, spatial *out-*, *un-*, and *re–* reflected distributionally in lower derivative-derivative similarities?

6.2 Methodology

We used the same methodology as in Study 3. We extracted additional corpus attestations for the four additional prefixes, choosing four base lemmas from the same verb class for each prefix except for spatial *out-*. The base lemmas are listed by prefix and base class in (16).

(16) a. *over-* + RUN class:
OVERDRIVE, OVERFLY, OVERRUN, OVERSTEP
b. spatial *out-* (various VerbNet classes):
OUTCROSS, OUTGAS, OUTLOAD, OUTSTREAM
c. *re-/un-* + TAPE class:
(i) REFASTEN, RELOCK, RESEAL, REWIND
(ii) UNFASTEN, UNLOCK, UNSEAL, UNWIND

As in Study 3, all vectors for the base verbs were created from the ukWaC sentences, while all vectors for the derivatives were created from the iWeb sentences. The absolute occurrences of forms with the additional prefixes in iWeb are given in Table 8.

Tab. 8: Derivatives with the additional prefixes in iWeb: absolute number of occurrences.

over-verb	occurrences	*out*-verb	occur.	*re*-verb	occur.	*un*-verb	occur.
overdrive	37629	outcross	1047	refasten	412	unfasten	2092
overfly	1495	outgas	2586	relock	1517	unlock	302674
overrun	35212	outload	64	reseal	7732	unseal	8591
overstep	6740	outstream	759	rewind	25894	unwind	54349

The number of overall occurrences varies considerably, with *outload* occurring just 64 times. For all other derivatives, as well as for all bases, the same downsampling to 100 items as in Study 3 was applied. Recall that comparing our approach to the word embeddings from Baroni et al. (2014) already included these pairs (see Section 5.2.4), and showed that downsampling successfully eliminates effects of absolute frequencies.

6.3 Results

Table 9 contrasts the results for spatial *over-* (left two columns) with those for comparative *out-* from Study 3 (right two columns), both with bases from the RUN-class.

Figure 4 shows the corresponding box plots, again with the p-values for the three target comparisons as bracket labels (with the graph for comparative *out-* again corresponding to the one presented in Study 3).

Spatial *over-* shows the same pattern as comparative *out-* with respect to base-derivative pairs being more similar than base-derivative non-pairs (W=42, p

Tab. 9: Average cosine similarites for the verbs from the RUN class, contrasting spatial *over-* and comparative *out-*.

	RUN (+ *over*)		RUN (+ *out*)	
	SIM	SD	SIM	SD
base-base	0.04	.004	0.04	0.01
base-derivative across pairs	0.04	.005	0.05	0.01
base-derivative pairwise	0.06	0.03	0.08	0.02
derivative-derivative	0.05	0.01	0.10	0.02

= .02967). The two prefixes are also similar in that for *over-*, derivative-derivative similarities are also higher than base-base similarities (W=1, p-value = 0.004). Noticeably, in both cases the difference between the conditions for comparative *out-* is more pronounced, with the similarities for the two *out-* conditions clearly higher than those of the corresponding *over-* conditions. In addition, while mean (and median) similarities for comparative *out-* are highest between derivatives (higher than for base-derivative pairs), for spatial *over-* the mean of base-derivative pairs are most similar, followed by the derivative-derivative ones, with the medians showing the same pattern as *out-*. Neither difference is significant.

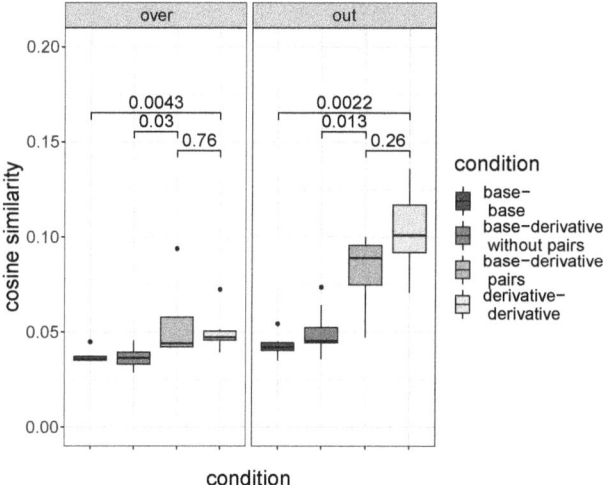

Fig. 4: Cosine similarites across the four different conditions for both *over-* and *out-* and the RUN class. The p-values for the target comparisons are given across the braces for the respective comparisons.

Table 10 contrasts the results for spatial *out-* with the across-classes results for comparative *out-* from Study 3 (see the 'all items' columns in Table 7). Figure 5 shows the corresponding figures with the p-values of the target comparisons.

Tab. 10: Average cosine similarites for spatial *out-* contrasted with comparative *out-*.

	spatial *out-*		comparative *out-*	
Pairings	SIM	SD	SIM	SD
base-base	0.03	0.01	0.04	0.01
base-derivative across pairs	0.03	0.01	0.04	0.01
base-derivative pairwise	0.05	0.03	0.06	0.02
derivative-derivative	0.04	0.01	0.07	0.03

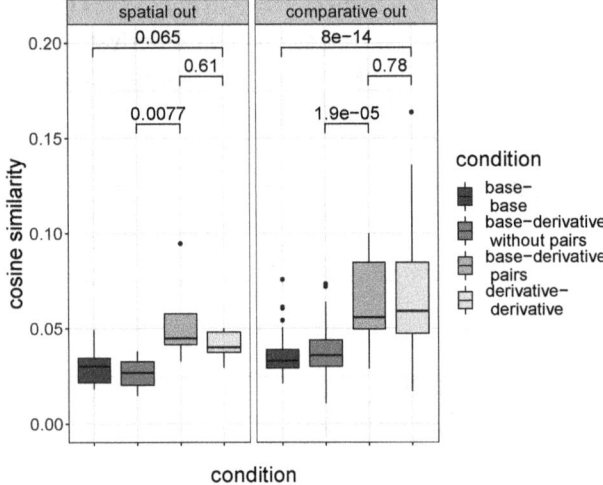

Fig. 5: Cosine similarites across the four different conditions for both spatial and comparative *out-*. The p-values for the target comparisons are given across the braces for the respective comparisons.

Similar to all results thus far, similarities of base-derivative pairs of spatial *out-* are higher than similarities of base-derivative non-pairs. This difference is significant (W = 45, p-value = 0.007692). Again, the base-base similarities are lower than the derivative-derivative similarities. This difference is not significant (W = 6, p-value = 0.06494). Importantly, just as for spatial *over-*, mean (and, in contrast to spatial *over-*, also median) pairwise base-derivative similarities are higher than derivative-derivative similarities for spatial *out-*. The difference is not significant (W = 15, p-value = 0.6095). As shown before, for comparative *out-*, this difference, while also not significant, goes in the opposite direction both across all classes and for each class individually.

The similarites for *un-* and *re-* with the same bases from the TAPE-class are shown in Table 11.

Tab. 11: Average cosine similarities for the bases from the TAPE class and their *un-* and *re-* derivatives.

	TAPE (+ *un*)		TAPE (+ *re*)	
	SIM	SD	SIM	SD
base-base	0.05	0.01	0.05	0.01
base-derivative across pairs	0.05	0.01	0.05	0.01
base-derivative pairwise	0.08	0.05	0.10	0.04
derivative-derivative	0.06	0.01	0.09	0.02

The prefixes *un-* and *re-* show the by now familiar patterns. Pairwise base-derivative measures are on average higher than pairless ones. However, the difference is not significant, neither for *un-* nor for *re-*, (both W = 40, p-value = .05824). The derivative-derivative similarities are higher than the base-base similarities. This is significant only for *re-* (W =1, p-value = .004). Importantly, the patterns again diverge from comparative *out-* in that base-derivative pairs show the highest similarities (both on means and medians), followed by derivative-derivative similarities. Just as before, this difference is not significant for either prefix.

6.4 Discussion

Based on our results, it is a general property of English deverbal verbs with a given prefix that they are more similar to each other than their respective bases are to each other. Likewise, base-derivative pairs are more similar than base-derivative non-pairs for all morphological processes. These properties are expected given the idea that any derivational process is characterized by a semantic core, and while they show up only partly significantly, they hold descriptively across the board. Regarding RQ4, an interesting difference between the prefixes emerges elsewhere: for comparative *out-*, derivatives are more similar to each other than base-derivative pairs. In this respect, the distributional behavior of *out-* clearly stands out among the prefixes we investigated.

This finding reinforces our interpretation that the word-formation process is by itself a highly pronounced semantic contributor to comparative *out*-derivatives, and arguably a more influential one than their respective bases. The most plausible reasons for the differences between prefixes are the change of semantic type and concurring argument structure alternation induced by comparative *out*-prefixation. In case this interpretation of the results of Study 4 is on the right track, it offers support for how we interpreted the findings of Study 3: the similarity differences we find between base-derivative pairs and across derivatives in *out*-prefixation follow from the prefix's applicative force, in particular with respect to licensed object arguments. At least relative to prefixes with different properties, this can be regarded as a peculiarity of comparative *out-*.

More generally, our results are of interest to distributional studies that deal with argument structure alternations. Recall that we are using distributional count models in this study (see section 5.2.4), and therefore cannot directly comment on prediction models. However, our findings that the one category that induces strong argument structural effects stands out is partly in line with Padó et al. (2016), who show that it is difficult to predict derivative semantics from the base for German derivational processes with argument structural effects. It is unclear to us, however, if there are other derivational processes in English with properties that are more similar to comparative *out-*'s and that would allow to further isolate argument structure as a core contributor to derivative similarity.

Finally, as remarked by one reviewer, a possibly confounding effect for our comparisons may be found in the differences of relative frequencies (see e.g. Hay 2001) and different degrees of lexicalization of the *out*-derivatives vis-à-vis the frequencies of the twelve additional prefixed lemmas. We chose our data largely on semantic grounds, and they do not allow for any conclusions in this respect. We can thus not exclude the possibility that relative frequency plays a role for the interpretation of Study 4.

7 Conclusion

In this paper, we have taken a decidedly quantitative approach for the investigation of a fundamental problem of derivational semantics, namely the semantic relatedness between different components of a word formation process. We have used English comparative *out*-prefixation as a testing ground and looked at the potential of bases to predict derivative semantics, at the relative uniformity of bases and derivatives, at similarities both across bases and across derivatives, and at comparisons with a number of further prefixes with diverging characteristics. Most generally, our results back up assumptions of comparative *out-*'s relative semantic richness as a word formation process, as well as assumptions of semantic relatedness being gradient in nature (cf. Spencer 2010a,b, 2013).

Studies 1 and 2 have shown that the resolution of systematic underspecification of *out-*'s comparative semantics is, largely, predicted by both base lemmas and by the semantic class of base lemmas, and that predictive power correlates with measures of the ambiguity of the members of these classes. We are not aware of studies that investigate such a form of underspecification for morphological processes. The findings are in line, however, with studies that show that the semantics of bases are crucial for constraining polysemy in derivation (e.g. Aronoff & Cho 2001; Kawaletz 2021; Plag et al. 2018).

Using distributional measures, Study 3 has revealed quantitative reflexes of two separate features of *out-*prefixation. First, derivatives and their bases show relative high degrees of similarity. Second, and more importantly, similarities between derivatives are far more pronounced. This constellation is peculiar to *out-*, as comparisons with four other prefixes have shown in the final study. Likely, this difference can be attributed to differences in the semantic structures that different word-formation processes systematically add to their respective bases. While our findings on differences of semantic coherence between the products of word formation processes are in line with other studies (see e.g. Wauquier 2020), we are not aware of studies that quantitatively reveal differences between base-derivative and derivative-derivative similarities of this kind.

A number of open issues require further investigation. As shown by, for example, Marelli & Baroni (2015) and Padó et al. (2016), different distributional measures are better suited for different word-formation processes. The role of lexicalization for frequent patterns, including fixed multi-word expressions (such as *to outstay one's welcome*), is likely to interfere with general ideas of compositionally derived vector representations in derivational semantics. Moreover, in all of our studies, we have generalized over base forms and, deliberately, not controlled for different senses. Possibly, sense selection for bases may allow for more accurate similarity measures between bases and derivatives from a distributional perspective. We leave these open issues to future research.

Acknowledgements

The research reported on in this article has been funded by the German Research Foundation (DFG project PL 151/11-1 'Semantics of derivational morphology' at Heinrich-Heine-Universität Düsseldorf and SFB 833 'The Construction of Meaning: The Dynamics and Adaptivity of Linguistic Structures' at Eberhard Karls Universität Tübingen). We thank Ingo Plag and two anonymous reviewers for helpful comments on earlier versions of the paper, and Ann-Sophie Haan for annotation work.

Bibliography

Ahn, Byron. 2022. Mapping *OUT*- argument structure. *Syntax* (to appear).
Aronoff, Mark. 1976. *Word formation in generative grammar.* Cambridge, MA: MIT Press.
Aronoff, Mark & Sungeon Cho. 2001. The semantics of -*ship. Linguistic Inquiry* 32. 167–173.
Baroni, Marco, Silvia Bernardini, Adriano Ferraresi & Eros Zanchetta. 2009. The WaCky wide web: A collection of very large linguistically processed web-crawled corpora. *Language Resources and Evaluation* 43(3). 209–226.
Baroni, Marco, Georgiana Dinu & Germán Kruszewski. 2014a. Don't count, predict! a systematic comparison of context-counting vs. context-predicting semantic vectors. *Proceedings of the 52nd Annual Meeting of the Association for Computational Linguistics, ACL 2014* 238–247.
Baroni, Marco, Georgiana Dinu & Germán Kruszewski. 2014b. Don't count, predict! Semantic vectors [Data set]. https://doi.org/10.5281/zenodo.2635544.
Bauer, Laurie, Rochelle Lieber & Ingo Plag. 2013. *The Oxford reference guide to English morphology.* Oxford: Oxford University Press.
Bird, Steven, Ewan Klein & Edward Loper. 2009. *Natural language processing with Python.* O'Reilly Media Inc.
Boleda, Gemma. 2020. Distributional semantics and linguistic theory. *Annual Review of Linguistics* 6. 213–234.
Bonami, Olivier & Matías Guzmán Naranjo. 2023. Distributional evidence for derivational paradigms. In Sven Kotowski & Ingo Plag (eds.), *The semantics of derivational morphology. Theory, methods, evidence* Linguistische Arbeiten, 219–259. Berlin: De Gruyter.
Bonami, Olivier & Denis Paperno. 2018. Inflection vs. derivation in a distributional vector space. *Lingue e Linguaggio* 17(2). 173–195.
Davies, Mark. 2018. The 14 billion word iWeb Corpus: Available online at https://corpus.byu.edu/iWeb/.
Haspelmath, Martin & Andrea D. Sims. 2013. *Understanding morphology. 2nd ed.* London and New York, NY: Routledge Taylor & Francis Group.
Hay, Jennifer. 2001. Lexical frequency in morphology: Is everything relative? *Linguistics* 39(6). 1041–1070.

Herweg, Michael. 2020. Motion verb constructions, frames, and profiling. *Questions and Answers in Linguistics* 6(1). 1–30.

Hill, Felix, Roi Reichart & Anna Korhonen. 2014. Simlex-999: Evaluating semantic models with (genuine) similarity estimation. *Computational Linguistics* 41(4). 665–695.

Kawaletz, Lea. 2021. *The semantics of English -ment nominalizations*. Düsseldorf: Heinrich-Heine-University Dissertation.

Kennedy, Christopher & Beth Levin. 2008. Measure of change: The adjectival core of degree achievements. In Louise McNally & Christopher Kennedy (eds.), *Adjectives and adverbs*, 156–182. Oxford: Oxford University Press.

Kennedy, Christopher & Louise McNally. 2005. Scale structure, degree modification, and the semantics of gradable predicates. *Language* (81). 345–381.

Kipper, Karin, Anna Korhonen, Neville Ryant & Martha Palmer. 2008. A large-scale classification of English verbs. *Language Resources and Evaluation* 42(1). 21–40.

Kisselew, Max, Sebastian Padó, Alexis Palmer & Jan Šnajder. 2015. Obtaining a better understanding of distributional models of German derivational morphology. In *Proceedings of the 11th international conference on computational semantics*, 58–63. London, UK: Association for Computational Linguistics. https://aclanthology.org/W15-0108.

Koefoed, Geert & Jaap van Marle. 2000. Productivity. In Geert E. Booij, Armin Burkhardt, Gerold Ungeheuer, Herbert Ernst Wiegand, Hugo Steger & Klaus Brinker (eds.), *1. Halbband: Ein internationales Handbuch zur Flexion und Wortbildung*, 303–311. Berlin: De Gruyter.

Kotowski, Sven. 2021. The semantics of English *out*-prefixation: A corpus-based investigation. *English Language and Linguistics* 25(1). 61–89.

Lapesa, Gabriella, Lea Kawaletz, Ingo Plag, Marios Andreou, Max Kisselew & Sebastian Padó. 2018. Disambiguation of newly derived nominalizations in context: A distributional semantics approach. *Word Structure* 11(3). 277–312.

Lapesa, Gabriella, Sebastian Padó, Tillmann Pross & Antje Rossdeutscher. 2017. Are doggies really nicer than dogs? The impact of morphological derivation on emotional valence in German. In *IWCS 2017 — 12th international conference on computational semantics — short papers*, https://aclanthology.org/W17-6922.

Lazaridou, Angeliki, Marco Marelli, Roberto Zamparelli & Marco Baroni. 2013. Compositional-ly derived representations of morphologically complex words in distributional semantics. In *Proceedings of the 51st annual meeting of the Association for Computational Linguistics (Volume 1: Long papers)*, 1517–1526. Sofia, Bulgaria: Association for Computational Linguistics. https://aclanthology.org/P13-1149.

Lieber, Rochelle. 2004. *Morphology and lexical semantics*. Cambridge: Cambridge University Press.

Lieber, Rochelle. 2016. *English nouns: The ecology of nominalization*. Cambridge: Cambridge University Press.

Maguire, Phil, Barry Devereux, Fintan Costello & Arthur Cater. 2007. A reanalysis of the carin theory of conceptual combination. *Journal of Experimental Psychology. Learning, Memory & Cognition* 33(4). 811–821.

Maienborn, Claudia. 2019. Flexible Bedeutungszuordnung im Lexikon: Polysemie – Unterbestimmtheit – Uminterpretation. In Yasuhiro Fujinawa & Jiro Inaba (eds.), *Wie entsteht Bedeutung? Semantik zwischen Grammatik, Kognition und Kontext*, 11–44. München: Iudicium Verlag.

Marchand, Hans. 1969. *The categories and types of present-day English word-formation*. 2nd ed. München: C.H. Beck.

Marelli, Marco & Marco Baroni. 2015. Affixation in semantic space: Modeling morpheme meanings with compositional distributional semantics. *Psychological Review* 122(3). 485–515.
McHugh, Marry L. 2012. Interrater reliability: the kappa statistic. *Biochemia Medica* 276–282.
McIntyre, Andrew. 2003. Preverbs, argument linking and verb semantics. In Geert Booij & Jaap Marle (eds.), *Yearbook of morphology 2003*, 119–144. Dordrecht and London: Kluwer Academic.
Mititelu, Verginica Barbu, Gianina Iordăchioaia, Svetlozara Leseva & Ivelina Stoyanova. 2023. The meaning of zero nouns and zero verbs. In Sven Kotowski & Ingo Plag (eds.), *The semantics of derivational morphology. Theory, methods, evidence*, 63–102. Berlin: De Gruyter.
Padó, Sebastian, Aurélie Herbelot, Max Kisselew & Jan Šnajder. 2016. Predictability of distributional semantics in derivational word formation. In *Proceedings of COLING*, 1285–1296. Osaka, Japan: The COLING 2016 Organizing Committee. https://aclanthology.org/C16-1122.
Plag, Ingo. 2003. *Word-formation in English*. Cambridge: Cambridge University Press.
Plag, Ingo, Marios Andreou & Lea Kawaletz. 2018. A frame-semantic approach to polysemy in affixation. In Olivier Bonami, Gilles Boyé, Georgette Dal, Hélène Giraudo & Fiammetta Namer (eds.), *The lexeme in descriptive and theoretical morphology*, 546–568. Berlin: Language Science Press.
Plag, Ingo, Lea Kawaletz, Sabine Arndt-Lappe & Rochelle Lieber. 2023. Analogical modeling of derivational semantics. Two case studies. In Sven Kotowski & Ingo Plag (eds.), *The semantics of derivational morphology. Theory, methods, evidence* Linguistische Arbeiten, 103–141. Berlin: De Gruyter.
Rainer, Franz, Wolfgang U. Dressler, Francesco Gardani & Hans Christian Luschützky. 2014. Morphology and meaning: An overview. In Franz Rainer, Francesco Gardani, Hans Christian Luschützky & Wolfgang U. Dressler (eds.), *Morphology and meaning*, 3–46. Amsterdam and Philadelphia: John Benjamins.
Rappaport Hovav, Malka & Beth Levin. 1992. *-er-*nominals: Implications for a theory of argument structure. In Tim Stowell & Timothy Stowell (eds.), *Syntax and the lexicon*, 127–153. New York, NY: Academic Press.
Rappaport Hovav, Malka & Beth Levin. 2001. An event structure account of English resultatives. *Language* 77(4). 766–797.
Schröder, Anne. 2011. *On the productivity of verbal prefixation in English: Synchronic and diachronic perspectives*. Tübingen: Narr.
Schäfer, Martin. 2020. Distributional profiling and the semantics of modifier classes. In Christopher Pinon & Laurent Roussarie (eds.), *Empirical issues in syntax and semantics 13*, 139–166. Paris: CSSP.
Schäfer, Martin. 2023. Splitting -*lys*: Using word embeddings to distinguish derivation and inflection. In Sven Kotowski & Ingo Plag (eds.), *The semantics of derivational morphology. Theory, methods, evidence* Linguistische Arbeiten, 261–296. Berlin: De Gruyter.
Solt, Stephanie. 2015. Measurement scales in natural language. *Language and Linguistics Compass* 9(1). 14–32.
Spencer, Andrew. 2010a. Factorizing lexical relatedness. In Susan Olsen (ed.), *New impulses in word-formation*, 133–172. Hamburg: Helmut Buske Verlag.
Spencer, Andrew. 2010b. Lexical relatedness and the lexical entry – a formal unification. In Stefan Müller (ed.), *Proceedings of the 17th international conference on head-driven phrase structure grammar*, 322–340. Stanford: CSLI Publications.
Spencer, Andrew. 2013. *Lexical relatedness*. Oxford: Oxford University Press.

Talmy, Leonard. 2000. *Toward a cognitive semantics. Vol.II: Typology and process in concept structuring*. Cambridge, MA: MIT Press.
Tolskaya, Inna. 2014. *Verbal prefixes: Selection and interpretation*. Tromsø: University in Tromsø Dissertation.
Varvara, Rossella. 2017. *Verbs as nouns: Empirical investigations on event-denoting nominalizations*. Trento: University of Trento dissertation.
Varvara, Rossella, Gabriella Lapesa & Sebastian Padó. 2021. Grounding semantic transparency in context. *Morphology* 31. 1–38.
Wauquier, Marine. 2020. *Confrontation des procédés dérivationnels et des catégories sémantiques dans les modèles distributionnels*. Toulouse: University of Toulouse Dissertation.
Wunderlich, Dieter. 2012. 84. Operations on argument structure. In Claudia Maienborn, Klaus von Heusinger & Paul Portner (eds.), *Semantics* Handbücher zur Sprach- und Kommunikationswissenschaft, 2224–2259. Berlin: De Gruyter.
Zwarts, Joost. 2008. Aspects of a typology of direction. In Susan D. Rothstein (ed.), *Theoretical and crosslinguistic approaches to the semantics of aspect*, 79–105. Amsterdam: John Benjamins.

Olivier Bonami & Matías Guzmán Naranjo
Distributional evidence for derivational paradigms

Abstract: This paper provides evidence from distributional semantics on the importance of paradigmatic relations in word formation systems. We argue that, if paradigmatic relations play a systemic role, that role should be measurable by examining whether pairs of lexemes derived from a common base (e.g. *baker* and *bakery* derived from *bake*) have semantic properties that are more readily predictable from one another than they are from the semantics of the base. We implement that idea using statistical models that predict the distributional vector of a lexeme based on that of another lexeme in the same derivational family. Applying the method on French data, we show that some (but by no means all) pairs of derivational processes give rise to undisputably paradigmatic properties and hence provide evidence of a systemic role for paradigmatic relations.

Keywords: derivational paradigms, semantics, analogical modeling

1 Introduction

There is a variety of ways lexemes may be morphologically related. Within a morphological family, some lexemes stand in a clear base-derivative relation, e.g. *lover* derives from *love*; others stand in a determinate but indirect relation, e.g. *lover* and *lovable* are indirectly related through their shared base *love*. In many other cases, while the two lexemes are clearly related, the exact nature of that relation is hard if not impossible to determine; think e.g. of accidental cases such as the relation between *social* and *society* or more systematic cases such as the relation between *pessimism* and *pessimist*. Clearly then, lexemes in a family entertain a variety of PARADIGMATIC RELATIONS, only some of which are base-derivative relations.

The idea that paradigmatic relations in general play an important role in word formation has received renewed interest by some, and skepticism by others, in the last few years; witness individual papers such as Štekauer (2014); Bauer (2019) as well as collections such as Hathout & Namer (2018, 2019); Fernández-Domínguez et al. (2020). The debate centers on two issues: the extent to which derivational families can be said to share properties of inflectional paradigms, and the existence and importance of predictability relations among members of a derivational family that cannot be reduced to their shared relationship to a common base.

In this paper we focus on the latter issue, and argue that hard quantitative evidence is needed to settle it and establish whether nontrivial paradigmatic relations play a systematic role in word formation. To this end, we deploy on French data methods from distributional semantics to assess the semantic interpredictability between pairs of lexemes derived from a common base, and compare it to semantic predictability from the base. We conclude that definitive evidence for nontrivial paradigmatic relations can be found in some but not all corners of the word formation system.

The structure of this paper is as follows. Section 2 presents an overview of the literature on derivational paradigms, and contextualizes our study. Section 3 gives a brief introduction to key ideas from distributional semantics, and formalizes our hypothesis. In Section 4 we present our dataset and the methods for this study. Section 5 contains the results, followed by a discussion of the results in Section 6. Section 7 concludes.

2 Derivational paradigms

2.1 Motivations for derivational paradigms

Conventional theories of word formation typically assume that derivational morphology is organized in terms of oriented (base, derivative) relationships, where each morphologically complex unit is motivated by a prior and morphologically simpler unit. This is formulated differently in different traditions: in a morpheme-based approach, the complex unit is formed by adding a morpheme to the simpler unit; in lexeme-based approaches of the tradition initiated by Aronoff (1976),[1] the meaning and shape of a derived lexeme is motivated by the application of a Lexeme Formation Rule to another base lexeme. Both approaches however share the view that derivational families are normally structured as rooted trees (Stump, 2019), with one unit serving as the ultimate ancestor for the whole family. Figure 1 illustrates this for the family of the English noun *center*.

A consequence of this view of derivational families is that not all situations of predictable morphological relatedness have the same value. As a case in point, consider the pair of lexemes (*centralizer*, *decentralizer*) from Figure 1: while there

---

[1] As Aronoff (1994, 7) clarifies, the term 'word-based' was an unfortunate choice for the approach developed there. We follow the more recent and accurate usage here.

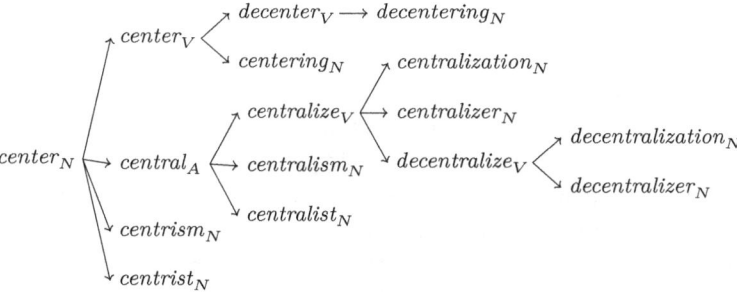

Fig. 1: Example of a derivational family structured as a rooted tree.

is a large series of pairs of English nouns that differ formally by the presence of the prefix *de-* and implement parallel semantic contrasts, this perceptible morphological relatedness is assumed not to be a derivational relation, but a consequence of the existence of a common base *centralize* from which both derive directly (*centralize→centralizer*) or indirectly (*centralize→decentralize→decentralizer*).

Yet there is ample and well-known evidence for the existence of situations where the rooted-tree model of derivational families fails to capture the full extent of morphological relatedness involving derivational processes. We document some of these in the remainder of this subsection (see also Bauer et al. 2013, chap. 23 for a compendium of the evidence from English). Our list is by no means meant to be exhaustive, but should give the reader a feel for the nature and importance of the phenomena under consideration; see among many others Marle (1984); Becker (1993); Bauer (1997); Booij (1997); Roché (2011b); Hathout & Namer (2014b); Strnadová (2014b) for more detailed discussion.

2.1.1 Back-formation

Probably the most well-known relevant situation is BACK-FORMATION. The term describes cases where there is clear historical or morphological evidence that the existence of a morphologically more complex unit motivated the coining of the simpler one rather than the other way around. A well-known example is English *bartend* from *bartender*: because English has NN compounds but no NV compounds, it is clear that the verb was modeled on the agent noun and not the other way around. While back-formation is usually considered to be an interesting but abnormal use of morphological resources, Namer (2012) provides compelling evidence for the highly productive use of backformation to coin verbs from neoclassical compounds in French.

2.1.2 Multimotivation

A different but important family of situations that challenges the received view are cases of MULTIMOTIVATION, where multiple members of a derivational family function as motivators for a derivative. The simplest subtype is the situation where it is undecidable which of two or more derivation trees should be postulated for a given derivative. Corbin (1976) famously discusses the case of French *assymétrique*, whose English cognate *asymmetrical* shares the same properties: it is undecidable whether it should be seen as deriving from *asymmetry* by suffixation of *-ical*, or from *symmetrical* by prefixation of *a-*. As Figure 2 illustrates, one would be tempted to model this by having two converging derivation relations leading to the same form, if that did not go against the rooted tree view of derivational families. Importantly however, while it is unpleasant to have to choose arbitrarily one of the two rooted trees (i.e. including one of the two dashed arrows in the figure but not the other), there is no morphological generalization that is not captured by both; hence arguably nothing valuable is lost by making that choice.

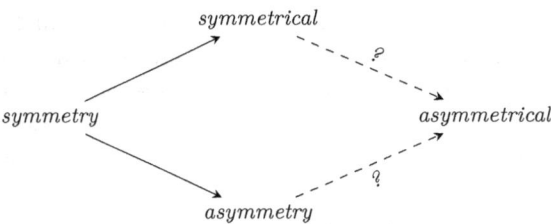

Fig. 2: The position of *asymmetrical* in its derivational family.

Multimotivation is more problematic in cases where it combines with a FORM-CONTENT MISMATCH (Hathout & Namer, 2014b). In such situations, the lexeme that is the manifest formal base for a derivative is distinct from the (related) lexeme from which the meaning of the derivative seems to follow. Hence *frequentist* is based formally on *frequent*, but its meaning is based on that of *frequency*: a frequentist values frequency, not things that are frequent. This is represented graphically in Figure 3. Likewise, *pessimistic* is based formally on *pessimist* but relates semantically more readily to *pessimism*. While such situations have a family resemblance with the case of *asymmetrical* discussed above, they crucially differ in that no choice of a rooted tree really captures the situation: since two lexemes in the family make complementary contributions to motivating the derivative, neither can be ignored.

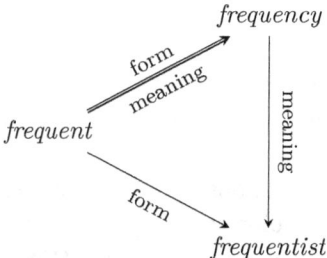

Fig. 3: The position of *frequentist* in its derivational family. Double arrows indicate convergent motivation by form and meaning, while single arrows indicate motivation in one dimension only.

More situations of multimotivation can and should be documented. In the preceding example, the two motivators make orthogonal contributions, since one is crucial for form and the other for meaning. Sometimes two motivators are crucial for meaning, with the derivative being ambiguous between a reading relating to one or the other (Strnadová, 2014b). For instance, *senatorial* has both a reading derived from *senator* (as in *senatorial family*, a family consisting of senators) and a reading derived from *senate* (as in *senatorial palace*, the palace hosting the senate). Because the two readings are closely related, it would be odd to treat this as a situation of homonymy, with two distinct lexemes derived independently, rather than polysemy, with a single derived lexeme. But if polysemy is posited, then we have a single lexeme whose semantics is jointly motivated by two separate other members of the derivational family. This is depicted in Figure 4.

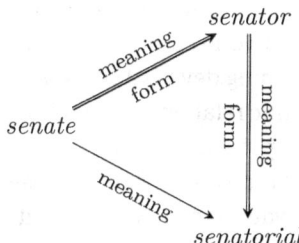

Fig. 4: The position of *senatorial* in its derivational family.

2.1.3 Cross-formation

Becker (1993) calls CROSS-FORMATION situations where pairs of lexemes stand in a relation of mutual motivation with no reason to assume that one direction of derivation is preferrable to the other.

As Becker notes, conversion is a prime source of situations of cross-formation. Since conversion pairs do not contrast in their morphological complexity, form provides no strong argument for directionality. As discussed by Marchand (1963), sometimes semantics does not help either: for instance, it makes just as much sense to see the nouns *judge* as deriving from the verb *judge*, by analogy to the derivation of *leader* from *lead*, or the verb *judge* as deriving from the noun *judge*, by analogy to the derivation of *deputize* from *deputy*. We may depict such a situation of cross-formation as in Figure 5.

Fig. 5: Conversion as cross-formation.

Reporting on a detailed investigation of verb-noun conversion pairs in French, Tribout (2020) shows that the situation exemplified with *judge* is general. She argues convincingly that the only unambiguous evidence for directionality in conversion comes from situations where the prior derivational history makes it obvious which member of the pair came first: for instance, *parlement* 'parliament' is the source for *parlementer* 'negotiate' rather than the other way around, because it obviously derives from *parler* 'speak' through the *-ment* noun-forming deverbal suffix; conversely, *décharge* 'dump, discharge' must derive from *décharger* 'unload, discharge', because of the presence of the verb-forming deverbal suffix *dé-*.[2] Analyzing 626 such cases with the help of a set of semantic relations derived from those of Plag (1999), Tribout observes that 85% of the pairs are related by a reversible semantic function with both directions of derivation attested. As a consequence, semantics does not motivate a direction of derivation in the vast majority of cases. Zooming out to the much larger set of conversion pairs where derivational history provides no motivation either, she concludes that absence of clear directionality is the rule rather than the exception in French verb-noun conversion pairs.

---

[2] Compare Barbu Mititelu et al. (2023), which relies on etymological information from the *Oxford English Dictionary* to establish directionality, a method Tribout explicitly argues against.

A different type of cross-formation involves substitutive morphology, and is nicely illustrated by *-ist*/*-ism* pairs and their cognates in various European languages. While there is no doubt that *-ist* and *-ism* derivatives can productively be formed by simple suffixation (witness *Trump, Trumpism, Trumpist*), it has long been observed[3] that the lexicon contains numerous pairs that are readily relatable to one another without being relatable to a common base (e.g. *fascism, fascist; optimism, optimist; masochism, masochist*). In addition, even where a common base clearly exists, the semantic relationship between the two derived terms is often more crisp and predictable than their relationship to their common base. For a telling example, consider the triple (*social, socialism, socialist*). While there is a nonarbitrary relation between *social* and its two derivatives, the meaning of the latter can hardly be predicted from that of the former. It is worth citing in full the Oxford English Dictionary's definition of the main reading of *socialism*,[4] to highlight the convoluted relation between its meaning and that of *social*.

> A theory or system of social organization based on state or collective ownership and regulation of the means of production, distribution, and exchange for the common benefit of all members of society; advocacy or practice of such a system, esp. as a political movement. Now also: any of various systems of liberal social democracy which retain a commitment to social justice and social reform, or feature some degree of state intervention in the running of the economy.

By contrast, *socialist* is simply defined as 'an advocate or supporter of socialism'; arguably, there is a transparent, bidirectional relationship between *socialism* (the doctrine of socialists) and *socialist* (an adherent to socialism), which is lacking between the two derivatives and their formal base. This is depicted graphically in Figure 6, with thicker lines indicating stronger motivation. Parallel observations hold for dozens if not hundreds of comparable triples of words.[5]

These observations suggest that speakers are attuned to a close relationship between *-ism* and *-ist* lexemes, allowing them to productively derive one from the other, independently of whether or to what extent a relationship to a common base can be inferred. That is, there is evidence for the existence of strong morphological regularities linking the two series of suffixed nouns in both directions, that are more reliable than those linking them to their formal base.

---

[3] Marle (1984) traces back observations to that effect in the Dutch tradition to a 1944 paper by Gerlach Royen. See also Roché (2011a) for extensive discussion of the French facts.
[4] Consulted online on December 21, 2021.
[5] See Rainer (2018) for a fascinating tour of the evolving meanings of *capitalist* and *capitalism* in European languages from the 17th century on, suggesting that the tight parallelism between *-ism* and *-ist* formations in the context of political doctrines is a relatively recent development.

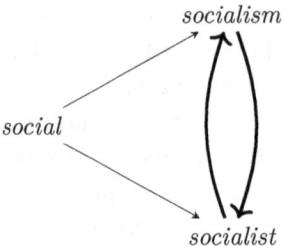

Fig. 6: The position of *socialism* and *socialist* in their derivational family.

2.2 Derivational paradigms

The existence of situations of back-formation, multimotivation, and cross-formation, has been documented for decades. Yet they have had limited impact of mainstream morphological theorizing. The most typical position, still held by many, is dismissal: while their existence is acknowledged, they are deemed not to fall within the scope of morphology, either as a matter of principle or because they are assumed to be rare exceptions.

The seminal study of Marle (1984) made a strong case that such phenomena should not be ignored by morphologists. Van Marle argues that PARADIGMATIC RELATIONS grounding what he calls SECONDARY or ANALOGICAL coinings need to be recognized, but that these are qualitatively different from derivational relations and should be treated outside the derivational system. This view was then popularized in the context of Construction Morphology (Booij, 2010) through the distinction between first-order (classical derivation) and second-order (paradigmatic relations) schemas, and adopted under a different name (daughter vs. sister schemas) by Relational Morphology (Jackendoff & Audring, 2020); see Audring (2019) for a recent and cogent discussion.

A more radical type of reaction is to conclude that unexpected word formation strategies should lead us to rethink entirely the architecture of the derivational system. Under this view, paradigmatic relations structure derivational families across the board, irrespective of whether it is possible to make sense of some of these relations in terms of oriented (base, derivative) relationships. Variants of this view are defended, among others, by Robins (1959); Becker (1993); Bochner (1993); Bauer (1997); Štekauer (2014); Bonami & Strnadová (2019); Hathout & Namer (2022). Crucial to this type of approach is the observation of parallels between inflectional paradigms and derivational families, leading to some notion of a DERIVATIONAL PARADIGM seen as a system of morphological relations that is parallel across derivational families. In particular, just as in inflection, the organization of derivationally-related words in terms of syntactic and semantic contrasts should be seen as conceptually orthogonal to the nature of the formal relationship they entertain.

There are important conceptual differences both between these two families of views and across studies within each of the two groups.[6] These are of little consequence for the present work, which focuses mostly on empirical evidence for a systemic role of paradigmatic relations in derivational morphology. For concreteness though, we will rely on Bonami & Strnadová's (2019) theoretical elaboration, according to which a paradigmatic system is a set of partial families of morphologically related words aligned using parallel contrasts of content. Figure 7 exhibits a simple example of a derivational paradigmatic system in this sense: the semantic contrasts between verb and agent noun, verb and action noun, agent noun and action noun, are the same (at some appropriate level of granularity) across all three derivational families, despite the use of different formal strategies (three different affixes for the action nouns, use of different types of stem allomorphs for the agent nouns). Once such broad semantic contrasts have been identified as motivating alignment across partial families, each collection of aligned lexemes can be seen as filling the same cell in a derivational paradigm. Bonami & Strnadová argue that this allows one to capture similarities between paradigmatic organization in inflection and derivation while doing justice to important differences such as the open-endedness of derivational families and the stronger semantic predictability of inflectional relations (Bonami & Paperno, 2018). Note that, in the spirit of abstractive word-based morphology (Blevins, 2006), there is no notion that some morphological relations between pairs of cells are prior to others: the fully connected graph of all pairs of cells is worthy of investigation, and any member of a paradigm is partially predictive of all other members; the focus of inquiry is in assessing quantitatively the strength of these predictability relations, without any preconception about some lexemes being more 'truly' connected than others.[7]

---

6 There are interesting parallels to be drawn here with the distinction, within approaches to inflection, between realizational approaches such as Paradigm Function Morphology (Stump, 2001, 2016), which use separate mechanisms to derive wordforms from stems and to capture direct implicative relations between wordforms, and abstractive word-based approaches (Blevins, 2006, 2016), which argue that all derivations from subword units are superfluous.

7 In this context, the representations in Figures 2–6 can all be seen as partial impressionistic representations of predictability relations within derivational paradigms.

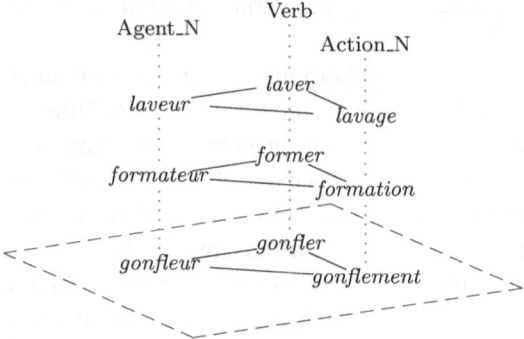

Fig. 7: Example of a derivational paradigmatic system. Horizontal planes represent partial derivational families; horizontal edges represent aligned semantic contrasts; and vertical dotted lines materialize aligned lexemes, filling the same cell in their respective derivational paradigms.

2.3 Towards systematic evidence for derivational paradigms

In the previous paragraphs we outlined some the main empirical arguments for the view that paradigmatic relations play an important role in the organization of morphological families. It is striking that, while some of these arguments have been on the table for decades, many morphologists remain unconvinced. We submit that one of the causes of that situation is the lack of quantitative evidence bearing on the issue: the debate is not whether some cases exist where morphological structure is used to coin new words that are not derivatives of a simpler base; rather, the debate is whether these are common enough to be considered part of the core of morphology, warranting radical changes to one's understanding of its architecture.

Hence we are on the lookout not just for paradigmatic effects in derivation, but for paradigmatic effects that are systematic. Bonami & Strnadová (2019) provide relevant evidence based on predictability of *form* rather than *meaning*. Building on previous quantitative work on the implicative structure of inflectional paradigms (Ackerman et al., 2009; Ackerman & Malouf, 2013), they examine how predictive the shape of words in each cell in a derivational paradigm is of the shape of words in other cells in that derivational paradigm, using conditional entropy of phonological shape classes as a measure of average predictability.[8] Focusing on French verbs and related agent and action nouns, they show that on

---

[8] More precisely, they examine the relationship between the phonological shape of citation forms, and rely on the modeling strategy detailed in (Bonami & Beniamine, 2016): reported num-

average, the shape of an agent noun is more readily predictable from that of the corresponding action noun than from that on the base verb; while the shape of an action noun is equally hard to predict from the base verb as from the agent noun. This is represented graphically in Figure 8, where a higher entropy value indicates more unpredictability. Note also the interesting observation that the derivatives provide better evidence for the shape of their base than the other way around.

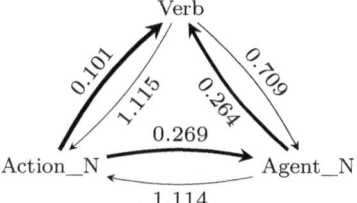

Fig. 8: Form predictability in French derivational paradigms, as measured by conditional entropy. Thicker lines correspond to higher predictability (and hence lower entropy).

Our goal in this paper is to explore whether similar evidence can be found looking at meaning rather than form. We focus on situations where two derivational processes[9] readily apply to the same base, making it possible to compare semantically triples of a base and two derivatives that are maximally similar from a formal point of view. Note that this is one of the configurations that led to the observation of cross-formations. In this situation, the mainstream view predicts that on average, the semantics of the base should be a better predictor of the semantics of each derivative than the derivatives are of each other.

Anecdotal evidence certainly points in the direction of that situation being common. Consider the two French triples in Figure 9. In the one on the left, the verb is polysemous with two main readings, and each of its two derivatives only has one reading, relating to one of the two readings of the verb. As a result, there is only a very loose semantic connection between the two derived nouns, while both relate very clearly to the base. In the one on the right, both derivatives have a

---

bers are the conditional entropy of the shape alternation linking two forms given relevant information on the shape of the predictor. All numbers were computed using Sacha Beniamine's Qumín package (Beniamine, 2018) applied to data from the Démonette database (Hathout & Namer, 2014a).

9 For the purposes of this study, we individualize derivational processes by form alternation and part of speech of the input and output; hence neither affix polysemy nor affix rivalry play a role in individualizing processes.

predictable meaning 'user of pumps', but both have been lexicalized with a much more specific reading. While predictability of the derived meaning from the base meaning is already lower in this case, the connection between the meaning of the two derivatives is even thinner.

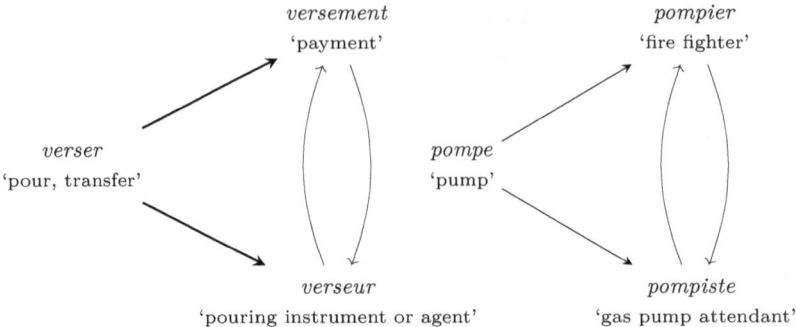

Fig. 9: Two French triples illustrating base predictiveness.

These two examples contrast directly with that of *social, socialism* and *socialist* pictured in Figure 6, where the semantic relationship between the two derivatives is both more transparent and more predictable than their relations to the adjectival base. What we do not know at this point is how prevalent each of these situations is: if we compare *-ment* and *-eur* (or *-ier* and *-iste*) suffixation in French, is it generally true that the base is a better predictor of derivative semantics, or did we just find a cute but isolated example? And what about *-isme* and *-iste*? Stated more broadly, our research question is then: are there pairs of processes applicable to the same bases where on average, the derivatives are more interpredictable than they are from the base? If the answer is yes, then this is strong evidence that paradigmatic relations between derivatives from the same base must be taken at face value.

Our assessment of the semantic interpredictability of morphologically related lexemes will rely on distributional semantics, to which we now turn.

3 Distributional semantics for morphology

In this paper we rely on a distributional representation of meaning (Harris, 1954; Firth, 1957). Under the distributional hypothesis, the meaning of a word is reflected in its distribution, so that words with similar meanings will appear in similar contexts. In practice, this view of semantics allows us to operationalize the meaning of a word as a numeric vector which we can induce automatically from large corpora. While current implementations of distributional models are not transparent in how they represent the meanings of words, the insight that words with similar meanings have similar distributions is directly captured in terms of the cosine similarity between two vectors (Lenci, 2008). Early work on distributional semantics employed count models, that is, the vector of a word was estimated directly by counting its coocurrences with other words in a corpus (Evert, 2014; Turney & Pantel, 2010; Turney, 2012; Miller & Charles, 1991; Erk, 2012; Baroni et al., 2014). More recent implementations of distributional semantics (e.g. Mikolov et al. 2013b) work by training a neural network to predict each word from its context, and then using the representation used by the network as the distributional vector of the word.[10] Since we are not interested in interpreting the individual vectors themselves, we will work with vectors induced using neural networks.

Distributional vectors have been put to use in all kinds of contexts in computational semantics and natural language processing. Interestingly for our purposes, one observation is that they can be used to draw semantic analogies to a surprising level of accuracy (Mikolov et al., 2013b; Pennington et al., 2014), to the point that accuracy of semantic analogies has quickly become a standard way of assessing the quality of a vector space. To take a concrete example, consider the situation depicted if Figure 10. We know the vectors for the words *Paris*, *France*, and *Colombia*, depicted in black, and we want to find a candidate vector for the word that is semantically to *Colombia* what *Paris* is to *France*. One simple way of doing this is to substract from the vector for *Paris* the vector for *France* and then add back the vector from *Colombia* (both operations depicted in blue). The empirical observation is then that this predicted vector is quite close in vector space (as measured by cosine similarity) to the actual vector for *Bogotá*, depicted in red. And there is a good reason for this: because $(France, Paris)$ and $(Colombia, Bogotá)$ stand in the same semantic relation, the difference vectors $\overrightarrow{Paris - France}$ and $\overrightarrow{Bogotá - Colombia}$ are expected to be nearly identical.

To illustrate semantic analogies we purposefully used an example where there is no morphological relation between the words under consideration. However if we move back to morphology, at least in simple cases, we expect pairs of words related by the same formal process to stand in the same relation, and hence for the difference vectors between bases and derivatives to be similar to one another (Marelli & Baroni, 2015). Figure 11 illustrates this idea with the example

---

10 Note that count models are still used in cases in which interpretability is more important that predictive accuracy (Boleda, 2020; Varvara et al., 2021).

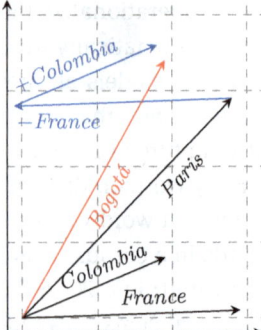

Fig. 10: Semantic analogies using distributional vectors: Bogotá is to Colombia as Paris is to France.

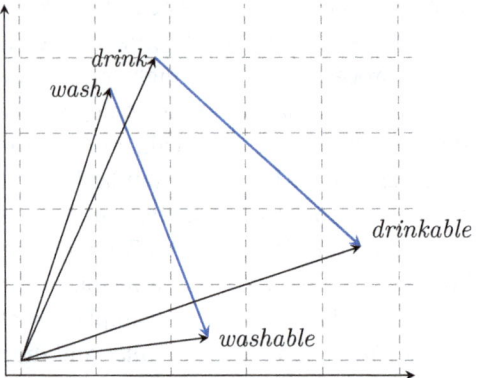

Fig. 11: Example of the distributional representation of *-able*.

of *able* adjectives in English. While *wash* and *drink* on the one hand and *washable* and *drinkable* on the other hand might be quite dissimilar, we expect the vector from *wash* to *washable* and the vector from *drink* to *drinkable* to be very similar to each other.

This fact effectively allows us to understand the semantics of a morphological process as a function linking the meanings of two words, as first advocated in detail by Marelli & Baroni (2015). For example, Bonami & Paperno (2018) compared the degree of predictability in derivational and inflection morphology. Their study showed that inflectional processes have more predictable semantics than derivational processes. Figure 12 illustrates this idea. In this example, the vectors from the infinitive to third singular are more consistent (more similar in length and di-

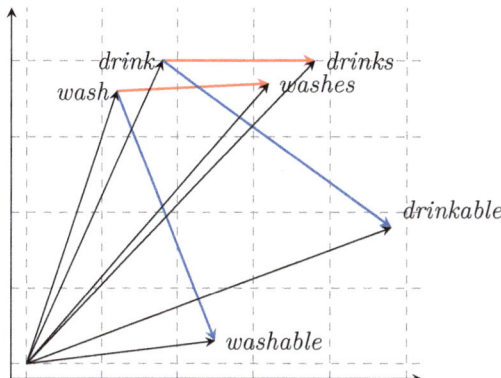

Fig. 12: Difference between derivation and inflection in distributional semantics.

rection) than the vectors going from the infinitive to the corresponding *-able* adjective.

Other examples of relevant studies leveraging distributional semantics to study semantic aspects of derivational processes are Padó et al. (2016); Lapesa et al. (2018); Amenta et al. (2020); Wauquier et al. (2020); Huyghe & Wauquier (2020, 2021); Varvara et al. (2021), whereas (Mickus et al., 2019; Guzmán Naranjo, 2020; Guzmán Naranjo & Bonami, 2021) use it to study inflection. We cannot do a complete review of literature on the matter in this paper, for a more exhaustive discussion of how distributional semantics has been used in linguistic theory see Boleda (2020).

We are now in a position to state our research question in terms of distributional semantics. Remember that we want, for a pair of processes that apply to the same bases, to compare the semantic interpredictability of two derivatives among themselves to how predictable each derivative is from its base. To this end we can set up partial paradigmatic systems in the sense of Bonami & Strnadová (2019) consisting of triples of words (x_i, y_i, z_i), such that all (x_i, y_i) pairs instantiate the same derivational process, and likewise all (x_i, z_i) pairs instantiate a second process, as shown in Table 1.

We now can tabulate the corresponding triples of distributional vectors $(\vec{x}_i, \vec{y}_i, \vec{z}_i)$ and compare the average predictability of each of the morphosemantic relations represented in the table. We are on the lookout for situations such as that illustrated in Figure 13: here, the $\vec{y}_i$s and the $\vec{z}_i$s relate to one another in a (more or less) uniform way, while the relations between $\vec{x}_i$s and the $\vec{y}_i$s vary widely; likewise for the relations between $\vec{x}_i$s and the $\vec{z}_i$s. If such situations can be documented, then they constitute strong evidence for models that take into

Tab. 1: Abstract representation of a set of triples of words exemplifying two processes applying to the same base.

Base	Process$_1$	Process$_2$
x_1	y_1	z_1
x_2	y_2	z_2
x_3	y_3	z_3
...	...	...

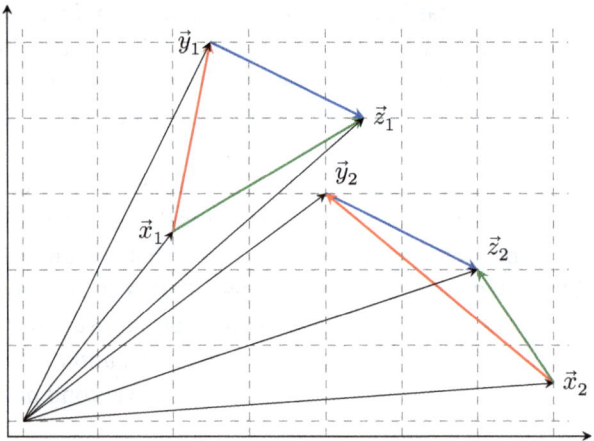

Fig. 13: Situations of interest, where derivatives are more interpredictable (blue vectors) than either is from their common base (red and green vectors).

account paradigmatic relations.[11] Note that what matters here is whether the difference vectors $\vec{z}_1 - \vec{y}_1$ and $\vec{z}_2 - \vec{y}_2$ are similar to one another, not whether $\vec{y}_1$ and $\vec{z}_1$ (or $\vec{y}_2$ and $\vec{z}_2$) are similar: we aim to assess the systematicity of contrasts across morphological families, not the proximity between members of a family.[12]

Before proceeding to explain how we implemented this idea, it is worth emphasizing what the structure of our argument is. Our aim is to compare the prediction of a classical view of derivation, where only (base, derivative) relations constitute linguistic knowledge, to that of a paradigmatic model, where all relations between pairs of lexemes in a family may constitute such knowledge. The prediction of a classical model is that a base should always be the best predictor of the properties of its derivatives; the prediction of a paradigmatic model is that this need not be the case, not that it can't be the case. Hence any situation of the type represented in Figure 13 is evidence for paradigmatic models. Situations where the base is the best predictor are irrelevant to the comparison, as the two types of models do not make contrasting predictions on these. Despite this, we will report on all the comparisons we have conducted, not just those that provide evidence on our main research question, as these turn out to raise interesting questions for future research.

---

11 Note that such situations are the analogue for predictability of meaning of the situations documented by Bonami & Strnadová (2019) for predictability of form: the base is a poorer predictor of properties of a derivative than another member of the derivational family.
12 In a study of eventive nominalizations in German, Varvara et al. (2021) rely on comparisons of base and derivative vectors to evaluate the average transparency of different rival processes. It is worth clarifying why we do not use the same methodology and follow instead the lead of Marelli & Baroni (2015); Bonami & Paperno (2018); Mickus et al. (2019). First, Varvara et al.'s methodology makes sense when comparing *rival* processes that have the same types of inputs and outputs. This is not the case for us, leading to problems: the similarity between pairs of vectors is bound to be heavily influenced by the corresponding words sharing a part of speech or ontological type. Hence we expect e.g. deverbal agent and event nouns to be more similar to one another than they are to their base, just by virtue of both being nouns. Likewise we expect verbs and event nouns to be more similar than verbs and agent nouns, because they both denote eventualities. Clearly these facts are orthogonal to our research question, which pertains to the diversity of semantic relations between pairs of words that stand in the same formal relation. Second, Varvara et al.'s (2021) careful study led to mixed results, and in particular did not confirm the hypothesis that average cosine similarity between base and derivative reflects intuitions on the relative transparency of different processes. This contrasts with the robust results of Marelli & Baroni (2015) and Bonami & Paperno (2018) relying on basically the same methodology we are adopting here.

4 Materials and methods

All materials used in this study (datasets, vector spaces, and R scripts) are available at https://zenodo.org/record/5799577.

4.1 Dataset

For this project we compiled a dataset of derivational processes in French by combining information from various sources: Hathout & Namer (2014a) for relations between verbs and nouns; Tribout (2010b) for nouns and verbs related by conversion; Koehl (2012) for deadjectival nouns; Strnadová (2014a) for derived adjectives; and Bonami & Thuilier (2019) for derived verbs in *-iser* and *-ifier*. To these we added new datasets on derived nouns in *-isme*, *-iste*, *-ier* and *-erie* automatically extracted from the GLÀFF lexicon (Hathout et al., 2014) and curated by hand.

The analysis focuses on the processes for which at least 50 (base,derivative) pairs were present in the resources, such that both lexemes are attested at least 5 times in the FRCOW corpus (Schäfer & Bildhauer, 2012). For those processes admitting bases in more than one part of speech, (e.g. *-age*: *laver* 'wash' > *lavage* 'washing', *feuille* 'leaf' > *feuillage* 'foilage'), if one part of speech accounts for 90% or more of the types, only types where the base has that part of speech were kept; this led to dismissing denominal *-age* and *-eur* derivatives but keeping *-isme* and *-iste* derivatives with both nominal and adjectival bases. Overall, this initial selection step resulted in a cumulative dataset of $21,990$ (base, derivative) pairs each exemplifying one of 35 derivational processes.

From this dataset we extracted paradigmatic systems corresponding to two processes sharing a base, and selected for analysis those for which more than 150 triples (base, process 1 derivative, process 2 derivative) were documented. Table 2 shows the selected pairs of processes and the number of triples documenting each. As can be seen, almost all processes derive nouns, with the exception of *-ant* which builds deverbal adjectives.

Table 3 shows a sample triple for each pair of processes. Note that action noun forming processes are overrepresented in the sample, and that some pairs of processes are rivals (e.g. age:V>N, ment:V>N) for which there happens to be a large enough number of doublets in our data sources for comparison to be possible.

We build a 100-dimensional vector space using a modified version of FrCow (Schäfer, 2016) and the skipgram variant of the Word2Vec algorithm (Mikolov

Tab. 2: Selected pairs of processes with the number of corresponding lexeme triples in the final datasets.

Process₁	Process₂	Sample size
age:V>N	conversion:V>N	833
age:V>N	eur:V>N	584
age:V>N	ment:V>N	354
ant:V>A	ment:V>N	302
conversion:V>N	eur:V>N	679
conversion:V>N	ment:V>N	377
ier:N>N	erie:N>N	151
eur:V>N	ion:V>N	514
eur:V>N	ment:V>N	342
isme:A/N>N	iste:A/N>N	277

Tab. 3: Sample triple for each selected pair of processes.

Processes	Base	Derivative₁	Derivative₂
(age:V>N, conversion:V>N)	givrer	givrage	givre
(age:V>N, eur:V>N)	racler	racleur	raclage
(age:V>N, ment:V>N)	encaisser	encaissage	encaissement
(ant:V>A, ment:V>N)	percer	perçant	percement
(conversion:V>N, eur:V>N)	découvrir	découverte	découvreur
(conversion:V>N, ment:V>N)	défausser	défausse	défaussement
(ier:N>N, erie:N>N)	verre	verrier	verrerie
(eur:V>N, ion:V>N)	dévorer	dévoreur	dévoration
(eur:V>N, ment:V>N)	porter	porteur	portement
(isme:A/N>N, iste:A/N>N)	Europe	européisme	européiste

et al., 2013a).¹³ These vectors are lexeme-based rather than word-based: we did not apply Word2vec, to the the wordforms, but to the concatenation of the word's lemma and its part of speech tag, as provided by the corpus. This is justified by the goal of studying lexeme-level derivational properties, and hence abstracting away from the special distributional properties of citation forms. It also maximizes the number of tokens representing each of the lexemes of interest.¹⁴

4.2 Assessing semantic predictability

To be able to compare semantic predictability across morphological relations, we first need to lay out a method for assessing precitability in each individual case. That is, given a set of pairs of derivationally related predictor and target lexemes $\{(p_1, t_1), \ldots, (p_n, t_n)\}$, we need to define a prediction algorithm mapping vectors for p_is to vectors for t_is, and assess the quality of the result for each pair.

The simplest way of doing this relies directly on Mikolov et al.'s ideas on semantic analogies already discussed in Section 3: To predict $\vec{t}_i$ from $\vec{p}_i$, pick another

---

13 We used the gensim implementation of Word2Vec (Řehůřek, 2010). Hyperparameters were as follows: 100 dimensions, 10 iterations, negative sampling, a window of 5 tokens and a minimum occurrence of 5 tokens. We chose these parameters after several tests, and based on previous experience. In particular, we experimented with both the cbow and the skipgram variant of the algorithm for this and other studies. Experience shows that vectors obtained with skipgram give rise to better performance for vector-to-vector prediction tasks. Both the skipgram and the cbow vector space are available for examination on the Zenodo repository.

14 Initial experimentation showed that vectors tend to overemphasize the role of grammatical gender: grammatical gender is by far the most prominent distributional distinction among nouns. Since our vectors are lexeme-based, this should not be the case (inflectional variation in determiners, adjectives and verbs agreeing in gender with nouns should be neutralized), and points to poor lemmatization. Although this is not crucial for the present study, it is for a separate study for which we used the same vectors. Accordingly, we slightly modified the corpus to compensate for that effect. First, portmanteau forms like *du* 'of_the.MAS', which had been tokenized as a single form and thus lemmatized as *du*, were re-lemmatized as *de* + *le*. This avoids an asymmetry between the lemmatization of masculine *du* and feminine *de la* 'of the.FEM'. Second, lemmatization of feminine nouns and adjectives was not coherent: sometimes feminine nouns (e.g. *institutrice* 'female teacher') were lemmatized to the corresponding masculine noun (e.g. *instituteur* 'male teacher') rather than seen as their own lemma; while sometimes feminine adjectives were lemmatized to the feminine (e.g. *gibbeuse* 'gibbous.FEM') rather than the conventional masculine form (e.g. *gibbeux* 'gibbous.FEM'). We corrected such cases to the extent possible by checking the lemmatization against the large lexicon in development in the Démonext project (Namer et al., 2019) and correcting automatically the lemmatization through string searches where that was possible. Examination of a random sample suggests that the number of remaining gender-related lemmatization errors is below 1%.

pair of words linked by the same morphological relation (p_j, t_j), and compute the vector $\vec{p}_i + \vec{t}_j - \vec{p}_i$. This simple method is quite noisy, as idiosyncratic properties of the pair of lexemes used for analogy (p_j, t_j) will inevitably have an influence on quality of prediction. This problem can be mitigated by using a set of pairs of lexemes rather than a single pair as our analogical base, and derive from this the average difference vector between predictors and targets. By adding this average difference vector to $\vec{p}_i$, we get a predicted value for $\vec{t}_i$ which evens out idiosyncratic differences between pairs of lexemes standing in the same morphological relation. This is the method used e.g. in Mickus et al. (2019).

Marelli & Baroni (2015) identify a potential problem with this and related methods and propose an elegant solution.[15] They note that derivational morphology often leads to predictably different outcomes depending on semantic properties of the base it applies to; for instance, the English prefix *re-*, giving rise to iterative readings when attached to an activity verb (*resing* means 'sing one more time') but to a restitutive reading when attached to an accomplishment verb (*reopen* means 'open what was previously closed'). Compare such a case with that of the polysemy of the suffix *-er*, which readily forms either agent or instrument nouns from verbs. In both cases we have a form of affix polysemy, but in the former, the output meaning is predictable from semantic properties of the base, whereas in the latter, it is not (or at least not to the same degree). This is precisely a difference in semantic predictability that the average difference vector method is unlikely to be able to capture.

To avoid that problem, Marelli & Baroni (2015) relate predictor and target vectors using a linear transformation. That is, instead of predicting each dimension in the target vector from just the same dimension in the predictor, each dimension in the target is predicted by a linear model taking all dimensions of the predictor as input. Thus there are as many linear models as there are vector dimensions; in our case this would lead to 100 models with the following structure in R formula notation:

```
target_val_1   ~ pred_val_1 + pred_val_2 + ⋯ + pred_val_100
target_val_2   ~ pred_val_1 + pred_val_2 + ⋯ + pred_val_100
         ⋮                        ⋮
target_val_100 ~ pred_val_1 + pred_val_2 + ⋯ + pred_val_100
```

---

15 Marelli & Baroni (2015) actually discuss this in the context of a critique of yet another way of addressing the semantics derivational morphology, by building a vector for an affix from the distribution of all words containing that affix, and then combining base and affix vectors using a linear model (Lazaridou et al., 2013). However their argument applies *mutatis mutandis* to the average difference vector approach.

With our data this tended to overfit the models, which resulted in relatively poor predictions of unseen test items. To compensate for this, we used a model structure that is conceptually similar to Marelli and Baroni's, but less rich. We first computed the 10 main principal components of the 100 dimensions for the vectors. Then we trained a single model predicting, for each dimension, the target value from the predictor value and the 10 principal components of the full predictor vector. This is shown in the formula below, where `dimension` is a nominal variable indicating the dimension of interest, `target_val` and `pred_val` are the respective values of the target and predictor vector for that dimension, and `PC1`, ..., `PC10` are the 10 main principal components of the input vector.

$$\texttt{target\_val} \sim \texttt{pred\_val} * \texttt{dimension} + \texttt{PC1} + \texttt{PC2} + \cdots + \texttt{PC10}$$

Note that there are two differences between our modelling strategy and Marelli & Baroni's: the use of principal components rather than full vectors, and the use of a single model to predict all dimensions rather than one model per dimension.

We then used 10-fold cross-validation to assess how well the model performed on unseen data. We split the data into 10 groups, and fitted the model using 9 of the groups. We then tried to predict the left out group, and repeated this for all 10 groups, and for all (predictor,target) pairs. To evaluate how well the model performed, we calculated the cosine similarity between the cross-validated predicted vector and the actual vector for each target.

4.3 Comparing predictability across morphological relations

Remember that we want to test the hypothesis that for some pairs of processes applicable to the same base, the semantic relationship between the derivatives is more predictable than the relationship of either derivative to their base. To that effect we need to assess semantic predictability between pairs of cells within a small paradigmatic system consisting of aligned sets of three forms, a base and two derivatives. This entails that, for each pair of processes under consideration, we have six sets of (predictor, target) pairs to consider; these are depicted graphically in Figure 14. Our main goal is to compare the accuracy of the $D_1 \to D_2$ and $D_2 \to D_1$ prediction relations to that of predictions from the base ($B \to D_1$, $B \to D_2$). However we will also comment on prediction of the base from the derivatives ($D_1 \to B$, $D_2 \to B$).

As a concrete example, for the process pair (*-eur*, *-ment*), we build six models (all with crossvalidation): base>eur, eur>base, base>ment, ment>base, ment>eur, and eur>ment. The model eur>ment learns to predict *-ment* from *-eur* forms, and we evaluate its performance as the cosine between the predicted vector and the

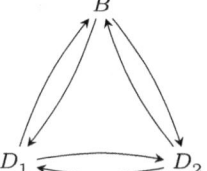

Fig. 14: The six prediction relations within a system of two derivational processes applying to the same bases.

Tab. 4: Illustration of model performance evaluated as cosine similarity between predicted actual target vectors.

Prediction relation	Sample predictor	Sample target	Sample performance	Average performance
base>eur	accorder	accordeur	0.640	0.676
eur>base	accordeur	accorder	0.753	0.689
base>ment	accorder	accordement	0.849	0.633
ment>base	accordement	accorder	0.869	0.637
eur>ment	accordeur	accordement	0.712	0.615
ment>eur	accordement	accordeur	0.493	0.600

actual observed vector. Table 4 shows the result on a sample triple of lexemes. Here we see that, for this triple, we get best performance for prediction of the -ment derivative from the base verb, and worse performance for prediction of the -eur derivative from the -ment derivative. Note also the asymmetry of performance scores, which varies from minimal when comparing base>ment to ment>base, to major when comparing eur>ment to ment>eur. This might seem counterintuitive but is to be expected: the first row in the table reports the cosine similarity between a predicted vector and the actual vector for *accordeur*, while the second reports the cosine between between a predicted vector and the actual vector for *accorder* (we are not using cosine to compare the vectors for two words, but two vectors for the same word). Likewise, the first and last rows report different sample performances, despite the fact that the target and hence the actual vector in the comparison is the same: on the first row the predicted vector stems from a model trained on base>eur pairs and applied to the actual vector for *accorder*, while on the last row the predicted vector stems from a model trained on ment>eur pairs and applied to the actual vector for *accordement*

We thus have an estimated cosine similarity between a predicted vector and an actual vector for each model and each (predictor,target) pair. At this point we could try to address our research question directly by comparing the average cosine similarity of each of the six models documenting a pair of process. By way of an example, The last column of Table 4 shows such averages for the models under consideration, suggesting a better accuracy of prediction of derivatives from their bases than among themselves.

We want to be more cautious, however, and to evaluate how certain we are about these average cosine similarities. We expect that there will be some degree of randomness in the prediction results stemming from at least two sources. First, the accuracy of the semantic distributional vectors themselves is not the same for all words, because Word2Vec models build better representations for more frequent words. Second, there is some random variation in the predictions stemming from the cross-validation. For this reason, comparing mean cosine distances directly would be careless. For example, considering again the numbers Table 4, we would want to know how confident we are that the predictive performance of the base>ment model, estimated at 0.633, is indeed higher than that of the eur>ment model, estimated at 0.615. Similarly, we want to take into account the variance around the mean: we can be more certain about a mean value if there is little variance across the individual estimates.

To quantify our uncertainty about the individual mean cosine estimates, we fit a separate Bayesian Beta regression for each of the 10 datasets under consideration. Remember that for each dataset we have 6 linear models producing predicted vectors for each of the 6 pairwise prediction relations between a base and two derivatives. The Bayesian model estimates the mean cosine similarity between predicted vector and actual vector on the basis of just a nominal variable indicating which of the 6 prediction relation this measurement exemplifies. That is, it predicts the Cosine column from the Relation column in the sample dataset in Table 5.[16]

Because we are working with cosine similarities, all values are bounded between 0 and 1, which means that we can use a Beta distribution as our likelihood.[17] We thus used brms (Bürkner, 2017, 2018) and Stan (Carpenter et al., 2017) to fit a Beta regression model to each of the 10 datasets. In addition to an estimation of mean cosine similarity for each of the 6 prediction relations, the model assesses

---

16 We tried adding the log frequency of the base and derived forms as predictors to see whether this had any effect the accuracy of the predictions but we were not able to find any noticeable effects.
17 Technically cosine similarities can include 0 and 1, which is not covered in Beta regression, but in practice our data contained neither zeroes nor ones.

Tab. 5: Sample input to the Bayesian model for the pair of processes (*-eur*, *-ment*). The predictor and target for which the performance observation was computed are shown for illustration, they are not part of the input to the model.

Relation	Predictor	Target	Cosine
base>eur	accorder	accordeur	0.640
base>eur	verser	verseur	0.580
...	...	...	...
base>ment	accorder	accordement	0.849
base>ment	verser	versement	0.737
...	...	...	...
textttment>eur	accordement	accordeur	0.493
ment>eur	versement	verseur	0.629
...	...	...	...

the uncertainty of that estimation in the form of a posterior distribution, which allows us to assess how strong the evidence for a difference in mean is.[18]

5 Results

In this section we discuss the results of the models. Instead of presenting coefficient tables we built conditional effects plots. A conditional effect plot shows the expected mean value for each predictor level, as well as the 95% uncertainty interval (the interval where 95% of the posterior probability density lies). We conclude that we have clear enough of a difference between two estimated means if the uncertainty intervals do not overlap. Figures 15-18 show the conditional effects plots for four pairs of processes which illustrate our findings. Plots for the remaining pairs of processes can be found in the appendix.

First, Figure 15 shows the conditional effects plot for (*-eur*, *-ment*). We observe that predictions between the base and *-eur* or *-ment* derivative are clearly better than predictions between the two derivatives. Hence this pair of processes do not provide evidence for the importance of a paradigmatic relation between derivatives: formal bases are the best predictors of their derivatives.

In contrast, Figure 16 shows the best example of paradigmatic effects in our sample. In this case, predicting the *-isme* lexeme from *-iste*, or the other way around, was considerably easier than predicting either from the base. Interest-

---
[18] See Gelman et al. (2013) and Gelman et al. (2020) for justification of the use of regression models rather than classical hypothesis testing to assess uncertainty.

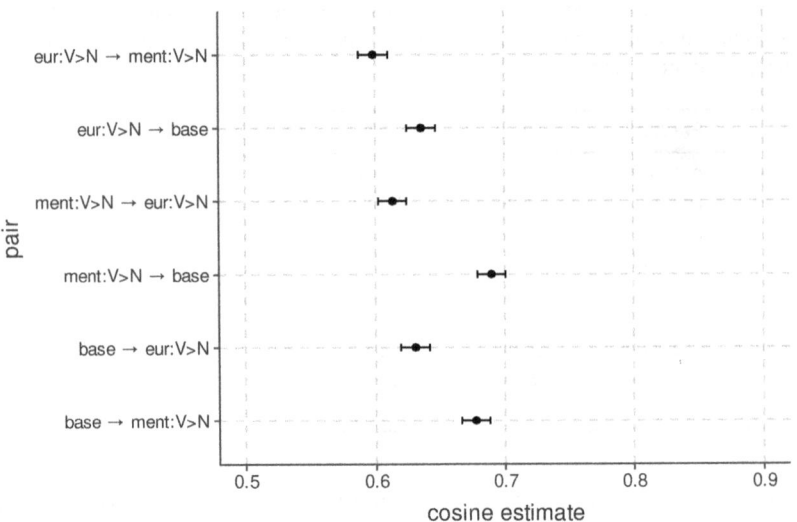

Fig. 15: Comparing *-eur* and *-ment* suffixation.

ingly, in this case we also see that going from the semantics of the *-isme* and *-iste* derived forms to the semantics of the base is considerably harder than going from the base to the derived form.

A similar, although less extreme situation, is visible with *-ier* and *-erie*, as shown in Figure 17. For this pair of processes, predicting between derived forms was easier than predicting from the base, but the evidence is far from being overwhelming: there is considerable overlap in the posterior distribution. Hence, even though we do not see a big asymmetry as with *-isme* and *-iste*, the evidence ponts in the direction of a paradigmatic effect. On the other hand, predicting the base semantics from the semantics of the derived forms was somewhat harder.

The cases discussed so far have one property in common, namely that predicting derivative from base is easier than or equally difficult as predicting base from derivative. Interestingly, this does not hold for all pairs of processes. Figure 18 shows the effects for conversion and *-ment*. In this case we see that predicting between the derivatives is harder than predicting from the base, but also that predicting the base semantics from derivatives is equally hard as the other way around. This suggests that there is not a clear directionality of prediction between base and derivative. While this is an interesting observation worthy of further investigation, it has no bearing on the theoretical distinction between classical and paradigmatic approaches.

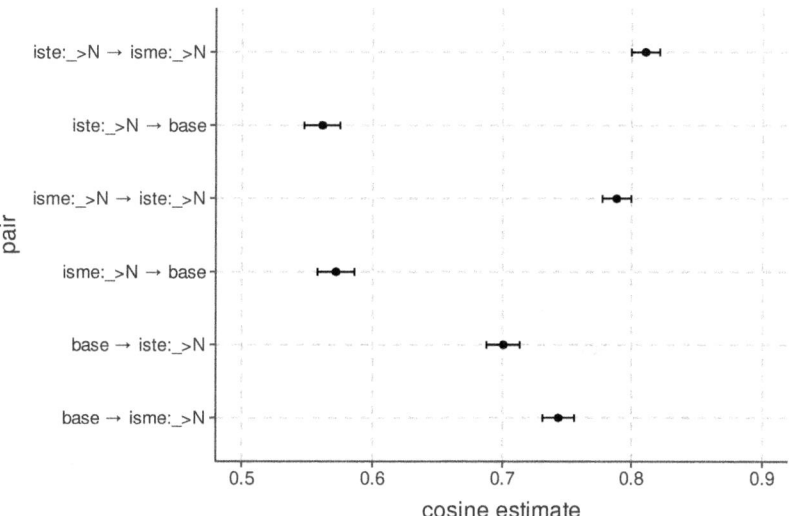

Fig. 16: Comparing *-isme* and *-iste* suffixation.

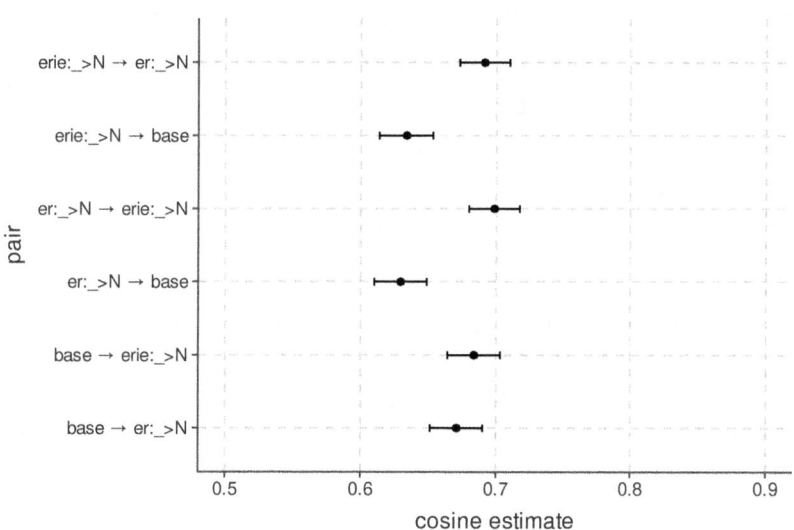

Fig. 17: Comparing *-ier* and *-erie* suffixation.

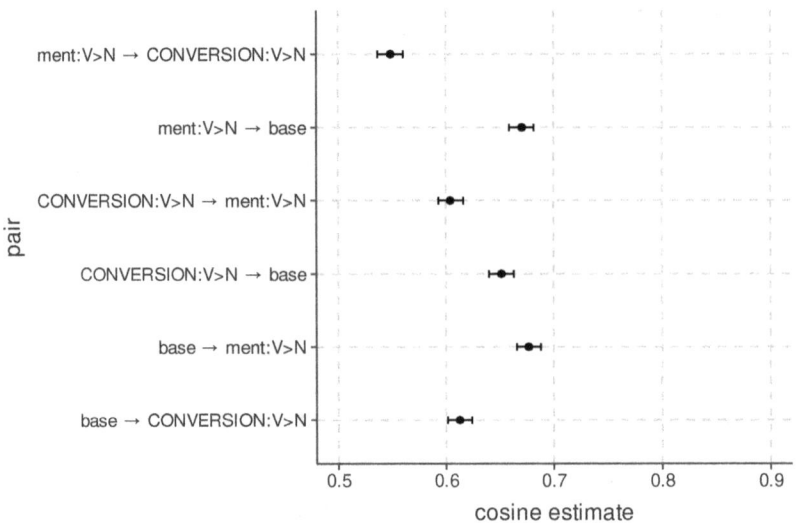

Fig. 18: Comparing conversion and *-ment* suffixation.

The preceding examples illustrate all the situations found in the data. Remaining plots can be found in the appendix, but are summarized in Table 6. For each pair of processes, the table indicates in the first two columns whether prediction of each derivative is easier from the other derivative or from the base; a superior sign ('>') indicates that there is clear evidence that it is, that is, the measured estimate is higher and the uncertainty intervals do not overlap. An equal sign indicates that there is no clear evidence either way, as the intervals overlap; an inferior sign indicates that the evidence goes in the opposite direction. Using the same conventions, the last two columns indicate whether prediction of a derivative from its base is easier than prediction of the base from the derivative.

As the reader can check verify, only 1 out of the 10 pairs of processes provides clear evidence for a paradigmatic effect (two '>' signs in the first two columns); however, only 4 are such that the base is clearly a better predictor of a class of derivatives than another member of the morphological family (two '<' signs in the first two columns). In the remaining 5 cases, the evidence is somewhat mixed, and the base has no clear privileged predictive status.

Tab. 6: Summary of the evidence for paradigmatic relations.

	D$_2$→D$_1$ vs. B→D$_1$	D$_1$→D$_2$ vs. B→D$_2$	B→D$_1$ vs. D$_1$→B	B→D$_2$ vs. D$_2$→B
(age:V>N, conversion:V>N)	<	<	=	<
(age:V>N, eur:V>N)	=	>	<	=
(age:V>N, ment:V>N)	<	<	<	=
(ant:V>A, ment:V>N)	<	<	=	=
(conversion:V>N, eur:V>N)	<	=	>	<
(conversion:V>N, ment:V>N)	<	<	>	=
(er:N>N, erie:N>N)	=	=	<	<
(eur:V>N, ion:V>N)	=	<	=	=
(eur:V>N, ment:V>N)	=	<	=	=
(isme:N>N, iste:N>N)	>	>	<	<

6 Discussion

In Section 2 we contrasted the predictions of a theory of morphology purely based on oriented base-derivative relations to one which recognizes other kinds of paradigmatic relations. The former entails that, although there can be accidental exceptions, at the level of the system the base should always be the best predictor of a derivative within its family. The latter view on the other hand suggests that for some processes this does not hold. Note the important lack of symmetry: the paradigmatic view does not entail that formal bases are *never* good predictors, but only that they need not be.

The results presented in section 4 hence provide exactly the kind of evidence we were looking for: paired nouns in *-isme* and *iste* are undoubtedly better predicted by each other than by their common formal base. The data for *-ier* and *-erie* nouns points in the same direction, although the evidence is less clear, probably because of a smaller dataset. Note that it is unsurprising that *-isme* and *-iste* exhibit paradigmatic effects, as they are the poster child for paradigmatic relations in derivation (see e.g. Becker 1993; Booij 2010; Roché 2011a). On the other hand, we are basing our conclusions here only on those cases where a formal base is present, whereas much of the usual argumentation on these nouns focuses on the large number of cases where no formal base is to be found. The novelty of this paper is to provide an operational method to investigate contrasts of semantic predictability in derivational families, which is only part of the relevant evidence. The fact that none of the remaining 8 pairs of processes led to similar results is not particularly concerning for the paradigmatic view, which predicts the exis-

tence of strong predictability among derivatives, not their high prevalence; after all, if they were highly prevalent, there would be no debate. However, the gradient of predictability we have observed suggests a direction for future work: once we have clearly established the reality of systematic paradigmatic relations among derivatives, it is worth exploring why these are on average less reliable than those between bases and derivatives.

While this does not directly address our main research question, another interesting observation concerns the interpredictability of bases and derivatives. Our expectation is that bases be better predictors of their derivatives than the other way around. Derivatives tend to be less polysemous than their bases, either because the derived meaning elaborates on a single sense of the base (Fradin & Kerleroux, 2003); or, when that is not the case, because the distribution of senses is less uniform in derivatives (Anselme et al., 2021). In addition, derivatives tend to be less frequent than their bases (Harwood & Wright, 1956; Hay, 2001), giving them less room for a variety of uses (and in particular for polysemy). Finally, Kotowski & Schäfer (2023) provide direct distributional evidence that derivatives resulting from the same process tend to be semantically less diverse than the bases they derive from. As a result of these observations, we expect the larger diversity of base semantics to impair the predictability of their meaning from the derivative's meaning.

This prediction is largely borne out in our data: we find clear evidence for higher predictability in the base-derivative direction in 8 cases out of 20, and clear evidence to the contrary in only 2 cases, which both correspond to different samples of verb to noun conversion. This is probably not an accident. First, conversion is generally assumed to be more polysemous than affixal processes (Plag, 1999; Tribout, 2010a), to the point that some have argued it to be essentially semantically unconstrained (e.g. Clark & Clark 1979 and Aronoff 1980 on noun to verb conversion). Second, deciding on the orientation of conversion is notoriously difficult: for the relationship between nouns and verbs in French, after careful empirical consideration, (Tribout, 2020) concludes that orientation is undecidable in a majority of cases. These two observations lead us to expect conversion to behave differently from other processes: while it would be very interesting to explore the situation in more detail, and understand why and how exactly conversion is different, the empirical results on directionality are overall compatible with our expectations.

One limitation of the present study is that we have not provided evidence that the cosine similarity between predicted and actual vectors does indeed reflect semantic unpredictability. Establishing this is not trivial: the quality of our vectors is clearly variable, all the more so because we used a very low frequency threshold for inclusion in the dataset, in the interest of getting enough types. As a result, there are many individual cases where it is unclear why the words are judged to be predictable or unpredictable. Given this situation, only a quantitative evaluation of average correlation between human unpredictability judgements and model predictions would truly allow us to assess quality. This is clearly beyond the scope of the present paper.

In the absence of such hard evidence, the best we can do here is to provide some circumstantial evidence that the models are capturing relevant distinctions. Focusing on *-isme* and *-iste* derivatives, we looked manually at extreme cases of quality of prediction of *-iste* derivatives from the base or from the *-isme* derivative. Among the 10 *-iste* derivatives that are best predicted from the base, we find cases like *biologiste* 'biologist' and *dynamiste* 'dynamist'. In the first instance, the corresponding *biologisme* names a specific philosophical doctrine. The noun *biologiste* can name a follower of that doctrine, but it also has a much more general and frequent meaning transparently related to that of the base *biologie* 'biology'. Conversely, *dynamiste* names a follower of the doctrine of *dynamisme*, but *dynamisme* 'dynamism' also has a more general and more frequent meaning that relates readily to the base adjective *dynamique* 'dynamic'. At the other end of the spectrum, cases where predictability of the *-iste* derivative from the *isme* derivative is maximal while predictability from the base is minimal typically involve an adjectival base with a fairly broad meaning (*social* 'social', *individuel* 'invidual') or that is clearly polysemous (e.g. *gauche* 'left side', 'political left') and the *-isme* and *-iste* derivatives name two closely related concepts of a doctrine and a follower of that doctrine, that is more specialized than the meaning of the base.

To sum up then, although a more thorough evaluation would be in order, a superficial examination of model predictions suggests that these do capture the relative predictability of different pairs of lexemes, and hence that these can be trusted as informing us on the existence of semantically stable paradigmatic relations.

A second limitation of this study is that we ignored two important phenomena at the core of contemporary research on derivational semantics, as is evident from other chapters in this volume. First, affix polysemy (see e.g. Lieber 2023; Plag et al. 2023; Schäfer 2023) is not taken into account directly: our vectors lump together tokens of a lexeme corresponding to different senses, and no effort has been made to select monosemous lexemes for analysis. It is hence possible that our results are influenced by different affixes exhibiting different degrees of polysemy, leading to different levels of predictability. Second, we also abstracted away from affix rivalry (see e.g.Plag et al. 2023; Huyghe et al. 2023), which could have an incidence on predictability among derivatives: if there is truly rivalry between two processes, then we expect the semantic contrasts between doublets to be random, leading to poor interpredictability. In both cases, we were limited by the lack of good operationalizations of the relevant variables (sense distributions in corpus data, degree of polysemy of affixes, degree of rivalry of affixes). We are hopeful that future research will overcome these limitations.

7 Conclusion

In this paper we first reviewed the literarure on derivational paradigms. After exhibiting various types of morphological facts that are taken as evidence for paradigmatic relations in derivation, we highlighted the existence of two different tradition for integrating these relations in morphological theory, typified by seminal work by Marle (1984) and Robins (1959) respectively. We then argued that while the literature provides many examples of anecdotal evidence for the importance of paradigmatic relations, systematic evidence was required for the relevant phenomena not to be dismissed as epiphenomenal and hence outside the focus of morphological theory.

We proposed to use distributional semantics to provide exactly that type of evidence: systematic paradigmatic relations should give rise to strong semantic predictability among derivatives, which can be operationalized using distributional methods. We went on to examine 10 pairs of processes in French derivational morphology, and showed that for at least one of these, we have clear evidence that on average, pairs of derivatives are more interpredictable than either is predictable from their common base. This is precisely the kind of systematic paradigmatic relation we were looking for. In that sense, we have thus provided strong evidence that paradigmatic relations among derivatives from a common base cannot be dismissed as epiphenomenal.

It is worth noting that we have only examined one type of evidence bearing on the reality of derivational paradigms. Although various configurations challenging the conventional view of derivation as grounded in oriented base-derivative relations were identified in section 2, we focused entirely on the particular situation of paired derivatives with a common and well-attested base. As such our conclusions are inherently limited: in particular they have little bearing on the distinction between approaches that take paradigmatic relations to be secondary to ordinary morphology, in the tradition of Marle (1984), and those that conceptualize all derivational relations as paradigmatic, in the tradition of Robins (1959). However, we have exemplified how distributional methods can be used to bear on investigating structured morphological relatedness quantitatively. We hope this study to lay the groundwork for a larger research program that would address empirically the challenges raised by paradigmatic structure in word formation.

Acknowledgment: We thank the audience at the workshop on Derivational Semantics, 2021 DGfS meeting, as well as two anonymous reviewers and the editors of the present volume for useful discussion and comments.

Funding: This research was partially conducted while Matías Guzman Naranjo was a postdoc at Université de Paris. This work was partially supported by the Démonext project (ANR 17-CE23-0005) as well as a public grant overseen by the French National Research Agency (ANR) as part of the "Investissements d'Avenir" program (reference: ANR-10-LABX-0083); and by the European Research Council (ERC) under the European Union's Horizon 2020 research and innovation programme (Grant agreement 834050).

Bibliography

Ackerman, Farrell, James P. Blevins & Robert Malouf. 2009. Parts and wholes: implicative patterns in inflectional paradigms. In James P. Blevins & Juliette Blevins (eds.), *Analogy in grammar*, 54–82. Oxford: Oxford University Press.

Ackerman, Farrell & Robert Malouf. 2013. Morphological organization: the low conditional entropy conjecture. *Language* 89(3). 429–464.

Amenta, Simona, Fritz Günther & Marco Marelli. 2020. A (distributional) semantic perspective on the processing of morphologically complex words. *The Mental Lexicon* 15(1). 62–78.

Anselme, Rémi, Olivier Bonami & Heather Burnett. 2021. Polysémie et troncation des noms en -ion en français. *Verbum* XLIII(1). 97–118.

Aronoff, Mark. 1976. *Word formation in generative grammar*. Cambridge, MA: MIT Press.

Aronoff, Mark. 1980. Contextuals. *Language* 56(4). 744–758.

Aronoff, Mark. 1994. *Morphology by itself*. Cambridge, MA: MIT Press.

Audring, Jenny. 2019. Mothers or sisters? The encoding of morphological knowledge. *Word Structure* 12(3). 274–296.

Barbu Mititelu, Verginica, Gianina Iordăchioaia, Svetlozara Leseva & Ivelina Stoyanova. 2023. The meaning of zero nouns and zero verbs. In Sven Kotowski & Ingo Plag (eds.), *The semantics of derivational morphology. Theory, methods, evidence*, 63–102. Berlin: De Gruyter.

Baroni, Marco, Georgiana Dinu & Germán Kruszewski. 2014. Don't count, predict! a systematic comparison of context-counting vs. context-predicting semantic vectors. In *Proceedings of the 52nd Annual Meeting of the Association for Computational Linguistics (Volume 1: Long Papers)*, 238–247. Baltimore, Maryland: Association for Computational Linguistics. https://aclanthology.org/P14-1023.

Bauer, Laurie. 1997. Derivational paradigms. In Geert Booij & Jaap van Marle (eds.), *Yearbook of morphology 1996*, 243–256. Dordrecht: Kluwer.

Bauer, Laurie. 2019. Notions of paradigm and their value in word-formation. *Word Structure* 12(2). 153–175.

Bauer, Laurie, Rochelle Lieber & Ingo Plag. 2013. *Oxford reference guide to English morphology*. Oxford: Oxford University Press.

Becker, Thomas. 1993. Back-formation, cross-formation, and 'bracketing paradoxes' in paradigmatic morphology. In Geert Booij & Jaap van Marle (eds.), *Yearbook of morphology 1993*, 1–25. Dordrecht: Kluwer.

Beniamine, Sacha. 2018. *Typologie quantitative des systèmes de classes flexionnelles*. Paris: Université Paris Diderot dissertation.

Blevins, James P. 2006. Word-based morphology. *Journal of Linguistics* 42. 531–573.

Blevins, James P. 2016. *Word and paradigm morphology*. Oxford: Oxford University Press.

Bochner, Harry. 1993. *Simplicity in generative morphology*. Berlin: De Gruyter.

Boleda, Gemma. 2020. Distributional semantics and linguistic theory. *Annual Review of Linguistics* 6(1). 213–234.

Bonami, Olivier & Sacha Beniamine. 2016. Joint predictiveness in inflectional paradigms. *Word Structure* 9(2). 156–182.

Bonami, Olivier & Denis Paperno. 2018. Inflection vs. derivation in a distributional vector space. *Lingue e Linguaggio* 17(2). 173–195.

Bonami, Olivier & Jana Strnadová. 2019. Paradigm structure and predictability in derivational morphology. *Morphology* 29(2). 167–197.

Bonami, Olivier & Juliette Thuilier. 2019. A statistical approach to affix rivalry: French *-iser* and *-ifier*. *Word Structure* 12(1). 4–41.

Booij, Geert. 1997. Autonomous morphology and paradigmatic relations. In Geert Booij & Jaap van Marle (eds.), *Yearbook of morphology 1996*, 35–53. Dordrecht: Kluwer.

Booij, Geert. 2010. *Construction morphology*. Oxford: Oxford University Press.

Bürkner, Paul-Christian. 2017. Brms: An R package for bayesian multilevel models using Stan. *Journal of Statistical Software* 80(1). 1–28.

Bürkner, Paul-Christian. 2018. Advanced bayesian multilevel modeling with the R package brms. *The R Journal* 10(1). 395–411.

Carpenter, Bob, Andrew Gelman, Matthew Hoffman, Daniel Lee, Ben Goodrich, Michael Betancourt, Marcus Brubaker, Jiqiang Guo, Peter Li & Allen Riddell. 2017. Stan: A probabilistic programming language. *Journal of Statistical Software, Articles* 76(1). 1–32.

Clark, Eve V & Herbert H Clark. 1979. When nouns surface as verbs. *Language* 55(4). 767–811.

Corbin, Danielle. 1976. Peut-on faire l'hypothèse d'une dérivation en morphologie? In Jean-Claude Chevalier (ed.), *Grammaire transformationnelle : syntaxe et lexique*, 47–91. Lille: Presses Universitaires de Lille.

Erk, Katrin. 2012. Vector space models of word meaning and phrase meaning: A survey. *Language and Linguistics Compass* 6(10). 635–653.

Evert, Stefan. 2014. Distributional semantics in R with the wordspace package. In *Proceedings of COLING 2014, the 25th International Conference on Computational Linguistics: System demonstrations*, 110–114. https://aclanthology.org/C14-2.

Fernández-Domínguez, Jesús, Alexandra Bagasheva & Cristina Lara Clares. 2020. *Paradigmatic relations in word formation*. Brill.

Firth, John R. 1957. Modes of meaning. In *Papers in linguistics, 1934-1951*, 190–215. Oxford: Oxford University Press.

Fradin, Bernard & Françoise Kerleroux. 2003. Troubles with lexemes. In Geert Booij, Janet De Cesaris, Sergio Scalise & Angela Ralli (eds.), *Selected papers from the third mediterranean morphology meeting*, 177–196. IULA-Universitat Pompeu Fabra (Barcelona). https://halshs.archives-ouvertes.fr/halshs-00122209.

Gelman, Andrew, John B Carlin, Hal S Stern, David B Dunson, Aki Vehtari & Donald B Rubin. 2013. *Bayesian data analysis*. 3rd ed. Boca Raton, Florida: Chapman & Hall/CRC.
Gelman, Andrew, Jennifer Hill & Aki Vehtari. 2020. *Regression and other stories*. Cambridge: Cambridge University Press.
Guzmán Naranjo, Matías. 2020. Analogy, complexity and predictability in the Russian nominal inflection system. *Morphology* 30(3). 219–262.
Guzmán Naranjo, Matías & Olivier Bonami. 2021. Overabundance and inflectional classification: Quantitative evidence from czech. *Glossa* 6(1). 88. https://doi.org/10.5334/gjgl.1626.
Harris, Zelig S. 1954. Distributional structure. *Word* 10. 146–162.
Harwood, F. W. & Alison M. Wright. 1956. Statistical study of English word formation. *Language* 32(2). 260–273.
Hathout, Nabil & Fiammetta Namer. 2014a. Démonette, a French derivational morpho-semantic network. *Linguistic Issues in Language Technology* 11(5). 125–168.
Hathout, Nabil & Fiammetta Namer. 2014b. Discrepancy between form and meaning in word formation: the case of over- and under-marking in french. In Franz Rainer, Wolfgang U. Dressler, Francesco Gardani & Hans Christian Luschützky (eds.), *Morphology and meaning (Selected papers from the 15th International Morphology Meeting, Vienna, February 2012)*, 177–190. Amsterdam: John Benjamins.
Hathout, Nabil & Fiammetta Namer (eds.). 2018. *Special issue of Lingue e Linguaggio XVII:2: Defining paradigms in word formation*.
Hathout, Nabil & Fiammetta Namer (eds.). 2019. *Special issue of Morphology 29:2: Paradigms in word formation: what are we up to?*
Hathout, Nabil & Fiammetta Namer. 2022. Paradis: a family and paradigm model. *Morphology* 32(2). 153–195.
Hathout, Nabil, Franck Sajous & Basilio Calderone. 2014. GLÀFF, a large versatile French lexicon. In *Proceedings of the Ninth International Conference on Language Resources and Evaluation (LREC'14)*, Reykjavik: European Language Resources Association (ELRA). http://www.lrec-conf.org/proceedings/lrec2014/pdf/58_Paper.pdf.
Hay, Jennifer. 2001. Lexical frequency in morphology: Is everything relative? *Linguistics* 39(6). 1041–1070.
Huyghe, Richard, Alizée Lombard, Justine Salvadori & Sandra Schwab. 2023. Semantic rivalry between French deverbal neologisms in *-age*, *-ion* and *-ment*. In Sven Kotowski & Ingo Plag (eds.), *The semantics of derivational morphology. Theory, methods, evidence*, 143–175. Berlin: De Gruyter.
Huyghe, Richard & Marine Wauquier. 2020. What's in an agent? *Morphology* 30(3). 185–218.
Huyghe, Richard & Marine Wauquier. 2021. Distributional semantic insights on agentive suffix rivalry in French. *Word Structure* 14(3). 354–391.
Jackendoff, Ray & Jenny Audring. 2020. *The texture of the lexicon*. Oxford: Oxford University Press.
Koehl, Aurore. 2012. *La construction morphologique des noms désadjectivaux suffixés en français*: Université de Lorraine dissertation.
Kotowski, Sven & Martin Schäfer. 2023. Quantifying semantic relatedness across base verbs and derivatives: English *out*-prefixation. In Sven Kotowski & Ingo Plag (eds.), *The semantics of derivational morphology. Theory, methods, evidence*, 177–217. Berlin: De Gruyter.
Lapesa, Gabriella, Lea Kawaletz, Ingo Plag, Marios Andreou, Max Kisselew & Sebastian Padó. 2018. Disambiguation of newly derived nominalizations in context: A distributional semantics approach. *Word Structure* 11(3). 277–312.

Lazaridou, Angeliki, Marco Marelli, Roberto Zamparelli & Marco Baroni. 2013. Compositionally derived representations of morphologically complex words in distributional semantics. In *Proceedings of the 51st Annual Meeting of the Association for Computational Linguistics (Volume 1: Long Papers)*, 1517–1526. Sofia, Bulgaria: Association for Computational Linguistics. https://aclanthology.org/P13-1149.

Lenci, Alessandro. 2008. Distributional semantics in linguistic and cognitive research. *Rivista di Linguistica* 20. 1–31.

Lieber, Rochelle. 2023. Ghost aspect and double plurality. In Sven Kotowski & Ingo Plag (eds.), *The semantics of derivational morphology. Theory, methods, evidence*, 15–35. Berlin: De Gruyter.

Marchand, Hans. 1963. On a question of contrary analysis with derivationally connected but morphologically uncharacterized words. *English Studies* 44. 176–187.

Marelli, Marco & Marco Baroni. 2015. Affixation in semantic space: Modeling morpheme meanings with compositional distributional semantics. *Psychological Review* 122. 485–515.

Marle, Jaap van. 1984. *On the paradigmatic dimension of morphological creativity*. Dordrecht: Foris.

Mickus, Timothee, Olivier Bonami & Denis Paperno. 2019. Distributional effects of gender contrasts across categories. In *Proceedings of the 2nd Meeting of the Society for Computation in Linguistics, Vol. 2*, New York, NY: Society for Computation in Linguistics. https://scholarworks.umass.edu/scil/vol2/iss1/19/.

Mikolov, Tomas, Kai Chen, Greg Corrado & Jeffrey Dean. 2013a. Efficient estimation of word representations in vector space. *arXiv* abs/1301.3781. http://arxiv.org/abs/1301.3781.

Mikolov, Tomas, Ilya Sutskever, Kai Chen, Greg S Corrado & Jeff Dean. 2013b. Distributed representations of words and phrases and their compositionality. In *Advances in neural information processing systems*, 3111–3119. Red Hook, NY, USA: Curran Associates Inc. http://papers.nips.cc/paper/5021-distributed-representations-of-words-and-phrases-and-their-compositionality.pdf.

Miller, George A & Walter G Charles. 1991. Contextual correlates of semantic similarity. *Language and Cognitive Processes* 6(1). 1–28.

Namer, Fiammetta. 2012. Nominalisation et composition en français: d'où viennent les verbes composés? *Lexique* 20. 173–205.

Namer, Fiammetta, Lucie Barque, Olivier Bonami, Pauline Haas, Nabil Hathout & Delphine Tribout. 2019. Demonette2 – Une base de données dérivationnelles du français à grande échelle : premiers résultats. In *26e Conférence sur le Traitement Automatique des Langues Naturelles*, Toulouse. https://halshs.archives-ouvertes.fr/halshs-02275652/document.

Padó, Sebastian, Aurélie Herbelot, Max Kisselew & Jan Šnajder. 2016. Predictability of distributional semantics in derivational word formation. In *Proceedings of COLING 2016, the 26th International Conference on Computational Linguistics: Technical Papers*, 1285–1296. Osaka: The COLING 2016 Organizing Committee. https://aclanthology.org/C16-1122.

Pennington, Jeffrey, Richard Socher & Christopher D Manning. 2014. Glove: Global vectors for word representation. In *Proceedings of the 2014 conference on empirical methods in natural language processing (EMNLP)*, 1532–1543. Doha, Qatar: Association for Computational Linguistics. https://aclanthology.org/D14-1162.

Plag, Ingo. 1999. *Morphological productivity: Structural constraints in English derivation*. Berlin: De Gruyter.

Plag, Ingo, Lea Kawaletz, Sabine Arndt-Lappe & Rochelle Lieber. 2023. Analogical modeling of derivational semantics. Two case studies. In Sven Kotowski & Ingo Plag (eds.), *The *semantics of derivational morphology. Theory, methods, evidence*, 103–141. Berlin: De Gruyter.

Rainer, Franz. 2018. Word formation and word history. The case of CAPITALIST and CAPITALISM. In Olivier Bonami, Gilles Boyé, Georgette Dal, Hélène Giraudo & Fiammetta Namer (eds.), *The lexeme in descriptive and theoretical morphology*, 43–65. Berlin: Language Science Press.

Řehůřek, Radim. 2010. Software framework for topic modelling with large corpora. In *Proceedings of the LREC 2010 Workshop on New Challenges for NLP Frameworks*, 45–50. Malta. http://www.lrec-conf.org/proceedings/lrec2010/workshops/W10.pdf.

Robins, R. H. 1959. In defense of WP. *Transactions of the Philological Society* 58. 116–144.

Roché, Michel. 2011a. Quel traitement unifié pour les dérivations en *-isme* et en *-iste*? In Michel Roché, Gilles Boyé, Nabil Hathout, Stéphanie Lignon & Marc Plénat (eds.), *Des unités morphologiques au lexique*, 69–143. Paris: Hermès Lavoisier.

Roché, Michel. 2011b. Quelle morphologie? In Michel Roché, Gilles Boyé, Nabil Hathout, Stéphanie Lignon & Marc Plénat (eds.), *Des unités morphologiques au lexique*, 14–39. Paris: Hermès Lavoisier.

Schäfer, Martin. 2023. Splitting *-ly*'s: Using word embeddings to distinguish derivation and inflection. In Sven Kotowski & Ingo Plag (eds.), *The semantics of derivational morphology. Theory, methods, evidence*, 261–296. Berlin: De Gruyter.

Schäfer, Roland. 2016. Commoncow: Massively huge web corpora from commoncrawl data and a method to distribute them freely under restrictive eu copyright laws. In Nicoletta Calzolari, Khalid Choukri, Thierry Declerck, Marko Grobelnik, Bente Maegaard, Joseph Mariani, Asuncion Moreno, Jan Odijk & Stelios Piperidis (eds.), *Proceedings of the tenth international conference on language resources and evaluation (lrec 2016)*, 4500–4504. Portorož, Slovenia: European Language Resources Association (ELRA). https://aclanthology.org/L16-1712.

Schäfer, Roland & Felix Bildhauer. 2012. Building large corpora from the web using a new efficient tool chain. In *Proceedings of the Eighth International Conference on Language Resources and Evaluation*, 486–493. http://www.lrec-conf.org/proceedings/lrec2012/pdf/834_Paper.pdf.

Strnadová, Jana. 2014a. *Les réseaux adjectivaux: Sur la grammaire des adjectifs dénominaux en français*. Paris: Université Paris Diderot and Univerzita Karlova V Praze dissertation.

Strnadová, Jana. 2014b. Multiple derivation in French denominal adjectives. In Sandra Augendre, Graziella Couasnon-Torlois, Déborah Lebon, Clément Michard, Gilles Boyé & Fabio Montermini (eds.), *Proceedings of the 8th décembrettes* (Carnets de grammaire 22), 327–346. Toulouse: CLLE-ERSS.

Stump, Gregory T. 2001. *Inflectional morphology. A theory of paradigm structure*. Cambridge: Cambridge University Press.

Stump, Gregory T. 2016. *Inflectional paradigms*. Cambridge: Cambridge University Press.

Stump, Gregory T. 2019. Some sources of apparent gaps in derivational paradigms. *Morphology* 29. 271–292.

Tribout, Delphine. 2010a. How many conversions from verb to noun are there in French? In Stefan Müller (ed.), *Proceedings of the 17th international conference on head-driven phrase structure grammar*, 341–357. Stanford, CA: CSLI Publications.

Tribout, Delphine. 2010b. *Les conversions de nom à verbe et de verbe à nom en français*. Paris: Université Paris Diderot dissertation.

Tribout, Delphine. 2020. Nominalization, verbalization or both? Insights from the directionality of noun-verb conversion in French. *Zeitschrift für Wortbildung/Journal of Word Formation* 4(2). 187–207.

Turney, Peter D. 2012. Domain and function: A dual-space model of semantic relations and compositions. *Journal of artificial intelligence research* 44. 533–585.

Turney, Peter D & Patrick Pantel. 2010. From frequency to meaning: Vector space models of semantics. *Journal of artificial intelligence research* 37. 141–188.

Varvara, Rossella, Gabriella Lapesa & Sebastian Padó. 2021. Grounding semantic transparency in context. *Morphology* 31. 409–446.

Štekauer, Pavol. 2014. Derivational paradigms. In Rochelle Lieber & Pavol Štekauer (eds.), *The Oxford handbook of derivational morphology*, 354–369. Oxford: Oxford University Press.

Wauquier, Marine, Nabil Hathout & Cécile Fabre. 2020. Semantic discrimination of technicality in french nominalizations. *Zeitschrift für Wortbildung/Journal of Word Formation* 4(2). 100–119.

Appendix: Remaining conditional effect plots

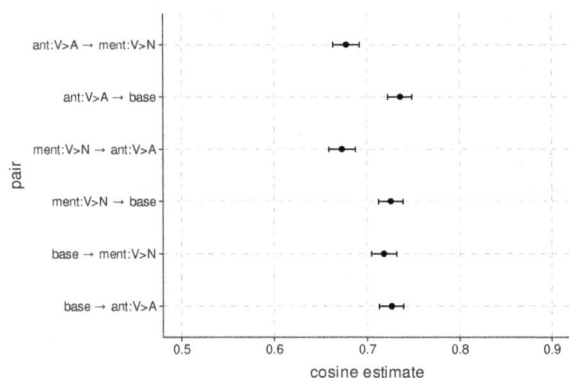

Fig. 19: Comparing -*ant* and -*ment* suffixation.

Distributional evidence for derivational paradigms — 257

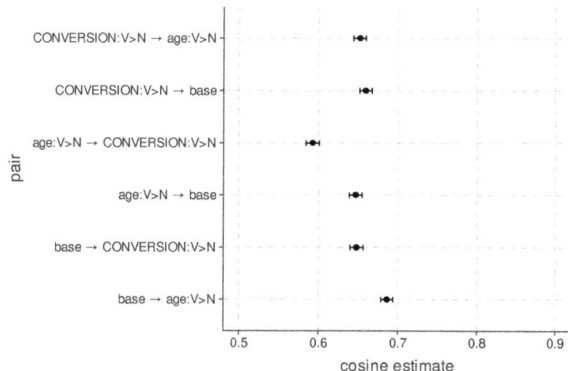

Fig. 20: Comparing conversion and *-age* suffixation.

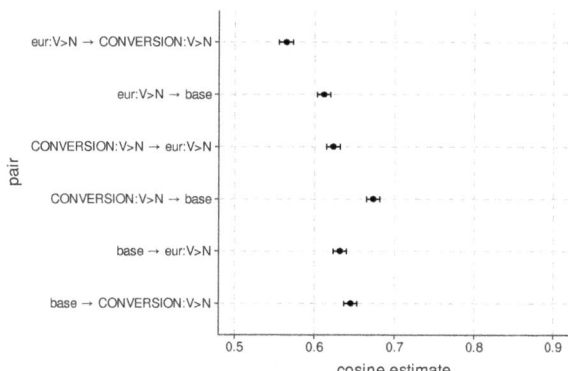

Fig. 21: Comparing conversion and *-eur* suffixation.

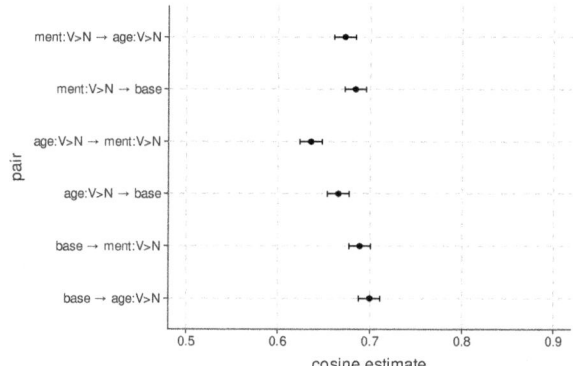

Fig. 22: Comparing *-age* and *-ment* suffixation.

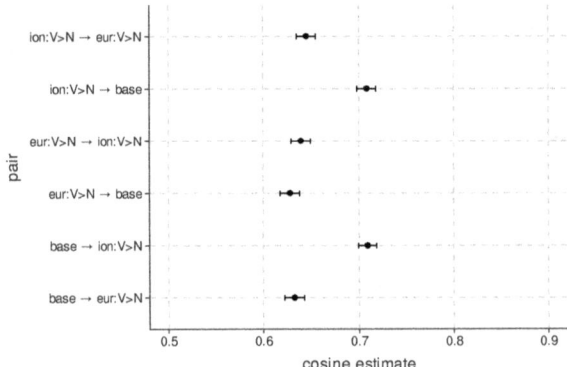

Fig. 23: Comparing *-eur* and *-ion* suffixation.

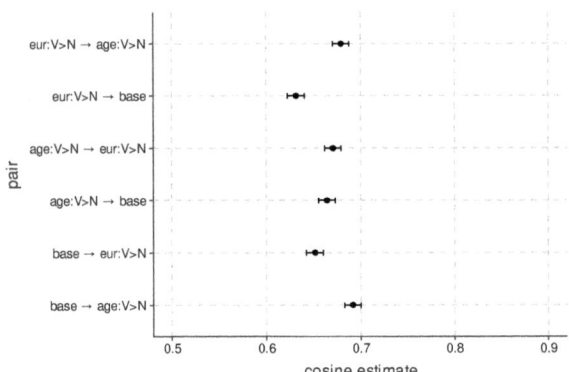

Fig. 24: Comparing *-age* and *-eur* suffixation.

Martin Schäfer
Splitting -*ly*'s: Using word embeddings to distinguish derivation and inflection

Abstract: Whether the relation of base and -*ly* forms in seemingly regular pairs like *quick/quickly* and *clever/cleverly* represents an instance of derivation or inflection has been widely debated. This paper starts from the observation that these two cases are actually not parallel, hypothesizing that pairs from the class of SPEED adjectives show features of inflection, but pairs from the class of HUMAN PROPENSITY adjectives show features of derivation. This hypothesis is explored using distributional semantics, employing different embeddings across three studies. Results show that the classes show a clear distributional difference in terms of the contribution of -*ly*, but the difference does not obtain across all studies, and not always as expected, indicating that a binary contrast inflection/derivation is too simplistic.

Keywords: derivation, inflection, semantics, distributional semantics, adjective, adverbial, English

1 Introduction

Whether the relation of bases and -*ly* forms in pairs like *quick/quickly* in English represents an instance of derivation or inflection has been widely debated, with Bauer et al. (2013, 536) "concluding that the evidence is inconclusive". As far as semantics is concerned, the relationship between the two forms is seen as completely regular (a few opaque exceptions aside), with -*ly* carrying no lexical meaning (Plag 2018, 200, Giegerich 2012). This complete regularity is surprising when considering that the items forming the pairs involved come from very different areas, and that the prototypical usage of the base form as attributive modifier and of the -*ly* form as adverbial modifier usually involves the combination with heads whose referents come from very different domains. To illustrate, take the examples in (1), with (1-a) showing pairs from the SPEED class and (1-b) showing pairs from the HUMAN PROPENSITY classes (for these classes, cf. Dixon 1982).

(1)   a.   quick/quickly, swift/swiftly
        b.   jealous/jealously, clever/cleverly

Martin Schäfer, Eberhard-Karls-Universität Tübingen, email: post@martinschaefer.info

Adjectives from the SPEED class in their attributive usage are typically combined with nouns referring to events, and in their adverbial usage, the verbs they combine with typically also refer to events. In contrast, adjectives from the HUMAN PROPENSITY class are typically combined with nouns referring to human referents, whereas verbs never have human referents. Intuitively, it therefore seems that going from usages of the base form to usages of the -*ly* form involves much less adjustment for the pairs in the SPEED class than for the pairs in the HUMAN PROPENSITY class.

In this paper, I argue that a closer look at the semantics involved suggests that the SPEED pairs show typical properties of inflection and the HUMAN PROPENSITY pairs typical properties of derivation. Three studies explore the extent to which this idea is reflected quantitatively when using distributional semantics measures.

2 Background

To set the stage for the empirical studies using distributional semantics, Section 2.1 outlines the relevant connections between adjective classes and the usage of their members as adverbial modifiers, Section 2.2 introduces distributional semantics and looks at approaches to the distinction between inflection and derivation in distributional semantics, and Section 2.3 outlines the expectations and hypotheses for the following studies.

2.1 Adjective classes and adverbial modification

That the relationship across base/base-*ly* pairs differs depending on the semantics of the adjectives involved is already discussed in Dixon (1982). He distinguishes seven semantic types for the word class 'adjective' in English: DIMENSION, PHYSICAL PROPERTY, COLOR, HUMAN PROPENSITY, AGE, VALUE, and SPEED. Discussing their properties as derived adverbs (under which term he also subsumes the -*ly* forms), he notes that only three of them, HUMAN PROPENSITY, VALUE, and SPEED, have the same, non-metaphorical lexical meaning as the adjective. In terms of their adverbial functions, HUMAN PROPENSITY forms occur as manner and sentence adverbials, and can also modify adjectives, cf. the examples in (2), drawn from the Corpus of Contemporary American English (COCA, Davies 2008–).

(2)   a.   When Nixon cleverly halted the draft of 18-year olds in the early 70s, that took the backbone out of the anti-war movement [...] [COCA]

b. This team was very cleverly assembled by Checketts. [COCA]
c. The monster itself is unique in design and cleverly ambiguous, making it all the more scary. [COCA]

Cleverly in (2-a) functions as a sentence adverbial, giving rise to paraphrases like *It was clever of Nixon that he halted the draft* .... In (2-b), *cleverly* functions as a manner adverbial (*...was assembled in a clever manner*). The semantic function of *cleverly* in (2-c) seems somewhat similar to that of a manner adverbial, but since no explicit eventive target is given, contextual contextual information is needed for successful interpretation, yielding plausible readings like *designed in a clever way to look ambiguous*.

VALUE forms can also modify adjectives, but otherwise occur only as manner adverbials. And SPEED forms only occur as manner adverbials, cf. (3).

(3) With an easy payment system, even a small business can quickly process payments. [COCA]

This study focuses on just the HUMAN PROPENSITY and the SPEED class, not only because they provide the clearest contrast within the three groups with non-metaphorical lexical meanings already on Dixon's criteria, but because they also show the clearest semantic differences: HUMAN PROPENSITY adjectives are predicates that apply prototypically to humans, that is, physical objects, while SPEED adjectives are prototypical predicates of events (Pustejovsky 1995, Bücking & Maienborn 2019, Schäfer 2021).

This difference places them at opposite ends when it comes to the prototypical functions of the base forms and the *-ly* forms: The prototypical usage of adjectives in their base forms is their usage as attributive modifiers in nominal modification. Prototypical noun referents, in turn, are physical objects. In contrast, the prototypical usage of *-ly* forms is their usage as verb modifiers, and prototypical verb referents are events.

In terms of semantic fit, it is straightforward for the SPEED class to modify verbs, because the adjectives are event predicates to begin with. In contrast, this is not straightforwardly possible for members of the HUMAN PROPENSITY class: there needs to be an intermediate step that allows one to connect them to events. This difference becomes apparent when taking a closer look at a few examples from each class.

Before turning to this difference, a quick reminder that both adjective classes also share an important property since they both are subsective adjectives whose interpretation is always relative to some scale or measure provided either by the linguistic or the extra-linguistic context: a quick answer by a child may take more time than a slow answer of an adult, and clever children are judged as such in comparison to the relevant age-group (see Schäfer 2018, 79–81 for discussion and literature).

So, where does the difference between the classes show up? Let's start with members of the SPEED class, cf. (4), and features related to them being event predicates.

(4) a. to run quickly/swiftly
    b. to answer quickly/swiftly

The combination between verb and -*ly* form gives rise to transparent and regular combinations: the event as a whole or subparts thereof only took a short amount of time. Depending on whether they relate to subparts of events or to events as a whole, or to the position of an event relative to a point in time they may receive different readings, but these readings are closely connected. In all cases, SPEED adjectives are directly connected to events, not to the 'way' or manner of an event. Further, across the usages, they target the same, temporal, dimension (hence the label 'one-dimensional' in Schäfer 2013, 55–57), and are consequentially given uniform analyses in the theoretical literature (cf. Rawlins 2013 and Koev 2017 on *quickly*).

As Schäfer (2021) shows for a subset of speed adjectives considered here (*quick, rapid, slow, speedy* and *swift*), speed adjectives in their prototypical attributive usages combine with nouns that refer to events. This preponderance of attributive combinations with heads referring to events is reflected in the existence of many instances where morphologically related heads occur across both forms, cf. (5).

(5) a. quick glance/to glance quickly
    b. swift movement/to move swiftly

Importantly, the events referred to are in both cases the same, only the realization via a nominal vs a verbal construction differs.

Combination of HUMAN PROPENSITY forms with verbs, in contrast, differ in all these respects from the SPEED adjectives: First, they do not give rise to transparent and regular combinations, cf. (6).

(6) a. to run cleverly/jealously
    b. to answer cleverly/jealously

It is relatively open which events would count as instances of clever or jealous running, and the same holds for answering events. This holds even more across the two events of running and answering: the actual properties of the events that lead to them being assessed as reflecting cleverness or jealousy might be very different.

Cooccurrence with morphologically related heads is possible, but only for those cases where the head nouns refer to events, cf. (7).

(7) a. jealous taunt/to taunt jealously
     b. clever answer/to answer cleverly

But prototypical attributive usages of HUMAN PROPENSITY adjectives combine with head nouns that refer to humans. By their very nature, these do not come with verbal counterparts, cf. (9).

(8) a. jealous husband/?
     b. clever girl/ ?

That *-ly* forms from the HUMAN PROPENSITY class are one step removed from the events they modify is also evident in the paraphrases for their usages as sentence and manner adverbials. For the sentential usage, the standard paraphrase *It was ADJ of X that ...* clearly ties the meaning contribution of the *-ly* form to a person. The paraphrases for the manner usage require the introduction of the underspecified way/manner placeholders *in an X manner/The way that ... was ADJ*. Again, what exactly counts as a clever/jealous manner or way is left open, and might, in addition, involve several aspects and dimensions of the event involved. Both adverbial usages are clearly distinct from each other. In fact, in a related language like German, which generally shows much similarity to English in its modification system, the two adverbial usages are typically realized by different forms, with the sentential usage employing the derivational suffix *-erweise*.

These clear differences between the two classes are behind the core idea of this paper: when a member of the SPEED class is used adverbially, it can be directly combined with the verb, no implicit intermediate step is necessary, the process is semantically regular and *-ly* only marks the grammatical function. In other words, it has all the hallmarks of a standard inflectional relationship. In contrast, for members of the HUMAN PROPENSITY class, an intermediate step is needed, the relationships between bases and *-ly* forms are not semantically regular, and *-ly* does not only mark grammatical function: these processes are thus similar to typical cases of derivation.

2.2 Derivation vs. inflection in distributional semantics

This paper explores two ideas to get at the derivation vs. inflection difference in distributional semantics. One rests on the link between derivation and inflection on the one hand and the stability of contrast on the other hand, following Bonami

& Paperno (2018). The second strain exploits different implementations of word embeddings to investigate the issue. Before introducing these two approaches in more detail, the next section provides a short introduction to distributional semantics and studies using it to investigate morphology.

2.2.1 Distributional semantics

Distributional semantics is based on the idea that the context in which a word appears characterizes its meaning. This approach easily lends itself to assessments of the meaning similarity of words; Sahlgren (2006, 21) captures this in his formulation of the distributional hypothesis: "Words with similar distributional properties have similar meanings".

Key to the computational implementation of this idea is the step of encoding the distribution of a word by means of a vector in geometrical space. We can illustrate this with the help of a toy example where we build vector representations for the three *-ly* forms *quickly*, *rudely* and *swiftly* by considering their occurrences in three different contexts: cooccurring with either the verbs *move*, or *decide*, or *follow*. Let's assume we tabulated the cooccurrences as in table 1, where the first cell tells us that *quickly* cooccurred 4 times with *move*.

Tab. 1: Toy example illustrating the first step in creating a simple distributional model: collecting cooccurrence counts for the target words, here the cooccurrences of the three *-ly* forms with the three verbs *follow*, *decide*, and *move*.

	move	decide	follow	total
quickly	4	3	1	8
rudely	2	1	4	7
swiftly	3	4	1	8
total	9	8	6	23

We now take the cooccurrence counts to represent vectors, so that the vector (4,3,1) represents the word *quickly*. Figure 1 illustrates how these vectors can be mapped into geometrical space: the context words, here *move*, *decide*, and *follow*, represent the dimensions of the vector space, and the cooccurrence counts with the *-ly* forms determine the length and directionality of three vectors, each of which encodes the distribution of the corresponding lexeme.

This simple three-dimensional space also allows us to demonstrate the most common measure to assess the semantic similarity between words: the cosine sim-

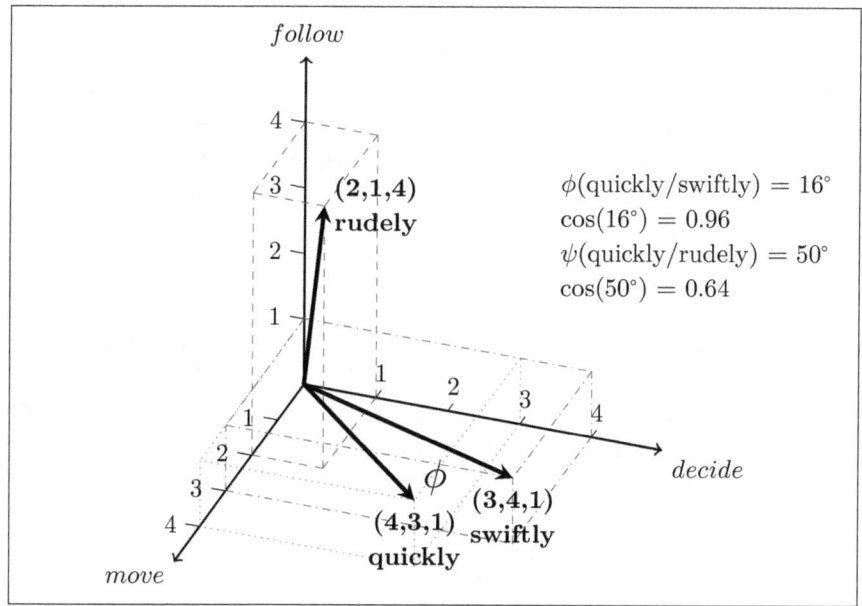

Fig. 1: A three-dimensional space showing the distributional vectors of *quickly*, *swiftly* and *rudely* based on the toy data in table 1. The three dimensions stand for the cooccurrences with the three verbs *move*, *follow*, and *decide*.

ilarity. The cosine similarity is simply the cosine of the angle that holds between any two vectors. In the example, the angle ϕ between the vector for *quickly* and the vector for *swiftly* is 16°, taking the cosine yields the cosine similarity of 0.96, very close to the highest possible value of 1. In contrast, the vectors of *quickly* and *rudely* are far less similar on this measure, the angle ψ of 50° resulting in a cosine similarity of 0.64.

Building on this simple model, it will become clear that this approach can now be fine-tuned in myriad ways. To start with, the context used for the cooccurrence counts can be varied. This parameter, often referred to as context window, can be set to anything from whole documents, paragraphs and sentences to just five, four, three, or even one word either to either side or one side of the target word. Further, the corpora used might be morphologically or syntactically pre-processed (e.g., part-of-speech-tagged, lemmatized, or parsed into dependency trees).

A further parameter is the context words themselves. Already early implementations of distributional semantics were based on a very large number of dimensions, for example the top 10,000 content words of a language, but other numbers are possible. And instead of raw cooccurrence frequencies, some sort of normalization is usually employed. A common method is the transformation of the raw counts into pointwise mutual information or similar measures. For example, the numbers in table 1 can be transformed from their raw frequencies to pointwise mutual information (with logarithm) by using the probabilities of the occurrences of the words involved in the corpus, cf. the formula in (9) (see Turney & Pantel 2010; this normalization is also used in Kotowski & Schäfer 2023 in this volume).

(9) $\quad pmi_{ij} = log\left(\dfrac{p_{ij}}{p_i p_j}\right)$

Using our toy example from above and taking the table to represent our whole corpus, the probability of encountering *quickly* in the context of *move* is 4/23, the overall probability of encountering our target word *quickly* is 8/23, and the probability of encountering the context word *move* is 9/23, leading to a pmi value of 0.35, cf. (10).

(10) $\quad pmi_{\text{quickly/move}} = log\left(\dfrac{p_{\text{quickly/move}}}{p_{\text{quickly}} \times p_{\text{move}}}\right) = log\left(\dfrac{4/23}{(8/23) \times (9/23)}\right) = 0.35$

A further common manipulation is the application of dimension reduction techniques by which the number of dimensions is reduced to smaller numbers, often 300 dimensions (cf. **L**atent **S**emantic **A**nalysis, Dumais 2004). Since the publication of the word2vec algorithm (Mikolov et al., 2013), word vectors are most often created via machine learning, and many thus trained vector sets are freely available. In a comparative study by Baroni et al. (2014), these vectors, often called embeddings, on average outperform the count models (cf. also there for comparisons of the effects of different parameter settings of many of the other parameters mentioned above). In this paper, three different sets of such pretrained vectors are used, two sets from Levy & Goldberg (2014), and, in Study 3, a set of vectors trained with fastText (Mikolov et al., 2017).

Within distributional semantics, there has been clear focus on word formation, either via derivation or via compounding. For an overview on work on derivation, cf. Boleda (2020) and, in this volume, Kotowski & Schäfer (2023) and Bonami & Guzmán Naranjo (2023). Reddy et al. (2011) is an early study comparing different means of vector composition and their relation to semantic transparency in English compound nouns. Vector composition in this context refers to various ways in which two vectors can be combined into a new vector, with perhaps the simplest way being vector addition: two vectors are combined by simply adding up their numbers. Taking again *quickly* and *swiftly* from our toy example above, vector addition would yield a new vector quickly+swiftly of ((4 + 3),(3 + 4),(1 +1)) = (7,7,2) . A slew of recent studies on compound nouns in English and German combines ideas from previous work on derivation in distributional semantics (Marelli & Baroni, 2015) with psycholinguistic approaches to conceptual combination (Marelli et al. 2017 and Günther & Marelli 2021 for English and Günther et al. 2020 for German). Inflection itself has not been focused on so much. Mikolov et al. (2013), the study introducing the word2vec algorithm, used a test set with words related by five semantic and nine syntactic relations to validate their approach. The syntactic part contains five different inflectional relations across the whole spectrum available in English (positive forms of adjectives compared to the corresponding comparative and superlative forms, plain forms of verbs compared to their *-ing*, past tense, and 3rd person sg forms, and nouns in the singular to their plural forms), as well as *-ly*, the affix of interest here. The analogy task they used will also be used in this paper, see Section 4. Together, these works convincingly show that both derivational as well as inflectional relationships can be captured with the help of distributional semantics. However, none of these works directly targets the difference between inflection and derivation. This is the focus of Bonami & Paperno (2018), to which we now turn, followed by the discussion of Levy & Goldberg (2014), whose work I will also use to explore possible differences in the behavior of base/*-ly* pairs.

2.2.2 Derivation and inflection in terms of stability of contrast

Bonami & Paperno (2018) provide a very careful operationalization of the differences between inflection and derivation in terms of quantitative aspects accessible through distributional semantics measures. They start out by discussing the list of five criteria from Stump (1998, 14–18), cf. (11), and it is helpful to go through this list again here for the special case of *-ly* forms.

(11)   a.   change in lexical meaning or part of speech
       b.   syntactic determination
       c.   productivity
       d.   semantic regularity
       e.   closure

Plag (2018, 200-201), who also goes through these criteria for *-ly*, acknowledges some exceptions (e.g. *hard/hardly*), but holds that pairs like *slow/slowly* and *aggressive/aggressively* show no change in lexical meaning. Is there a part of speech change? Plag argues that this could be called into question on the grounds that there are theories taking adjectives and adverbs to belong to the same underlying category. But even if one accepts that there are two distinct wordclasses adjective and adverb, this criterion is still not helpful for the base/*-ly* pairs, because the answer clearly hinges on the overall decision inflection/derivation. Since inflection by definition never leads to a part of speech change, an analysis of the relation between base and *-ly* form as inflection amounts to no change in part of speech, the *-ly* form would count as just a further adjectival form. In contrast, when one adheres to the traditional classification of forms like *slowly* and *aggressively* as belonging to the separate lexical category of adverbs, there is of course a part of speech change. But since this issue, that is, whether the relation between base and *-ly* forms resembles one of inflection or one of derivation, is exactly what we are investigating here, the criterion of part-of-speech-change by itself cannot be used as a diagnostic. For syntactic determination, Plag points to the requirement to use the *-ly*-form in adjectival and verbal modification, and, in contrast, the unacceptability of the *-ly* form in attributive position.

As far as productivity is concerned, he notices only few exceptions (*fastly, *goodly), and semantic regularity, discussed by him in terms of semantic transparency, is again given, save exceptions like the above-mentioned *hardly*. Finally, *-ly* closes the word for further derivational processes, assuming that comparative and superlative formation are themselves instances of inflection. While Plag (2018) concludes that most points speak against a classification as a derivational suffix, he notes that this data shows that the distinction is not categorical. Taking a stronger stance, Giegerich (2012) argues that the evidence is solidly in favor of an inflectional analysis. Payne et al. (2010) are proponents of a derivational analysis. While my focus here will be on the semantic aspects, Payne et al. (2010) show that the criteria of syntactic determination, productivity, and closure are in fact not so clear-cut guiding posts to distinguish between inflection and derivation.

Bonami & Paperno (2018) point out that Stump's criteria are "formulated in terms of high-level morphological notions that are not easy to operationalize". Of special interest for the present paper is their point that it is unclear how to decide on what is lexical vs. not-lexical in meaning, and what counts as semantic regularity. They focus on this last point and provide an operationalization of the semantic regularity criterion in terms of stability of contrasts, as given in (12) (= Bonami & Paperno's (2)):

(12) **Stability of contrast:** the morphosyntactic and semantic contrasts between pairs of words related by the same *inflectional* relation are more similar to one another than the contrasts between pairs of words related by the same *derivational* relation.

Bonami & Paperno explored this criterion by looking at sets of triplets of <pivot, inflectionally related form, derivationally related form> in French. They found that overall the contrasts between inflectionally related forms were more stable.

Approaching a single affix, here -*ly*, in terms of derivation and inflection requires a slight adaption of their approach, since I am interested in whether the stability of contrast is different across *ly*-pairs from different semantic classes.

2.2.3 Inflectional and derivational contrasts in terms of topical and functional similarity

The second approach I use to explore the difference between the lexical classes exploits differences between different types of word embeddings, one focusing topical similarity, and one focusing functional similarity. Levy & Goldberg (2014) compare word embeddings trained using a standard bag-of-words SKIPGRAM model on the English Wikipedia as a corpus with embeddings arrived at by using a generalization of that model trained on a dependency-parsed version of the same corpus. They note that "[...], the bag-of-words nature of the contexts in the 'original' SKIPGRAM model yield *broad topical similarities*, while the dependency-based contexts yield more *functional similarities* of a *cohyponym* nature" Levy & Goldberg (2014, 303). They "expect the syntactic contexts to yield more focused embeddings, capturing more functional and less topical similarity." The reason for this expectation is that bag of words embeddings (henceforth: **bow**) ignore the syntactic function of context words, while dependency based embeddings (henceforth: **deps**) take the syntactic function into account.

In their own qualitative evaluation, they compare the five most similar words, the nearest neighbors, of a set of six target words. If there are differences between the embeddings, the **bow** embeddings usually find associates, and **deps** embeddings find words that behave similarly. For example, the top five nearest neighbors for the adjective *object-oriented* are exclusively other adjectives on the **deps** embeddings, while on the two **bow** embeddings tested they contain two nouns each. In a quantitative investigation, Levy & Goldberg used the WordSim353 dataset (Finkelstein et al., 2002), split for similarity and relatedness (Agirre et al., 2009). Among the topmost similar pairs in this dataset are mostly synonyms, e.g. *midday/noon*, *money/cash*, and *journey/voyage*. In other words, items that have the same meanings and can be used in the same syntactic contexts. Examples for highly related pairs in this dataset are *environment/ecology*, *money/bank*, and *law/lawyer*. These pairs are highly associated with each other but clearly differ in meaning. They can often not be used in the same syntactic contexts. **Deps** embeddings have a clear tendency to rank the similar words higher (in terms of the cosine similarity of the pairs) than **bow** embeddings.

How does this relate to the -*ly* pairs of interest here? The link becomes obvious when taking clear cases of inflection and derivation, and the first criterion from

Stump's list, cf. (11), change in lexical meaning or part of speech. Word pairs related by derivation are typically semantically associated, but they are not semantically similar. Prototypically, their meanings and their part of speech changes (*law/lawless*), they cannot occur in the same syntactic contexts and are in this way functionally different. In contrast, inflectionally related forms keep the same meaning and are, in terms of semantic similarity, on par with synonyms. That means that on **deps** embeddings, wordpairs related by inflection should be more similar to each other than wordpairs related by derivation in comparison to the same word pairs on **bow** embeddings. Consequently, if the hypothesis is correct that the relation between pairs from the SPEED class resembles inflection and the relation between pairs of the HUMAN PROPENSITY class resembles derivation, the pairs are expected to show marked differences when comparing the similarities across the two types of embeddings.

2.3 Expectations and hypotheses

Because I expect the SPEED pairs to show characteristics typical of inflection and the HUMAN PROPENSITY pairs to show characteristics typical of derivation, I hypothesize that
1. Regardless of the embeddings used, the SPEED pairs show stable contrasts, while the HUMAN PROPENSITY pairs do not show stable contrasts.
2. Any contrast between the two classes will in general be clearer on the **deps** embeddings than on the **bow** embeddings.

These expectations are explored in two studies. Study 1 focuses on similarities and correlations within the classes, and Study 2 focuses on the performance of the pairs in the two classes in an analogy task. These two studies are complemented by a third study that uses distributional vectors containing information about the internal make-up of the words represented by the vectors.

3 Study 1: Within-class similarities and correlations in bow and deps embeddings

The first study explores differences relating to the stability of contrast by comparing the two adjective classes in terms of:
a) their variation in average similarity and
b) their pair internal correlations.

In both cases, differences between the **bow** and **deps** embeddings are additionally considered.

Hypothesizing that HUMAN PROPENSITY pairs behave like derivationally connected forms and SPEED pairs like inflectionally related forms, the expectation is that the latter show stable contrasts in direct comparison. More concretely, I predict:

a) Stability of contrasts across pairs
   On average, the relationship between base and *-ly* forms is more stable for pairs from the SPEED class. The semantic similarities between the members of each pair should be more similar for the SPEED class. Therefore, the variation around the mean similarities should be lower for these pairs than for the pairs from the HUMAN PROPENSITY class.

b) Stability of contrasts for pairs within their classes
   Class internal similarities should be kept intact for the SPEED class, but not for the HUMAN PROP class. For example, if *quick* within its class is most similar to *rapid*, then I expect that similarly *quickly* is within its class most similar to *rapidly*. This expectation follows from the stability of contrasts: since the shift in the semantic space is expected to be similar across the pairs, the relative similarities should remain the same.

Both predicted results are expected regardless of the embedding, but I expect a clear difference between the two embeddings with regard to each other: For hypothesis a), I expect that when directly comparing the similarities between the pairs on the **deps** embeddings with those on the **bow** embeddings, the SPEED pairs are more similar, but the HUMAN PROP pairs are less similar. This expectation comes from the focus on functional similarity of the **deps** embeddings and the complementary focus on topical similarity of the **bow** embeddings. Since the pairs of the SPEED class are expected to show characteristics of inflection, they should be more similar on the **deps** embeddings then on the **bow** embeddings. For hypothesis b), the contrast between the two classes is expected to be more clear on the **deps** embeddings. Again, this follows from the functional vs. topical focus of the two embeddings and the hypothesis that the SPEED class pairs show characteristics of inflection. With their focus on functional similarity, the **deps** embeddings should show even less variation in the rankings across the pairs for the SPEED class, while there should be more variation across the pairs in the HUMAN PROPENSITY class, again in comparison to the **bow** embeddings.

3.1 Study 1: Materials and techniques

To represent the two adjective classes, samples of 11 pairs of SPEED and 11 pairs of HUMAN PROPENSITY base/-*ly* pairs were used, cf. table 2 for the 22 base forms.

Tab. 2: Adjective base forms by class

adjective class	adjectives
SPEED	brisk, hasty, hurried, prompt, quick, rapid, rhythmical, slow, speedy, sudden, swift
HUMAN PROP	clever, cruel, eager, generous, greedy, happy, intelligent, jealous, proud, rude, shrewd

The sample contains the maximum number of pairs that fall into the SPEED class; Dixon himself just gives *fast*, *quick*, and *slow* as examples and speaks of a few more (*fast* is not used here because it does not form a base/-*ly* pair). Extending the class to 11 was achieved by selecting similar terms using thesauri. Note that this procedure led to the inclusion of items like e.g. *rhythmical* and *sudden*, which at first might strike one as odd members of this class. But considering the underlying semantics, both fit quite well: *rhythmical* is clearly targeting only the temporal dimension of an event, or more specifically, of subevents within a larger event, and *sudden* likewise targets the temporal dimension, this time not of subparts of the event, but of an event in relation to a contextually given point in time. Both of these aspects also occur in usages of *quick*, which served as a prototypical example above: a quick decision often refers to a decision made after a short amount of time relative to a contextual reference point, it is here similar to typical usages of *sudden*, and a quick beat refers to a beat with sequences repeating after short intervals in time, similar to *rhythmical* in targeting repeated subevents. To keep the sample sizes comparable, the HUMAN PROPENSITY pairs were also capped at 11 (of these, seven are already listed by Dixon).

Two sets of pre-trained vectors from Levy & Goldberg (2014)[1] were used (cf. their paper for further details):
- **bow:** 183,870 embeddings trained on the English Wikipedia using a 5-word window and the original word2vec skip-gram implementation, with the negative sampling parameter set to 15, and 300 dimensions.

---

[1] See https://levyomer.wordpress.com/2014/04/25/dependency-based-word-embeddings/.

– **deps:** 174,015 embeddings trained using a modified skip-gram algorithm, trained on the dependency-parsed version of the same corpus, again with 300 dimensions.

Levy & Goldberg (2014) also provide embeddings using a 2-word window. As their own study shows that the results from using these fall in-between the 5-word window and the dependency trained vectors in their qualitative and quantitative assessments, they are not considered here, as I am interested in maximal differentiating behavior.

To assess the similarity of two vectors, cosine similarity is used. All calculations of cosine similarities and vector manipulations were done with Python, all statistical analysis was done with R. All code used in producing the analyses here and in Studies 2 and 3 is available here: https://doi.org/10.6084/m9.figshare.19093496.v2.

3.2 Study 1: Results

3.2.1 Hypothesis a): contrasts across pairs

Table 3 shows the average similarities along with the standard deviations between the pairs in the SPEED and HUMAN PROPENSITY classes.

Tab. 3: Average pairwise similarities in the two classes of adjectives by embedding

adjective class	BOW			DEPS		
	mean	median	SD	mean	median	SD
SPEED	0.45	0.44	0.143	0.47	0.48	0.108
HUMAN PROP	0.48	0.47	0.072	0.40	0.39	0.052

The standard deviation in the HUMAN PROP class similarities is lower than the standard deviation for the SPEED class. This holds across both embeddings. The differences in variation are significant in both cases ($F = .26$, $p = .04274$ and $F = .23$, $p = .02981$, respectively). This finding is not in line with hypothesis a), which predicted less variation within the SPEED class. When we turn to the changes in average differences resulting from using the different embeddings, the results are in line with the prediction: On the **deps** embeddings, the SPEED pairs are on average more similar than on the **bow** embeddings (0.47 vs. 0.45). For the HUMAN PROPEN-

Tab. 4: Beta regression model for the cosine similarities between the pairs on both embeddings, with the pairs as random effects and the HUMAN PROPENSITY class and the **bow** vector space as reference levels. (Parametric coefficients with logit link function, adjusted R-squared: 0.749)

	Estimate	Std. Error	z value	Pr(>|z|)
(Intercept)	-0.08235	0.12457	-0.661	0.508585
adjective class	-0.11512	0.17661	-0.652	0.514485
vector space	-0.30877	0.08866	-3.483	0.000497
adjective class:vector space	0.38317	0.12594	3.043	0.002346

SITY pairs, the **deps** embeddings show less similarity than the **bow** embeddings (0.40 vs. 0.48).

When modeling the pairwise similarities with a beta regression with the pairs as random effects, a significant interaction of vector space and class emerges, cf. the model in table 4 and the interaction plot in Figure 2.

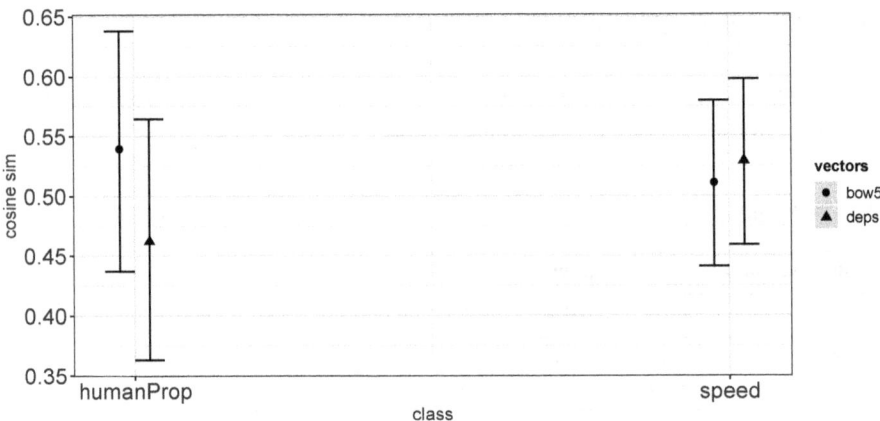

Fig. 2: Interaction of vector space and adjective class when modeling the cosine similarities between base and -*ly* forms

The figure clearly shows the differentiated effect of vector space on the two semantic classes: for the HUMAN PROPENSITY pairs, the **deps** embeddings show significantly less similarity than the **bow** embeddings. In contrast, for the SPEED pairs, the **deps** embeddings show slightly but not significantly higher similarities than the **bow** embeddings.

3.2.2 Hypothesis b): The internal correlations

To what extent are class internal similarities kept intact across forms in the two classes of interest? Table 5 exemplifies the data of interest, using the pair *quick/quickly* and cosine similarities from the **bow** embeddings. The first two columns show the cosine similarities between *quick* and all the other bases from the SPEED pairs. The third and fourth columns shows the cosine similarities between *quickly* and the *-ly* forms of the other speed pairs.

Tab. 5: Cosine similarities of the **bow** embeddings of *quick* and *quickly* and the other bases and *-ly* forms in the SPEED class. Items are ranked by the similarity of *quick* to the other base forms.

quick to	similarity	*quickly* to	similarity
slow	0.54	slowly	0.69
hasty	0.45	hastily	0.41
prompt	0.42	promptly	0.62
rapid	0.42	rapidly	0.70
sudden	0.39	suddenly	0.51
swift	0.39	swiftly	0.75
hurried	0.39	hurriedly	0.42
brisk	0.38	briskly	0.35
rhythmical	0.26	rhythmically	0.25
speedy	0.17	speedily	0.25

The table is ordered by the cosine similarity between *quick* and the other base forms in the SPEED class, with the second column showing the corresponding similarity values between *quickly* and the *-ly* forms. The measure of interest is the correlation between the two rankings, in this case, Pearson's **r** = 0.726, with p = 0.018. This correlation was also calculated for the same pair on the **deps** embeddings, and the same two calculations were performed for all other pairs from the SPEED class and from the HUMAN PROPENSITY class. Table 6 summarizes the data across all pairs and both embeddings by showing the mean correlations and the standard deviations for both classes on both embeddings.

As the table shows, the mean correlations on the **deps** vectors are across the board smaller. When comparing the two adjective classes, the mean correlations are in both cases higher for the SPEED vectors, with a mean difference of .11 on the **bow** embeddings and of 0.03 on the **deps** embeddings. When modeling the correlations with a beta regression, only the effect of vector spaces as such emerges as significant, cf. table 7.

Tab. 6: Summary of the correlations between the base and *-ly* similarities to the other class members per pair.

	bow		deps	
class	mean cor	sd	mean cor	sd
SPEED	0.70	0.16	0.26	0.23
HUMAN PROPENSITY	0.59	0.26	0.23	0.35

Tab. 7: Beta regression model for the class-wise correlations across pairs on both embeddings, with pairs as random effects and the **bow** vector space as reference level. (Coefficients (mean model with logit link), adjusted R-squared: 0.732)

	Estimate	Std. Error	z value	Pr(>|z|)
(Intercept)	1.5517	0.1466	10.586	< 2e-16
vector space	-1.0446	0.1346	-7.761	8.42e-15

In other words, there is no significant difference due to the classes, but the **bow** embeddings show significantly higher average correlations in comparison to the **deps** embeddings.

3.3 Study 1: Discussion

Looking at the two hypotheses, we observe mixed results: Against the expectation of hypothesis a), the HUMAN PROPENSITY class shows less variation in the pairwise similarities on either embedding, although this difference is only significant for the **bow** embeddings. The expectation that on the DEPS embeddings the SPEED pairs should be more and the HUMAN PROPENSITY less similar than on the **bow** embeddings is confirmed: the factors vector space and class significantly interact in predicting the similarities, showing a non-significant higher similarity for SPEED pairs on the **deps** embedding and significantly lower similarities for the HUMAN PROPENSITY pairs on the **deps** embedding.

The class internal correlations considered in hypothesis b) go in the expected directions for both embeddings, that is, on average, the correlation is higher for the pairs from the SPEED class than for the pairs from the HUMAN PROPENSITY class. But class does not emerge as a significant factor when modeling the data. The effect of vector space again emerges as significant here: **bow** embeddings lead to higher correlations across the board. This is unexpected, as I hypothesized that the focus on functional similarity should yield comparatively higher correlations for the SPEED class pairs on the **deps** embeddings.

Trying to understand the many unexpected patterns in the results of Study 1 necessitates a closer look at the data. I will first discuss an interesting pattern in the data underlying the correlations reported, and then explore the behavior of the embeddings further by looking at nearest neighbors across the spectrum of base/-*ly* pairs.

The correlations of interest for hypothesis b) were based on pairwise similarities between each base form and all other base forms within a class, and the corresponding pairwise similarities of the -*ly* forms. Looking not at the correlations but instead zooming in on the average similarities between the base forms and the -*ly* forms reveals a very interesting pattern, cf. table 8.

Tab. 8: Average similarities per form within their classes, on both embeddings.

		average similarities	
class	vector space	base forms	-*ly* forms
SPEED	**bow** embeddings	0.29	0.38
HUMAN PROPENSITY	**bow** embeddings	0.41	0.31
SPEED	**deps** embeddings	0.50	0.75
HUMAN PROPENSITY	**deps** embeddings	0.88	0.42

Strikingly, a uniform split by adjective class emerges on both embeddings: For the SPEED class, the average similarities are higher for the -*ly* forms, on the **bow** embedding rising from 0.29 to 0.38, on the **deps** embedding from 0.5 to 0.75. In contrast, for the HUMAN PROPENSITY class, the average similarities are higher for the non-*ly* forms, with 0.41 to 0.31 on the **bow** embeddings, and 0.88 to 0.42 on the **deps** embeddings. One attractive speculation is that the average similarities across the forms are higher whenever the class members are in their semantically natural environment: the event predicates of the SPEED class when functioning adverbially, and the object predicates of the HUMAN PROPENSITY class in all non-*ly* environments. Note, though, that this cannot be decisively concluded from the data. As mentioned in Section 2.1, SPEED adjectives in their attributive usages also prototypically modify nouns that refer to events.

To arrive at a better understanding of the behavior of the embeddings with regard to the target words, and to get an idea of what lies behind the wide variation in the results across the pairs, table 9 shows the nearest neighbors for a representative selection of the items. The table shows the top five words that are most similar in terms of cosine similarities to three pairs from each adjective class. The three pairs are chosen to represent the spectrum of pairwise similarities, using the **bow** embeddings as a reference point. That is, *swift/swiftly* and *eager/eagerly* show the lowest similarity, *brisk/briskly* and *happy/happily* represent the median, and *rhythmical/rhythmically* and *generous/generously* show the highest similarity. The table does not show very clear patterns. While for *swift* on the **bow** embeddings proper names obscure the picture (*Taylor/Gulliver*), the other sets of nearest neighbors also show considerable variance. For example, the vectors for the top five nearest neighbors for *brisk* in the **bow** embedding seem split into two groups, the two other speed adjectives *fast* and *slow* and *frenetic/leisurely/lively*. The nearest neighbors for *briskly* on the same embedding have an even greater semantic spectrum, including *crazily* and *noisily*. When comparing the SPEED and *human propensity* pairs, the latter seem overall more coherent in that they mostly contain other items from this class. Perhaps this is partially an effect of the small size of the SPEED class. The difference in focus on topical similarity vs. functional similarity across the two vector spaces becomes clearest when looking at the words most similar to the *-ly* forms: the **deps** vectors only pick out other *-ly* forms, whereas the **bow** embeddings include other forms, for example just the base forms. Finally, across the board the top five items are very different both across base and *-ly* forms as well as across embeddings. They also vary in the numbers of antonyms included in the top five. The next study explores whether switching to a different paradigm, the analogy task, brings out the differences between the two classes in a more consistent way.

4 Study 2: An analogy task

In the second study, I approach the difference between the two classes by using an analogy task. The task is first described in Mikolov et al. (2013), who queried the relationship between words by using the question in (13) (the comparison of *aggressive/aggressively* to *rapid/rapidly* is one out of the nine pairs they use to test word-to-word syntactic relationships).

(13) "What is the word that is similar to *aggressive* in the same sense as *rapidly* is similar to *rapid*?"
= Which word d is similar to word c in the same sense as word b is to word a?

The question can be answered via word embeddings in two simple steps:
1. A probe vector is calculated by subtracting the vector for a from the vector for b and adding the vector for c, e.g. $vector_{rapidly} - vector_{rapid} + vector_{aggressive}$
2. Cosine similarity is used to rank all the word vectors in the vector space in terms of their similarity to the probe vector.

Tab. 9: Top five nearest neighbors to six selected target word pairs on either embedding. The first three pairs are from the SPEED class, with low, median, and high pairwise similarity. The last three pairs are from the HUMAN PROPENSITY class, again with low, median, and high pairwise similarity.

target pair	bases		-ly forms	
	bow	deps	bow	deps
SPEED class				
swift/swiftly	taylor	tardy	quickly	promptly
	farley	quick	promptly	forcefully
	rutter	spry	slowly	amicably
	cooke	hick	rapidly	gracefully
	gulliver	brisk	gradually	expeditiously
brisk/briskly	frenetic	languid	zipping	noisily
	leisurely	hectic	crazily	fluidly
	lively	desultory	noisily	uneventfully
	fast	adroit	gently	painlessly
	slow	frenetic	leisurely	erratically
rhythmical/ rhythmically	declamatory	polyrhythmic	melodically	sonically
	melismatic	dance-like	harmonically	melodically
	syncopated	gestural	syncopated	harmonically
	contrapuntal	melismatic	rhythmical	cognitively
	polyrhythmic	bell-like	polyrhythmic	aerodynamically
HUMAN PROPENSITY class				
eager/eagerly	anxious	anxious	anxiously	earnestly
	willing	willing	enthusiastically	fervently
	reluctant	hesitant	warmly	anxiously
	wanting	loath	joyfully	strenuously
	unwilling	reluctant	gratefully	vociferously
happy/happily	glad	ecstatic	gladly	unhappily
	pleased	glad	unhappily	silently
	happier	anxious	joyfully	discreetly
	thankful	thankful	cheerfully	peacefully
	thrilled	hesitant	quietly	quietly
generous/ generously	gracious	gracious	generous	ably
	generously	amiable	graciously	enthusiastically
	frugal	judicious	liberally	sympathetically
	compassionate	agreeable	handsomely	handsomely
	handsome	courteous	gifts	cordially

3. The word vector that is most similar to the probe vector, that is, the vector that is on the first rank, is the answer to the question in (13).

Recall the example of vector addition using the toy vectors in Section 2.2.1: the procedure here is not more complicated, involving only subtraction and addition of the corresponding vector components.

Thinking about the implementation of the analogy task in terms of the role of the *-ly*, the first step itself consists essentially of the isolation of the meaning contribution of *-ly*: subtracting the vector of *rapid* from the vector of *rapidly* yields a vector that stands for the contribution of *-ly*. Adding the vector of a different adjectival base, here *aggressive*, yields the probe vector. As my interest here is not in testing a specific pair, but to explore the behavior of the contribution of *-ly* averaged across the two sets of vectors drawn from the SPEED and HUMAN PROPENSITY classes, I will explore the effect of this approach at class-level. That is, I will first isolate the contribution of *-ly* in each of the pairs of interest here, and then use the resulting vector presentations to compare the meaning contribution of *-ly* averaged over each of the two classes as well as over both classes, that is, all pairs.

Recall the finding presented in the discussion of Study 1 that on both embeddings the *-ly* forms of the SPEED pairs are more similar to each other then the corresponding base forms while the opposite holds for the HUMAN PROPENSITY pairs. Based on that finding, I expect that a single meaning contribution of *-ly* can only be successful in the analogy task for the SPEED pairs. A second expectation, deriving from the tables of the top five nearest neighbors considered in the discussion of Study 1, is that this will work better on the **deps** embeddings, which consistently had *-ly* forms as nearest neighbors of the six *-ly* forms of the target pairs. In addition, the average vectors themselves allow again to assess the stability of contrast aspect from hypothesis a) in Study 1.

4.1 Study 2: Materials and techniques

Study 2 uses the same set of pairs and the same set of word embeddings as Study 1. The probes for the analogy task were calculated as follows (always separately for both the **bow** and the **deps** embeddings):
1. To isolate the contribution of *-ly* across a pair, the vector for the base form was subtracted from the vector for the *-ly* form. This yields 22 *-ly* vectors, or, in the terminology of Bonami & Paperno (2018), 22 vector offsets, one for each pair. These 22 vectors were used to calculate two average vectors. One average vector was calculated using the 11 vectors from the SPEED class, the second av-

erage vector was calculated using the 11 vectors from the HUMAN PROPENSITY class.
2. From the 22 individual vectors, two average -*ly* vectors were calculated for every base, using a leave-one-out approach. One 'all-*ly*' vector, encompassing the individual -*ly* vectors from both classes, and one class-specific vector, depending on the class of the base: either 'SPEED-ly' or 'HUMAN PROPENSITY -*ly*':
    a) all-*ly*: a vector for class-unspecific -*ly*, created by averaging across all individual -*ly* vectors except the -*ly* vector from the target pair itself. I.e., for *quick/quickly*, the all-*ly* vector is calculated by averaging over the 10 other SPEED class -*ly* vectors and all the HUMAN PROPENSITY -*ly* vectors.
    b) SPEED-*ly*: a class specific vector calculated by averaging across the 10 other -*ly* vectors from the SPEED class.
    c) HUMAN PROPENSITY-*ly*: a class specific vector calculated by averaging across the 10 other -*ly* vectors from the HUMAN PROPENSITY class.
3. For every base, the two average -*ly* vectors resulting from the previous step were used to calculate two probes: the general probe using the all-*ly* vector, and the class-specific -*ly* probe using the class-specific -*ly* vectors. This was done by simply adding the corresponding -*ly* vector to the vector of the base form.

The resulting vectors are explored in three different ways:
1. by comparing the variation of the individual -*ly* vectors,
2. by comparing the ranks in the analogy task, and
3. by comparing the similarities in the analogy task.

The first is the most straightforward assessment: the variance of the similarities between the individual vector offsets, and the average vector offset within a class is compared. This method is adapted from Bonami & Paperno (2018), who use it to investigate the different relations in their triplets of one pivot form and one derivationally and one inflectionally related other form. They hypothesize that when comparing inflectional and derivational relations this way, the vector offsets from the inflectional relations should show less dispersion around the average vector offset, and thus less variance, in line with the idea that inflection is connected to stable contrasts. Derivational relations, in comparison, should show more dispersion and hence more variance. Here, of course, there is no pivot, and the forms to be compared are the members of the two different semantic classes. As described above, the individual vector offsets are the 22 vectors arrived at by subtracting the vector of the base of a pair from the -*ly* form of that pair. The average vector offset for a class is the average of each 11 -*ly* vectors of a class which are simply added together and then divided by 11.

The second and third are two aspects of the same task: when using the leave-one-out-vectors to construct analogy probes, I want to know how well these probes work in identifying the expected target. This is assessed in two different ways: first, by looking at the rank of the target among the nearest neighbors of the probe, and second, by looking at the cosine similarity of the target to the probe. For both measures, the probes using the all-*ly* vectors are compared to the class-specific -*ly* vectors. I am using both ranks and absolute similarities because these two aspects are in principle independent of each other and therefore both of interest. The comparison of the ranks is the standard way to assess the success of the analogy task: only if the target is the nearest neighbor of the probe is the analogy task correctly answered. Whether this success comes about with a relative high or relative low cosine similarity between the probe and the target depends on the overall distribution of items in the vector space. The absolute similarities are therefore independently of interest.

As before, for all three comparisons both vector spaces are explored. In line with the hypotheses explored in Study 1 and the remarks at the end of the previous section, there should be a more marked contrast between the two classes on the **deps** embeddings. The SPEED class should show less variation for its -*ly* vectors and better performance on the analogy task in comparison to the results from the **bow** embeddings.

4.2 Study 2: Results

4.2.1 Variance in the vector offsets

Recall that the variance in the vector offsets is simply the variance in the cosine similarities between the 11 individual -*ly* vectors per class (SPEED or HUMAN PROPENSITY) and the average -*ly* vector per the respective class. For the **bow** vectors, the variance in the cosine similarities is bigger for the SPEED class (0.018) than for the HUMAN PROPENSITY class (0.004). This difference is significant (F = 4.9641, p = 0.01838). For the **deps** vectors, the SPEED class shows a variance of 0.0030, compared to a variance of 0.0025 in the HUMAN PROPENSITY class. This very small difference is not significant (F 1.1908, p = 0.7878). This finding is not in line with expectations, as for both embeddings less variation, that is, less dispersion, was expected for the members of the SPEED class. Note also that across the two vector spaces the results are unexpected: only on the **bow** embeddings is there a significant difference in the variances (in an unexpected directions), whereas the **deps** embeddings show no difference.

4.2.2 Ranks in the analogy task

When the target -*ly* form is the nearest neighbor of the probe, the task is considered a success. For example, after calculating a probe for *swiftly* by adding an average -*ly* vector to the base *swift*, the task is successful if the vector for *swiftly* is placed on the first rank in the set of all vectors in the vector space ranked by cosine similarity to the probe. Mikolov et al. (2013) implicitly acknowledge that this task is hard, because they discard the words used to construct the probes when looking for the closest nearest neighbor. That is, for them, if the base form *swift* is on the first rank and the target *swiftly* on the second rank, it would still count as a success. Here, I will count as successes only true first ranks, but I will report on the top five ranks. This allows to assess how close the targets were to success, that is, to the first rank, even if the first rank itself is missed.

To conveniently assess the performance of the probes across the different classes, average vectors, and vector spaces, the results are always presented by using the same types of graphs. The ranks are shown on the y-axis, with the first rank on top, going down to the fifth rank and finally collecting all targets outside the top five range in the category 'out'. The -*ly* targets are represented on the x-axis, first the targets from the SPEED class, second the targets from the HUMAN PROPENSITY class. Both are ordered alphabetically, and the dots showing their place in the ranking are color-coded for the two classes: blue for the SPEED class and red for the HUMAN PROPENSITY class.

Figure 3 shows the ranking of the -*ly* targets when using the **bow** probes and the *ly*-vector generalized across all 22 pairs except the respective probe pair.

The task is not successful for any of the pairs, but the overall performance for the SPEED probes is better. For the SPEED class, the majority of the targets, six, are on the second rank, the vector for *suddenly* is on the third rank, and the probe for *slowly* on the 5th rank. The vectors for *promptly*, *speedily*, and *swiftly* are outside of the top five range. In contrast, only two of the HUMAN PROPENSITY targets are on the second rank, one is occupying the third rank and another the fourth rank. Seven out of eleven are outside the top five. In all cases, that is, for both the SPEED as well as the HUMAN PROPENSITY targets, it is always the base form that occupies the first rank. In other words, the contribution of the all-*ly* vector does not manage to move the probe vector far enough from the vector of the adjectival base, indicating that the contributions of -*ly* across all 21 other items are too different from each other and the target -*ly* to yield a specific enough average vector.

When instead using the probes calculated using the class-wise averaged -*ly* vectors, the rankings clearly improve for the SPEED class, but also for the HUMAN PROPENSITY class, cf figure 4.

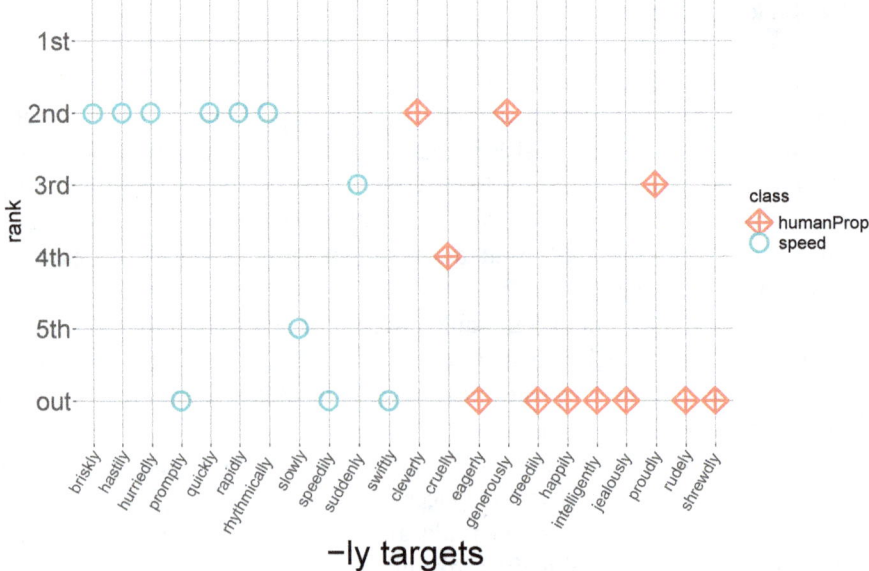

Fig. 3: Rankings of the *-ly* targets in terms of their cosine similarity to the probes. Using the **bow** embeddings, with the *-ly* vector averaged across all other pairs using the leave-one-out technique.

For the SPEED class, all three vectors that were outside the top five using the all-*ly* probes are now within the top five, with the vector for *promptly* in second place, the vector for *swiftly* in third place and the *speedily* vector in fifth place. Only the *briskly* vector falls in ranks, from second to fourth. For the HUMAN PROPENSITY class, three are in second place, with the *shrewdly* vector previously outside the top-five. The *intelligently* vector also moves from outside the top five to rank three. At the same time, the vector for *cruelly*, on rank four with the all-*ly* probe, is now also outside of the top five, so that the number of items in this class outside of the top five ranks only decreases by one. Just as before, when looking at the items ranked first, these are always the base forms.

Figure 5 shows the result when averaging *-ly* across both classes using the **deps** embeddings. The result is clearly worse than the results obtained with the **bow** vectors. Within the **deps** embeddings, the results for the SPEED class are better, but for both classes, the majority of targets, seven and nine, respectively, are ranked outside the top five. For the SPEED class, there are two second ranks, and two fifth ranks. For the HUMAN PROPENSITY class, the *rudely* vector is ranked second, and the *cruelly* vector is ranked fourth.

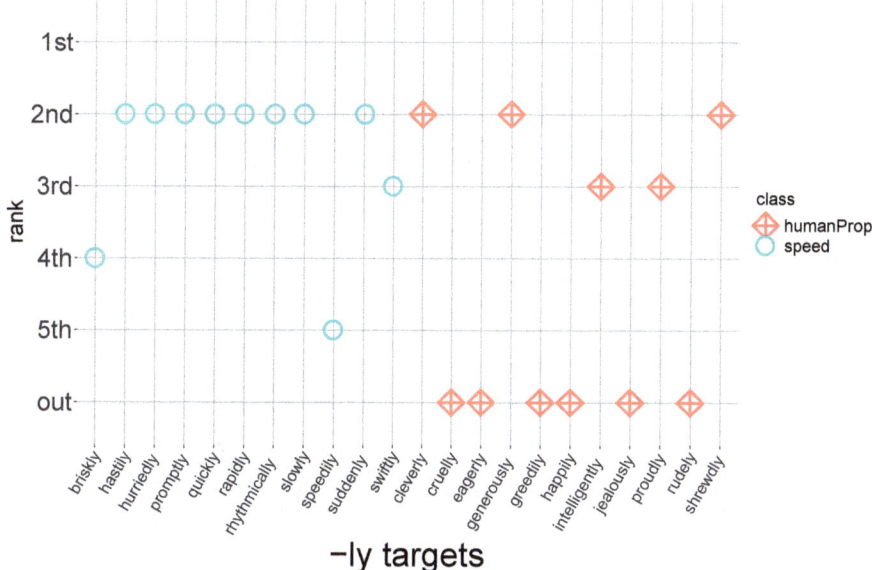

Fig. 4: Rankings of the *-ly* targets in terms of their cosine similarity to the probes. Using the **bow** embeddings, with the *-ly* vector averaged by class.

That these probes behave notably different from the **bow** probes is already apparent in that the vectors for *speedily* and *rudely*, two of the overall three vectors ranked second, are ranked outside of the top-five on the **bow** embeddings. Another notable contrast when looking in more detail at the nearest neighbors of the probes emerges when considering the words whose vectors are on rank one in this task, cf. the second column in table 10. For both classes, only six first-ranked items each correspond to the base forms, and five first-ranked items each are *-ly* forms, although not the target forms. Of these, some forms in the SPEED class seem notably off, e.g. *laboriously* as closest to the *quickly*-probe.

Figure 6 shows the results for the class-specific *-ly* vectors on the **deps** embeddings. This constitutes a notable improvement, again with an advantage for the SPEED pairs. The vector for *briskly* is successfully predicted, and the vectors for *speedily* and *swiftly* are ranked second, the one for *rapidly* fourth and the vector for *hastily* fifth. For the HUMAN PROPENSITY class, the improvements are limited to the vectors already ranked within the top five. The *rudely* vector is also a success, as expected placed on the first rank. The *cruelly* vector is now on the second rank, but all other vectors remain outside of the top five. Intriguingly, the two successful items performed relatively badly on the class-specific **bow** embeddings, with the *briskly*-probe ranked fourth and the *rudely*-probe outside of the top five.

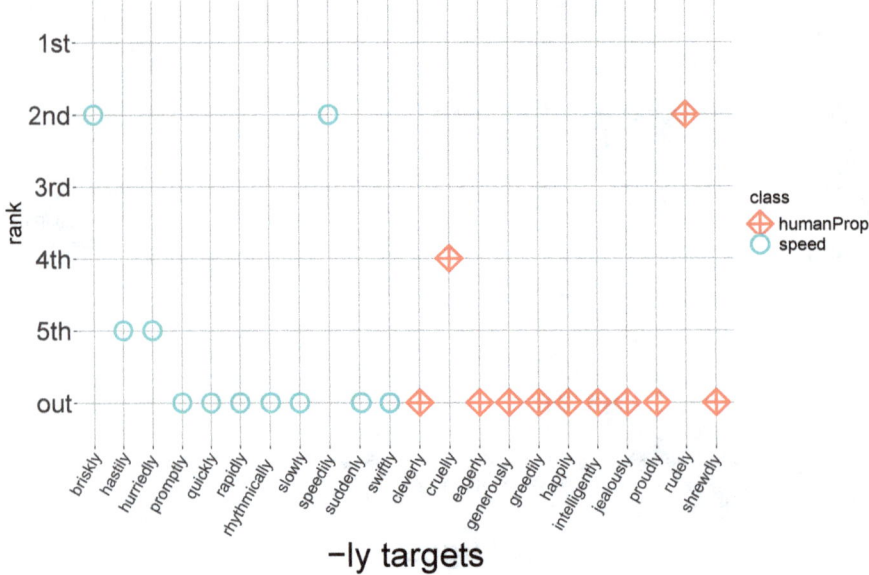

Fig. 5: Rankings of the *-ly* targets in terms of their cosine similarity to the probes using the **deps** embeddings. *-ly* vector averaged across all pairs using the leave-one-out technique.

Just as for the probes using the all-*ly* vector, the actual items on the first rank in this task are not just the corresponding base forms, in contrast to the results from the **bow** embeddings. All first ranked items for the class-specific *-ly* probes are shown in the third column in table 10. For the SPEED class, besides the single success in the form *briskly*, there are the same six base forms that already showed up for the all-*ly* probes. The remaining four first ranked items are all *-ly* forms, three times *swiftly*, and again *self-consciously* for *rhythmical*. While these are not the expected words, they are clearly closer in meaning than the first ranked items for the all-*ly* probes as *swiftly* is itself part of the SPEED class. For the HUMAN PROPENSITY class, all first ranked items are now *-ly* forms, mostly coming from the HUMAN PROPENSITY class.

4.2.3 The similarities in the analogy task

Table 11 shows the average cosine similarities between probes and targets for both types of *-ly* vectors, all-*ly* and class-specific *-ly*, on both embeddings.

For the **bow** embeddings, the similarity between probe and target for the items in the SPEED class is higher when using the class-specific *-ly* vectors than

Tab. 10: Analogy task: most similar words to the probe for the generalized -*ly* vectors and the separated -*ly* vectors under the **deps** embedding, using the leave-one-out approach

target relation	depsAll	depsSep
brisk-briskly	erratically	briskly
hasty-hastily	rudely	swiftly
hurried-hurriedly	hurried	hurried
prompt-promptly	prompt	prompt
quick-quickly	laboriously	swiftly
rapid-rapidly	rapid	rapid
rhythmical-rhythmically	self-consciously	self-consciously
slow-slowly	slow	slow
speedy-speedily	speedy	speedy
sudden-suddenly	irreversibly	swiftly
swift-swiftly	swift	swift
clever-cleverly	tactfully	concretely
cruel-cruelly	cruel	jealously
eager-eagerly	eager	royally
generous-generously	cordially	cordially
greedy-greedily	tactfully	tactfully
happy-happily	happy	cheerfully
intelligent-intelligently	maturely	flexibly
jealous-jealously	jealous	impulsively
proud-proudly	proud	graciously
rude-rudely	rude	rudely
shrewd-shrewdly	ably	ably

Tab. 11: Similarities in the analogy task: descriptive overview

| class | lyVector | bow | | deps | |
		sim	sd	sim	sd
speed	all-*ly*	0.562	0.0868	0.744	0.0701
speed	speed-*ly*	0.590	0.0726	0.742	0.0577
human propensity	all-*ly*	0.561	0.0749	0.735	0.0459
human propensity	human propensity -*ly*	0.559	0.0776	0.768	0.0392

when using the all-*ly* vectors. In contrast, for the items from the HUMAN PROPENSITY class, the all-*ly* result in very slightly higher similarities between probes and targets in comparison to the class-specific -*ly* vectors. For the **deps** embeddings, it is exactly the other way around: For the SPEED class, the all-*ly* vectors produces slightly higher similarities than the class-specific -*ly* vectors. For the HUMAN PROPENSITY class, the class-specific vectors produce higher similarities between

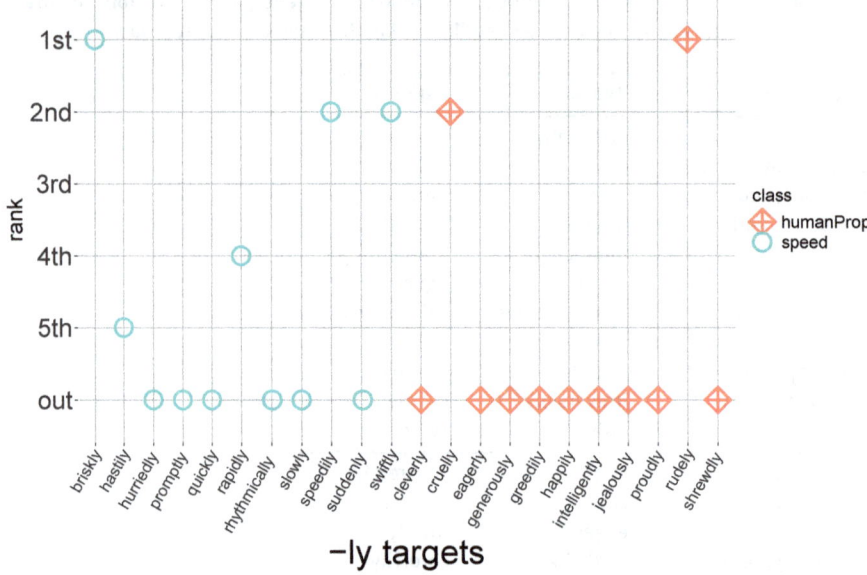

Fig. 6: Rankings of the -*ly* targets in terms of their cosine similarity to the probes using the **deps** embeddings. -*ly* vector averaged by class using the leave-one-out method.

probes and targets. Across the board, the similarities on the **deps** embeddings are notably higher than the similarities on the **bow** embeddings.

When modeling the similarities for each vector space with beta regression models, we see for both embeddings significant interactions of semantic classes and -*ly* vectors, cf. the models in tables 12 and 13 and the interaction plots in figure 7.

Tab. 12: Beta regression model for the cosine similarities probe-target and the bow embeddings, with pairs as random effects, and the HUMAN PROPENSITY class and the all-*ly* vectors as reference levels. (Parametric coefficients with logit link, R-squared adjusted: 0.732)

	Estimate	Std. Error	z value	Pr(>|z|)
(Intercept)	0.251095	0.097536	2.574	0.0100
adjective class	0.001197	0.137940	0.009	0.9931
-*ly* vector	-0.008422	0.038421	-0.219	0.8265
adjective class:-*ly* vector	0.128437	0.054484	2.357	0.0184

Tab. 13: Beta regression model for the cosine similarities probe-target and the **deps** embeddings, with pairs as random effects and the HUMAN PROPENSITY class and the all-*ly* vectors as reference levels. (Parametric coefficients with logit link, R-squared adjusted: 0.902)

	Estimate	Std. Error	z value	Pr(>|z|)
(Intercept)	1.02944	0.08896	11.572	< 2e-16
adjective class	0.06169	0.12592	0.490	0.624225
-*ly* vector	0.17790	0.03872	4.594	4.34e-06
adjective class:-*ly* vector	-0.18993	0.05455	-3.482	0.000498

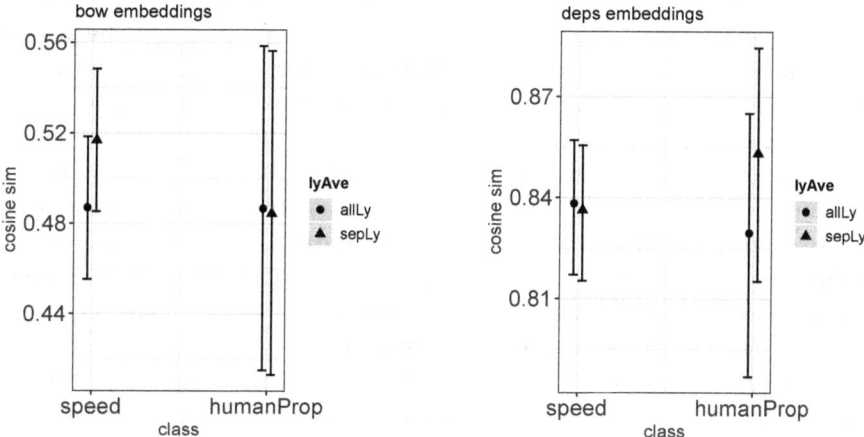

Fig. 7: Interaction plots for average vectors and adjective class on the **bow** embeddings (left hand side) and on the **deps** embeddings (right hand side).

The two interaction plots clearly show the difference between the results in the two vector spaces, with the prediction of the two average -*ly* vectors for each class almost completely overlapping for the HUMAN PROPENSITY class on the **bow** embeddings but for the SPEED class on the DEPS embeddings. Also of interest is the clear difference in the confidence bands between the two semantic classes on both embeddings: the confidence bands for the SPEED class are consistently much smaller than those for the HUMAN PROPENSITY class.

4.3 Study 2: Discussion

Study 2 brought differentiated results that are again only partially in line with expectations. Against expectations, the offset vectors using the **bow5** embeddings showed less variation for the HUMAN PROPENSITY class, with no difference on the **deps** embeddings.

For the rankings in the analogy task, the **bow** embeddings turned out to be more successful than the **deps** embeddings: While the task was not successful in its final step with the highest ranked targets only on the second ranks, the results show that the embeddings are able to pick up a difference at the class level, with the difference in the expected direction: probes from the SPEED class performed better overall, and there was more improvement in the rankings for this class in comparison to the HUMAN PROPENSITY class when switching to class-specific *-ly* vectors. The pairs in the SPEED class seem to have more in common so that a vector averaged over these forms is more meaningful than using the same method for the HUMAN PROPENSITY class. For the **deps** vectors, the results were comparatively weak, although SPEED targets were overall ranked higher and again improved more on the class-specific vectors.

When looking at the absolute cosine similarities for the targets on the **bow** embedding, the **bow** embeddings behave mostly as expected: only for the SPEED class is there a clear difference when comparing the results using the all-*ly* vectors to the results from using the class-specific *-ly* vector. As the model shows, the interaction between class and type of vector is significant. The clear difference in the confidence bands between the semantic classes in the interaction plot also shows very clearly that the model is more confident when it comes to predicting the behavior of the items from the SPEED class. Comparing the absolute similarities with the rankings, it is notable that when using the all-*ly* vectors there is no significant difference between the two semantic classes in terms of the absolute similarities of the targets to the probes, while we saw that the targets from the SPEED class are ranked higher than those from the HUMAN PROPENSITY class. This underscores the usefulness of employing both rankings and absolute values together, suggesting that the items from the two semantic classes clearly occupy very differently structured areas in the semantic space.

The pattern for the absolute cosine similarities on the **deps** embeddings is exactly opposite, and therefore clearly against expectations. The only commonality with the model for the **bow** results are the tighter confidence bands for the items from the SPEED class. It is not clear to me how meaningful these results are, especially since this set-up on the whole did not perform well as far as the rankings are concerned. At the same time the rankings still showed an advantage of the SPEED class items when using the class-specific *-ly* probes, and a better performance of the SPEED class items in general. This does not line up with the absolute similarities. Overall, as we saw from investigating the first ranked items for this class, the **deps** embeddings show more unexpected, and at the moment unexplainable, behavior.

5 Study 3: Analogy and -*ly* aware embeddings

The results so far have been mixed; the only result that went mostly as expected were the ranking and cosine similarities for the **bow** embeddings in the analogy task. With one intriguing twist: in all cases, the first rank in the analogy task on the **bow** embeddings are occupied by the base forms. Intuitively, this is highly unexpected: the target is very obviously a -*ly* form, so non-*ly* forms should not be selected.

The embeddings used so far don't represent information concerning the forms of the words themselves. What happens when we switch do embeddings that do exactly this?

Mikolov et al. (2017) implement one way of including word internal structure in embeddings, in their terminology subword information. The words are broken down into character-ngrams (with characters simply the orthographic characters), which are in turn represented as vectors, the sum of which is added to the standard word vector. Study 3 employs these enriched embeddings in the analogy task.

Note that, conceptually, including word internal structure in the embeddings is a clear step away from the original distributional slogan "You shall know a word by the company it keeps!" from Firth (1957, 11). Crucially, when using the embeddings as stand-in for meanings, it lets form aspects of the word contribute to its meaning. I will come back to this issue in the discussion.

5.1 Study 3: Material and techniques

Study 3 uses the exact same materials and techniques for the analogy task as Study 2, with the only difference being the embeddings used. These are now the pretrained fasttext (= **fast**) embeddings including subword information, wiki-news-300d-1M-subword.vec.zip, from https://fasttext.cc/docs/en/english-vectors.html. These vectors have been trained on a corpus of 16 billion tokens, using Wikipedia 2017, the UMBC webbase corpus and the statmt.org news dataset. For details of the training, cf. Mikolov et al. (2017). As the vector space contains considerably more embeddings (1 million vs. 183,870 (**bow**) and 174,015 (**deps**), only the embeddings for the most frequent 175,000 words were used to search for the nearest neighbors in order to keep the results comparable.

5.2 Study 3: Results

5.2.1 Rankings in the analogy task

When using the general *-ly* probes, two of the SPEED targets and three of the HUMAN PROPENSITY targets are correctly identified. Seven of both the SPEED targets and the HUMAN PROPENSITY targets are ranked second. Finally, two SPEED targets and one HUMAN PROPENSITY target are ranked third. All non-target first ranks are occupied by the respective non-*ly* forms.

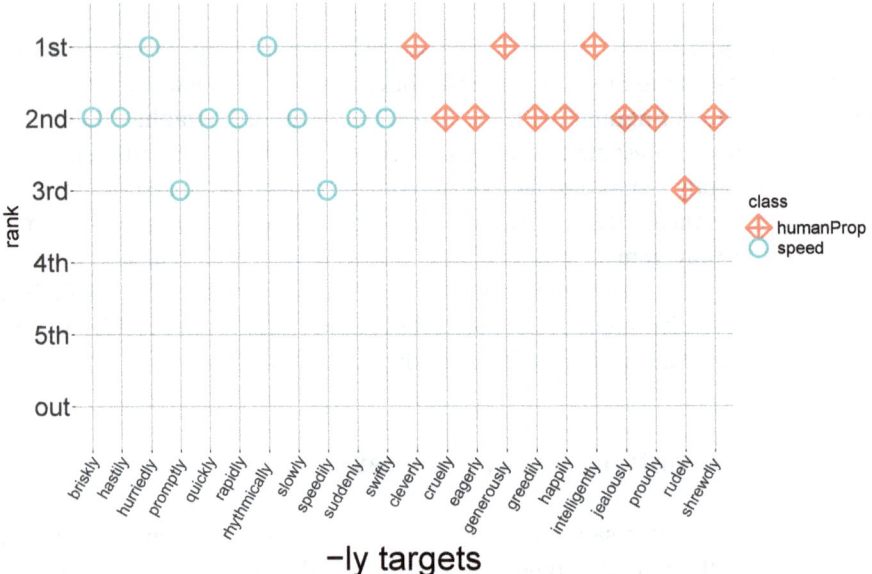

Fig. 8: Rankings of the *-ly* targets in terms of their cosine similarity to the probes using the **fast** embeddings, with the *-ly* leave-one-out vector averaged across both classes.

Switching to the class-specific *-ly*-vectors results in a slight improvement for the SPEED vectors, where the target vector for *hastily* moves from second to first rank. The ranks for the HUMAN PROPENSITY targets remain unchanged.

Just as for the all-*ly* probes, the other first ranks are occupied by the respective base forms.

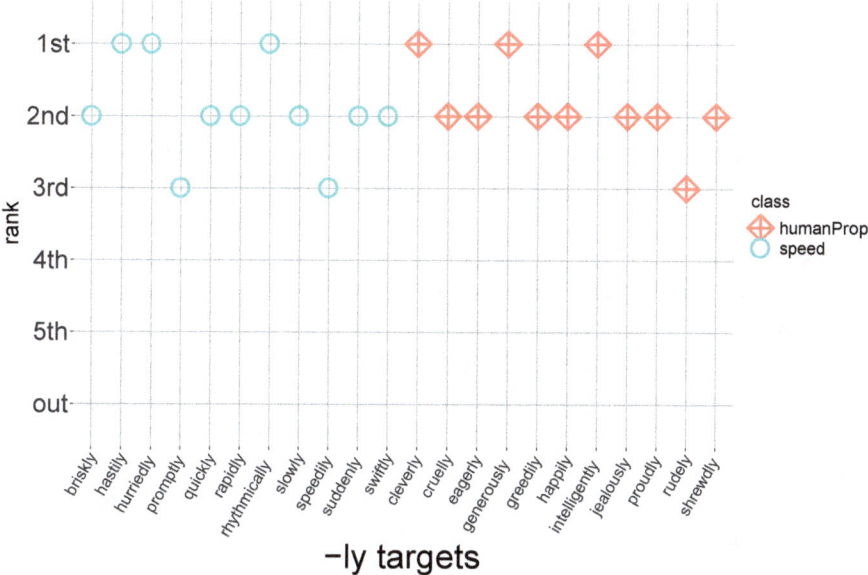

Fig. 9: Rankings of the -*ly* targets in terms of their cosine similarity to the probes using the **fast** embeddings, with the -*ly* leave-one-out vector averaged by class.

5.2.2 Similarities in the analogy task

The average similarities of the targets to the probes are shown in table 14.

Tab. 14: Average cosine similarities between probe and target vectors on the **fast** embeddings.

class	-*ly* vector	cosine similarity	standard deviation
speed	all-*ly*	0.755	0.0709
speed	speed--*ly*	0.750	0.0859
human propensity	all-*ly*	0.786	0.0484
human propensity	human propensity-*ly*	0.800	0.0445

For the SPEED class, the cosine similarities between targets and probes are minimally more similar when using the all-*ly* vector than when using the class-specific speed -*ly* vector. In contrast, the opposite effect, slightly larger this time, can be observed for the HUMAN PROPENSITY vectors. Modeling the similarities with beta regression yields no significant effects neither for the interaction between class and *ly*-vectors nor for adjective class or average vector used individually.

5.3 Study 3: Discussion

The aim of Study 3 was to explore whether including subword information might result in more targets being successfully identified in the analogy task. This was indeed the case, and the vector space gave overall the best results across all pairs and for both classes. However, using this vector space also eroded all differences observed so far for the two different classes and for the effect of a switch of all-*ly* vectors to class specific vectors: neither made a significant difference.

This leveling of all differences brings us back to the nature of these embeddings. As mentioned above, the very fact that the **fast** embeddings use subword information makes them conceptually very different from the classic idea behind distributional semantics. That *swift* and *swiftly* share patterns in their orthographic form is not a feature of their distribution, but simply a feature of their form. And this form feature is not linked to any differences in lexical semantics of the adjectival base forms, therefore it is not surprising that encoding subword information in the embeddings weakens any effect of semantic class membership encoded in the embeddings via the distribution of the words. In effect, using the base/-*ly* pairs with the **fast** embeddings, the analogy task is no longer merely about semantic or syntactic similarity, but about these similarities in conjunction with form overlap.

6 General discussion

The three studies presented here explored the hypothesis that the relations between base and -*ly* forms for SPEED adjectives behave like instances of inflection whereas the relations between bases and -*ly* forms of HUMAN PROPENSITY adjectives behave like instances of derivation in terms of their distributional semantics. Two specific aspects were investigated: a) is there evidence for SPEED adjectives to show more stable contrasts than HUMAN PROPENSITY adjectives and b) is there evidence for a vector space more sensitive to functional similarity to show clearer differences for these two classes than a vector space focusing on topical similarities.

The results from Study 1 and Study 2 only yield partial evidence for this. In particular, assessing the difference between the two classes by looking at variance, either in the similarities across the pairs in Study 1, or in terms of the dispersion of the offset vectors in Study 2, has shown that the HUMAN PROPENSITY class shows less variance (except for the offset-dispersion on the **deps** embeddings, which showed no difference). Support for the hypothesis that SPEED pairs behave more like inflection came via the second aspect of comparison in Study 1: the HUMAN PROPENSITY pairs are less similar and SPEED pairs more similar when comparing the **deps** embeddings to the **bow** embeddings. Not significant, but in the expected direction was the final finding from Study 1: class internal correlations are higher for the SPEED class. Another chance finding from Study 1 was the overall higher mean similarity of -*ly* forms from the SPEED class to each other in comparison to the base forms, with the opposite pattern obtaining for the HUMAN PROPENSITY class: this shows that the difference in semantic class has reflexes in the distribution, although these particular reflexes cannot straightforwardly be related to the general issue of inflection versus derivation.

The analogy task in its original form, that is, focusing on the ranks of the targets within the nearest neighbors of the probes, shows the clearest pattern in line with the original hypothesis: switching from the non-specific all-*ly* vectors to the class specific vectors comes with a very clear improvement for the targets from the SPEED class, notably on the **bow** embeddings. For the **bow** embeddings, this finding goes together with the effect of the switch for the absolute similarities of the targets, while yielding opposite results for the **deps** embeddings. The latter result, however, is perhaps not so relevant given that this vector space performed so poorly on this task overall.

Study 3 explored whether the failure of the best performing embeddings in the analogy task in study 2 to produce any successes could be overcome by using the **fast** embeddings, which also encode subword information. This was expected to help answer the analogy task successfully, as except for the -*ly* ending itself and some minor adjustments (hasty/hastily etc.) the words of a pair completely overlap orthographically. This expectation turned out to be correct. This vector space overall performed best on the analogy task, but the comparison of the results from the all-*ly* vectors to those of the class-specific vectors showed virtually no effect. In a way, this result links back very nicely to the starting point of this paper: -*ly* forms are interesting, because the theoretical literature cannot decide whether they should be treated as inflectional or derivational. The clear semantic differences between the members of pairs of the SPEED class on the one hand and the HUMAN PROPENSITY class on the other hand outlined in section 2.1 are not immediately obvious and require close semantic analysis. They are obscured by the pairs sharing the same affix to link their forms, and the fact that they both occur in the prototypical adjectival and adverbial patterns.

These semantic differences are at least partially accessible via the classic distributional paradigm, that is, when using the distribution of a word to characterize its meaning. They are again hidden when a distributional approach adds form-based word-internal information, like the subword information in the **fast** embeddings used here.

Were the number of items to small to show a quantitative difference? It is clear that purely distributional approaches often use far higher numbers of items. For example, the work by Bonami & Paperno (2018) on French is based on 100 triples each containing the pivot form and a inflectionally and a derivationally related form, whereas I just compared 22 pairs. I believe that the very fact that clear distributional reflexes were found shows that the set of items was not too small. At the same time, widening the approach to encompass larger numbers is certainly desirable, but was bound here by the few overall numbers of pairs from the SPEED class. But 11 pairs is already a considerable improvement when compared to typical theoretical works in semantics, where the focus is usually on at most a handful of words (compare many of the works cited in Section 2.1). A further desirable extension of the methods used in this paper suggests itself when looking at Schäfer (2020). There, I only looked at four pairs, *quick/quickly*, *slow/slowly*, *wise/wisely* and *lucky/luckily*, but I compared their vectors across six distinct usages, three using the base form, and three using the *-ly* form. This approach allows to tease apart usage details necessarily glossed over in the current study and might lead to more consistent results across tasks.

A final issue concerns the internal consistency of the two classes compared here: just as for the number of pairs considered overall, the very fact that clear differences could be found without taking further steps shows that the classes were consistent to a sufficient degree. But there are two steps that should be taken in future research to put these results on a more solid footing. On the one hand, this investigation would ideally be complemented by a purely quantitative approach that explores whether the distribution of pairs by themselves would also establish these same classes, or whether perhaps other classifications might capture the internal semantic structure of the system of English adjectives more adequately. On the other hand, it would also be useful to validate this paper's methodology on datasets that show similar characteristics. One such dataset of interest are the *-ing* nominalizations discussed in this volume by Lieber (2023), where she finds a clear difference of the effect of *-ing* depending on whether the base verbs are durative or not. If the approach presented here is on the right track, this difference should also show up in a distributional analysis.

7 Conclusion

In this paper, I argued that a closer look at the semantics involved across base/*-ly* pairs such as *quick/quickly* on the one hand and *clever/cleverly* on the other hand suggests that only the SPEED pairs are instances of inflection whereas the HU-

MAN PROPENSITY pairs are instances of derivation. The overall mixed results of the three distributional semantics studies show that there clearly are differences in the semantic contribution of -*ly* across the two semantic classes. But these differences are more complex than hypothesized. This suggests that a binary distinction between inflectionally and derivationally related forms does not do justice to the data, and gives yet more evidence why the relation encoded across base/-*ly* pairs remains a challenge. This challenge is made even more difficult by the finding that embeddings including word-internal information perform best on the analogy task but are insensitive to any semantic distinction between the SPEED and HUMAN PROPENSITY class. Given that these two specific adjective classes were selected because they show the clearest and most systematic contrasts according to theoretic accounts, these results also show that there is still a long way to go when it comes to understanding the relationship between lexical classes established in theoretical works and possible reflections of these classes in distributional semantics.

Acknowledgements

Many thanks to Sven Kotowski and two anonymous reviewers for helpful comments on earlier versions of the paper and to Dominic Schmitz for a similarly helpful beta regression starter file in R. Work on this paper was partially funded by the Deutsche Forschungsgemeinschaft (DFG, German Research Foundation) – SFB 833 – Project ID 75650358.

Bibliography

Agirre, Enekoand, Enrique Alfonseca, Keith B. Hall, Jana Kravalova, Marius Pasca & Aitor Soroa. 2009. A study on similarity and relatedness using distributional and wordnet-based approaches. In *Proceedings of Human Language Technologies: The 2009 Annual Conference of the North American Chapter of the Association for Computational Linguistics*, 19–27.

Baroni, Marco, Georgiana Dinu & Germán Kruszewski. 2014. Don't count, predict! A systematic comparison of context-counting vs. context-predicting semantic vectors. *52nd Annual Meeting of the Association for Computational Linguistics, ACL 2014 - Proceedings of the Conference* 1. 238–247.

Bauer, Laurie, Rochelle Lieber & Ingo Plag. 2013. *The Oxford reference guide to English morphology*. Oxford: Oxford University Press.

Boleda, Gemma. 2020. Distributional semantics and linguistic theory. *Annual Review of Linguistics* 6. 213–234.

Bonami, Olivier & Matías Guzmán Naranjo. 2023. Distributional evidence for derivational paradigms. In Sven Kotowski & Ingo Plag (eds.), *The semantics of derivational morphology. Theory, methods, evidence*, 219–259. Berlin: De Gruyter.
Bonami, Olivier & Denis Paperno. 2018. Inflection vs. derivation in a distributional vector space. *Lingue e Linguaggio* 17(2). 173–195.
Bücking, Sebastian & Claudia Maienborn. 2019. Coercion by modification. The adaptive capacities of event-sensitive adnominal modifiers. *Semantics and Pragmatics* 12(9). 1–39. 10.3765/sp.12.9.
Davies, Mark. 2008–. The corpus of contemporary American English: 450 million words, 1990–present. Available online at http://corpus.byu.edu/coca/.
Dixon, Robert M. W. 1982. *'where have all the adjectives gone?' and other essays in semantics and syntax*. Berlin: De Gruyter.
Dumais, Susan T. 2004. Latent semantic analysis. *Annual Review of Information Science and Technology* 38(1). 188–230. 10.1002/aris.1440380105. http://dx.doi.org/10.1002/aris.1440380105.
Finkelstein, Lev, Evgeniy Gabrilovich, Yossi Matias, Ehud Rivlin, Zach Solan, Gadi Wolfman & Eytan Ruppin. 2002. Placing search in context: The concept revisited. *ACM Trans. Inf. Syst.* 20(1). 116–131. 10.1145/503104.503110. https://doi.org/10.1145/503104.503110.
Firth, John R. 1957. *Papers in linguistics: 1934 –1951*. Oxford: Oxford University Press.
Giegerich, Heinz J. 2012. The morphology of -*ly* and the categorial status of 'adverbs' in English. *English Language and Linguistics* 16(3). 341–359. 10.1017/S1360674312000147.
Günther, Fritz & Marco Marelli. 2021. Caoss and transcendence: Modeling role-dependent constituent meanings in compounds. *Morphology* 1–24. 10.1007/s11525-021-09386-6. https://doi.org/10.1007/s11525-021-09386-6.
Günther, Fritz, Marco Marelli & Jens Bölte. 2020. Semantic transparency effects in German compounds: A large dataset and multiple-task investigation. *Behavior Research Methods* 52(3). 1208–1224. 10.3758/s13428-019-01311-4.
Koev, Todor. 2017. Adverbs of change, aspect, and underspecification. In Dan Burgdorf, Jacob Collard, Sireemas Maspong & Brynhildur Stefánsdóttir (eds.), *Proceedings of the 27th semantics and linguistic theory conference*, 22–42. Washington, DC: Linguistic Society of America. Https://doi.org/10.3765/salt.v27i0.4123.
Kotowski, Sven & Martin Schäfer. 2023. Quantifying semantic relatedness across base verbs and derivatives. english *out*-prefixation. In Sven Kotowski & Ingo Plag (eds.), *The semantics of derivational morphology. Theory, methods, evidence*, 177–217. Berlin: De Gruyter.
Levy, Omer & Yoav Goldberg. 2014. Dependency-based word embeddings. In *Proceedings of the 52nd annual meeting of the association for computational linguistics (volume 2: Short papers)*, 302–308. Baltimore, MN: Association for Computational Linguistics. 10.3115/v1/P14-2050. https://www.aclweb.org/anthology/P14-2050.
Lieber, Rochelle. 2023. Ghost aspect and double plurality. on the aspectual semantics of eventive conversion and -ing nominalizations in English. In Sven Kotowski & Ingo Plag (eds.), *The semantics of derivational morphology. Theory, methods, evidence*, 15–35. Berlin: De Gruyter.
Marelli, Marco & Marco Baroni. 2015. Affixation in semantic space: Modeling morpheme meanings with compositional distributional semantics. *Psychological Review* 122(3). 485–515. 10.1037/a0039267.
Marelli, Marco, Christina L. Gagné & Thomas L. Spalding. 2017. Compounding as abstract operation in semantic space: Investigating relational effects through

a large-scale, data-driven computational model. *Cognition* 166. 207 – 224. https://doi.org/10.1016/j.cognition.2017.05.026. http://www.sciencedirect.com/science/article/pii/S0010027717301440.

Mikolov, Tomas, Kai Chen, Greg Corrado & Jeffrey Dean. 2013. Efficient Estimation of Word Representations in Vector Space. *ArXiv e-prints* .

Mikolov, Tomás, Edouard Grave, Piotr Bojanowski, Christian Puhrsch & Armand Joulin. 2017. Advances in pre-training distributed word representations. *CoRR* abs/1712.09405. http://arxiv.org/abs/1712.09405.

Payne, John, Rodney Huddleston & Geoffrey K. Pullum. 2010. The distribution and category status of adjectives and adverbs. *Word Structure* 3(1). 31–81.

Plag, Ingo. 2018. *Word-formation in english* Cambridge Textbooks in Linguistics. Cambridge: Cambridge University Press 2nd edn.

Pustejovsky, James. 1995. *The generative lexicon*. Cambridge, MA: The MIT Press.

Rawlins, Kyle. 2013. On adverbs of (space and) time. In Boban Arsenijević, Berit Gehrke & Rafael Marín (eds.), *Studies in the composition and decomposition of event predicates*, 153–193. Dordrecht: Springer Netherlands. 10.1007/978-94-007-5983-1_7. https://doi.org/10.1007/978-94-007-5983-1_7.

Reddy, Siva, Diana McCarthy & Suresh Manandhar. 2011. An empirical study on compositionality in compound nouns. In *Proceedings of the 5th international conference on natural language processing*, 210–218. Chiang Mai, Thailand: AFNLP.

Sahlgren, Magnus. 2006. *The word-space model: Using distributional analysis to represent syntagmatic and paradigmatic relations between words in high-dimensional vector spaces*. Stockholm: Stockholm University dissertation.

Schäfer, Martin. 2013. *Positions and interpretations: German adverbial adjectives at the syntax-semantics interface*. Berlin: De Gruyter.

Schäfer, Martin. 2018. *The semantic transparency of English compound nouns*. Berlin: Language Science Press. 10.5281/zenodo.1134595.

Schäfer, Martin. 2020. Distributional profiling and the semantics of modifier classes. In Christopher Pinon & Laurent Roussarie (eds.), *Empirical issues in syntax and semantics 13*, 139–166. Paris: CSSP. http://www.cssp.cnrs.fr/eiss13/.

Schäfer, Martin. 2021. From quick to quick-to-infinitival: on what is lexeme specific across paradigmatic and syntagmatic distributions. *English Language and Linguistics* 25(2). 347–377. 10.1017/S1360674320000167.

Stump, Gregory T. 1998. Inflection. In A. Spencer & A. Zwicky (eds.), *The handbook of morphology*, 13–43. London: Blackwell.

Turney, P. D. & P. Pantel. 2010. From frequency to meaning: Vector space models of semantics. *Journal of artificial intelligence research* 37. 141–188.

Index

accomplishment, 15–17, 20–25, 27, 29, 31, 33, 112–114, 179
achievement, 15–17, 20–25, 27, 28, 30–33, 112–114, 179
activity, 17, 21–24, 26–31, 33, 112–114, 179
adjective
– differences to adverbs, 267, 295
– human propensity, 259–297
– speed, 259–297
adverbial
– manner, 260–263
– sentence, 260–263
affix
– -able (English), 3, 4, 178
– -age (French), 8, 10, 143–170, 236–250
– -al (English), 65, 178
– -ance (English), 65
– -ant (French), 236–250
– -ate (English), 67
– -ation (English), 37, 39, 65
– -ee (English), 8, 10, 37–60
– -erie (French), 236–250
– -erweise (German), 263
– -er (English), 2, 41, 66, 178
– -eur (French), 8, 236–250
– -ical (English), 3
– -ic (English), 3
– -ier (French), 236–250
– -ifier (French), 236–250
– -ify (English), 67
– -ing (English), 2, 4, 6, 9, 10, 15–34, 65, 103–123
– -ion (English), 4
– -ion (French), 8, 10, 143–170, 236–250
– -iser (French), 236–250
– -isme (French), 236–250
– -iste (French), 236–250
– -ity (English), 2
– -ive (English), 4
– -ize (English), 5, 67
– -ly (English), 8, 10, 11, 259–297
– -ment (English), 9, 10, 37, 38, 41, 59, 65, 123–137
– -ment (French), 8, 10, 143–170, 236–250
– -ness (English), 2
– -or (English), 4
– -ship (English), 3, 4
– -s (English), 178
– out-, comparative (English), 8, 177–214
– out-, spatial (English), 181, 182, 184, 205–212
– over- (English), 184, 205–212
– re- (English), 180, 184, 205–212
– un- (English), 184, 205–212
affix competition, 2, 8–11, 103–123, 143–170
affix polysemy, 15–34
agent, 123–137, 178, 186
agentive, 144, 153, 154, 164, 169
ambiguity, 143, 145, 147, 149–152, 169
AML, Analogical Modeling of Language, 7, 9, 103–105, 107, 109–112, 118, 119, 124, 125, 128, 129, 131–137
analogical modeling, 7, 11, 103–137
analogical set, 109, 110, 118, 119, 122, 131–133, 135–137
analogy, 7, 9, 103–137, 224, 226, 231, 232, 235, 238, 239, 278–296
animate, 123–137
argument structure, 180–182, 184, 186, 197, 205–214
aspect, 15–34, 103–123
– lexical, 15–34
aspectual class, 17, 18, 21–24, 33, 111–114, 179–180
aspectual features, 9, 112–123, 179–181

Baysian model, 242, 243

causation, 123–137, 180–182, 192, 196
change-of-state, 10, 123–137, 179, 180
class
– aspectual, *see* aspectual class

– noun, *see* noun class
– verb, *see* verb class
cluster analysis, 165, 166
coherence, *see* semantic coherence
comparison, *see* scalarity
competition, *see* affix competition
compositionality, 3, 6
Construction Morphology, 6
conversion, 2, 3, 6–10, 15–34, 63–95, 103–123, 178, 236–250
– directionality of, 3, 63–95
cosine similarity, 231, 235, 240–242, 248
count, 16–20, 22, 23, 111–123

Distributed Morphology, 5, 6
Distributional Semantics, 6, 8, 9, 11, 179, 183–184, 196–214, 219–251, 259–267
– analogy, 278–296
– stability of contrast, 267–278
– topical vs. functional similarity, 269–296
– cosine similarity, 184, 199–204, 209–211
– count vector, 264, 265
– count vector, 198–202, 212
– downsampling, 199–202, 208
– semantic vector, 184, 196–202, 205, 208, 213, 219, 231–236, 238–242, 248, 249
– word embedding, 200–202, 212, 264, 278, 280, 297
durative, 9, 15, 16, 19, 21, 23, 25, 27–33, 112–123, 149, 151, 158–161, 164, 169
dynamic, 10, 19, 21, 22, 112–123

endpoint, 20, 21, 25, 112–123
event, 180–184, 186, 191, 195, 206, 207
– property of, 181, 183, 186, 191, 195
event modification, *see* modification
event structure, 181–184, 196, 197, 206
eventive, 16–19, 22, 24, 31, 111–123
eventuality, 10, 37–60, 143, 146, 149, 159, 161
experiencer, 178

frame semantics, 6, 8, 10, 40, 42, 43, 46–48, 50–55, 59, 124–128, 131, 133, 135, 136

gap, *see* lexical gap

homonymy, 2, 186, 191
HPSG, 6

imperfective, 15, 16, 18, 19
inflection
– differences to derivation, 1, 4, 7, 9, 11, 259–297
– properties, 267–269
instrument, 123–137, 178

lexical aspect, 10, 143, 147, 160, 161, 169, 179
lexical gap, 131, 135–137
Lexical Semantic Framework, 6
location, 123–137, 178

mass, 111–123
measure, 178
modeling
– analogical, *see* analogical modeling
modification
– adverbial, 259–263, 268, 277
– attributive, 259–263, 268, 277
– of events, 259–263, 272, 277

neologism, 143–170
nominalization, 219–251
– denominal, 8, 37–60
– deverbal, 8, 9, 15–34, 65–67, 103–137, 143–170
– non-deverbal, 39, 40, 45
noun class
– semantic prime (WordNet), 64–66, 68–69, 78–91, 93–94

paradigm
– derivational, 4, 10, 219–251
– inflectional, 4, 219, 226, 228
paradigmatic relation, 4, 8, 10, 11, 219–251
patient, 3, 123–137, 178, 180
polysemy, 2, 3, 9, 10, 103–137, 149, 169, 178, 185, 186, 191, 213

predicate
– of events, 261, 277
– of objects, 261, 277
predictability
– semantic, 182–196, 220, 227–230, 232, 233, 235, 238–240, 247–250
prefix, *see* affix
product, 123–137
progressive, 15–19

random forest, 160–163
referential, 16, 111–123
referential shift, 39–43, 47, 48, 55, 58, 59
Relational Morphology, 6
result, 123–137
resultative, 181
rivalry, *see* affix competition

scalarity, 180–182, 196
– dimension, 182–196, 204, 205
semantic coherence, 3, 4, 8, 10, 11, 177–214
semantic relatedness, *see* semantic coherence
semantic vector, *see* Distributional Semantics
semelfactive, 15–17, 20–25, 27–34, 112–114, 179
stability of contrast, *see* Distributional Semantics
state, 15–17, 20–25, 112–114, 123–137, 179
stative, *see* state
stimulus, 123–137, 178
suffix, *see* affix

t-SNE, 166, 167
telic, 17, 18, 21, 33, 149, 151, 154–156, 160, 161, 163, 168, 169
theme, 3, 123–137, 178, 180, 182, 186
TiMBL, Tilburg Memory-based Learner, 7, 107
transitive, 144, 147, 150–153, 168, 169
transposition, 123–137

underspecification, 177–179, 182–196, 213

verb class, 9, 18, 22, 23, 127, 132, 134
– semantic prime (WordNet), 64, 66–69, 78–91, 93–94
– VerbNet, 183–196, 202, 203, 205, 206, 208

WordNet, 63–95
– word sense pair, 63–65, 73, 76, 90, 94
– morphosemantic relation
  – agent, 64, 66, 70, 71, 76–78, 80–83, 87, 89, 92–94, 98
  – body-part, 70, 71, 76, 77, 79
  – by-means-of, 70, 71, 74, 76–78, 80, 81, 86, 90, 92–94, 101
  – destination, 70, 71, 76, 77, 79
  – event, 64, 70–72, 76–78, 80–83, 91–94, 99
  – instrument, 64, 66, 70, 71, 76–78, 80, 81, 87, 90, 92–94, 101
  – location, 64, 70, 71, 76, 77, 80, 81, 87, 90, 92–94, 101
  – material, 70, 71, 76, 77, 79, 90
  – property, 64, 70–72, 76, 77, 80, 81, 83, 92–94, 99
  – result, 64, 70–72, 76–78, 80, 81, 83, 84, 92–94, 100
  – state, 64, 70, 71, 76, 77, 80, 81, 87, 88, 92–94, 102
  – undergoer, 70, 71, 76–78, 80, 81, 83–85, 90, 92–94, 100
  – uses, 70, 71, 74, 76–78, 80, 81, 87, 88, 92–94, 102
  – vehicle, 70, 71, 76, 77, 79

zero derivation, *see* conversion
zero noun, *see* conversion (directionality of)
zero suffix, 65, 67
zero verb, *see* conversion (directionality of)

www.ingramcontent.com/pod-product-compliance
Lightning Source LLC
Chambersburg PA
CBHW060350190426
43201CB00044B/1977